Feature Distribution in Swedish Noun Phrases

Publications of the Philological Society, 32

Feature Distribution in Swedish Noun Phrases

Kersti Börjars

Publications of the Philological Society, 32

Oxford UK & Boston USA

ISBN 0–631–208712

First published 1998

Blackwell Publishers
108 Cowley Road, Oxford, OX4 1JF, UK

and
350 Main Street,
Malden, MA 02148, USA.

British Library Cataloguing in Publication Data
A catalogue record for this publication is available from the British Library

Library of Congress Cataloging-in-Publication Data
Applied for

Printed in Great Britain by
Whitstable Litho Printers Ltd., Whitstable, Kent

Explicit hoc totum:
Pro Christo da mihi potum
Fifteenth-century scribe

CONTENTS

ACKNOWLEDGEMENTS

My sincere thanks for the original thesis version were due especially to the following: my supervisor, John Payne, probably the best supervisor in the world. Martin Barry for providing equal portions of helpful advice and sarcasm whenever I had problems with the computers; all other members of the Department of Linguistics at the University of Manchester: a damn' fine linguistics department; Onderzoeksinstituut voor taal en spraak, which gave me a good home for six months in the autumn of 1992. (I am especially grateful to Martin Everaert, Janet Grijzenhout and Ellen-Petra Kester. *Ik heb het bij jullie prima naar mijn zin gehad.*); my parents, Elof and Gun Brit Börjars, I am amazed at the many ways in which they have always supported me, even though they must at times have been very doubtful about the wisdom of my next project; Robin for his help with organizing the maternity leave during which I got a fair amount of writing done; most of all the marvellous Andrew Masters for his help with this thesis (this involved proofreading, a lot of washing up and many other things), but mainly for just about everything else.

My sincere thanks for this version are due to: all the above; my examiners, Bob Borsley, Elisabet Engdahl and Nigel Vincent for providing helpful discussion and advice both during the viva and afterwards, and to Nigel for providing detailed comments for the published version; the British Academy, for giving me a personal research grant which allowed me to attend the ESSLLI summer school in Barcelona – many of the things which I learned there have been useful for the revision of this book; the Council of the Philological Society, and particularly Max Wheeler and Keith Brown, for their involvement in the publication of this book; Zeth Alvered and Lars-Olof Delsing for the points, both detailed and general, which they raised; two anonymous referees for their comments; and finally, the staff at Blackwell Publishers, particularly to Joanna Wade for her patience.

LIST OF TABLES

ABBREVIATIONS

1	first person
2	second person
3	third person
ACC	accusative case
AVM	attribute-value matrix
BSE	base form of verb
CAP	Control Agreement Principle (Gazdar et al. 1985: 89)
CG	Categorial Grammar
COM	common gender (i.e. non-neuter)
COMP	complementizer
CMP	comparative
DAT	dative case
DEF	I use this abbreviation to refer to the definite ending which may occur on nouns in Swedish, and also to the definite feature of which the ending is a manifestation
EFP	Edge Feature Principle (Halpern 1992a and b, Miller 1992a, Svenonius 1992c)
F	feminine gender
FG	Functional Grammar
GEN	genitive case
HFC	Head Feature Convention (Gazdar et al. 1985: 97)
HFP	Head Feature Principle (Pollard and Sag 1994: 18)
HPSG	Head-driven Phrase Structure Grammar
INDEF	indefinite
INF	infinitive
LFG	Lexical-Functional Grammar
M	masculine
NOM	nominative case
NT	neuter gender
OBJ	object form
OBL	oblique case
PART	participle
PASS	passive
PL	plural
POSS	possessive
PRD	predicative
PRON	pronominal
PRT	particle
PST	past tense
REFL	reflexive
SPR	superlative
SG	singular
STR	strong form of adjectives in Swedish (and nouns and determiners in other languages)
SUBJ	subject form
SUP	supine (the Swedish equivalent of English perfect participle)
WK	weak form of adjectives in Swedish (and nouns and determiners in other languages)

1

INTRODUCTION

The aim of this book is to study in some detail a number of aspects of the syntactic structure of Swedish noun phrases. This study should lead to a theoretical analysis of Swedish noun phrases. Ideally, the resulting analysis should have a number of important characteristics. Firstly, each step of it should be empirically motivated by the data discussed and the analysis should make the correct predictions about what is a possible Swedish noun phrase and what is not. Even though I will focus almost exclusively here on the syntactic structure, the syntactic analysis must not contradict semantic facts. Secondly, the account should be formulated in precise terminology so as to make it possible to define categories, to state generalizations in exact terms, and also to make it easier to verify the account against further data. Finally, the analysis should make it possible to compare Swedish noun phrases with those of other languages to reveal differences and similarities. The last two goals can most easily be achieved if an established theoretical framework is used for the analysis. However, before a particular framework is chosen, a number of basic facts about Swedish noun phrases need to be established. The framework which most naturally captures these basic facts can then be selected. In line with this methodology, I begin my study by examining in some detail some aspects of Swedish noun phrases in as theory-independent a way as possible. In chapters 2, 3 and 4 I am therefore aiming to consider a very limited set of data, partly in order to define the issues that need to be dealt with and partly to establish certain basic facts about Swedish noun phrases without being hindered by the assumptions of any particular theory. I am thinking here especially of the status of the definite ending on nouns, to be dealt with in chapter 3, and the headedness of noun phrases, which will be discussed in chapter 4.

The approach that I have chosen necessarily means that the pre-analysis groundwork is given more prominence than in studies which set out from a more precise set of theoretical assumptions.[1] A necessary consequence of this approach is that my eventual analysis will only be applied to a limited subset of Swedish noun phrases. However, I believe that the result of my pre-analysis investigation should be respected in any account of Swedish noun phrases. Therefore, I consider that the analysis proposed in this book forms a good starting point for a more complete treatment of Swedish noun phrases.

An instance of the limitation in data is the fact that I will focus on the prenominal elements within the noun phrase. With respect to feature distribution, this is the most interesting aspect of the Swedish noun phrase. The marking for (in)definiteness on nouns and adjectives interacts in interesting and far from straightforward ways with the (in)definiteness of the determiner. Post-nominal elements are less interesting from the point of view of feature distribution. Most post-nominal modifiers in Swedish are not inflected for definiteness, gender and number. There is little interaction between the presence of post-nominal elements and the presence or absence of a determiner.

One of the first issues that needs to be considered is how many types of prenominal elements there are. Both in traditional accounts (such as Loman 1956) and in more recent ones (such as Delsing 1991 (but compare Delsing 1993: 185–224) and Santelmann 1992) it is assumed that there are a number of classes of prenominal elements, not just determiners and adjectives. If more than two classes of prenominal elements can be identified on the basis of syntactic criteria, then this must be represented in the structure proposed for Swedish noun phrases. Therefore, in chapter 2, I will attempt to establish some criteria for determiner and modifier status. In this discussion, I will take articles to be typical determiners, and adjectives to be the typical modifiers. The established criteria will then be applied to elements which are not obviously either determiners or adjectives. The aim is to decide whether further syntactic categories of prenominal elements are justified, and if so, how many.

A second piece of necessary groundwork is to decide on the status of the definite ending on Swedish nouns. This permits the noun to function as a full referential noun phrase without a syntactic determiner, even when the noun is a singular count noun. This is illustrated in (1.1).[2]

(1.1) a. **Mus-en** åt upp osten.
mouse-DEF ate up cheese.DEF
'The mouse ate all the cheese.'

b. **Murmeldjur-et** somnade.
marmot-DEF fell asleep
'The marmot fell asleep.'

The fact that the definite ending appears to do the job of a syntactic determiner in these examples has led a number of linguists to assign it syntactic status (such as Delsing 1988, 1989, 1992, Santelmann 1992 and Taraldsen 1990, 1991 (for Norwegian)). On the other hand, the definiteness marker is morphologically bound. Furthermore, it can co-occur with a syntactic determiner, which is unexpected if it is itself a syntactic determiner. On the basis of this, other linguists have concluded that the definite ending is the morphological manifestation on a noun of a feature [+DEF], and hence does not have any independent status in the syntax. This approach is most striking in the work of Cooper (1984, 1986) and Svenonius (1992a, 1992c), but it has also been adopted for certain constructions by Delsing (1993). In chapter 3 I will consider carefully the characteristics of the definite ending in order to establish which of these analyses is the most appropriate.

An issue relating to the representation of noun phrases which has received a lot of attention in the last ten years or so is the notion of headedness. Traditionally, the head of a noun phrase has been assumed to be the noun. This tradition has been so strong that very few discussions about the head status of noun phrases can be found in the literature before the 1980s. Notable exceptions are J. Lyons (1977: 391) and Vennemann and Harlow (1977). However, in the mid-eighties, more and more proposals started to appear to the effect that the head of the noun phrase is in fact the determiner, so that the category of a noun phrase is DP. This discussion took place mainly in the transformational literature and appears to have been started by Abney (1987).[3,4] There were, however, also other earlier proposals to this effect, and one especially relevant to a discussion of Scandinavian noun phrases is due to Hellan (1986). For a few years after 1987, a number of arguments which were assumed to point in favour of a DP analysis appeared in the transformational literature. The discussion has now more or less died down and the standard assumption in most works on noun phrases is that they are indeed DPs. However, for me the question is still open, and in chapter 4 I will discuss arguments for and against a DP analysis of Swedish noun phrases.

Having considered these three issues: the number of categories of prenominal elements within the noun phrase, the status of the definite ending, and the headedness of Swedish noun phrases, I turn to the actual analysis of Swedish noun phrases. In chapter 5 I give an account of definite noun phrases, and in chapter 6 I provide an analysis of indefinite noun phrases. Within this analysis, a number of notorious difficulties with Swedish noun phrases will have to be accounted for.

Firstly, an account must be provided for the fact that a definite noun can function as a full noun phrase, as in (1.1). This will be done in section 5.2. Secondly, even though the definite ending appears to function as a determiner in the sense that it allows a singular count noun to function as a full noun phrase, it can still co-occur with definite determiners, as in (1.2a). The issue is further complicated by the fact that some definite determiners require the following noun **not** to carry the definite ending, as in (1.2b). This issue will be dealt with in section 5.3.

(1.2) a. den mus-en / *mus
that mouse-DEF mouse
'that mouse'

b. denna mus / *mus-en[5]
this mouse mouse-DEF
'this mouse'

When a definite singular count noun is preceded by a modifier, a syntactic determiner must be present, as in (1.3). If the noun phrase does not contain any other syntactic determiner, then a syntactic definite article *den*, homophonous to the demonstrative determiner in (1.2a) is used.[6] In this position, the adjective carries a special marking which is usually referred to as the weak ending in the literature on Germanic languages. The issues of why the determiner is required and how the adjective receives the weak ending will be considered in section 5.4.

(1.3) *(Det) sömnig-a murmeldjur-et somnade.
the/that sleepy-WK marmot-DEF fell asleep
'The sleepy marmot fell asleep.'

The generalization that all prenominal elements which are not themselves determiners in definite noun phrases need to be preceded by a syntactic determiner appears to be violated in a number of Swedish noun phrases. Examples are provided in (1.4).

(1.4) a. **Vit-a** hus-et måste repareras.
white-WK house-DEF must repair.PASS
'The White House must be repaired.'

b. **Norr-a** sida-n skadades av stormen.
north-WK side-DEF damage.PASS by storm.DEF
'The north side was damaged by the storm.'

c. **Alla** (de) hus-en måste repareras.
all those house-DEF must repair.PASS
'All (those) houses must be repaired.'

I will claim that these are, in fact, not counter-examples to the generalization. An account of these types of noun phrases will be given in section 5.5.1.

Singular indefinite count nouns differ from the corresponding definite forms in that they cannot occur in argument positions in Swedish unless they are accompanied by a syntactic determiner. This difference between definite and indefinite nouns, which is illustrated by the contrast between (1.1b) and (1.5), will be accounted for in section 6.2.3.

(1.5) *(Ett) murmeldjur somnade.
a marmot fell asleep
'A marmot fell asleep.'

In predicative positions, certain indefinite singular count nouns need not be preceded by a syntactic determiner, as (1.6a) shows. This class of nouns will be discussed in section 6.4.4. However, if the noun is preceded by an adjective, then a determiner must be present, as in (1.6b) and (1.6c). This means that the restriction illustrated in (1.3) for definite noun phrases holds also for indefinite ones. Note that in indefinite noun phrases the adjective carries strong inflection, which shows gender and number distinctions. A discussion of how the behaviour of adjectives in indefinite noun phrases fits into my general account of Swedish noun phrases is given in section 6.3.

(1.6) a. Torun är **journalist**.
Torun is journalist
'Torun is a journalist.'

b. Torun är *(en) duktig journalist.
Torun is a.COM capable.WK.COM.SG journalist(COM)
'Torun is a capable journalist.'

c. Gazza är *(ett) överbetalt fotbollsproffs.
Gazza is a.NT over-paid.STR.NT.SG professional football player(NT)
'Gazza is an over-paid professional football player.'

It is not only in predicative positions, as in (1.6a), that indefinite nouns can occur without syntactic determiners. There are some other exceptions as well, as the examples in (1.7) illustrate. The special properties of these constructions, and the issues involved in indefinite noun phrases lacking determiners will be discussed in section 6.3.

(1.7) a. **Möss** äter gärna ost.
mice eat gladly cheese
'Mice like to eat cheese.'

b. **Bil** är dyrt.
car(COM) is expensive.NT
'Owning a car is expensive.'

c. Morfar röker **pipa**.
granddad smokes pipe
'Grandad is a pipe smoker.'

d. Vi vill köpa **hus**.
we want buy house
'We want to buy a house.'

One of the issues which falls outside this book, because of the focus on prenominal elements, is that of relative clauses. This is by no means because they are uninteresting, or indeed easy to account for. In fact, restrictive relative clauses do interact with the use of the definite form of the noun and the presence of prenominal determiners in ways which are not usually accounted for in analyses of Swedish noun phrases. I refer to van der Auwera (1990) for an interesting discussion of the different types of restrictive relative clauses which are permitted in Swedish. Holmberg (1987) discusses some of the issues involved in a transformational framework. For an account in terms of Categorial Grammar of Swedish noun phrases containing different types of relative clauses, see Payne and Börjars (1994).

Another interesting and challenging aspect of Swedish noun phrases which is hardly dealt with in this book is the role of prenominal genitives and possessive pronouns. The complexity of the issues involved in these constructions means that it is not possible to propose a satisfactory analysis on the basis of a superficial discussion of the facts and space does not permit a detailed discussion. I will give a brief account of some of the issues involved in section 2.2.4. I refer to Börjars (1990) for a syntactic analysis of certain aspects of prenominal genitives.

2

DETERMINERS AND MODIFIERS

2.1. Previous studies of prenominal elements

In phrases like the ones in (2.1), there is some agreement in the literature that the non-italic words should be labelled DET, ADJ and N as in the examples.

(2.1) a.

halva	den	kakan
half	that	cake.DEF
	DET	N

'half that cake'

b.

hans	*många*	*sådana*	små	möss
his	many	such	little	mice
			ADJ	N

'his many such little mice'

c.

alla	de	*många*	röda	bilarna
all	the/those	many	red	cars.DEF
	DET		ADJ	N

'all the/those many red cars'

d.

sin	*egen*	bok
his/her.REFL	own	book
		N

'his/her own book'

e.

den	*ena*	*andra*	idén
the	one-out-of-two	other	idea.DEF
DET			N

'one of the other two ideas'

f.

ingen	*likadan*	blå	bil
no	same	blue	car
		ADJ	N

'no identical blue car'

g.

det	*enda*	*tidigare*	försöket
the	only	previous	attempt.DEF
DET			N

'the only previous attempt'

The words in italics in (2.1) are more difficult to characterize and different labels have been assigned to them.

Within a framework of traditional Scandinavian *field grammar* (Diderichsen 1946), Loman (1956) provides a detailed study of prenominal elements in Swedish. He claims that the italic elements in (2.1), which he calls 'attributive pronouns', together with the determiners, belong to the DETERMINER FIELD (*bestämningsfält*), whereas the adjectives are found in the DESCRIPTION FIELD (*beskrivningsfält*). He divides the attributive pronouns into six POSITION CLASSES (PKs) on the basis of word order and distributional facts. Members of each of these classes are shown in table 2.1. Loman relates the position classes to semantic aspects of the words. To each position class he assigns a label referring to its semantic properties: 'totality', 'determination', 'possession', 'quantity', 'selection' and 'comparison'. Even though Loman's classification is thirty years old, it provides a good basis for a study of prenominal elements, firstly, because he provides an extensive list of the kind of elements that any analysis must be able to deal with. Secondly, he makes a claim that can be tested, namely, that there are a number of classes of elements which share certain properties with determiners; they are all assumed to belong to the determiner field. These classes of elements are also

Table 2.1 Loman's position classes

Determiner field						Description field
PK1	PK2	PK3	PK4	PK5	PK6	Adjectives
hela	*dessa*	*min*	*mycken*	*annan*	*sådana*	
whole	these	my	much	another	such	
halva	*den (här)*	*din*	*båda*	*övriga*	*likadana*	
half	this	your.SG	both	other	identical	
alla	*den (där)*	*sin*	*bägge*	*enstaka*	*dylika*	
all	that	reflexive possessive	both	few	such	
båda	*den*	*hans*	*mången*	*sista*	*slika*	
both	the/those	his	many a	last	such	
bägge	*en*	*hennes*	*många*	*senaste*		
both	a(n)	her	many	most recent		
samtliga	*någon*	*dess*	*talrika*	*senare*		
all	some	its	numerous	later		
	varje	*ens*	*få*	*tidigare*		
	each	one's	few	previous		
	var	*vår*	*otaliga*	*enda*		
	each	our	innumerable	only		
	ingen	*er*	*fåtaliga*	ordinals		
	no	your.PL	few			
	somliga	*deras*	cardinals above one			
	some	their				
	åtskilliga	*allas vår/er*				
	several	all our/your				
	vissa	possessive NPs				
	certain					

assumed to be different from descriptive elements like adjectives. This division is meant to make predictions about ordering constraints. For a modern analysis of prenominal elements, the division in table 2.1, if it is empirically justified on the basis of syntactic facts, might mean that the elements in PK3 to PK6 should belong to the same syntactic category as determiners. It would, however, certainly mean that these elements should not belong to the same syntactic category as adjectives. In this subsection I will therefore use Loman's classification as a basis for my initial investigation of the prenominal elements within the noun phrase. In section 2.2.1 I will discuss some of the problems with the position classes in general and with some of their members in particular.

Other approaches to the same kind of elements can be found in the literature on Swedish noun phrases. Allén (1958) aims to characterize the whole class of pronouns. Most of the prenominal elements discussed in Loman (1956) are assumed to belong to this class. Allén's division of pronouns is based purely on semantic factors. He arrives at an initial division into definite and indefinite pronouns, both of which are subject to further subdivisions. The labels of the subcategories are reminiscent of the ones used by Loman (1956).

Within an early transformational framework (Chomsky 1965), Teleman (1969) sets out to define the categories of the 'pronominal attributes' that are needed to generate correct noun phrases. Even though the approach is outdated and a number of the assumptions strike one as entirely arbitrary and unmotivated, this is an excellent source of data. Some of the generalizations made are also directly relevant to any modern account of prenominal elements in Swedish noun phrases.

In traditional grammars of Swedish, the italicized words in (2.1) are assigned to a number of different categories. Beckman (1952) uses terms such as definite and indefinite numerals and definite and indefinite pronouns. The dictionary of the Swedish Academy (SAOL 1981) assigns labels such as PRONOMINAL NUMERAL, PRONOMINAL ADJECTIVE and ADJECTIVE.

All these treatments present their problems. The traditional grammars and Allén (1958) give no unified account of the items that can precede the nuclear noun in a noun phrase. Loman (1956) and Allén (1958) assume without argument that the distinction between adjectives and the elements in the determiner field is clear cut. Furthermore, Allén and, to a lesser extent, Loman base their categories on vague semantic distinctions.[1] Teleman (1969) relies heavily on assumptions made within the theory he uses. For instance, he does not give evidence why some of the pronominal attributes which always precede the head in the surface structure should be generated under a node to the right of the head noun.

I will assume that there is a class of prenominal elements which have a special status semantically and also syntactically, namely the determiners. In Loman's system, this class corresponds to PK2. In section 2.2.2 I will attempt to establish a number of criteria for defining the class of determiners and I will also consider some of the problems involved in applying these criteria. In section 2.3 I will look at some characteristics of elements which are assumed to be the core members of the description field, namely adjectives. In section 2.4 I will examine the members of Loman's position classes PK1 and PK4 to PK6 and other relevant elements with respect to the characteristics of the core members of the determiner field and the description field. In this subsection, I hope to establish whether a distinction should in fact be made between the 'description field' and the 'determiner field' and, if so, whether the members of PK1 and PK4 to PK6 do indeed belong in the determiner field. Before providing a syntactic analysis of Swedish noun phrases, I need to know whether a division into these two major categories is justified on the basis of syntactic considerations, and hence whether the distinction should be represented in the syntactic structure of Swedish noun phrases.

2.2. The determiner field

2.2.1. *Problems with Loman's (1956) position classes*

The use of two distinct classes of prenominal modifiers makes predictions about word order relations. Indeed, the classes are defined largely on the basis of word order facts. This is problematic not only as far as the position classes (PKs) are concerned, but also with respect to the two major fields.[2] As the examples in (2.2) show, adjectives, that is, members of the description field, can precede members of the determiner field. *Smutsig* 'dirty' is a typical adjective, for instance, in that it carries the adjectival ending *-ig*, it can occur in the comparative and superlative forms: *smutsigare*, *smutsigast* and it can be turned into an adverb by the addition of the derivational suffix *-t*. *Längsta* is the superlative form of *lång* 'long'.

(2.2) a. en smutsig sådan mus
a dirty such[PK6] mouse
'a dirty mouse of that kind'

b. det längsta sista försöket
the longest last[PK5] attempt
'the longest last attempt'

Similar problems also occur with the ordering between the elements of the position classes. There are notoriously flexible elements like *båda* which occur in PK1 and PK4 in Loman's system, but which can also follow elements in PK5 (as in (2.3a)) and must therefore also belong to PK6. However, as (2.3b) and (2.3c) show, there are also other examples to indicate that the ordering constraints are less strict than the use of position classes may imply.

(2.3) a. de andra båda syskonen
the[PK2] other[PK5] both[PK1/4] siblings
'the other two siblings'

b. sådana andra karameller
such[PK6] other[PK5] sweets
'sweets of that other kind'

c. de andra två förslagen
the[PK2] other[PK5] two[PK4] suggestions
'the other two suggestions'

Furthermore, even though complementary distribution is one criterion used by Loman to establish these classes, several examples can be found of noun phrases containing two elements from the same position class. Examples are given in (2.4).

(2.4) a. andra tidigare förslag
other[PK5] previous[PK5] suggestions
'other previous suggestions'

b. två talrika arter
two[PK4] numerous[PK4] species
'two species with numerous members'

There is one further problem associated with the notion of co-occurrence as used by Loman. *Mången* 'many a', which combines only with singular count nouns, is assumed to belong to PK4 just like *många* 'many', which combines with plural nouns. Unlike *många*, *mången* cannot co-occur with core determiners, the members of PK2.[3] This is illustrated in (2.5).

(2.5) a. de många mössen
the[PK2]many mice
'the many mice'

b. *den / *en / *ingen mången mus
the[PK2] / a[PK2] / no[PK2] many a mouse

In a historical perspective, this may not be a surprising fact since *mången* can be assumed to be the result of *många* 'many' merging with the indefinite article. However, we are considering the data here in a synchronic perspective, and the issue is what the function of *mången* is in present day Swedish. One reason why Loman assumes that *mången* belongs in PK4 is that it cannot co-occur with any other members of PK4; hence the co-occurrence criterion could be said to support the assumption that *mången* belongs in PK4. However, all elements in PK4, except *mycken*, may co-occur only with plural nouns. *Mycken* occurs only with non-count nouns. This means that there are independent reasons not to expect *mången*, which requires a singular count noun, to occur with any of the members of PK4.

The placement of *mången* with *många* in PK4 illustrates a further problem with Loman's position classes. He uses order and co-occurrence restrictions as the major criteria for membership of a particular position class. This means that the classes are basically syntactic in nature. Still, one reason why *mången* is in PK4 is because of its semantic similarity with the other elements. This means that the classes are not motivated entirely on syntactic criteria. If these classes are to be used to motivate syntactic structure, one would prefer them to be based on syntactic arguments only. I see no reason why elements that are from a semantic point of view basically quantifying in nature should behave identically with respect to syntactic constraints. I do not want to exclude the possibility that there might be three elements whose basic semantics is quantifying, but which still function as a determiner, as an adjective and as some intermediate category, respectively.

The problems pointed out here do not by any means invalidate Loman's position classes. Loman's work still shows that certain ordering and co-occurrence restrictions hold between the non-descriptive prenominal elements. These constraints are, however, rather weak for all the elements except those belonging to PK2 and PK3, that is, the core determiners, and the genitives and possessive pronouns. The conclusion based on the discussion here is then that in the determiner field, the members of PK2 and PK3 seem to have certain properties which set them apart from the members of the other position classes. What remains to be seen is whether or not the members of the other position classes are sufficiently similar to the core determiners and sufficiently different from the adjectives to justify a distinction between a determiner field and a description field.

2.2.2. *Criteria for determiner status*

I will follow the common assumption that articles are core determiners. As articles, I will consider *den* 'the', *en* 'a(n)' and also the unstressed *någon* 'some [sm̩]'. For an element to be considered a determiner it must share certain crucial properties with the articles. For the notion of determiner field to be relevant to a syntactic description, the elements which are assumed to belong in this field must have at least some of these properties too. In this section, I will try to establish what the crucial properties are.

The crucial semantic characteristic of (extensional) determiners is that they represent functions from properties to a set of properties. In terms of Boolean Semantics (Keenan and Faltz 1985), they are functions from P to P*. Using terminology from Functional Grammar (FG), they are elements that turn a nominal into a term (see Siewierska 1991 and van der Auwera 1990). This property is reflected in the syntax by the fact that the core determiners can combine with an indefinite singular count noun to allow the resulting category to function as a full referential noun phrase.[4] In Categorial Grammar (CG) (Wood 1993) this is shown in the fact they are of the category

NP/N, that is, they may combine with a nominal to form a noun phrase. The ability to turn an indefinite singular count noun into a noun phrase is then one crucial criterion for determiner status. By this criterion, we can show that the bold elements in (2.6a) are determiners, but that those in (2.6b) are not.

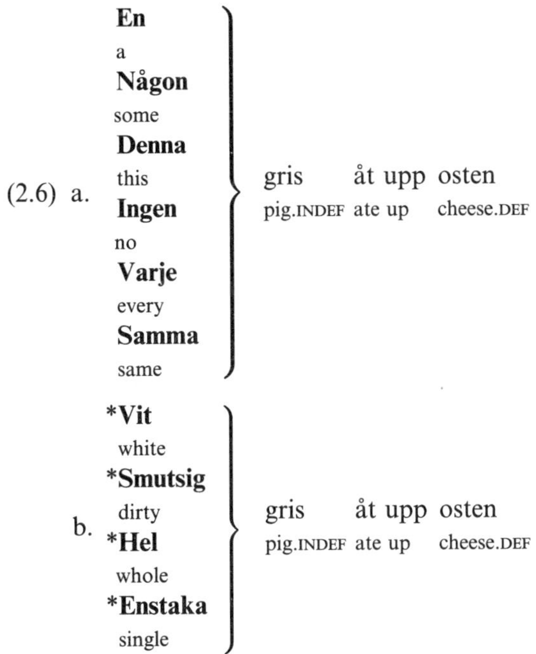

(2.6) a.
En
a
Någon
some
Denna
this
Ingen
no
Varje
every
Samma
same
gris åt upp osten
pig.INDEF ate up cheese.DEF
b.
*Vit
white
*Smutsig
dirty
*Hel
whole
*Enstaka
single
gris åt upp osten
pig.INDEF ate up cheese.DEF

This may be a surprising result, particularly with respect to *varje* 'every/ each', which is clearly a quantifier semantically. However, I am attempting to distinguish classes entirely by syntactic criteria. There are many examples in grammar where elements share syntactic properties without sharing semantic properties, and vice versa.

Plural, non-count and definite nouns can function as full referential noun phrases on their own. This criterion can therefore not be applied to all prenominal elements since some of them may occur only with plural or non-count nouns. In fact, since the independent definite article *den* cannot occur with an indefinite noun, this criterion does not even apply to one of the core determiners. Hence we need further criteria. A common assumption is that any one noun phrase can contain only one determiner. This seems a justifiable assumption with respect to the semantic nature of core determiners. We would not expect a noun phrase to be able to contain two elements which represent functions from properties to a set of properties. First of all, the two functions would yield different, often contradictory results. Secondly, the functions could presumably not apply simultaneously. On the other hand, they could not apply consecutively either, since the output of each function is different in nature from the input. When one function has applied, the nominal does not represent properties any more, but sets of properties. The second function would therefore not have the correct input. A second syntactic criterion for determiners is then that they occur in complementary distribution with other determiners. If an element can co-occur with the elements assigned determiner status by the first criterion, then this element is not itself a determiner. By this criterion, the bold elements in (2.7a) may be determiners, but those in (2.7b) cannot be.

(2.7) a.

***Samma**	en			
same	a			
***Vilka**	dessa	mus / möss	åt upp	osten
which	these	mouse/mice.INDEF	ate up	cheese.DEF
***Varje**	denna			
every	this			

b.

Alla	dessa			
all	these			
Båda	dessa	möss	åt upp	osten
which	these	mice.INDEF	ate up	cheese.DEF
Några	**sådana**			
some	such			

With respect to both criteria discussed so far, *mången* which was one of the problem elements that I discussed in section 2.2.1, behaves like a determiner. Examples are provided in (2.8).

(2.8) a. Mången mus har knaprat på osten.
many a mouse has nibbled on cheese.DEF
'Many a mouse has nibbled on the cheese.'

b. *varje mången mus som knaprade på osten
every many a mouse which nibbled on cheese.DEF

This confirms that *mången* does not belong in Loman's PK4, but in the class of core determiners.

A characteristic of determiners which is peculiar to Swedish (and Norwegian and Danish) is their ability to 'license' an adjective. In Swedish, definite singular count nouns can function as full noun phrases, and there are also contexts where indefinite singular count nouns may occur without a determiner. Examples are provided in (2.9). This aspect of definite nouns will be dealt with in detail in section 5.2, indefinite nouns as used in (2.9b) will be discussed in section 6.4.4.

(2.9) a. **Musen** åt upp osten.
mouse.DEF ate up cheese.DEF
'The mouse ate all the cheese.'

b. Torun är **journalist.**
Torun is journalist
'Torun is a journalist.'

However, when the noun is preceded by an adjective, a determiner must be present. In this sense determiners license adjectives. Examples are provided in (2.10).

(2.10) a. ***(Den) gamla musen** åt upp osten.
the old mouse.DEF ate up cheese.DEF
'The old mouse ate all the cheese.'

b. Torun är ***(en) skicklig journalist**.
Torun is a skilful journalist
'Torun is a skilful journalist.'

In (2.10), the articles have been used, but any other determiner would have permitted the presence of the adjective in the same way.

It should be pointed out that, with respect to the criteria proposed here, pronouns like *vi* 'we' and *ni* 'you.PL' are determiners. They cannot co-occur with other determiners and they license adjectives in the way that other determiners do. Examples are found in (2.11).

(2.11) a. { *Dessa (these) / *Inga (no) / *Samma (same) } **vi** hundägare vägrar betala skatt
we dog owners refuse pay tax

b. **Vi hungriga studenter** kräver ökade studielån.
we hungry.WK students demand increased study loans
'We hungry students demand increased study loans.'

Payne (1993c: section 2.1) proposes a more general characteristic which distinguishes determiners from other prenominal elements; determiners cannot be modified. However, if the two criteria discussed above are taken to be definitional of determiners, then certain elements are classified as determiners in Swedish which do not have this characteristic. According to the first criterion, *varje* 'each' and *samma* 'the same' are determiners. The examples in (2.6a) showed that these elements can combine with a singular non-definite count noun to form a full referential noun phrase. However, these two elements appear to accept at least one modifier, namely *nästan* 'almost', as the examples in (2.12) show.

(2.12) a. **Nästan varje student** hade skrivit färdigt sin C-uppsats i tid.
almost every student had written ready his/her C-essay in time
'Almost every student had finished their undergraduate dissertation in time.'

b. Karin köpte **nästan samma byxor** som Anna.
Karin bought almost same trousers as Anna
'Karin bought almost identical trousers to Anna.'

One way of reconciling the 'no modifier criterion' with the other two determiner criteria would be to assume the constituent structure in (2.13a) rather than (2.13b) for the bold noun phrases in (2.12). This would make these examples similar to those containing the modifier *bara* 'only' as in (2.13c). The structure indicated by the brackets in (2.13c) is motivated by the fact that *bara* appears to be able to modify any maximal projection in Swedish, as in (2.14) (see (4.45) in section 4.4).

(2.13) a. [nästan [DET NOMINAL]]

b. [nästan DET] NOMINAL]

c. **Bara [den kjolen]** finns i storlek 38.
only that skirt.DEF exists in size 38
'Only that skirt is available in size 38.'

(2.14) a. Oscar äter bara [$_{NP}$ den bananen].
Oscar eats only that banana.DEF

b. Oscar vill bara [$_{VP}$ äta den bananen].
Oscar wants only eat that banana.DEF

c. Oscar verkar bara [$_{AP}$ arg på henne].
Oscar seems only angry with her

d. Oscar verkar arg bara [$_{PP}$ på henne].
Oscar seems angry only with her

Some of the sentences in (2.14) are possible also with *nästan*, as in (2.15), but the argument for assuming the structure in (2.13a) is not at all as strong for *nästan* as it is for *bara*.[5]

(2.15) a. Oscar nästan grät.
Oscar almost cried

b. Oscar nästan slukade bananen.
Oscar almost wolfed down the banana

c. Oscar ville nästan döda henne.
Oscar wanted almost kill her

d. Oscar verkar nästan arg på henne.
Oscar seems almost angry with her

I cannot really think of any more convincing syntactic arguments in favour of either of the two structures in (2.13a) and (2.13b) for the bold noun phrases in (2.12). If arguments to support (2.13a) can be found, then, of course, these examples do not form exceptions to the three criteria. Otherwise, a number of possible solutions suggest themselves. We could assume that for an element to be a syntactic determiner, it has to fulfil all three criteria. This would mean that *varje* and *samma* are not determiners. A disadvantage with this assumption is that the noun phrases in (2.6a); *varje gris* 'each pig' and *samma gris* 'the same pig' would lack a determiner. This would make them unique amongst Swedish noun phrases in that they are determinerless noun phrases with singular indefinite count nouns as their nuclei. Such noun phrases are normally not permitted except under very special semantic circumstances (see sections 6.4.2, 6.4.3 and 6.4.4). Another possible explanation could be sought in a distinction between notions such as syntactic determiner and semantic determiner. A syntactic determiner can then be assumed to be defined by the first two criteria: the ability to make a noun phrase out of a singular indefinite count noun and complementary distribution with other determiners. This class includes *varje* and *samma*. Semantic determiners are then those elements whose semantics is such that they do not permit modification. The elements *varje* and *samma* would then be the kind of elements which are not semantic determiners.

At least for the time being, I will maintain the first two criteria for determiner status, as well as the characteristic that determiners cannot normally be modified. A caveat will have to be added to the effect that there is one modifier, *nästan*, which can modify a small number of the elements which are syntactic determiners according to the other criteria. Even with examples like (2.12) in mind, the near total lack of modification does seem to be quite a striking characteristic of determiners.

There are also conflicts between the first two criteria. As (2.16a) shows, *hurdan* 'what kind of' is a determiner according to the first criterion discussed. On the other hand, the data in (2.16b) indicate that *hurdan* can co-occur with another determiner, and can therefore not itself be a determiner according to the second criterion discussed above.

(2.16) a. **Hurdan** **bil** köpte ni?
what kind of car bought you
'What kind of car did you buy?'

b. **En hurdan** **bil** köpte ni?
a what kind of car bought you
'What kind of car did you buy?'

In this case, I will assume that the examples in (2.16) exemplify two distinct uses of *hurdan*, one in which it is a determiner – (2.16a) – and one in which it is a modifier (2.16b).

In Swedish as in many other Germanic languages, the indefinite article derives from the numeral 'one'. However, it seems clear that the indefinite determiner *en* is a determiner, and has a different syntactic status from the numerals. The most striking example of this is the fact that all numerals can follow a possessive pronoun or prenominal genitive noun phrase (for a discussion of the role of these elements, see section 2.2.4).[6] The indefinite article *en*, on the other hand, cannot occur in that position. This is exemplified in (2.17).

(2.17) a. *min / *Johans en mus
my Johan's one mouse

b. mina / Johans två möss
my Johan's two mice
'my/Johan's two mice'

There are forms related to *en*, *ena* 'one out of two (or more)' and *enda* 'single', which can be used to express the intended meaning of (2.17a).[7] These forms can co-occur with determiners and hence do not function as determiners themselves, as the examples in (2.18) show. They are similar to numerals in that they can follow prenominal genitives and possessive pronouns, as in (2.19).

(2.18) a. en enda mus
a single mouse
'a single mouse'

b. den ena musen
the one out of two (or more) mouse.DEF
'one of the two (or more) mice'

(2.19) a. min enda mus
my single mouse
'my only mouse'

b. Johans ena mus
Johan's one out of two mouse
'one of Johan's mice'

The issue of determiner status is further complicated by prenominal elements such as those exemplified in (2.20).

(2.20) a. **Ovannämnda** institution har erkänts.
above-mentioned institution has recognize.PASS
'The above-mentioned institution has been recognized.'

b. **Fel** löpare diskvalificerades.
wrong runner disqualify.PASS
'The wrong runner was disqualified.'

I will return to these examples in section 5.5.1.3, where I argue that these elements are, in fact, syntactic determiners.

The class of determiners as I have defined it here is then rather a big and semantically heterogeneous one.[8] It includes at least all the elements in (2.21) (this is not meant to be an exhaustive list). I will not attempt any sub-distinctions into semantic subclasses, because all I am interested in at present is the fact that they all behave syntactically like the core determiners.

(2.21)

en	någon	den	denna	ingen
a(n)	some	the/that	this	no
intet	varje	var	samma	vilken
no	every	every	same	which
vilkas	vars	mången	varsin	varannan
whose	whose	many a	one each	every other
varenda	hurdan	ovannämnda	fel	
every	what kind of	above-mentioned	wrong	

2.2.3. *Lexically complex determiners*

Some of the criteria established in the previous subsection can be applied to certain lexically complex elements and will classify these as syntactically simple determiners. In some of these cases, the exact status of the elements in question is a complicated issue. One example is the bold string in (2.22). According to the first criterion discussed in section 2.2.2, it is a determiner, since in (2.22a), it permits a singular indefinite count noun to function as a full noun phrase. On the other hand, in (2.22b) the string co-occurs with another determiner, and should therefore not be considered a determiner according to the second criterion for determiner status. The issue is further complicated by the fact that the first element of the string can be separated from the rest to form what appears to be a discontinuous determiner, as in (2.22c). This makes an analysis of *vad för en/någon* as a syntactically simple element difficult to defend.

(2.22) a. **Vad för** bil köpte ni?
what for car bought you
'What kind of car did you buy?'

b. **Vad för en** bil har ni?
what for a car have you
'What kind of car have you got?'

c. **Vad** har ni **för (en) bil**?
what have you for a car
'What kind of car have you got?'

I will not discuss this issue further here. I refer to Börjars (1992) for a detailed discussion of the issues involved and for a proposed analysis in terms of *wh*-movement from the specifier position of a noun phrase. This type of construction in Swedish has also been discussed by Teleman (1969). Parallel constructions are found in the other Scandinavian languages, German and Dutch. Corver (1990: 123–56) provides an account of a similar Dutch construction, and also gives an overview of analyses previously suggested for it.

Another, to my mind less problematic, example of a lexically complex determiner is *den här/den där*. Examples are provided in (2.23).

(2.23) a. **den här** musen
this mouse.DEF

b. **det där** murmeldjuret
that marmot

Den här/den där show identical distribution to semantically related determiners like *denna* 'this' and *den* 'that', the only difference being that *denna* requires the following noun not to occur in its definite form.[9]

Unlike the case of *vad för* (*en*), the two parts of *den här/den där* cannot be separated, as the examples in (2.24) indicate.

(2.24) a. ***den** gamla **där** bilen
that old there car.DEF

b. ***de** tre **där** bilarna
those three there cars.DEF

The example in (2.25) is grammatical, and this may give the appearance that *den här/den där* may be discontinuous.

(2.25) den bilen där
that car.DEF there

However, I would like to argue that what we have in (2.25) is not a discontinuous version of the determiner *den där*, but the demonstrative determiner *den* in combination with the adverbial *där*. Even though it seems obvious that *där* and *här* in *den där/här* have developed from the adverbials *där* and *här*, I think that there are good reasons to assume that the combinations have been reanalysed as one lexical unit of the category determiner. *Den* is not a distal demonstrative in *den där/här* as it is in *den . . . där*. Even though (2.25) is acceptable, (2.26a) is not, in contrast to (2.26b).

(2.26) a. ??den bilen här
that car.DEF here

b. den här bilen
that car.DEF

The noun phrase in (2.26a) is unacceptable for the same reason that the English ??*that car here* is infelicitous. I presume that this can be ascribed to a clash between the distal demonstrative *den* and the proximal adverb *här*. If *den här* is considered a combination of the distal demonstrative and a prenominal adverbial, then the difference in acceptability between (2.26a) and (2.26b) is mysterious.

Also, because of the spatial connotations of the adverbs *här* and *där*, they sound odd when used with abstract nouns which cannot usually be located in space. This is illustrated in (2.27). The same examples can, however, be used with *den här/den där*, as in (2.28).

(2.27) a. ??den noggrannheten där
that carefulness there

b. ??den förhoppningen där
that expectation there

(2.28) a. den där noggrannheten
that carefulness

b. den där förhoppningen
that expectation

The status of *den där/här* is controversial. Delsing (1989: 1–15) refers to Abney (1987: 301f.) for the claim that adverbs can be treated as adjectives, and assumes that the structure of *den där musen* is identical to that of *den gamla musen* 'the old mouse'. Delsing does not provide further arguments for this position, but, if *här* and *där* are considered to be adjectives, then on his analysis the double definiteness in these examples can be straightforwardly accounted for. In later work, Delsing (1993) classifies all demonstratives as adjectives (see section 5.3.2.1). Santelmann (1992: 102) argues for the same position as Delsing (1989): 'because these expressions always have double determiners, I shall assume that *här* and *där* in these cases do not differ syntactically from other attributive adjectives, even though they do not take adjectival agreement forms and they function semantically as demonstratives.' I believe that assigning the same status to *här* and *där* as to an adjective, and hence giving (2.26b) the structure [*den* [*här bilen*]], makes incorrect predictions. For instance, it would predict that the two elements can be co-ordinated in the same way that adjectives can. As (2.29) compared with (2.30) shows, this is incorrect.

(2.29) a. *den **här** och/eller **där** bilen
this.SG and/or car.DEF.SG

b. *de **här** och/eller **där** bilarna
these and/or car.DEF.PL

(2.30) a. Köpte ni den **röda eller gröna** bilen?
bought you the red or green car.DEF
'Did you buy the red or the green car?'

b. *Köpte ni den **här eller där** bilen?
bought you that here or there car.DEF

c. Köpte ni **den här eller den där** bilen?
bought you this or that car.DEF
'Did you buy this car or that one?'

Contrary to what would be expected if *här* and *där* were analysed in a way parallel to adjectives, these elements do seem to form a constituent with the preceding *den* as in (2.30c).

Furthermore, an adjective forms a constituent with the following noun, and can therefore be co-ordinated with another such string, as in (2.31a). As (2.31b) shows, however, this is not the case with *här* and *där*.[10]

(2.31) a. Köpte ni den **röda bilen eller gröna bilen**?
bought you the red car.DEF or green car.DEF
'Did you buy the red car or the green car?'

b. *Köpte ni den **här bilen eller där bilen**
bought you that here car.DEF or there car.DEF

I conclude therefore that *den här* and *den där* are two lexically complex, but syntactically simple, demonstrative determiners which select a definite noun, like a number of other determiners in Swedish (see section 5.3).

Another type of element which has been analysed as a lexically complex determiner of some sort is exemplified in (2.32) (see Loman 1956 and Allén 1958).

(2.32) a. **ett par** möss
a.NT pair(NT).SG mice(COM).PL
'a couple of mice'

b. **ett antal** möss
a.NT number(NT).SG mice(COM).PL
'a number of mice'

Such examples can be contrasted with the superficially similar ones in (2.33).

(2.33) a. **en kanna** öl
a.COM jug(COM) beer(NT)
'a jug of beer'

b. **ett glas** mjölk
a.NT glass(NT) milk(COM)
'a glass of milk'

The two types have in common their structure, Det+N+N. In both types, the determiner agrees in number and gender with the first noun rather than the second. However, a number of differences can be established (for more extensive discussion of the differences, see Teleman 1969: 22–36 and Delsing 1991a, 1993: 200–24). In examples like (2.32), any element that has to agree with the noun phrase as a whole tends to agree with the second noun; in (2.33), agreement is normally with the first noun. In both types, the second noun can be quite freely modified, whereas it is only in examples such as those in (2.33) that the first noun can be freely modified. The indications are then that *ett par* and *ett antal* form tight units that could plausibly be considered determiners. In (2.33), on the other hand, there is evidence that the first noun is the head noun of that noun phrase, whereas the second noun is a modifier. The modifier status of the second noun in this type is supported by the fact that it can usually be replaced by a preposition phrase consisting of a preposition and the noun.

Even though there is evidence that *ett par* and *ett antal* should be analysed similarly to determiners, a solution in which *ett par* forms a lexical unit in the same way that *den här* does is not plausible. The reason is that, even though these nouns cannot be modified as freely as the second noun in the same constructions, there are some limited possibilities of modification (for examples see Teleman 1969: 25 and Delsing 1993: 205). In the discussion here, I have been assuming that determiners will be analysed as belonging to a lexical category. However, if one assumes that determiners are, in fact, pronouns and hence of the same phrasal category as such elements (presumably NP or DP, depending on the type of analysis), then syntactically complex determiners could be accepted.[11] I will not deal with this issue in any further detail here, but I refer to Delsing (1993: 207–13) for a modern analysis of these elements within a transformational framework.

2.2.4. *Prenominal genitives and possessive pronouns*

In Swedish, possessive pronouns and prenominal genitive noun phrases – I will use the term PrenGen to refer jointly to both types – function like determiners in that they can combine with an indefinite singular count noun to form a full referential noun phrase. Examples are found in (2.34).

(2.34) a. **Min övertygelse** står fast.
my conviction remains

b. **Vår kommittés slutgiltiga beslut** framförs till regeringen.
our committee's final decision is put forward to the government

From data like (2.34), one can conclude that the Swedish PrenGens are DETERMINER GENITIVES rather than ADJECTIVAL GENITIVES, in terms of Lyons (1985, 1986, 1989, 1992) (for a discussion of this distinction, see also Plank

1992). However, as the examples in (2.35) show, these PrenGens can co-occur with other determiners, namely, *denna*, *varje* and *var*. This means that according to the second criterion, the PrenGens are not determiners.[12]

(2.35) a. **denna** min övertygelse
this my conviction

b. **detta** vår kommittés slutgiltiga beslut
this our committee's final decision

c. **varje** / vart mitt beslut
every every my decision

Delsing (1989: 14, 1993: 137–8) claims that *denna* in (2.35) is in fact not the determiner *denna*, but a quantifier *denna*. I will return to Delsing's analysis of demonstratives in section 5.3.2.1.

There are also other difficulties with analysing a phrase such as *vår kommittés* as a determiner. Since it is a phrasal element of syntactic complexity, and since a determiner is assumed to be a lexical element, the whole phrase cannot be the determiner, but some part of it will fulfil that specific function. This problem occurs mainly in a DP analysis. In an NP analysis, determiners could be assumed to be basically pronominal in nature and therefore of category NP themselves.[13] Such an analysis could accommodate phrasal determiners as already pointed out in section 2.2.3.

In line with recent proposals for a DP analysis of noun-phrase structure, the D slot of DPs containing PrenGens would be filled by the morphological element *-s* or by a feature, say [POSS] or [GEN], which assigns genitive case to the PrenGen noun phrase, as in *min övertygelse* and *vår kommitté* in (2.34).[14] The subject noun phrases in (2.34) are definite, and the standard assumption in any analysis would be that this definiteness feature is associated with the D position. The nominal head in these constructions does not carry the definite ending. Hence the definiteness of the phrase must be assumed to come from the D. For examples like (2.34), this would mean that *-s* or [GEN] must be a definite determiner. This assumption, however, causes difficulties for another type of noun phrase in Swedish. In this type of construction, which is quite productive, an indefinite determiner co-occurs with a genitive noun (or nominal phrase). Examples are provided in (2.36).[15]

(2.36) a. en synd-en-s kvinna
a.COM sin-DEF.COM-GEN woman(COM)
'a woman of sin'

b. ett ondska-n-s vapen
a.NT evil-DEF.COM-GEN weapon(NT)
'a weapon of evil'

The fact that the indefinite article determines the head noun rather than the noun of the PrenGen is made clear by (in)definiteness agreement and in

(2.36b) also by gender agreement. There are structural differences between the genitives in this type of construction and those in (2.35). Possessive pronouns cannot be used, for instance, in the indefinite noun phrases. Examples like (2.37a) and (2.37b) are ungrammatical. The possibilities of modifying the nominal are also very limited, though there are examples like (2.37c) (see Thorell 1973: 47).

(2.37) a. *en hans kvinna
a his woman

b. *ett vårt vapen
a our weapon

c. ett tredje klass-en-s hotell
a.NT third class-DEF.COM-GEN hotel(NT)
'a third rate hotel'

It seems obvious that the possessive phrase should not be considered a determiner in these cases. However, if *-s* or [GEN] is considered a determiner in (2.34) and (2.35), we would have to say that we have a different *-s* or a different [GEN] feature in (2.36) and (2.37c). An alternative available within an NP analysis would be to adopt the position of Lyons (1985, 1986, 1989, 1992) and describe the differences between (2.34) and (2.35), on the one hand, and (2.36) and (2.37c), on the other, in terms of the position of the prenominal genitive.

There is a further problem related to PrenGens and definiteness. Holmberg (1992: 67–71) points out the rarely noted fact that noun phrases with PrenGens can denote a property and hence occur in truly predicative positions. His example which shows that the construction really is predicational and not identificational is repeated in (2.38).[16] Because *Johans lärare* represents a property it can be ascribed to two individuals. This would not be possible in an identificational construction.

(2.38) Per är Johans / min lärare och Lisa är också Johans / min lärare.
Per is Johan's my teacher and Lisa is also Johan's my teacher
'Per is Johan's/my teacher and Lisa is also Johan's/my teacher.'

It is not clear that one would want to analyse these noun phrases containing PrenGens as definite noun phrases either, since definite noun phrases cannot usually occur in predicative positions.

I will not discuss the status of prenominal genitives further here, and I will not propose an analysis for the noun phrases which contain them. I refer to Börjars (1990) for a discussion of the possibilities within a non-transformational DP analysis. Delsing (1993: 147–84) discusses possessive constructions at some length and provides a transformational account of noun phrases containing them, though as far as I can tell, he does not provide any account for examples like (2.36).

2.3. The description field

The first step on the road to providing a syntactic description of Swedish noun phrases is to establish whether the distinction between a determiner field and a description field is justified syntactically. In section 2.2.2 I discussed a number of syntactic characteristics of the core members of the determiner field. In this section I will do the same for the core members of the description field, namely adjectives. Obviously, the class of adjectives has vague boundaries, maybe even more so than most other categories. In this section, I will use adjectives like *vit* 'white' and *smutsig* 'dirty', which can be assumed to be central members of the class. My list of criteria is obviously not intended to be exhaustive. I refer to Malmgren (1990) for a detailed discussion of various elements which can fulfil adjectival functions and of their different properties.

The main characteristic established for determiners in section 2.2.2 is the fact that they can change the basic semantic status of a nominal. In syntactic terms they turn nominals into full noun phrases. Adjectives do not have this ability; they are category-preserving, they combine with a nominal to form a nominal element of the same level. The addition of an adjective does not change the syntactic status of the nominal with which it combines. This is illustrated in (2.39).

(2.39) a. *Mus åt osten.
mouse ate cheese.DEF

b. *Vit(a) mus åt osten.
white mouse ate cheese.DEF

An adjective can occur in one of two positions in Swedish: in attributive position, preceding the noun it modifies, but following the determiner; or in predicative position, in which case one of a restricted number of verbs must occur between the noun it modifies and the adjective. Examples are given in (2.40).

(2.40) a. den vita / smutsiga musen
the white dirty mouse.DEF

b. den musen är vit / smutsig
that mouse.DEF is white dirty

c. en vit / smutsig mus
a white dirty mouse

d. en mus är ofta vit / smutsig
a mouse is often white dirty

Adjectives are introduced by a recursive rule, so that, in principle, any number of adjectives can co-occur within one noun phrase, as in (2.41). This contrasts with the behaviour of determiners, which occur in complementary distribution.

(2.41) den lyckliga lilla vita smutsiga musen
the happy little white dirty mouse

A further characteristic of adjectives is that, when they occur recursively, the internal order is quite free. In certain cases there is a preferred order, and any other order may sound emphatic or marked, as in (2.42). In each example, the preferred order is given first, and if there is a possible order that is less common this is also given. If only one order is provided, any other order sounds decidedly odd. For proposed explanations for the ordering restrictions of adjectives in Swedish, see Loman (1964) and Malmgren (1990: 177–82).

(2.42) a. ett stort rött äpple vs. ett rött stort äpple
a big red apple a red big apple

b. två stora sorgsna ögon vs. två sorgsna stora ögon
two large sad eyes two sad large eyes

c. en ny svensk politisk strid
a new Swedish political battle

d. ett modernt musikaliskt lexicon
a modern musical lexicon

Morphologically, adjectives are distinct in two ways. Firstly they can be compared, with an ending of (V)*re* in the comparative and (V)*st* for the superlative. No similar ending exists for the determiners. Secondly, adjectives are inflected for definiteness. The definite and indefinite forms are what are usually referred to as the adjective's weak and strong forms. The different adjectival forms are summed up in table 2.2. In addition to these forms, there is a weak ending *-e* which can be used on adjectives occurring in noun phrases headed by a noun with a male human referent. As table 2.2 shows, the distinction between weak and strong forms is only visible in singular noun phrases. Examples are provided in (2.43). The weak and strong forms will be discussed in more detail in sections 5.4 and 6.3, respectively.

Table 2.2 Paradigm for adjectival weak–strong inflection in Swedish

gender	number	weak	strong
common	singular	*hungrig**a***	*hungrig*
	plural	*hungrig**a***	*hungrig**a***
neuter	singular	*hungrig**a***	*hungrig**t***
	plural	*hungrig**a***	*hungrig**a***

(2.43) a. ett smutsig-**t** murmeldjur
a.NT dirty-NT.STR marmot(NT)

b. det smutsig-**a** murmeldjuret
the.NT dirty-WK marmot(NT)

c. en smutsig-Ø mus
a.COM dirty-COM.STR mouse

d. den smutsig-**a** musen
the.COM dirty-WK mus.DEF

Another characteristic of adjectives is the fact that they can occur in elliptical constructions.[17] Examples of such noun phrases are given in (2.44).

(2.44) a. Karin köpte den vita musen och Anders **den gråa**.
Karin bought the white mouse and Anders the grey.WK
'Karin bought the white mouse and Anders the grey one.'

b. Den vita musen kliade sig i örat, men det gjorde inte **den gråa**.
the white mouse scratched REFL in ear.DEF but it did not the grey.WK
'The white mouse scratched his ear, but the grey one didn't.'

In both sentences in (2.44), *mus* is the understood and retrievable noun in the bold noun phrase. Similar constructions are possible with a number of determiners. When the definite article and the demonstratives are used in the same way, the resulting NP seems to be deictic and one would only expect it to be used when speakers can use extra-linguistic means of indicating what they are referring to. Examples are provided in (2.45). It seems to me that, in the example in (2.45a), the final *den* could refer to, for instance, a dog or a bag of nuts for the mouse, if the speaker pointed at one. Such a free interpretation is not possible in (2.44). Also, whereas the first use of *den* in (2.45a) and (2.45b) is ambiguous between a definite and a demonstrative reading, the second instance can in both cases only be demonstrative.

(2.45) a. Karin köpte den vita musen och Anders **den**.
Karin bought that white mouse.DEF and Anders that
'Karin bought that white mouse and Anders that (one).'

b. Den vita musen kliade sig i örat, men det gjorde inte **den**.
the white mouse.DEF scratched REFL in ear.DEF but it did not that
'The white mouse scratched its ear, but that (one) didn't.'

An adjective that occurs in an elliptical construction like this can carry the genitive ending that would normally go on the noun. In the examples in (2.46), the final genitive ending belongs semantically to the understood noun *mus*.

(2.46) a. Karin tvättade den vita musens bur och Anders
Karin cleaned the white mouse.DEF.GEN cage and Anders
tvättade **den gråas**.
washed the grey.WK.GEN
'Karin cleaned the cage of the white mouse and Anders cleaned the grey one's.'

b. Den vita musens bur är ren men inte **den gråas**.
the white mouse.DEF.GEN cage is clean but not the grey.WK.GEN
'The cage of the white mouse is clean, but not the grey one's.'

This ability to carry the genitive article that 'belongs' to an understood nominal seems to be unique to the adjective. As the examples in (2.47) show, determiners and demonstratives cannot function in this way even though some of them have genitive forms.[18]

(2.47) a. *Karin tvättade en hamsters bur men Anders tvättade **ingens**.
Karin cleaned one hamster.GEN cage but Anders cleaned no.GEN
'Karin cleaned one hamster's cage, but Anders didn't clean any hamster's cage.'

b. *Karin tvättade några hamstrars burar, men hon
Karin cleaned some hamsters.GEN cages but she
tvättade inte **varjes**.
cleaned not every.GEN
'Karin cleaned some hamsters' cages, but not every hamster's cage.'

c. *Karin tvättade den hamsterns bur men inte **dens**.
Karin cleaned that hamster.DEF.GEN cage but not that.GEN
'Karin cleaned the cage of that hamster, but not that one's.'

The elliptical noun phrase in which a determiner is followed by an adjective with a genitive *-s* ending can occur in the determiner slot of a noun phrase, as in (2.48).

(2.48) a. Karin tvättade den bruna musens bur
Karin cleaned the brown mouse.DEF.GEN cage
men inte **den vitas hus**.
but not the.COM white.GEN house.NT
'Karin cleaned the brown mouse's cage, but not the white one's house.'

b. Den svarta kattens öron var rena men det
the black cat.DEF.GEN ears were clean but it
var inte **den randigas svans**.
was not the.SG striped.GEN tail
'The black cat's ears were clean, but the striped one's tail wasn't.'

Another difference between determiners and adjectives is the fact that the adjectives can be modified by adverbs and prepositional phrases. Examples are given in (2.49a) and (2.49b). As discussed in section 2.2.2, the possibilities, if any, for modification of determiners are extremely limited.

(2.49) a. den **helt** **vita** musen
the completely white mouse.DEF

b. den **i hans ögon väldigt smutsiga** musen
the in his eyes very dirty mouse.DEF

A final characteristic of adjectives is the fact that they can be co-ordinated with other adjectives, as in (2.50).[19]

(2.50) a. de **gamla** och **vita** mössen
the old and white mice.DEF

b. det **fallfärdiga** men **charmiga** huset
the ramshackle but charming house.DEF

Conjunctions involving a determiner and an adjective are impossible.

It should be added here that many of the Swedish words that have traditionally been unhesitatingly assigned the label adjective lack one or more of these characteristics. In (2.51a) an example is given of an adjective which does not show any morphological change for agreement. The adjective also lacks the comparative and superlative forms, even though semantically, the adjective seems gradable. Examples are also given of an adjective that can occur only in attributive position, (2.51b), and one which may occur only in predicative position (2.51c).

(2.51) a. en stilla kväll
a.COM quiet evening(COM)
ett stilla möte
a.NT quiet meeting(NT)
stilla kvällar
quiet evening.PL
*stillare / *mest stilla kvällar
quieter most quiet evening

b. stackars pojke / *pojken var stackars
poor boy boy.DEF was poor

c. mjölken är slut
milk.DEF is used up
'there is no more milk'
*(*en) slut mjölk / *den sluta mjölken
a used up milk the used up milk.DEF

2.4. The determiner field vs. the description field

If a syntactic distinction between different types of prenominal elements is to be maintained, syntactic evidence supporting such a distinction must be found. In terms of Loman (1956), for the division between determiner field and description field to be maintained, the elements of the determiner field must be shown to share a number of properties with determiners rather than with archetypal descriptive elements like adjectives. In more modern terms, we need to find syntactic evidence motivating separate syntactic classes like Q(uantifier) and Num(eral). The criteria which can be used to distinguish determiners and adjectives can be summarized schematically as in table 2.3. This table involves simplifications, and I refer back to the discussion in sections 2.2.2 and 2.3 for further details.

With only a couple of minor exceptions, the determiners behave consistently with respect to these criteria, but very few adjectives fulfil all the criteria. This means that, for an element to fall into the category of determiner, it must behave like a determiner with respect to all the criteria. In order to be classified as an adjective, on the other hand, the element need not satisfy all the criteria. In this section, I will apply the criteria established for determiners and for descriptive elements to the members of PK1 and PK4 to PK6; I use Loman's terminology here because the position classes provide a convenient shorthand way of referring to different types of prenominal elements. Lødrup (1989: 63–111) provides a discussion of similar issues in Norwegian, but less from a syntactic point of view than is my aim here.

The main syntactic characteristics of determiners is that in combination with a singular indefinite count noun they can form a complete noun phrase which can occur in the subject position of a sentence. This criterion is, of course, only relevant to elements that can combine with such a noun. The members of PK1 and PK4 to PK6 which can occur with an indefinite singular count noun do not function like determiners in this respect. In (2.52) a number of examples illustrating this point are given.

Table 2.3 Characteristics of determiners and adjectives

	Det	Adj
Status changing	+	–
License adjectives	+	–
Recursive	–	+
Ordering	not appl	weak
Accepts modification	–	+
Predicative position	–	+
Morphological marking WK/STR CMP/SPR	–	+
Accepts genitive *-s* in elliptic constructions	–	+
Can be co-ordinated with adjectives	–	+

(2.52)

*Annan other *Enda only *Sådan such *Likadan same	mus mouse	skrattade laughed	åt at	katten cat.DEF

Another characteristic of determiners is that they occur in complementary distribution with each other. The examples in (2.53) support the conclusion based on (2.52) that these elements are not determiners.

(2.53)

En a	annan other enda only sådan such likadan same	mus mouse	skrattade laughed	åt at	katten cat.DEF

This criterion is also important for elements to which the first criterion cannot be applied because they cannot co-occur with a single indefinite count noun. Such prenominal elements can still be argued not to be determiners on the basis of data like (2.54), (2.55) and (2.56).

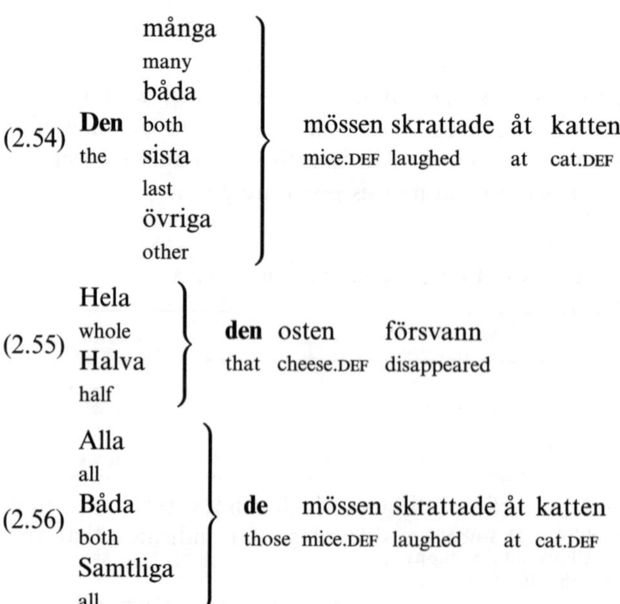

(2.54)

Den the	många many båda both sista last övriga other	mössen mice.DEF	skrattade laughed	åt at	katten cat.DEF

(2.55)

Hela whole Halva half	**den** that	osten cheese.DEF	försvann disappeared

(2.56)

Alla all Båda both Samtliga all	**de** those	mössen mice.DEF	skrattade laughed	åt at	katten cat.DEF

When the elements follow determiners, they will often carry the same marking for weak and strong forms as adjectives. I have only given a few examples here, but the argument can be applied to all members of PK1 and PK4 to PK6 in table 2.1 (section 2.1) except *mången* which I argued in section 2.2.2 to be a determiner.

The predicative position which is characteristic of adjectives can be filled by many of the elements from the determiner field, even though the determiners themselves cannot occur predicatively. Examples are provided in (2.57), (2.58) and (2.59). Some of these examples are only possible when the element is postmodified by a preposition phrase or a clause.

(2.57) Mössen var { likadana / många / talrika / få / otaliga }
mice.DEF were { same / many / numerous / few / innumerable }

(2.58) Glädjen var mycken.
joy.DEF was much

(2.59) a. Karins cykel är **sådan** att man måste bromsa med pedalerna.
Karin's bicycle is such that one must brake with pedals.DEF
'Karin's bicycle is such that one must use the pedals to brake.'

b. Den löparen var **först** / **sist** över mållinjen.
that runner was first/last over finishing line.DEF
'That runner was the first to cross the finishing line.'

c. Mötet var **tidigare/senare** än det andra.
meeting.DEF was earlier/later than the other
'The meeting was later/earlier than the other one.'

d. Mössen var **fler** än jag väntat mig.
mice.DEF were more than I expected REFL
'There were more mice than I had expected.'

Not all members of the relevant position classes can occur in predicative positions. However, this does not necessarily mean that the behaviour of those elements distinguishes them from the members of the description field. In (2.51b) I gave an example of an adjective which cannot itself occur in a predicative position. The evidence considered so far indicates that the members of position classes 1 and 4 to 6 share more properties with adjectives than with determiners.

The recursion which is characteristic of adjectives does not apply in the same way to the members of the position classes. On the other hand, co-occurrence restrictions for the members of the position classes are not as strict as for the determiners. Even though the position classes are based on complementary distribution, the examples in (2.4) in section 2.2.1 showed that in, a few cases, members of the same class can co-occur. Furthermore, if we assume that the members of the position classes all belong to one syntactic category, such as Q(uantifier), then quite long strings of attributes can be formed – not as long as some possible adjectival strings, but that may be due to the fact that the number of combinations of semantically compatible but not tautologous attributes is quite limited. This means that, even though the attributes under discussion here are more restricted than the members of the description field, they are certainly not as restricted as the determiners.

The use of position classes also implies a rigid ordering between the different elements and also especially between the elements of the determiner field and the description field. The elements of the determiner field could therefore be distinguished in two ways. Firstly they will always precede the descriptive elements and, secondly, they will occur in a rigid internal order. However, neither of these characteristics could actually be used to distinguish the members of the determiner field from those of the description field. The examples in (2.60) show that adjectives can, in fact, precede members of the determiner field. In (2.61) there are examples showing that the order between the position classes is not as rigid as implied by the class system. (These examples are repeated from (2.2) and (2.3) in section 2.2.1.) Furthermore, in section 2.3, I showed that ordering restrictions also apply between members of the description field.

(2.60) a. en smutsig sådan mus
a dirty such[PK6] mouse
'a dirty mouse of that kind'

b. det längsta sista försöket
the longest last[PK5] attempt
'the longest last attempt'

(2.61) a. de andra båda syskonen
the other[PK5] both[PK1/4] siblings
'the other two siblings'

b. sådana andra karameller
such[PK6] other[PK5] sweets
'the other kind of sweets'

c. de andra två förslagen
the other[PK5] two[PK4] suggestions
'the other two suggestions'

A characteristic unique to adjectives (and adverbials) is the comparative and superlative forms. Of course, the comparative and superlative forms are limited to gradable adjectives, in Swedish as in other languages. Some of the members of the determiner field can actually occur in comparative and superlative forms. The ending *-st*, characteristic of superlatives in Swedish, is found in *först* 'first' and *sist* 'last', which could be considered 'semantic superlatives'. That is to say that they indicate the extreme ends of a spectrum, like superlatives do. The other position classes contain examples of comparative and superlative use of attributes. *Många* 'many' (PK4) has the suppletive comparative and superlative forms *fler* and *flest*. *Få* 'few' (PK4) has *färre*. Östergren (1919) even cites the superlative form *färst* but does add that it is extremely rare. Morphologically, *senaste* 'most recent' in PK5 is the superlative form of *sen* 'late', and there is a comparative form *senare*. The morphology of *tidigare* 'previous' in PK5 indicates that it is the comparative form of *tidig* 'early', with the superlative form *tidigast*. However, there are changes in meaning involved. The words *senare* and *senaste* tend to mean 'more/most recent', rather than stressing the lateness of the event. In the same way, *tidigare* may be used to mean roughly the same as the prefix *ex-* in Swedish and English.

Östergren (1919) also gives examples of how *talrika*, *fåtaliga* and *otaliga* can be used like gradable adjectives and have comparative endings. Examples from Östergren are given in (2.62).

(2.62) a. lika otalig som sanden är i havet
as numerous as sand.DEF is in sea.DEF

b. de kom tillbaka otaligare än någonsin
they came back more numerous than ever

It seems, then, that the members of PK4 to PK6 which are semantically gradable do have inflections for at least the comparative form and often for the superlative.

In section 2.3 I showed that adjectives can occur in elliptical constructions where the noun is elided. However, this criterion is problematic as a test for adjective status, because determiners too can occur in this type of construction. There is, I claimed, a difference in the semantics of the result. The examples with determiners are not true examples of ellipsis in that there is not always an obvious retrievable nominal. A more important difference in behaviour between determiners and adjectives in this respect is the fact that adjectives can carry the genitive *-s* of an understood nominal. The members of PK6, even though they may occur in elliptical constructions, do not seem to be able to carry the genitive *-s*, as the examples in (2.63) show.

(2.63) a. Karin vill ha en sådan mus men inte en **sådan**.
Karin wants have a such mouse but not a such
'Karin wants to have such a mouse (as this), but not such a one (as that).'

b. ?Karin gör gärna rent en sådan katts korg, men inte en **sådans**.
Karin make gladly clean a such cat.GEN basket but not a such.GEN
'Karin would be happy to clean the basket of such a cat as this, but not that of such a one as that.'

Many of the attributes belonging to the other position classes, but not all, function like adjectives in this way. Examples are provided in (2.64), (2.65) and (2.66).

(2.64) a. Jag kan rätta några elevers uppsatser, men inte **samtligas**.
I can mark some pupils' essays but not all.GEN
'I can mark the essays of some pupils, but not those of all (pupils).'

b. Jag kan rätta den ena elevens uppsats, men inte **bådas**.
I can mark the one pupil's essays but not both.GEN
'I can mark the essays of one of the pupils, but not (the essays) of both of them.'

(2.65) a. —Kan du rätta båda elevernas uppsatser?
can you mark both pupils' essays
—Jag kan rätta den **enas**, men inte den **andras**.
I can mark the one-out-of-two.GEN but not the other.GEN
'I can mark one of the pupils' essays, but not the other's.'

b. Jag kan rätta några få elevers uppsatser, men vill du
I can mark some few pupils' essays but want you
ha **mångas** rättade får du fråga någon annan.
have many.GEN marked may you ask somebody else
'I can mark the essays of a few pupils, but if you want the essays of many pupils marked, you'll have to ask somebody else.'

(2.66) a. Jag kan rätta den här elevens uppsats men ingen **annans**.
I can mark this pupil's essay but nobody other's
'I can mark this pupil's essay, but nobody else's.'

b. Anders gratulerade den förste och den andre löparens fruar,
Anders congratulated the first and the second runner's wives
men inte **den tredjes**.
but not the third.GEN
'Anders congratulated the first and second runners' wives, but not the third one's.'

c. Jag har det förra mötets rapport men inte **det senastes**.
I have the previous meeting's report but not the latest.GEN
'I have the report from the previous meeting, but not the one from the most recent one.'

d. Karin hittade de yngsta elevernas matsal, men inte **de övrigas**.
Karin found the youngest pupils' dining hall but not the other's
'Karin found the youngest pupils' dining hall but not that of the other pupils.'

Many of these elliptical NPs can also fill the determiner slot, in the same way that elliptical NPs with adjectives can. Some examples are provided in (2.67).

(2.67) a. en annans uppsats
a other.GEN essay
'another one's essay'

b. den tredjes fru
the third.GEN wife
'the wife of the third one'

c. de övrigas matsal
the other.GEN dining hall
'the other ones' dining hall'

d. den enas uppsats
the one-out-of-two.GEN essay
'the essay of one of them'

Even though a number of the attributes can take the genitive ending *-s* in elliptical noun phrases, some of them cannot. Like the other criteria discussed in this section, this one cannot be used to defend the adjective status of all the prenominal elements under discussion here. On the other hand, if the attributes discussed were all grouped with the determiners, then the fact that so many of them function similarly to adjectives would be surprising.

Another feature that distinguishes between adjectives and determiners is modification. Determiners cannot be preceded by a modifier (though see the discussion of the examples in (2.12) in section 2.2.2), whereas adjectives can be modified quite freely. As the examples in (2.68) show, the attributes in position classes 1 and 4 to 6 can be modified. They are often modified by elements that could also modify adjectives.

(2.68) a. en **alldeles likadan** mus
a totally same mouse
'a mouse which was exactly the same'

b. en **helt annan** mus
a completely other mouse
'a different mouse altogether'

c. det **allra senaste** mötet
the totally latest meeting
'the absolutely most recent meeting'

d. hans **numera knappt femtio** frimärken
his presently hardly fifty stamps
'his collection of stamps which now do not even number fifty'

e. de **beklagligtvis ytterst få** intresserade
the deplorably extremely few interested
'the sadly extremely few interested people'

f. **på tok för många** gäss
on crazy too many geese
'far too many geese'

g. de **enligt hans mening talrika** gästerna
the according to his opinion numerous guests
'the guests, which were numerous in his opinion'

h. **knappt halva** den kakan
hardly half that biscuit
'just less than half that biscuit'

The last characteristic feature of adjectives discussed in section 2.3 was the fact that they, unlike determiners, can be co-ordinated with other adjectives. As the examples in (2.69) show, attributes from all the position classes under discussion can be co-ordinated with adjectives.

(2.69) a. **halva** och **alldeles för torra** kakor
half and completely too dry biscuits
'biscuits which have been broken in half and which are far too dry'

b. **få** och **för små** möss
few and too small mice

c. **andra** och **bättre** böcker
other and better books

d. en **likadan** och **lika dyr** kaka
a same and equally expensive biscuit

In this respect too, the members of position classes 4 to 6 and possibly those of class 1 behave more similarly to adjectives than to determiners.

2.5. Conclusions

The purpose of this chapter was to decide how many categories of prenominal elements can be distinguished on the basis of syntactic criteria. Two categories were taken as a starting point: determiners and adjectives. The aim was to discover whether the elements found in Loman's (1956) position classes 1 and 4 to 6 share a sufficient number of properties with either of these categories to be assigned to the same category, or whether an independent category, say Q(uantifier) or Num(eral), is required. The discussion was formulated in terms of Loman's position classes because they provide both a convenient terminology and a useful list of elements. The discussion is equally relevant to a more modern approach to noun phrase structure.

The criteria I used were summarized in table 2.3 in section 2.4. Of the elements tested, only one (*mången*) satisfies all the criteria for determiner status. Since determiners are much more consistent in their behaviour with respect to the tests than adjectives, the behaviour of these elements (apart from *mången*) is untypical of determiners. The conclusion I draw on the basis of the data discussed in this chapter is therefore that there is no clear distinction with respect to syntactic behaviour between the non-determiner members of Loman's determiner field and members of the description field. This means that there is no syntactic motivation for classifying the 'non-determiners' discussed here with the determiners.

I found that there was one word in Loman's PK4, which did behave consistently like a determiner, namely *mången* 'many a'. With respect to all other elements under discussion, the determiner criteria indicate that the elements function syntactically in a fundamentally different way from determiners. I therefore conclude that the members of Loman's PKl and 4 to 6 do not belong to the same syntactic category as determiners.

With respect to the characteristics of adjectives in table 2.3, quite a different pattern emerges. There is no element in the position classes which behaves like an adjective in relation to every characteristic. On the other hand, there are few 'real' adjectives which have all of these characteristics. Each element in the position classes under discussion shows some characteristics of adjectives. Therefore, I see no reason to posit a separate syntactic category for these elements. I will assume that elements like *alla* 'all', *få* 'few', *enda* 'only' and *sådana* 'such' (see table 2.1 in section 2.1) belong to the syntactic category A, which, when modified, can form an AP. The ordering restrictions between these adjectives will need to be specified somewhere in the grammar. However, this also holds, albeit to a lesser extent, for core adjectives referring to concepts like colour and size. A possible way of doing this might be to make limited use of some version of Field Grammar within a category-based phrase-structure grammar. For suggestions to this effect to deal with other ordering problems, see for instance Ahrenberg (1992) and Hellan (1993).

3
DEFINITE FEATURE OR DEFINITE ARTICLE

3.1. Introduction

In traditional Swedish grammars, there is no consensus view of the status of the definite ending -*(e)n* / -*(e)t* / -*na*. Hulthén (1948) uses the term 'definite end-article' (*bestämd slutartikel*). Thorell (1973: 19–23) refers to *musen* 'mouse.DEF' as the 'definite form' of the noun, but then lists -*en* under articles. The same terminology is used in Ljung and Ohlander (1971: 39). Historically, DEF developed from an independent demonstrative pronoun, even though there is still some discussion about the precise form it developed from. For discussions of the historical development and the forms involved, see for instance Haugen (1976: 297–299, 1982: 95–99) and Wessén (1970: 29–49), Anward and Swedenmark (1997) discuss different ways of modelling this development. Perridon (1989) provides a detailed overview of the different historical arguments.

The reason for the confusion in a synchronic approach is that a noun like *musen* can function as the subject of a sentence without an independent determiner. On the other hand, such a noun can also co-occur with, for instance, demonstrative determiners, as in *den musen* 'that mouse.DEF'. The term 'definite form' points to a tree like (3.1a), whereas the notion of -*en* as a definite article is best captured by (3.1b). In (3.1), I have assumed that the syntactic category of a noun phrase is NP, but both types of analyses could be captured in a DP structure. I will return to the issue of which syntactic category to assign to noun phrases in Chapter 4.

(3.1)

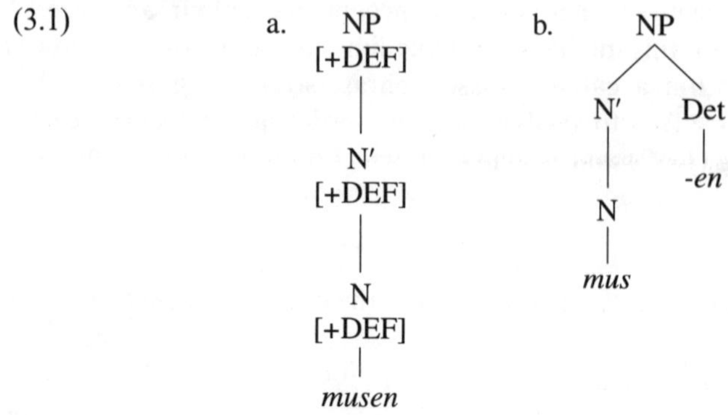

In (3.1a) DEF is part of the morphology, whereas in (3.1b), it has syntactic status. This means that in a theoretical, rather than purely descriptive, approach to Swedish noun phrases, the confusion of terminology must be resolved. For the time being, I will refer to it as DEF.

In an analysis where DEF is assigned syntactic status, it cannot be given exactly the same status as a word since it is morphologically bound. In such an analysis, DEF would be relevant both to the syntax and the morphology. Items that have this intermediate status between syntax and morphology are often referred to as CLITICS. Elements which do not have syntactic status, like DEF in (3.1a), are referred to as AFFIXES in the same tradition.[1] In the literature, this distinction has been discussed in depth, notably by Klavans (1979, 1983, 1985), Zwicky (1977, 1985b) and Zwicky and Pullum (1983).[2] In this chapter, I will apply these criteria to DEF in order to decide which of the types of analysis represented in (3.1) is more appropriate.

In section 3.2 I will discuss the ways in which DEF has been dealt with in previous analyses of Swedish noun phrases. I consider tests that have been put forward for clitics and affixes in section 3.3, and look at how these apply to the Swedish DEF. The consequences if DEF was assigned independent syntactic status as in (3.1b) are explored in section 3.4. In 3.5 the behaviour of DEF is compared to that of another element in Swedish that has often been assigned clitic status, namely the genitive ending *-s*. In section 3.6 the distribution of the Swedish DEF is compared to similar elements in other languages.

3.2. PREVIOUS ANALYSES

In theoretical analyses of Swedish noun phrases, both types of representation in (3.1) have been suggested. Nilsson (1968) assumes that the ending is an article, as in (3.1b). Furthermore, she argues that the indefinite article *en/ett* and the definite end article *-en/-et* are not two distinct lexemes, but just one article which can yield either a [+DEF] or a [–DEF] noun phrase, depending on whether it is generated before or after the noun. Nilsson's article is written in the spirit of enthusiasm for unwieldy transformations characteristic of the early transformational grammarians. I have not seen it taken up in any more recent articles and I will not discuss it further here.

Without arguing the issue, Cooper (1984, 1986), Hellan (1986) and Svenonius (1992c) assume that DEF does not have syntactic status, but is the instantiation of a feature [+definite].[3] The analyses which result provide quite different accounts of the fact that a noun which carries this feature can function as a full noun phrase. I will return to the details of these analyses in section 5.2.2.2.

In recent transformational accounts of Scandinavian noun phrases, DEF is standardly assumed to have syntactic status, for example, Holmberg (1987),

Delsing (1988, 1989), Santelmann (1992), Taraldsen (1990, 1991) and Sigurðsson (1992). One exception is Holmberg (1992: 64) who positions a noun like *musen* under an N node. Delsing (1993) assumes that in some constructions DEF is base generated on the noun, under the N node, and in other cases it has independent syntactic status and is generated under D. In analyses where DEF has independent syntactic status, the account of why a definite noun like *musen* can function as a full noun phrase is straightforward: *musen* contains a syntactic determiner, just like *the mouse* does. In section 5.2.2.1 I will discuss these analyses in more detail.

Holmberg (1987) is one of the few linguists aiming at a theoretical analysis of Scandinavian noun phrases who also explicitly discusses the status of DEF. Since such arguments are so rare in the literature on Scandinavian, I will discuss two of the arguments briefly here, even though Holmberg has since published a different account of Swedish noun phrases (Holmberg 1992). Two of Holmberg's (1987: 4–5) arguments are summarized in (3.2).

(3.2) (i) If DEF is considered the manifestation of a [+DEF] feature, this implies that definiteness is a lexical property of head nouns. This would mean that a definite noun like *musen* would be found in the lexicon as an N[+DEF], in the same way as pronouns and proper nouns. This would, of course, be an unwanted consequence, since a definite noun has many morphological and syntactic characteristics which pronouns and proper nouns do not have.

(ii) The fact that the definite ending always attaches outside derivational and inflexional affixes and that it cannot occur inside a compound is a further sign that the affix cannot be the manifestation of a feature.

In his first argument, Holmberg seems implicitly to discard the possibility of morphological rules. The claim on which Holmberg bases his first argument can be summed up as follows; the N+DEF combination is either a lexical, inherently definite unit, or it is a combination governed by syntactic rules on a par with a combination of an independent determiner and a noun. This appears to be an over-simplification. Analyses like those of Cooper (1984, 1986) and Hellan (1986), where DEF is the manifestation of a feature, do not necessarily imply that a noun with a feature [+definite] has the same status as a proper noun. In the case of *musen* 'mouse.DEF', we could assume that there are two lexical entries: *mus* and *-en*, but no lexical entry *musen*, and still claim that the combining of the two elements is not governed by syntactic rules, but by morphological rules. A distinction could be made between elements like proper nouns, which are inherently [+DEF], and elements like *musen*, which have received their feature value [+DEF] through morphological processes.

As regards Holmberg's second argument, it should be noted that, whereas

DEF follows the plural affix, it always occurs inside the possessive *-s* when the two co-occur. I will return to this in sections 3.3.3 and 3.5. Furthermore, if the fact that DEF does not occur internally in compounds is interpreted as an indication that it is a syntactic element, then this will have far-reaching consequences for many elements in Swedish that have traditionally not been considered part of the syntax. In the example that Holmberg uses (see (3.3a)), it might be more logical to expect the first part of the compound to contain the plural suffix, rather than DEF. After all, car thieves are more naturally thought of as thieves that steal cars (plural) in general, rather than a specific, definite car. Still, as (3.3b) shows, the plural affix cannot occur either.

(3.3)	a.	biltjuv	biltjuven	*bil**en**tjuv	*bil**en**tjuven
		car.thief	car.thief.DEF	car.DEF.thief	car.DEF.thief.DEF
	b.	biltjuvar	*bil**ar**tjuv	*bil**ar**tjuvar	
		car.thief.PL	car.PL.thief	car.PL.thief.PL	

Holmberg (1987: 4) does say that he considers the status of the plural affix as a lexical property dubious. Holmberg's argument can also be extended to adjectival endings. An adjective modifying a neuter noun in an indefinite noun phrase carries a neuter agreement marker, or strong morphology, *-t*. As the examples in (3.4) show, when the adjective forms a compound with a neuter noun, it does not carry the agreement marker it would otherwise have carried when combined with a neuter noun.

(3.4)	a.	ett	blek-**t**	ansikte
		a.NT	pale-NT	face(NT)
		*ett	blek**t**ansikte	
		a.NT	pale.NT.face	
		ett	blekansikte	
		a	pale.face	
	b.	ett	vit-**t**	vin
		a.NT	white-NT	wine(NT)
		*ett	vit**t**vin	
		a.NT	white.NT.wine	
		ett	vitvin	
		a.NT	white.wine	

If the argument were to be extended to adjectives, then the agreement marker would also be assumed to have syntactic status. Holmberg's argument relating to compounds, taken to its extreme, would give rise to what could be called a radical 'non-lexicalism'. All inflections become elements of the syntax, and the distinction between syntax and morphology fades into virtual non-existence. This is, of course, exactly the direction in which recent transformational theory has moved (an early example is Baker

1988), but it is still true in more recent versions of the theory like Minimalism (Chomsky 1995). However, in the remainder of this chapter, I will argue that in order to make possible a correct account of the facts relating to the Swedish DEF, the distinction between syntax and morphology must be preserved.

3.3. WHAT IS A CLITIC?

In the previous section, we saw that most recent analyses of Scandinavian languages assign syntactic status to DEF (Delsing (1988, 1989, 1993), Holmberg (1987), Santelmann (1992), Taraldsen (1990, 1991) and Sigurðsson (1992)). This means that DEF is analysed as a clitic. The term 'clitic' refers to a category of items that share certain properties with affixes, mainly that of being bound. On the other hand, clitics are assumed to share certain other properties with words, particularly, they are assumed to be governed by syntactic rules.[4] The behaviour of affixes, on the other hand, is governed by morphological rules.

A theory-independent definition of 'clitic' has not been established. Still, there is some agreement about what characteristics distinguish clitics from affixes. Criteria for such a distinction have been proposed and discussed, in largely theory-independent terms, by, for instance, Carstairs (1981: 1–44), Klavans (1983, 1985), Sadock (1991: 48–77) and Spencer (1991: 375–84) and in an Optimality Theory approach by Anderson (1996), but maybe most influentially by Zwicky and Pullum (1983).[5] These criteria have been developed on the basis of a wide range of phenomena in a large number of languages and most of them are generally applicable. In this section, I will consider the behaviour of DEF in the light of these criteria.

There are problems with applying criteria of the type proposed by Zwicky and Pullum. The biggest of these is the main assumption that the criteria divide bound elements into two discrete classes. The behaviour of elements is often not totally consistent. This means that in order to arrive at the conclusion that an element is either a clitic or an affix, certain criteria must be assumed to be less crucial.[6] I am not expecting the criteria to provide conclusive evidence that the Swedish DEF is either a clitic or an affix. I am hoping that the criteria used by others to distinguish affixes from clitics, when applicable to the Swedish DEF, will point in one direction rather than the other with a certain degree of consistency.

The criteria for morphological status can be used without the assumption that they will distinguish two discrete classes of elements.[7] If the criteria are applied to a number of elements and the elements behave differently, even without any of them behaving consistently as a clitic or an affix, then an analysis must represent these distinctions, regardless of whether the elements are referred to as clitics and affixes. For this reason, in this chapter, I will apply the criteria not only to DEF, but also to the Swedish possessive *-s* (in section 3.5) and to DEFs in other European languages (in section 3.6).

In this introduction, I have, without discussion, introduced a distinction between morphology and syntax. This distinction is by no means generally accepted and the existence of morphology as a separate module has been debated in the literature (for instance by Anderson 1982). If we disregard clitics and simplify the issue, we can say that morphology is the set of rules which governs word formation, and syntax is the set of rules which governs the formation of phrases. The question is then whether the two sets are sufficiently different to warrant the existence of two different modules: morphology and syntax. If the answer to this question is no, then the distinction between clitics and affixes disappears. The two categories will be non-distinct and similar to any other unit of the syntax except in so far as they are bound. If the answer to the question is that we do need a morphology module, then we can recognize affixation and cliticization as two kinds of word formation, one type governed by morphological rules and one by syntactic rules. This means that in this chapter, I am not only investigating whether Swedish DEF is an affix or a clitic, but indeed whether such a distinction is justified at all.

3.3.1. *Phrasal host*

Probably the most generally accepted characteristic of clitics is the fact that they are positioned relative to a phrasal unit rather than in relation to a specific syntactic category (see for instance, Carstairs 1981, Klavans 1983, 1985, Spencer 1991 and Zwicky and Pullum 1983). Klavans (1985) refers to clitics as PHRASAL AFFIXES. She calls the phrasal element which is the domain of a clitic its HOST PHRASE. Phonologically, the clitic is attached to a word, and this is termed the HOST WORD by Klavans (1985). Klavans's terminology offers a possibility of defining more strictly what it means to be positioned in relation to a phrasal category. She provides a description in terms of three parameters of how a clitic is positioned in relation to its host phrase and host word. These positioning parameters can, in Klavans's view, be seen as constraints on clitics, that is, if an item is a clitic, there should be a way of describing its position in terms of the three parameters. (This is made explicit in Klavans 1983: 104–8.) The three parameters are given in table 3.1. According to Parameter 1 (P1), the position of a clitic is specified in relation to the initial or final element of its host phrase. Parameter 2 (P2) indicates whether the clitic occurs before or after the element set by P1. Finally, Parameter 3 (P3) specifies whether the clitic attaches phonologically to the left (enclitic) or to the right (proclitic). The three parameters thus allow a clitic to be phonologically attached to a word outside its domain; for instance, if it has the value ‘initial’ for P1, ‘before’ for P2 and ‘enclitic’ for P3. An example of such a clitic is the object noun phrase in Kwakwala

Table 3.1 Klavans's parameters constraining the position of clitics

	TYPE	VALUES
Parameter 1	dominance	initial/final
Parameter 2	precedence	before/after
Parameter 3	phonological liaison	proclitic/enclitic

(Klavans 1985: 106–8). Contracted auxiliaries in English may be another example of elements which cliticize to something outside their phrasal hosts (see Kaisse 1983).

If the Swedish DEF is a clitic, we expect a definition of its placement in terms of P1, P2 and P3 to be possible. DEF always attaches at the end of a word; this means that the value for P3 must be 'enclitic'. The position of DEF in the subject noun phrase of (3.5) can be defined either by P1 'initial' and P2 'after', or P1 'final' and P2 'after'.

(3.5) [Gris-**en**]$_{NP}$ grymtade.
pig-DEF grunted
'The pig grunted.'

The first possibility, 'initial, after, enclitic', is, however, ruled out by the example in (3.6). Here DEF does not attach to the right of the initial element of its phrasal host.

(3.6) [Den här gamla smutsiga gris-**en**]$_{NP}$ grymtade.
this old dirty pig-DEF grunted
'This dirty old pig grunted.'

The values 'initial, after, enclitic' actually describe the Wackernagel position if the domain is the sentence (Wackernagel 1892). In section 3.6 I will give examples of languages that appear to have a 'Wackernagel position' within the noun phrase.

The other possible combination: 'final, after, enclitic', would correctly predict the position of DEF in (3.5) and (3.6). However, the same parameter values would, incorrectly, predict that DEF would also follow postmodification in Swedish noun phrases. As the examples in (3.7) show, this is not the case.

(3.7) a. [Gris-**en** med lång svans]$_{NP}$ grymtade.
pig-DEF with long tail grunted
'The pig with the long tail grunted.'

b. [Gris-**en** med lång svans som tycker om gröt]$_{NP}$ grymtade.
pig-DEF with long tail who likes porridge grunted
'The pig with a long tail who likes porridge grunted.'

It seems unlikely that a satisfactory way of describing the position of DEF in Swedish noun phrases in terms of Klavans's parameters can be found. Thus, from this discussion of Klavans's parameters in relation to the position of DEF within Swedish noun phrases, we can conclude that either Klavans's parameters are wrong, or the Swedish DEF is better analysed as an affix than a clitic. Klavans's distinction is based on thorough research into a large number of unrelated languages. Furthermore, the notion that the position of a clitic is defined in terms of a phrasal unit is generally accepted in this tradition. This means that unless we can find some other strong evidence that DEF behaves like a clitic, we can conclude that the difficulties with applying Klavans's parameter here arise from the fact that DEF is not a clitic, but an affix.

3.3.2. *Selectivity*

Another typical feature of a clitic is that its relation to its host word is weak. The relation is weak in the sense that a clitic typically disregards the syntactic category of its host word as long as the structural criteria, defined in relation to its host phrase, are fulfilled (Carstairs 1981, 1987, Sadock 1991: 52ff., Spencer 1991: 350–1, Zwicky and Pullum 1983). An affix, on the other hand, attaches to items belonging to a specific class of words. As the examples in (3.8) indicate, DEF cannot be attached to a word of any other category than noun. In (3.8a), the potential host word is a preposition, in (3.8b), a verb, and in (3.8c), it is a verb particle.

(3.8) a. flicka-**n** framför / *flicka framför-en
girl-DEF in.front girl in.front-DEF
'the girl in front'

b. flicka-**n** jag träffade / *flicka jag träffade-n
girl-DEF I met girl I met-DEF
'the girl I met'

c. brev-**et** hon slängde bort / *brev hon slängde bort-et
letter-DEF she threw away letter she threw away-DEF
'the letter she threw away'

In Swedish, when a noun is understood, rather than overtly present, in a noun phrase containing an adjective, this adjective can carry morphemes that are otherwise typical of nouns. This was discussed in section 2.3. The example in (3.9b) shows that DEF cannot be carried by an adjective in this way. Instead, a prenominal determiner must be used, as in (3.9c).[8]

(3.9) Den här flaska-n drack vi fort, men . . .
this bottle-DEF drank we quickly but

a. . . . förra flaska-**n** drack vi långsamt.
last bottle-DEF drank we slowly

b. *. . . förra-n drack vil ångsamt.
last-DEF drank we slowly

c. . . . **den** förra drack vi långsamt.
the last drank we slowly
'This bottle we drank quickly, but the last bottle we drank slowly.'

An adjective in Swedish can only carry DEF when it has been fully nominalized. An example is provided in (3.10a). In this example, the adjective has been fully nominalized and has acquired a specific meaning. Compare this to (3.10b), where the same adjective occurs in an elliptical construction rather than as a nominalized adjective.

(3.10) a. Vänster**n** krånglar igen.
left.DEF is.awkward again
'The political left is being awkward again.'

b. —Vilken sida av gatan bor ni på? —**Den** vänstra.
which side of street.DEF live you on the left.WK
—*Vänstern.
left.DEF
'—Which side of the street do you live on? —The left one.'

From the examples used so far, we can conclude that DEF can attach only to nouns. This means that it is unlike a clitic in being selective about the syntactic category of the element to which it attaches. DEF is, in fact, even more selective with regard to its host than this. In (3.11) and (3.12) examples are given where the head noun is followed by post-modification that has a noun as its final element. Still, DEF cannot attach to the end of these noun phrases.

(3.11) a. [[Gris-en] med lång svans $]_{NP}$ grymtade.
pig-DEF with long tail grunted

b. *[[Gris med lång svans] -en $]_{NP}$ grymtade.
pig with long tail -DEF grunted
'The pig with a long tail grunted.'

(3.12) a. [[Gris-en] som har lång svans] grymtade.
pig-DEF that has long tail grunted

b. *[[Gris som har lång svans] -en] grymtade.
pig that has long tail -DEF grunted
'The pig which has a long tail grunted.'

The behaviour of the Swedish DEF is most untypical of a clitic in that its possible host words are restricted not only to a particular category, N, but even further to head nouns only. The position of DEF is then better defined relative to a particular category rather than a particular phrase. This is typical of affixes rather than clitics.

Related to the notion of selectivity as used by Zwicky and Pullum (1983) is a characteristic difference between affixes and clitics proposed by Carstairs (1981). Carstairs distinguishes between two types of bound forms: those whose position is fixed relative to a syntactic category (Carstairs's Characteristic 2a) and those whose position is defined in terms of a phrasal unit (Carstairs's Characteristic 2b).[9] He suggests another five characteristics that bound forms may have. The most important one for my discussion here is Characteristic 5: the shape of the bound form is often affected by the grammatical features (such as number, gender, conjugation-type or declension-type) of the item which governs its position. In the Insensitivity Claim, Carstairs (1981: 7) posits that no bound form can have both characteristics 2b and 5. He gives evidence from a variety of languages to support his claim. In the terms used here, this means that the form of a clitic is not expected to be influenced by the grammatical features of the host word (or host phrase if the host word is not a constituent of the host phrase). Clitics may have allomorphs, as long as the form of these is defined by general phonological rules only. The form of affixes, on the other hand, is often influenced by grammatical features.[10]

In the case of DEF the host word, that is, the noun, is the governor. Nouns in Swedish belong to one of two gender categories; neuter and common gender (often referred to as *neutrum* and *utrum*, respectively, in Swedish). In the plural, this distinction is absent. Which form DEF takes depends on the gender and the number of the noun with which it occurs, and also on its declension as (3.13) and (3.14) show.[11]

(3.13) a. råtta-**n** kanin-**en**
rat[COM]-DEF rabbit[COM]-DEF

b. öga-**t** bi-**et**
eye[NT]-DEF bee[NT]-DEF

(3.14) a. råttor-**na** kaniner-**na**
rat.PL-DEF rabbit.PL-DEF

b. ögon-**en** bin-**a**
eye.PL-DEF bee.PL-DEF

In Carstairs's terms we can conclude from the data in (3.13) and (3.14) that Swedish DEF has Characteristic 5 and, according to the Insensitivity Claim, this means it cannot simultaneously have Characteristic 2b, but must have 2a. In more conventional terms, it means that DEF behaves like an affix rather than a clitic in this respect.

From Klavans's description of cliticization as phrasal affixation it follows that the distinction can be made in terms of the type of subcategorization frame which defines the elements' distribution. This is illustrated in (3.15), adapted from Klavans (1983: 105).

(3.15) a. $[[\_]_{X''} = \text{enclitic}]_{X''}$ $\quad$ $[\text{proclitic} = [\_]_{X''}]_{X''}$
b. $[[\_]_{X}\ \text{suffix}]_{Y}$ $\quad$ $[\text{prefix}\ [\_]_{X}]_{Y}$

In (3.15a), X″ could possibly be X′, in (3.15b) X and Y could refer to the same category, or different categories, depending on whether the affix is inflectional or derivational. The symbol = refers to the link between a clitic and its host. From the evidence presented above it follows that the subcategorization frame of DEF must have the form given in (3.16), that is, the basic shape of (3.15b).

(3.16) $[[\quad]_{N}\ \text{DEF}]_{N}$

This can be compared with the frames Klavans (1983: 107) provides for the Classical Greek post-lexical proclitic determiner (3.17a) and the Irish lexical 'proclitic' possessive (3.17b) (following an analysis given by McCloskey 1982: 86, who claims that there is no evidence to indicate that the Irish possessive is attached to its noun outside the lexicon).

(3.17) a. $[\text{DET} = [\_]_{N'}]_{N''}$
b. $[\text{DET} = [\_]_{N}\ ([\_]_{A''}\ \ldots)]_{N''}$

In Classical Greek, modifiers can precede the head noun, and the DET attaches to whichever element fills the leftmost position. The Irish possessive is attached to a member of the lexical category N. The frame in (3.17b) shows that the DET, which according to McCloskey (1982) is a morphological element without independent syntactic status, can still allow the noun, with its modification, to function as a full noun phrase. In other words, an element which is judged not to have any independent syntactic status still appears to be able to do the same job as a syntactic determiner like the English definite article *the*. How this is represented is a matter to which I will return in section 5.2. So far then, the evidence has pointed in the direction of a lexical rather than syntactic analysis of DEF in Swedish.

3.3.3. *Ordering*

Another property ascribed to clitics relates to the ordering between clitics and affixes: a clitic attaches outside any form of inflexion. The ordering restriction rests on particular theoretical assumptions about the organization of the components within the grammar, but is still widely used as a criterion for clitic or affix status. The restriction follows directly in analyses which assume a linear model of grammar and which define affixes as lexical and clitics as post-lexical (like Zwicky and Pullum 1983 and Klavans 1983, but unlike Sadock 1991). Since affixes are attached to their stems in the lexicon, and clitics attach to hosts outside the lexicon, and since once an element has left the lexicon it is beyond the reach of the lexical rules, proclitics must occur before prefixes and enclitics after suffixes.[12]

Unfortunately, the ordering of DEF in relation to affixes and clitics in Swedish does not offer any conclusive indication of the status of DEF. Below, I compare the position of DEF relative to the plural suffix on the one hand, in (3.18), and the genitive *-s* on the other, in (3.19). In (3.20), the only grammatical form of a noun phrase containing all three morphemes is provided.

(3.18) a. katt-er-na
cat-PL-DEF

b. *katt-en-er
cat-DEF.SG-PL

c. *katt-na-er
cat-DEF.PL-PL
'the cats'

(3.19) a. katt-en-s
cat-DEF-GEN

b. *katt-s-en
cat-GEN-DEF
'the cat's'

(3.20) katt-er-na-s
cat-PL-DEF-GEN
'the cats''

Since a clitic is more syntactic than an affix, and since the most syntactic of affixes are inflexional affixes, I only compare DEF with an inflexional affix here. Most of the criteria for clitic status which are applied to DEF in this section can be applied to the possessive *-s* in Swedish and then they indicate quite clearly that the genitive *-s* is a clitic. This will be demonstrated in section 3.5. From (3.18) to (3.20) we can then conclude that the order in Swedish is as in (3.21a), and that the orders represented in (3.21b) and (3.21c) are illicit.

(3.21) a. host > inflexional affix > DEF > clitic

b. *host > DEF > inflexional affix

c. *host > clitic > DEF

In Swedish, more than one affix may attach to the same host. When this happens, only one order is possible. Many languages that have syntactic clitics can have a number of clitics clustered together, and then the clitics are usually placed according to a strict ordering. This means that the order represented by (3.21a) is consistent with the status of DEF as an affix, but also with DEF being a clitic. So, (3.21a) could be taken as evidence that DEF is an affix – one that must follow the plural affix when they co-occur; or it could be seen as an indication that it is a syntactic clitic – one that must always precede the syntactic clitic *-s* when they co-occur.

3.3.4. *Irregularities*

When a distinction between morphological and syntactic elements is made, one of the motivations for doing so is the fact that there appear to be two kinds of rules: morphological and syntactic. Elements whose behaviour is governed by the type of rules termed morphological are part of the morphology and likewise for syntax. A satisfactory definition of the distinction between the two types of rules has, as far as I am aware, not been given. However, a number of characteristics for the two types can be provided. For instance, morphological rules often yield paradigms (in the traditional sense), while syntactic rules do not. The paradigms governed by morphological rules often contain irregularities and arbitrary gaps, where one particular combination fails to occur for no principled reason. Patterns created by syntactic rules, on the other hand, do not usually contain arbitrary gaps and other irregularities.

Thus, if DEF is a clitic, and is adjoined to its host by syntactic rules, we expect there to be no arbitrary gaps. However, if we compare DEF with the prenominal definite article *den* in Swedish, we find that there are a number of unexpected gaps.[13] In Swedish, when a common noun without premodification is followed by a restrictive relative clause, it can either occur with DEF, as in (3.22a), or with the prenominal article *den* without DEF, as in (3.22b). A non-restrictive relative clause, on the other hand, can only follow a N+DEF combination; see (3.23a) and (3.23b).

(3.22) a. **Musen** som inte hade ätit av ostenö verlevde,
mouse.DEF COMP not had eaten of cheese.DEF survived
men den andra dog.
but the other.one died

b. **Den mus** som inte hade ätit av osten överlevde,
the mouse COMP not had eaten of cheese.DEF survived
men den andra dog.
but the other.one died
'The mouse which had not eaten any of the cheese survived, but the other one died.'

(3.23) a. **Musen**, som förresten hade ätit av osten, dog.
mouse.DEF COMP by.the.way had eaten of cheese.DEF died

b. *Den mus, som förresten hade ätit av osten, dog.
the mouse COMP by.the.way had eaten of cheese.DEF died
'The mouse, which, by the way, had eaten some of the cheese, died.'

When proper nouns occur with a non-restrictive relative clause, they occur without any definiteness marker, as in (3.24).

(3.24) a. Klas, som förresten hade ätit av osten, dog.
Klas COMP by.the.way had eaten of cheese.DEF died
'Klas, who, by the way, had eaten some of the cheese, died.'

In certain contexts, a proper noun can also occur with restrictive modification. In such cases, one might want to say that the proper noun is reanalysed as a common noun, since it behaves in certain respects as a common noun. In English, proper nouns used with a restrictive relative clause can be determined by a definite article and can take the plural ending *-s*, just like common nouns. Examples are given in (3.25).

(3.25) a. The Oscar I know just sleeps all day.

b. All the Andrews that I know are very clever.

We might therefore expect a reanalysed Swedish proper noun to behave like the common noun in (3.22) with respect to determination. However, as the examples in (3.26) show, only the prenominal article can be used. This can then be considered an arbitrary gap in the distribution of DEF. Note that this holds also for proper nouns which are homophonous to common nouns. An example like (3.26b) is ungrammatical also with the proper noun *Björn*, even though there is a common noun *björn* 'bear' which can occur with DEF: *björnen*.

(3.26) a. *Klas som jag känner hade ätit av osten.
Klas COMP I know had eaten of cheese.DEF

b. *Klasen som jag känner hade ätit av osten.
Klas.DEF COMP I know had eaten of cheese.DEF

c. **Den Klas** som jag känner hade ätit av osten.
the Klas COMP I know had eaten of cheese.DEF
'The Klas who I know had eaten some of the cheese.'

Geographical names provide another illustration of seemingly arbitrary gaps. As an example, I use the Swedish names for foreign rivers. The names for the rivers Rhine and Seine cannot take DEF as (3.27) and (3.28) show. Instead, the name of the river may be preceded by the definite form of *flod* 'river', as in (3.27c) and (3.28c).

(3.27)
a. Ren
Rhine
b. *Renen
Rhine.DEF
c. Floden Ren
river.DEF Rhine
} flyter genom Bonn.
flows through Bonn
'The Rhine flows through Bonn.'

(3.28)
a. Seine
Seine
b. *Seinen
Seine.DEF
c. Floden Seine
river.DEF Seine
} flyter genom Paris
flows through Paris
'The Seine flows through Paris.'

However, as the example in (3.29) shows, there are names of foreign rivers which can occur with DEF, and therefore, the ungrammaticality of (3.27b) and (3.28b) seems to lack a principled explanation and can be considered an instance of an arbitrary gap.[14]

(3.29)
a. Themsen
Thames.DEF
b. Floden Thames
river.DEF Thames
} flyter genom London.
flows through London
'The (river) Thames flows through London.'

Note that this is not a restriction against determination in general since both alternatives in (3.30) are grammatical.

(3.30) Den {Ren / Seine} som flöt förbi mitt hotellrum för 40 år sedan
the {Rhine / Seine} that flowed past my hotel room for 40 years ago
var inte full av rostiga kundvagnar.
was not full of rusty customer trolleys
'The Rhine/Seine that flowed past my hotel room 40 years ago was not full of rusty supermarket trolleys.'

There are also a few plural nouns in Swedish that cannot occur with DEF, as in (3.31). In these sentences, a definite interpretation of the noun phrases is not possible (examples from Thorell 1973: 32).

(3.31) a. Ge mig **fakta**, är du snäll.
give me fact.PL are you kind
'Give me facts, please.' It could not mean 'Give me the facts, please.'

b. **Akademici** har protesterat.
academic.PL have protested
'Academics have protested.' It could not mean 'The academics have protested.'

Certain nouns ending in a vowel followed by *-n* seem to have a zero allomorph of DEF in colloquial Swedish, as in (3.32).[15]

(3.32) a. Kan du möta mig vid **station** / station-en.
can you meet me at station.DEF station-DEF
'Can you meet me at the station?'

b. Han sänkte **grammofon** / grammofon-en.
he lowered record.player.DEF record.player-DEF
'He turned the record player down.'

Since the examples in (3.31), unlike those in (3.32), do not allow a definite interpretation, the noun phrases in (3.31) cannot be claimed to contain a zero DEF. It should also be noted that there is nothing in the semantics of *fakta* and *akademici* that makes them incompatible with a definite reading, as the examples in (3.33) show.

(3.33) a. **Dessa fakta** visar tydligt hur allvarlig situationen är.
these facts show clearly how serious situation.DEF is
'These facts clearly show how serious the situation is.'

b. **Dessa akademici** har sett sin köpkraft minska med
these academics have seen their purchasing power decrease with
8% sedan 1980.
8% since 1980
'These academics have seen their purchasing power decrease by 8% since 1980.'

In the theories of grammar assumed by Zwicky and Pullum (1983) and Klavans (1983, 1985), a clitic is adjoined to its host in the syntax. This means that morphological rules, which are prone to yield irregularities, cannot apply to host–clitic combinations. The stage at which such units are formed is beyond the reach of morphological rules. This leads Zwicky and Pullum (1983: 503) to define their characteristic C: morpho-phonological idiosyncrasies are more characteristic of affixed words than of clitic groups.

Thus, if DEF is an affix, we can expect a fair amount of irregular behaviour within combinations of N+DEF. If, on the other hand, DEF is a clitic, we expect such irregularities to occur to a lower degree. As the examples in (3.34) show, irregularities do occur.

(3.34) a. |segel+et| → seglet
sail.DEF

b. |gymnasium+et| → gymnasiet
secondary.school.DEF

c. |centrum+et| → centret, centrat OR centrumet
centre.DEF

An irregularity of the type found in (3.34a) may be considered a regular, phonologically motivated change. The words in (3.34b) and (3.34c), on the other hand, exemplify the kind of irregular behaviour that we would not expect of a clitic combination. As regards this criterion then, DEF behaves more like an affix than a clitic. However, in section 3.6.2.4, I will show that in languages where DEF behaves like a clitic with respect to all other criteria, N+DEF combinations still show irregular behaviour of this kind. It was, in fact, this kind of problem which led Börjars and Vincent (1993) to propose a different way of categorizing bound elements. In their account, irregularities are taken to be characteristic of any element which is bound, that is, which shows phonological liaison with another element.

3.3.5. *Phonological processes*

Some of the criteria for a distinction between clitics and affixes do not apply to the Swedish nouns. This is the case as far as I can tell with phonological rules and rules of stress assignment.

In Swedish, stress assignment is not influenced by the addition of the definite article. I have also been unable to discover any phonological process which distinguishes clitics from affixes. An example of a process that can take place across a stem–affix border in Swedish is retroflexion. If the stem ends in /r/ and the initial sound of the affix is a dental, i.e. /t, d, n, s, l/, then this cluster is realized as a retroflex, [ʈ, ɖ, ɳ, ʂ, ɭ], just as it would be word internally. Examples are given in (3.35).

(3.35) a. pärla [pæɭa] fors [fɔʂ]
pearl brook

b. skör-t /ʃœːr/ + /t/ → [ʃœːʈ]
brittle-SG.NT

c. kör-d /çœːr/ + /d/ → [çœːɖ]
drive-PST.PART

As (3.36) shows, this retroflexion also takes place when a noun ending in /r/ is followed by /n/, an allomorph of DEF. However, nothing can be concluded from this, since retroflexion also applies across word boundaries as in (3.37).

(3.36) mutter-n /mɯtːər/ + /n/ → [mɯtːəɳ]
nut-DEF

(3.37) a. skör tavla /ʃœːr/ + /taːvla/ → [ʃœːʈaːvla]
brittle painting

b. kör dåligt /çœːr/ + /dɔːlɪt/ → [çœːɖɔːlɪt]
drives badly

I have not been able to find a phonological process that could apply to N+DEF combinations and that is specific to stem–affix boundaries.

3.3.6. *Conclusions based on the clitic–affix distinction*

Of all the evidence presented in this section, nothing points towards the Swedish DEF being a clitic. A few of the criteria discussed cannot be applied to Swedish, or do not provide evidence for it being either an affix or a clitic. However, all the tests that can be used and that do point in either direction indicate that the distribution and other properties of DEF are determined by morphological rather than syntactic rules.

We could still, in principle, maintain that DEF is a clitic in Swedish, if we could demonstrate that there is something in the rules of Swedish grammar which prevents clitics in general in Swedish from fulfilling the criteria for clitic status discussed here. However, in section 3.5 I will show that this is not the case. There I will give examples of an element in Swedish which does satisfy the criteria for clitic status which I have discussed in this section.

Many of the criteria for clitic status discussed in this section were developed for and applied to syntactic items like negation, objects, auxiliary verbs, etc. It could be claimed that the reason why DEF does not satisfy the criteria is the fact that it is a determiner. Conceivably, there could be something in its status as a determiner that makes it different from other types of clitics in some respects. In order to investigate this issue, in section 3.6, I will compare the Swedish DEF with elements in some other languages that share with the Swedish DEF the property of being morphologically bound while functioning like a determiner semantically.

3.4. **DEF as a syntactic element**

3.4.1. *The issues*

In analyses where DEF is assigned syntactic status, it fills the same structural position as any other (definite) determiner at least at some level of derivation (e.g. Delsing 1988, 1989, 1993, Holmberg 1987, Santelmann 1992, Taraldsen 1990, 1991 and Sigurðsson 1992).[16] This means that such analyses of DEF could be supported by evidence indicating that DEF behaves in a similar way to non-clitic definite determiners.

3.4.2. *Word order*

In Swedish, DEF would be the only determiner occurring to the right of the noun. For some linguists, the surface word order would be seen as an indication that DEF should not be analysed as a syntactic determiner, since noun phrases containing DEF would then be structurally different from noun phrases containing any other determiner. However, in the analyses under discussion here the word order differences are due to syntactic movement (with the exception of Holmberg 1987, who does assume that DEF is generated to the right of the noun, but the independent definite determiners to the left). Underlyingly, DEF occupies the same position as the other determiners. The movement involved in noun phrases containing DEF is a consequence of DEF's being a bound morpheme. DEF is thus generated to the left of the noun, but the noun moves to the left to provide a host for the bound morpheme.

3.4.3. *Co-occurrence with other determiners*

In section 2.2, I showed that a class of prenominal determiners could be identified which all occur in complementary distribution. This class contains, for instance, the prenominal definite article, the indefinite article and the demonstrative determiners (see table 2.1 in section 2.1). Presumably, if DEF is assumed to be a syntactic, underlyingly prenominal, determiner, it would belong to this class, and we would expect it to occur in complementary distribution with the other members. If, on the other hand, there is so-called double determination, this weakens the case for assigning syntactic status to DEF.[17] As the examples in (3.38) show, it can co-occur with some, but not all of the other definite determiners.

(3.38) a. **den** vita mus**en**
the white mouse.DEF

b. **den** mus**en**
that mouse.DEF

c. *denna musen
this mouse.DEF

d. **den där** mus**en**
that mouse.DEF

e. *samma musen
the.same mouse.DEF

If DEF is a syntactic definite determiner with the same position in the structure as any other determiner, then we would expect (3.38a), (3.38b) and (3.38d) to be ungrammatical. In section 5.3.2.1, I will discuss the solutions to this problem that have been offered within these transformational analyses.

3.4.4. *Co-ordination*

If the definite affix is a determiner like *den* 'the' or 'that', *denna* 'this', and *den där* 'that', then one might also expect it to behave similarly to these other determiners with regard to co-ordination. The examples in (3.39) show how the definite article *den* (in all cases it could also be interpreted as the demonstrative *den*) and the demonstrative *denna* in their plural forms can determine two co-ordinated nominals (N or N′ in traditional X-bar terms). In both cases it is clear that the prenominal determiner functions as the determiner for both conjuncts, since even a definite or a plural noun preceded by an adjective needs a prenominal article to form a noun phrase in Swedish.

(3.39) a. de höga bänkarna och de låga stolarna →
the.PL high benches and the.PL low chairs
de höga bänkarna och låga stolarna
the.PL high benches and low chairs

b. dessa höga bänkar och dessa låga stolar →
these high benches and these low chairs
dessa höga bänkar och låga stolar
these high benches and low chairs

As the parallel example in (3.40) shows, this does not work with the definite affix. In (3.41) I provide examples of co-ordinated noun phrases which are considered close units in Swedish. As the examples show, the definite affix cannot determine the co-ordinated nouns even when they form such a close unit of meaning. In (3.42) an English example of a similar type of construction is provided. If a separate determiner is used for each of the conjuncts in (3.42), then the 'unit meaning' is lost.

(3.40) bänkarna och stolarna ↛ bänkar och stolarna[18]
bench.PL.DEF and chair.PL.DEF [benches and chairs].DEF

(3.41) a. hink och spade[19] + DEF ↛ hink och spaden
bucket and spade → hinken och spaden

b. mamma och pappa + DEF ↛ mamma och pappan
mother and father → mamman och pappan

(3.42) fish and chips + definite article → the fish and chips (which I ate)

The fact that DEF cannot determine the co-ordinated nominals *hink och spade* and *mamma och pappa* cannot be due to gender discrepancies, since in both combinations, both nouns are of the same gender. Furthermore, it cannot be due to the fact that the co-ordinated structure should be treated as a plural nominal, since there are noun phrases in Swedish where a singular determiner determines a co-ordinated nominal. This is possible only when the two nominals form a close semantic unit. The example in (3.43a) shows that a co-ordinated noun phrase requires plural adjective agreement.[20] It can therefore be assumed that a co-ordinated nominal element such as *mamma och pappa* carries a [PL] feature. Still, the singular indefinite determiner *en* 'a' can determine the conjoined nouns, as in (3.43b).

(3.43) a. Hennes [mamma och pappa]$_{N'[PL]}$ är trevliga / *trevlig.
her mother.SG and father.SG are nice.PL nice.SG

b. Hon har en trevlig [mamma och pappa]$_{N'[PL]}$
she has a.SG nice.SG mother and father

This means that it cannot be argued that the inability of DEF to determine a co-ordinated phrase arises because the determiner has the feature [SG], whereas a co-ordinated noun phrase would usually be [PL].

3.4.5. *Conclusions based on a comparison with syntactic determiners*

In this section, I have compared DEF's behaviour with that of syntactic determiners. I found that with respect to co-occurrence restrictions and the ability to determine a co-ordinated nominal element, DEF behaves differently from the syntactic determiners. The data discussed in this section can therefore be seen as evidence against a syntactic analysis of DEF.

Some of the differences described in this section turn out to be due to the fact that DEF is bound rather than free, so that the differences between DEF and syntactic determiners do not actually give any indication of whether DEF is a clitic or an affix. I will return to this issue in sections 3.5.2 and 3.6.3, where I investigate the syntactic behaviour of another bound element in Swedish, and of the DEF elements of some other European languages.

3.5. A COMPARISON WITH THE POSSESSIVE *-S* IN SWEDISH

3.5.1. *Criteria for an affix–clitic distinction*

The English possessive *'s* is generally treated as a clitic (see for instance Klavans 1985, and Bauer 1988: 99).[21] The Swedish genitive *-s* behaves in many important ways like the English *'s*, and can therefore also be assumed to be a strong candidate for clitic status. In this section and the next, I will examine the Swedish genitive *-s*, and compare its behaviour with that of DEF in relation to the criteria for clitic and affix status discussed in sections 3.3 and 3.4.

As discussed in section 3.3.1, a clitic is often described as a bound morpheme, whose position is defined in relation to a phrasal unit rather than a particular syntactic category. Its position in relation to this phrasal category can be described in terms of Klavans's (1983, 1985) parameters. These parameters are repeated here for the sake of convenience.

Table 3.1 Klavans's parameters constraining the position of clitics (from section 3.2.1)

	TYPE	VALUES
Parameter 1	dominance	initial/final
Parameter 2	precedence	before/after
Parameter 3	phonological liaison	proclitic/enclitic

The examples in (3.44) show that the possessive *-s* in Swedish consistently occurs on the right edge of the noun phrase, attached phonologically as an enclitic to the last word of the phrase (see (3.5)–(3.7)).

(3.44) a. $[$grisen$]_{NP}$ -s grymtande
pig.DEF -GEN grunting
'the pig's grunting'

b. $[$den här gamla smutsiga grisen$]_{NP}$ -s grymtande
this old dirty pig.DEF -GEN grunting
'the grunting of this dirty old pig'

c. $[$grisen med knorr på svansen$]_{NP}$ -s grymtande
pig.DEF with a curly tail -GEN grunting
'the grunting of the pig with the curly tail'

d. $[$grisen med knorr på svansen som tycker om gröt$]_{NP}$ -s grymtande
pig.DEF with a curly tail who likes porridge -GEN grunting
'the grunting of the pig with a curly tail who likes porridge'

These data show that the position of *-s* in Swedish can be defined in terms of Klavans' parameters as 'final, after, enclitic'. The subcategorization frame of *-s* would be as in (3.45).

(3.45) $[[\ \_\ ]_{N''} = s\ ]_{N''}$

The frame in (3.45) is typical of a clitic (see Klavans 1983: 105 and the discussion in section 3.3.2), and in this respect, the Swedish *-s* behaves like a clitic.

Another criterion for clitic status that DEF failed to satisfy relates to the degree of selectivity that a bound form displays with regard to the word to which it is phonologically attached. A clitic typically disregards the syntactic category of its host word as long as the structural criteria, defined in relation to its host phrase, are fulfilled. In (3.44) we saw that, unlike DEF, *-s* can attach to nouns other than the head noun. The examples in (3.46) show that like a typical clitic, *-s* can also attach to words of other syntactic categories, as long as these occur as the final element of a noun phrase. As in English, these examples are less likely to occur in written than in spoken Swedish. However, since Swedish does not have an obvious alternative, like the English *of*-construction, I suspect they are more frequent in Swedish than in English. In (3.46a) *-s* is phonologically attached to a preposition, in (3.46b) to a verb, and in (3.46c) to a verb particle. In (3.47a), the possessive is attached to a personal pronoun. As Carstairs (1981: 5) points out for English, the combination of a personal pronoun and the possessive *-s* is otherwise ungrammatical. This is illustrated in (3.47b).

(3.46) a. pojken framför-**s** pappa
boy.DEF in.front-GEN father
'the boy in front's father'

b. pojken jag träffade-**s** pappa
boy.DEF I met-GEN father
'the boy I met's father'

c. pojken som kom bort-**s** pappa
boy.DEF that came away-GEN father
'the boy who got lost's father'

(3.47) a. pojken som slog mig-**s** pappa
boy.DEF that hit me-GEN father
'the father of the boy who hit me'

b. pojken som slog *mig-s / OKmin pappa
boy.DEF that hit me-GEN my father
'the boy who hit my father'

As discussed in section 2.3, when a noun is understood and not overtly present in a noun phrase, and an adjective is the final element of the remaining noun phrase, the possessive *-s* can attach to this adjective. An example is given in (3.48). This can be compared with the behaviour of DEF in (3.9)

(3.48) Den här flaskan-**s** kork sitter fast, men . . .
this bottle.DEF-GEN cork sits tight but

a. . . . den förra flaskan-**s** kork fick vi lätt ur.
the last bottle.DEF-GEN cork got we easily out

b. . . . den förra-**s** kork fick vi lätt ur.
the last-GEN cork got we easily out

'The cork of this bottle is stuck, but the cork of the last one we got out easily.'

With regard to Carstairs's (1981) Insensitivity Claim (see section 3.3.2) the possessive *-s* behaves like a clitic in that its form is not influenced by the grammatical features of the host. Swedish does not make use of a construction of the English *of*-type to express possession, so the possessive *-s* is used for animate and inanimate nouns alike. Regardless of the number and gender of the noun, the possessive has just one form. The only possible exception to this is when the noun ends in /s/. In this case, no extra *-s* is added. This could, however, be considered a phonologically motivated zero allomorph.

I have not been able to discover any morphological or semantic irregularities or arbitrary gaps in combinations of a host and the possessive *-s*. Nor have I found any examples where any changes take place in the word to which the possessive is added. In section 3.3.4, we saw that such irregularities do occur with combinations of N+DEF.

3.5.2. *Possessive* -s *as a syntactic element*

In section 3.4, I discussed two ways in which DEF failed to behave like other syntactic determiners. Firstly, whereas the syntactic determiners do not co-occur, DEF can, or indeed must, co-occur with other definite determiners. Secondly, DEF is unlike the syntactic determiners in that it cannot determine a co-ordinated nominal element. I concluded section 3.4 by suggesting that DEF's failure to behave like a syntactic determiner might possibly be related to the nature of clitics. If this were the case, the data in that section could not be used to argue against a syntactic analysis of DEF. I want to evaluate this suggestion here by comparing DEF's syntactic behaviour with that of the possessive *-s*, which I established as a clitic in section 3.5.1. In this subsection, I will deal only with the behaviour of possessive *-s* with regard to co-ordination.

The examples in (3.49) show that possessive *-s* can attach to co-ordinated nominal elements of different kinds. The fact that this is possible even when it is not a question of 'joint ownership', at least in certain registers, is illustrated in (3.50).

(3.49) a. Björn Borg och John McEnroe-**s** första match
Björn Borg and John McEnroe-GEN first match
'the first match that Björn Borg and John McEnroe played against each other (or, in principle, that they played together)', that is, 'Björn Borg and John McEnroe's first match'

b. den dumma ankan och den söta lilla musen-**s**
the stupid duck.DEF and the sweet little mouse.DEF-GEN
äventyr i Kalle Anka
adventures in Kalle Anka
'the adventures of the stupid duck and the sweet little mouse in Donald Duck'

(3.50) Gustav och Karin-**s** näsor hade blivit röda
Gustav and Karin-GEN noses had become red
av den kalla vinden.
by the cold wind
'The cold wind had made Gustav and Karin's noses go red.'

3.5.3. *Conclusions*

The evidence presented in this subsection indicates that the Swedish possessive *-s* is a clitic. With respect to all criteria for clitic status which apply to *-s*, it behaves like a clitic. The expectation expressed in section 3.4.4, that if a bound element has syntactic status it will behave like a syntactic element with respect to co-ordinated structures, was borne out for the possessive *-s*. This indicates that there is nothing inherent in Swedish clitics to prevent them from applying to a co-ordinated phrase. From the data presented so far, we can conclude that the possessive *-s* is a clitic and that DEF behaves in almost every respect differently from the possessive. It seems unlikely therefore that an analysis in which DEF is assigned clitic status will be capable of reflecting these crucial differences satisfactorily.

3.6. A COMPARISON WITH 'ENCLITIC ARTICLES' IN OTHER LANGUAGES

3.6.1. *The issues*

In sections 3.3 and 3.4, I applied criteria for clitic status to the Swedish DEF. All the evidence from these sections pointed away from an analysis of Swedish DEF as a clitic. In section 3.5, we saw that Swedish does have an element, the possessive *-s*, which has the characteristics we expect of a clitic according to the criteria discussed. It is still conceivable that the criteria discussed in sections 3.3 and 3.4 are not applicable to determiner-like elements, but only to items like pronouns, auxiliary verbs and negations to which they have been most commonly applied. In order to establish whether the failure of the Swedish DEF to satisfy the clitic criteria is due to the fact that it is a semantic determiner, I will compare its behaviour with that of similar elements in other languages.

I will be concerned here with the other Scandinavian languages: Danish (D) and Norwegian (N) (which, with Swedish, will be referred to as Mainland Scandinavian), and Faroese (F) and Icelandic (I) (Insular Scandinavian), and with those Balkan languages which have a DEF-element that can occur as a bound element on a noun, namely Albanian (A), Bulgarian (B), Macedonian (M) and Romanian (R).[22] Naturally, it is beyond the scope of this book to provide a detailed analysis of DEF in each language. The purpose of this section is to record the main characteristics of DEF in these languages and to contrast these with those discussed for Swedish in sections 3.3 and 3.4. In section 3.6.2, I will apply the criteria discussed in section 3.3 to these other DEF elements, and in section 3.6.3, I will consider the syntactic status of these DEFS. For the Balkan languages, I refer to Lunt (1952), Elson (1976) and Scatton (1980) for Bulgarian and Macedonian; to Dobrovie-Sorin (1987), Grosu (1988) and Renzi (1989) for Romanian; and to Morgan (1984) for more data on Albanian noun phrases and discussion of the issues involved here.

The Scandinavian and Balkan languages are not the only ones which have a bound element which can function as a determiner semantically. There are several other languages which have an element similar to the Swedish DEF, for example Basque and Armenian. I have, however, decided to focus my comparison on the Scandinavian and Balkan languages, since these can, to some extent, be classed together in two groups.

3.6.2. *Clitic vs. affix status*

3.6.2.1. *Phrasal host*

With respect to Klavans's (1985) parameters, all the other Scandinavian languages behave like Swedish. In these languages too, DEF is not positioned relative to a phrase. The position of DEF cannot be defined in terms of Klavans's parameters.

In Macedonian and Bulgarian, DEF occurs quite consistently in second position (though compare the data in (3.59) and (3.60) in 3.6.2.2). This means that its position can be defined in Klavans's terms as 'initial, after, enclitic'. This is illustrated for Macedonian in (3.51).

(3.51) a. čovek-**ot** M
man-DEF
'the man'

b. dobr-**iot** čovek
good-DEF man
'the good man'

c. dobr-**iot** mal čovek
good-DEF little man
'the good little man'

d. *dober čovek-**ot**
good man-DEF

e. *dober mal-iot čovek
good little-DEF man

In Romanian, it is also the case that DEF occurs in second position, though there are some complications. In Romanian, there are three ways of expressing the meaning of (3.51b); these are given in (3.52).

(3.52) a. om-**ul** bun R
man-DEF good

b. bun-**ul** om
good-DEF man

c. om **cel** bun
man PRT.DEF good
'the good man'

In (3.52a) and (3.52b), the position of DEF can be defined in terms of Klavans's parameters as 'initial, after, enclitic', that is, in the same way as the Macedonian and Bulgarian DEFs. In (3.52c), the *l* in *cel* can also be considered a form of DEF which is attached to a particle *ce*. If this line of argument is followed, the position of DEF cannot easily be defined as 'initial, after, enclitic'. However, within a transformational framework, Dobrovie-Sorin (1987) argues that *cel* should be analysed as a unit, occupying the same position in the structure as DEF or a syntactic determiner. If we follow her analysis, then (3.52c) poses no difficulty for a definition of the position of Romanian DEF in terms of Klavans's parameters. I will return to the status of *cel* in section 3.6.3.1. Further problems with assuming that DEF occurs in the second position in Romanian noun phrases will be discussed in section 3.6.2.2.

In Albanian, the data is even less clear than in Romanian, as illustrated by (3.53).

(3.53) a. djal-**i** i mirë A
boy-DEF ? good

b. i mir-**i** djalë
? good-DEF boy
'the good boy'

If the element which I have not glossed in (3.53) is considered to form a close constituent with the adjective, then the parameter values 'initial, after, enclitic' can be maintained also for Albanian. I will return to the status of this element in section 3.6.3.1. There are, however, further problems with Albanian DEF, as (3.54) illustrates.

(3.54) a. (të) katër djem-**të** A
PRT four boy.PL-DEF
'the four boys'

b. (të) gjithë djem-**të**
PRT all boy.PL-DEF
'all the boys'

The initial particle *të* is optional in these noun phrases and we could therefore decide not count it as a word for the purpose of Klavans's parameters. However, even if this element is disregarded, DEF still does not occur in second position. The numeral *katër* 'four' and the quantifier *gjithë* 'all' precede the noun, like the adjective in (3.53b), but still DEF cannot attach to either of these elements. Instead it occurs attached to the element in third position, which could also have been an adjective.

From what has been said in this subsection, it can be concluded that DEF in the Scandinavian languages behaves radically differently from that of the Balkan languages. The data from Albanian slightly blur the picture, but apart from this, the position of the Balkan DEF can be defined in terms of Klavans's parameters, as 'initial, after, enclitic'. For the Scandinavian languages, this is not possible. If these parameters are taken as a constraint on clitics, then the Balkan DEFs behave like clitics, whereas the Scandinavian ones behave like affixes.

Within a sentence, the parameter values 'initial, after, enclitic' define a position known as the Wackernagel Position (Wackernagel 1892). In many languages, this second position in the sentence is filled by clitics such as sentence particles, pronouns or auxiliary verbs. This is the case with some auxiliaries in a number of south Slavonic languages like, for instance, Bulgarian (see Halpern and Zwicky 1996 for a number of articles on this phenomenon, Halpern 1992a for a prosodic analysis of second position clitics and Anderson 1993, 1996 for a morphological approach, the latter within an Optimality Theory framework). We could therefore refer to the position of the Balkan DEF as a Wackernagel position within the noun phrase.

3.6.2.2. *Selectivity*

The Scandinavian languages behave similarly to Swedish in that DEF can attach to the head noun only. A combination of an adjective and DEF is possible only when the adjective has been thoroughly nominalized.

In section 3.6.2.1 (examples (3.51), (3.52) and (3.53)), we saw that in the Balkan languages, DEF can attach also to adjectives. In these languages, DEF behaves like a clitic in that its position is defined in terms of a phrasal unit rather than a particular word class. As the example in (3.55a) shows, the Albanian DEF can also attach to adjectives used without a noun, even when these have not been highly nominalized and taken on a narrow meaning as in Swedish (see (3.10)). DEF can also attach to a *wh*-word in Albanian, as in (3.55b).

(3.55) a. i bekuar-**i** A
? blessed-DEF
'the blessed one'

b. cil-**i** djalë
which-DEF boy
'which boy'

In Romanian, DEF can occur on adjectives (3.52) and on a restricted number of numerals (3.56a). However, there are premodifiers, such as most numerals and quantifiers that cannot be host to the DEF clitic. Instead, DEF occurs in third position, attached either to the head noun or an adjective. This is illustrated (3.56b), (3.56c) and (3.56d). As (3.56e) shows, the quantifier can also follow the noun, and when it does, DEF cliticizes onto the noun, in second position (see Renzi 1989: 220–1).

(3.56) a. întîi-**ul** etaj R
first-DEF floor
'the first floor'

b. *tot-**ul** oraş
all-DEF city

c. tot oraş-**ul**
all city-DEF

d. tot sărac-**ul** oraş
all poor-DEF city

e. oraş-**ul** tot
city-DEF all
'the whole (poor) city'

In Romanian, it is also not possible for DEF to attach to an adverb, as shown in (3.57a). When a noun is preceded by an adjective modified by an adverb, DEF attaches instead to the adjective, as in (3.57b) (see Scatton 1980: 210, n. 3).

(3.57) a. *foart-**ul** sărac oraş R
very-DEF poor city

b. foarte sărac-**ul** oraş
very poor-DEF city
'the very poor city'

In Macedonian, nouns and adjectives can host DEF as already demonstrated in section 3.6.2.1. Furthermore, it can occur on a prenominal possessive as in (3.58a). DEF can even combine with a word in initial position that is not a modifier of the noun. This is illustrated by the contrast between (3.58b) and (3.58c).

(3.58) a. moj-**ot** časovnik M
my-DEF watch
'my watch'

b. četiri-stotini lug'e
four-hundred people
'four hundred people'

c. četiri-**te** stotini lug'e
four-DEF hundred people
'the four hundred people'

However, if the initial element is an adverb, as in (3.59), then DEF cannot occur in second position. As (3.59b) shows, the adjective phrase of which the adverb is a part cannot host DEF either. Instead the alternative construction (3.59c), containing a non-clitic demonstrative functioning as an independent definite article, is used.[23]

(3.59) a. *mnogu-**ot** golem čovek M
very-DEF big man
b. *mnogu golem-**iot** čovek
very big-DEF man
c. **onoj** mnogu golem čovek
that very big man
'the very big man'

The example in (3.60a) shows that the restriction which applies to Macedonian in (3.59a) also applies to Bulgarian. However, as illustrated in (3.60b), Bulgarian does allow DEF to attach to the adjective phrase as a whole in these cases. This was also shown to be the case in Romanian in (3.57).

(3.60) a. *mnog-**ət** star teatər B
very-DEF old theatre
b. mnogo starij-**ət** teatər
very old-DEF theatre
'the very old theatre'

As in section 3.6.2.1, we can conclude that there is a difference in nature between the DEFs of the Scandinavian languages on the one hand, and those of the Balkan ones on the other. In the Scandinavian languages, only a head noun, or a totally nominalized adjective can function as a host for DEF. The Balkan languages are more permissive. Even though none of them allows DEF to attach indiscriminately to any category, DEF does behave like a clitic in that its position is defined in relation to a phrasal unit rather than a particular syntactic category. We can express this as follows: in the Balkan languages, the basic principle states that DEF occurs in the second position of the noun phrase, sometimes not counting semantically insignificant particles. However, there are in each language a number of categories that cannot host a DEF. Thus a conflict may arise between two incompatible principles. Each language has a different way of resolving the conflict. In Albanian, when DEF cannot find a host in the initial position, it may attach instead to the second element, thereby itself ending up in third position within the noun phrase (see (3.54)). In Bulgarian, when the first **word** is not a legal host, DEF instead cliticizes onto the first **constituent**. This also leaves DEF in the third, rather than second, position if words rather than constituents are counted (see (3.60b)). In Macedonian, the rule seems to be that if DEF cannot occur in the second position, then it cannot occur at all. Instead, a prenominal determiner is used, as in (3.59c). Finally, in Romanian a conflict can arise with certain quantifiers and also with adverbs. In the case of the quantifier *tot* 'all', Romanian may use the same strategy as Albanian (see (3.56)). If the noun phrase contains adverbs modifying adjectives, then Romanian follows the same principle as Bulgarian and DEF attaches to the first constituent rather than the first word (see (3.57)). It is also possible to shift the noun around the illegal element, to initial position. If the word order is changed in this way, both principles can be satisfied: DEF attaches to the noun and is in second position in the noun phrase. This strategy was followed in (3.56e).

If we take Carstairs's (1981) narrower view of selectivity, all languages fail this criteria. In all languages the shape of DEF depends on the grammatical features (at least on the gender and number, and in some languages also on the case) of the head noun of the noun phrase in which it occurs, i.e. all these instances of DEF have characteristic 5. According to the Insensitivity Claim (Carstairs 1981: 7), no item can have both characteristics 5 and 2b. Characteristic 2b defines the set of items that have their position defined in terms of a phrasal unit rather than a syntactic category. This can be loosely stated as 'if the form of DEF depends on the grammatical features of the head noun, it cannot be a clitic.' This definition of selectivity then does not distinguish between the DEFs of the different languages discussed here, whereas the more conventional view of selectivity does divide the languages quite clearly into two groups: the Scandinavian languages and the Balkan ones.

3.6.2.3. *Ordering*

Theories of grammar which assume that affixation takes place in the lexicon, and cliticization outside it, and which do not assume morphological or syntactic movement, predict that an affix will always occur closer to the root than a clitic (see Klavans 1983, 1985 and Zwicky and Pullum 1983). In section 3.3.3, I showed that this constraint on the ordering of clitics and affixes does not provide any evidence for or against clitic status being assigned to the Swedish DEF.

In the other Mainland Scandinavian languages, the situation is much the same as in Swedish, that is, DEF follows plural markers, which are usually considered affixes, but precedes clitic-like elements such as the possessive. This means that the criterion cannot be used as an argument for or against clitic status for these languages either.

Icelandic and Faroese, on the other hand, have more complex noun morphology. In the indefinite forms, the noun is inflected for number and gender, and within each gender, there is also a distinction between strong and weak inflexion (or between subclasses, as, for instance, Lockwood 1977: 28–38 prefers to call them). The definiteness marker always follows this inflexion. However, since there is no phrasal possessive *-s* like the one in the Mainland Scandinavian languages and English, there is no clitic element to which the position of DEF can be compared in Insular Scandinavian. It can be claimed, however, that case affixes can follow DEF. If these case markers were considered affixes on the noun, then this would be an indication that DEF was an affix too, since we do not expect endoclitics to be possible (see Klavans 1985: 114–16). However, Klavans (1979) provides evidence that clitics of category X may be inflected in the same way as words of category X. Since prenominal determiners in Insular Scandinavian are inflected for case (and number/gender/class), it is plausible to assume that DEF, if it is a clitic, can also be inflected for case. This means that the case markers which follow DEF in Insular Scandinavian can be used as evidence that DEF is in fact a clitic.

An example of a noun paradigm from Faroese is given in (3.61). I have introduced the ∅ where there is traditionally assumed to be a zero realization of a morpheme. The part of each noun which is printed in bold is used as the indefinite form. The paradigm is similar in Icelandic.[24]

(3.61)	**bát-ur**-in	**bát-ar**-nir	F
	boat-M.SG.STR.NOM-DEF.M.SG.NOM	boat-M.PL.NOM-DEF.M.PL.NOM	
	bát-∅-in	**bát-ar**-nar	
	boat-M.SG.STR.ACC-DEF.M.SG.ACC	boat-M.PL.ACC-DEF.M.PL.ACC	
	bát-i-num	**bát-un**-um (indef: bátum)	
	boat-M.SG.STR.DAT-DEF.M.SG.DAT	boat-M.PL.DAT-DEF.M.PL.DAT	
	(**bát-s**-ins)	(**bát-a**-nna)	
	boat-M.SG.STR.GEN-DEF.M.SG.GEN	boat-M.PL.GEN-DEF.M.PL.GEN	

In this inflection pattern, an element *-(i)n* can be recognized which can be considered the DEF. This is followed by a case inflexion which varies for gender and number as in (3.62) (Barnes 1994: 198–202). This can be compared to the forms of the demonstrative prenominal determiners *hesin*, *hasin* and *hin* in Faroese. The pattern for *hin* is given in (3.63). The demonstrative which is also used as prenominal definite article, *tann*, has a slightly different pattern.

(3.62)	SG	NOM	∅	PL	NOM	*-ir*	F
		ACC	∅		ACC	*-ar*	
		DAT	*-um*		DAT	*-um*	
		(GEN	*-s*)		(GEN	*-na*)	

(3.63) *hin* 'the other' F

SG	NOM	*hin*	PL	NOM	*hinir*
	ACC	*hin*		ACC	*hinar*
	DAT	*hinum*		DAT	*hinum*
	(GEN	*hins*)		–	

These correspondences make an analysis in which DEF is assumed to be inflected for case (and number/gender/class) plausible. Especially in the genitive the clitic analysis seems reasonable, since both the stem and DEF carry the genitive *-s*. A corresponding Icelandic example is provided in (3.64).

(3.64) hest-s-inn-s I
horse-GEN-DEF-GEN

The alternative is to assume that DEF is an affix in these languages; either an affix which precedes the affix marking case (and number/gender/class) or an affix which has one form for each case (and gender/number/class). In the latter case, the fact that *-(i)n* recurs, and that the endings are similar to that of other determiners would then be more or less coincidental. This strikes me as a less attractive account, but which of these two analyses is chosen may depend on other aspects of the behaviour of DEF in these two languages as contrasted with that of Mainland Scandinavian.

In the Balkan languages, it is not clear to me that anything can be concluded from facts relating to the order of affixes and clitics. In Albanian, for instance, the plural affix always precedes DEF, but a case ending appears to follow it, as in (3.65a). However, as the examples in (3.65b) show, one would have to resort to an artificial and abstract analysis in order to make it possible to derive the forms in (3.65b) from those in (3.65a) in this way. The same holds for the plural forms, as given in (3.65c) and (3.65d).

(3.65)				A
a.	djal-i-∅	djal-i-n	djal-i-t	
	boy-DEF-NOM	boy-DEF-ACC	boy-DEF-OBL	
b.	djalë	djalë	djal-i	
	boy.NOM	boy.ACC	boy-OBL	
c.	djem-të	djem-të	djem-ve	
	boys-DEF.NOM	boys-DEF.ACC	boys-DEF.OBL.PL	
d.	djem	djem	djem-ve	
	boys.NOM	boys.ACC	boys-OBL.PL	

Again, the data in (3.65) is compatible both with an analysis of DEF as a clitic and with DEF as an affix.

Few conclusions about the affix or clitic status of DEF can be drawn from facts relating to ordering. In Swedish and other Mainland Scandinavian languages, it is positioned to the right of an affix, but to the left of a clitic. This is consistent with both a clitic and an affix analysis of DEF. In some of the other, more inflected, languages, DEF can be followed by a case ending. In some of these languages, such as Albanian, the combination of DEF and the case marker seems unanalysable in terms of two separate parts. Instead, DEF can be assumed to have separate forms for the different cases. Both affixes and clitics may have different forms, so again this does not allow us to choose between a clitic and an affix analysis. However, in Icelandic and Faroese, the ordering data makes a clitic analysis of DEF the most plausible option.

3.6.2.4. *Irregularities*

With respect to arbitrary gaps and morpho-phonological idiosyncrasies, the other Scandinavian DEFs seem to behave much like the Swedish one. In (3.66) and (3.67), some examples from Icelandic and Faroese are provided. In Icelandic, if a stem ends in *-ur* and DEF (*-inn* (M and F) or *-ið* (NT)) is added, then there is a change in the stem, but only if the noun is not masculine (3.66). In Faroese, the shape of DEF may vary within one gender/case/number paradigm, as in (3.67).

(3.66) a. |hestur+inn| → **hestur**inn I
horse(M).DEF

b. |lifur+inn| → **lifr**in
liver(F).DEF

c. |hreiður+ið| → **hreiðr**ið
nest(NT).DEF

(3.67) a. staður staður-**in** stað-**num** F
place(M) place-DEF.NOM place-DEF.DAT

b. seyður seyður-**in** seyð-**inum**
sheep(M) sheep-DEF.NOM sheep-DEF.DAT

In the Balkan languages, morpho-phonological irregularities also occur, though they are probably less common. Lunt (1952: 42), for instance, says for literary Macedonian that 'very few substantives undergo a change in stem before the article.' This change in the stem is the only form of irregularity that Lunt discusses. An example of changes in the stem of Macedonian nouns is given in (3.68a). This shows how masculine nouns ending in -C*a*C may drop the vowel before the consonant. An example of irregularity in Romanian is given in (3.68b). Here, a feminine noun ending in *-ii* appears in an irregular form when DEF(GEN or DAT) is added. This in spite of the fact that nouns can end in *-iii* as (3.68c) shows. Finally, in (3.68d), an example from Albanian is provided. In this case, an old form of DEF may be used as an alternative and this is accompanied by a change in the stem.[25]

(3.68) a. teatar+ot → **teatr**ot M
theatre.DEF

realisam+ot → **realism**ot M
reality.DEF

turisam+ot → **turisam**ot M
tourism.DEF

b. |familii+i| → famil**iei** R
family(F).GEN/DAT.DEF

c. cop**iii** R
children.DEF

d. krye krye-t kre-u A
head head-DEF head-DEF

Arbitrary gaps are also harder to find in the Balkan languages than in the Scandinavian ones. A case in point is proper nouns. Even though Macedonian would normally use the definite form in (3.69a), (3.69b) is possible in poetic use. In an emotional statement like (3.69c), DEF can also be added to the name of a city. In this emotional use, this is the only possibility, according to my informant.

(3.69) a. reka-**ta** Dunav M
river-DEF Danube

b. Dunav-**ot**
Danube-DEF
'the Danube'

c. Skopje**vo** e ubavo
Skopje.DEF is beautiful
'Skopje is beautiful!'

In Albanian, DEF regularly occurs on proper nouns, as in (3.70a). As (3.70b) shows, DEF can also be added to foreign names. The form of DEF used in the case of foreign names follows regular patterns. The choice of form is based on the final sound of the name (or the closest Albanian approximation of it).

(3.70) a. Agim-**i** A
Agim-DEF

b. Çarlz-**i**
Charles-DEF

3.6.2.5. *Conclusions*

A comparison of the data presented in this subsection with those discussed in section 3.3 shows that the reason why the Swedish DEF does not behave like a clitic in so many ways cannot be ascribed to its semantic nature. Other languages, especially the Balkan ones, have a bound determiner element that does fulfil (most of) the criteria for clitic status discussed in section 3.3.[26] I have found in this section that it is with respect to the phrasal host and to the degree of selectivity of the host word that the Scandinavian and the Balkan languages differ most clearly. With regard to these criteria, we can distinguish two distinct types of languages: the Scandinavian ones, where

DEF behaves like an affix, and the Balkan languages, where DEF shows clear clitic properties.

With respect to the other criteria (discussed in sections 3.6.2.3 and 3.6.2.4), the results are less clear cut. As far as the morphological complexity of DEF is concerned, the Insular Scandinavian languages side with the Balkan ones. The inflectional properties of DEF in the Insular Scandinavian languages can be seen as evidence of its clitic status. Arbitrary gaps are less common in the Balkan languages, but morpho-phonological irregularities seem to occur in all the languages discussed. From this it can be concluded that a purely linear model of cliticization cannot provide a satisfactory analysis of the facts discussed. Since all the languages contain irregularities such as changes of the stem, a linear model would predict that DEF must be combined with the stem in the morphology, thus that it is an affix in all cases. This does not, however, fit with the facts discussed in sections 3.6.2.1 and 3.6.2.2. Instead, it seems to me, the irregularities arise from the fact that DEF is, in all languages, a bound form. This is actually as predicted by the parameters for a distinction between different classes of meaningful elements proposed by Börjars and Vincent (1993).

3.6.3. *DEF as a syntactic element*

3.6.3.1. *Co-occurrence with other determiners*

With respect to the co-occurrence of DEF and other determiners, all the other Scandinavian languages differ from Swedish, and from each other. Of the other Scandinavian languages, Norwegian resembles Swedish most closely. However, there are fewer circumstances in Norwegian where independent definite determiners occur with a noun without DEF. As (3.71a) shows, *denne* is used with DEF. This should be contrasted with standard Swedish, where *denna* cannot occur with DEF as in (3.38c), repeated here as (3.71b).[27]

(3.71)	a.	**denne**	mann**en**	N
		this	man.DEF	
	b.	*denna	musen	S
		this	mouse.DEF	

Fjeldstad and Hervold (1989: 39) claim about the co-occurrence of definite determiners and DEF, (the so-called double determination) that it 'is more commonly used in *Nynorsk* than in *Bokmål*, and many use it consistently'. However, Strandskogen and Strandskogen (1980: 57) in their grammar of *Bokmål* signal an increased use of double determination also in this variety of Norwegian. It seems then as if the official varieties of Norwegian, like many dialects of Swedish, are already in, or are moving towards, a situation in which definite independent determiners always co-occur with DEF. This means that if DEF is analysed as a syntactic determiner, all definite

Norwegian noun phrases containing an independent determiner must have two determiner nodes.

The co-occurrence of DEF and possessive noun phrases is complicated in Norwegian. If we limit ourselves to possessive pronouns, there are two possibilities. If the possessive precedes the noun, the noun must not carry DEF (3.72a), but if the possessive follows the noun, DEF must occur (3.72b).

(3.72) a. **min** bok — N
my book

b. bok**en** **min**
book.DEF my
'my book'

This difference, and the further complications which arise if proper nouns and full noun phrases are taken into account, have often formed the starting point for analyses of Norwegian noun phrases (for example Fiva 1987 and Taraldsen 1990). However, I will only note the facts here and not discuss them further. Suffice it to say that if *min* in (3.72a) is best considered a determiner, then it is unusual amongst Norwegian determiners in that it requires the noun not to carry DEF.

In Danish, DEF occurs in complementary distribution with independent determiners, as illustrated by the examples in (3.73).

(3.73) a. mand-**en** — D
man-DEF

b. **den** unge mand / *mand-en
the young man man-DEF

c. **den** mand / *mand-en
that man man-DEF

d. **denne** mand / *mand-en
this man man-DEF

e. **mit** / **Johans** hus / *hus-et
my Johans house house-DEF

In Icelandic, DEF does not usually co-occur with an independent prenominal determiner, as in (3.74). One difference between Icelandic (and to some extent Faroese) and the other Scandinavian languages is that a noun can be premodified by an adjective phrase without a prenominal modifier. An example of this is found in (3.74e).

(3.74) a. maður-**inn** — I
man-DEF

b. **þessi** maður
this man

c. **sá** maður
that man

d. **hinn** mikli maður[28]
the great man

e. mikli maður-**inn**
great man-DEF
'the great man'

However, there are two cases in which DEF can be used with a prenominal determiner in Icelandic. Firstly, there is a determiner homonymous with the independent definite article (except in NT.SG.NOM/ACC) which requires the noun which follows it to carry DEF. This is exemplified in (3.75). Secondly, DEF can be used with prenominal determiners for emphatic effect, as in (3.76).

(3.75) **hinn** maður**inn** / *maður I
the.other man-DEF man
'the other man'

(3.76) a. **þau** ár(-**in**) I
those years-DEF
'those (very) years'

b. **þetta** ár(-**ið**)
this year-DEF
'this (very) year'

Faroese follows a less restrictive pattern than any of the other Scandinavian languages. If the noun is preceded by an adjective phrase, the prenominal demonstrative *tann* must be used (see (3.77b)). Usually DEF is retained, but 'the suffix is occasionally omitted' (Lockwood 1977: 107). This is illustrated in (3.78). Other prenominal determiners may also occur with or without DEF, apparently without a change of meaning. Examples are provided in (3.79).

(3.77) a. kettlingur-**in** F
kitten-DEF.NOM

b. *svarti kettlingur-in
black kitten-DEF.NOM

(3.78) a. **tann** svarti kettlingur-**in** F
the black kitten-DEF.NOM

b. **tann** svarti kettlingur
the black kitten
'the black kitten'

(3.79) a. **henda** genta(-**n**)F
this girl-DEF

b. **tann** tíð(-**in**)
that time-DEF

To a certain extent, Barnes (1994) confirms this picture of the co-occurrence of independent determiners and DEF in Faroese. He does, however, give some indication of preferences: 'where definite noun phrases contain an adjective or a demonstrative, or both, Faroese prefers double definition . . . but single definition also occurs' (Barnes: 207).[29] Barnes also gives an example of a definite noun phrase in Faroese that contains a premodifying adjective, but no prenominal article. His example is given in (3.80). According to Barnes, this construction 'occurs widely in written Faroese, and is especially common in the press'. In the spoken language the pattern appears to be restricted to names or set phrases as in Swedish.

(3.80) gamli bátur**in** F
old boat.DEF
'the old boat'

In spite of Barnes's clarification, it can still be said that Faroese is less restrictive as far as co-occurrence or non-co-occurrence of determiners and DEF goes than all other Scandinavian languages.

In general in Faroese, the existence of several alternative structures is often the result of Danish influence. One original type of construction may exist, frequently similar to an Icelandic type, and in addition to this a structure borrowed from Danish may occur. Because of this influence, Faroese often appears more permissive than other Scandinavian languages. One example of this is the word-order restrictions in main and subordinate clauses. Often Faroese permits both the so-called Mainland Scandinavian and the Insular Scandinavian orders (for a summary of the facts, see Börjars 1991). In the case of the co-occurrence restrictions within the noun phrase, it is not obvious that an explanation can be found in terms of this mixture of original constructions and Danish influence. In Danish, there is no co-occurrence of DEF and an independent determiner and in Icelandic the possibilities of co-occurrence are very limited.

Albanian, like Faroese, appears to have optional co-occurrence of DEF and syntactic determiners. Examples are provided in (3.81).

(3.81) a. **ky** djalë / djal-**i** A
this boy boy-DEF

b. **ai** djalë / djal-**i**
that boy boy-DEF

Since the demonstrative elements *ky* and *ai* may function as determiners without the presence of DEF, the examples in (3.81) must be considered cases of co-occurrence of determiners.

There are further potential cases of co-occurrence of determiners in Albanian which involve DEF. In noun phrases containing an adjective, the initial element, which can be either the noun or the adjective, carries DEF. Regardless of which element is initial, the adjective must be preceded by an apparently free element *i*.[30] This is illustrated in (3.82a) and (3.82b). (Albanian examples are borrowed and adapted from Morgan 1984. My discussion of the Albanian data owes a lot to Morgan's article.)

(3.82) a. djal-**i** **i** mirë A
boy-DEF ? good
b. **i** mir-**i** djalë
? good-DEF boy
'the good boy'

Some possessive constructions pose similar problems. Possessive pronouns follow the noun in Albanian, and the noun that precedes it must carry DEF (see (3.83a)). The same holds for proper noun possessors, as (3.83b) shows. In this case, the construction is even further complicated by the fact that the proper noun must itself carry DEF and be preceded by the particle -*i*.

(3.83) a. djal-**i** im A
boy-DEF my
'my boy'
b. djal-**i** **i** Agim-**it**
boy-DEF ? Agim-DEF.OBL
'Agim's boy'

However, it is not clear how to analyse this element *i*. A seemingly obvious possibility is to assign it the status of a non-bound version of DEF since the two are homonymous. Under this analysis, the free *i* would be a determiner and (3.82a), (3.82b) and (3.83b) would be examples of co-occurring determiners.

There is a serious problem with the assumption that the independent *i* is a syntactic determiner. If it is considered a determiner in (3.82), it must presumably be a definite determiner. This is, however, a problematic conclusion, since *i* also occurs in indefinite noun phrases. This is illustrated in (3.84).

(3.84) një djalë **i** mirë A
a boy ? good
'a good boy'

Since the bound -*i* in (3.81) and (3.82) only occurs in definite noun phrases, we could then conclude that the free *i* is not actually a syntactically independent version of *-i*. If *i* is not just a non-bound version of the bound DEF *-i*, then it is not clear that it should be analysed as a determiner at all. Hence, it is not obvious that (3.82a), (3.82b) and (3.83b) do in fact provide examples of co-occurrence of DEF.

A further complication of the matter is the fact that the form of the independent *i* may vary between definite and indefinite noun phrases. In certain parts of the paradigm for *i*, there are two alternate forms.[31] This is only the case for the definite paradigms. If one wanted to argue that the definite *i* is different from the one occurring in indefinite noun phrases, then one might want to use this as supporting evidence. However, since one of the alternates in the definite paradigm is always identical to the corresponding form in the indefinite paradigm, it is certainly not a compelling argument. I conclude instead that the free *i* is not a definite determiner, and that therefore the noun phrases in (3.82) do not exemplify co-occurrence of determiners. What I have glossed with a question mark in these examples should be glossed as PRT rather than DEF. Still, I claim that Albanian does have double determination, namely when DEF occurs with the syntactic demonstratives, as in (3.81).

In Macedonian, DEF does not occur with other determiners. This is illustrated for demonstratives in (3.85). DEF does co-occur with possessive pronouns, as in (3.85c) (repeated from (3.58a)).

(3.85) a. **toj** čovek / *čovek-ot M
that man man-DEF

b. **ovoj** čovek / *čovek-ot/-ov
this man man-DEF

c. moj-**ot** časovnik
my-DEF watch
'my watch'

However, there are reasons to assume that the possessive in (3.85c) is actually not a determiner, but an adjective. In terms of C. Lyons (1985, 1989, 1992, in press), it is an adjectival genitive. The possessive *moj* is like an adjective for instance in that it may take the standard adjectival gender markers. We can also say that the very fact that DEF can attach to it is a sign that it is an adjective. Lunt (1952: 36) describes the possessives in relation to the personal pronouns as follows: '[The personal pronouns] are paralleled by a set of slightly irregular adjectival forms, which function in every way like adjectives (except that they cannot be modified by an adverb) but have the meaning "belonging to the 1st (2nd, 3rd, general) person".' I conclude then that in Macedonian (and Bulgarian), there are no cases of co-occurrence of determiners.

In Romanian, DEF may co-occur with a syntactic demonstrative. As (3.86a) shows, the morphological determiner does not occur if the demonstrative precedes the noun. This means that we would have to regard *acest* as the determiner in (3.86a). If this analysis of *acest* carries over into noun phrases like (3.86b), then this is a case of co-occurrence. In (3.86b), the demonstrative follows the noun, which obligatorily carries DEF. However, the demonstrative does in this case have a different form. In fact, the ending on the demonstrative in this case could be viewed as an indication that it functions as an adjective. Its position is also one commonly filled by an adjective. For these reasons, I rule out (3.86b) as an example of co-occurrence of determiners.

(3.86) a. **acest** om — R
this man
'this man'

b. om-**ul** acesta
man-DEF this
'this man'

A further Romanian candidate for double determination is exemplified in (3.87) (from Plank 1995).

(3.87) cîne-**le** (ce**l**) biet — R
dog-DEF PRT.DEF poor

Unlike the Albanian *i*, *cel* occurs only when the adjective follows the noun. When the adjective is in its prenominal position, DEF attaches to the adjective, which is then not preceded by *cel*.[32] Furthermore, *cel* cannot occur in indefinite noun phrases. None of the arguments I put forward for not analysing the Albanian (3.82) and (3.83) as co-occurrence of determiners seems to apply to Romanian, and I can see no reason why (3.87) should not be considered a case of co-occurring determiners. I would claim then that Romanian does provide examples of co-occurrence of determiners, but not in cases which involve DEF and a demonstrative (see (3.86)). If we assume that *cel* should be analysed as an instance of DEF attached to a particle (or 'dummy host'), then the co-occurrence takes the form of two instances of DEF. Alternatively, if one accepts Dobrovie-Sorin's (1987) conclusion that *cel* is itself a determiner, then this is an example of co-occurrence between an independent syntactic determiner and DEF.

The data relating to co-occurrence of DEF with other determiners, or with other instances of DEF, are the least clear of all the aspects of DEF discussed so far. In Swedish and Norwegian DEF can co-occur with a syntactic determiner; both languages appear to be moving towards a situation in which all definite determiners require a definite nominal. Romanian also has co-occurrence. Depending on how *cel* is analysed, the co-occurrence is either of two instances of DEF or of DEF and a syntactic determiner. Danish, Icelandic, Macedonian and Bulgarian do not have any cases of co-occurrence that would make an analysis of DEF as a syntactic determiner implausible. Faroese and Albanian, finally, appear to have optional co-occurrence of determiners. Especially with respect to Romanian and Albanian, it is difficult to judge whether certain elements should be assigned the status of determiner or not. Furthermore, the extent to which co-occurrence is truly optional in Albanian and Faroese remains to be established.

3.6.3.2. *Co-ordination*

In section 3.4.4, I showed that, with respect to co-ordination, the Swedish DEF does not behave like the prenominal independent determiners. The host to which DEF is attached cannot consist of two co-ordinated nouns. The data in section 3.5.2 make clear that this cannot be ascribed to the fact that DEF is a bound morpheme, since the possessive *-s* can attach to a co-ordinated nominal element.

I have not been able to find an example of DEF attaching to a co-ordinated host in any of the other languages considered here. They are maybe not the kind of examples one would expect to find in a grammar, and I have not had access to a native speaker for all these languages. However, not even in Macedonian, where DEF satisfies most of the criteria for clitic status and can therefore be considered part of the syntax, is it possible to let DEF determine a co-ordinated nominal, as (3.88) shows.

(3.88) a. *[maži i ženi] -te M
husbands and wives -DEF

b. *[maži-te i ženi]
husbands-DEF and wives

c. maži-**te** i ženi-**te**
husbands-DEF and wives-DEF
'the husbands and wives'

In (3.88a), DEF is found in second position if the co-ordinated nouns are counted as one unit. If, on the other hand, each part of the conjunct counts as one unit for the purpose of the position of DEF, the DEF is in second position in (3.88b). However, no matter how 'second position' is defined, as these two examples show, DEF cannot have a co-ordinated host. Instead, DEF must be repeated on each conjunct, as in (3.88c).

3.6.3.3. *Conclusions*

With respect to restrictions on the co-occurrence of independent determiners and DEF, the languages discussed here show interesting differences. Norwegian, and Swedish appear to be moving towards a situation in which if an independent definite determiner is present, the noun it determines must also carry DEF. In such a language, it would be difficult to maintain that DEF was a syntactic determiner on a par with the independent ones.[33] Rather, DEF would be better analysed as some kind of morphological agreement marker; the morphological manifestation of a syntactic feature. In Icelandic, the distribution of independent definite determiners and DEF is almost complementary. When the two co-occur, this has the effect of emphasis, except in one case. In Danish, DEF and independent determiners do actually occur in fully complementary distribution. The facts about Faroese are slightly more complicated. The pattern sketched by Lockwood (1977) implies that there is never obligatory co-occurrence, nor obligatory non-co-occurrence, of DEF and an independent determiner. However, it is not clear whether this implies that some speakers use the two in complementary distribution and others do not, whether the two options belong to different registers, or whether every speaker uses a noun with or without DEF in free variation with independent definite determiners. Barnes (1994) does give some indications of preference and relative frequency of the different options, but it still leaves Faroese less restrictive than any of the other Scandinavian languages.

In Macedonian and Bulgarian, DEF and independent determiners occur in complementary distribution. This is true if the possessive is considered an adjective, and in section 3.6.3.1 I claimed that there are good reasons to do so. In Romanian, the situation is more complicated. Whether or not DEF can be said to occur in complementary distribution with independent definite determiners depends on how certain elements, like post-nominal demonstratives and *cel/cea*, are viewed. Albanian, finally, is similar to Faroese in that DEF is optional with certain determiners.

With respect to the criteria discussed in sections 3.3 and 3.6.2, the languages seem to divide quite neatly into two classes: the Scandinavian languages, where DEF is an affix; and the Balkan languages, where DEF is a clitic.[34] However, with respect to co-occurrence, all the languages seem to differ. With respect to the other syntactic criterion discussed in sections 3.4 and 3.6.3, namely, co-ordination, all the languages discussed behave like Swedish in that they do not allow DEF to attach to a co-ordinated host.

3.7. CONCLUSIONS ABOUT THE STATUS OF THE 'ENCLITIC ARTICLE'

All tests applied to Swedish DEF in section 3.3 pointed in the same direction: in no way does DEF behave like a clitic. Furthermore, as the evidence in section 3.4 indicated, DEF does not behave like a syntactic determiner with respect to co-occurrence with other determiners and co-ordination. The possibility that clitics in Swedish behave differently from those on which the criteria for clitic status have been developed was refuted in section 3.5. In this section, I showed that the Swedish possessive *-s* does satisfy a convincing number of the criteria for clitic status. The comparison with other languages in section 3.6 showed that the failure of Swedish DEF to satisfy the clitic criteria cannot be ascribed to the fact that it is a determiner. In this section, I showed that DEFs in other languages satisfy the same criteria. I showed that even the closely related languages Icelandic and Faroese appear to satisfy some of the criteria. The one exception to this was related to co-ordination. In none of the languages discussed can DEF modify a co-ordinated nominal.

In table 3.2, the behaviour of the different DEFs is represented schematically. Naturally, this table gives a simplified picture of the facts, but it can still give some impression of the complexity of the distinction between affixes and clitics with respect to the data. A large bold tick indicates that with respect to this criterion, DEF in the language in question behaves like a clitic. A smaller tick indicates that this DEF is probably best analysed as a clitic, but that there are slight problems with such an analysis. A minus sign indicates that in this language, with respect to this criterion, DEF behaves like an affix. Where the sign ± occurs, the criterion does not give evidence either way. When a box has been left empty, I have not been able to find any relevant data.

A number of comments on the criteria used in table 3.2 and throughout this chapter are in order. Firstly, as pointed out in section 3.6.2.2, if we take 'selectivity' in terms of Carstairs's (1981: 7) Insensitivity Claim, then all languages fail the test. According to the Insensitivity Claim, if the shape of DEF depends on the grammatical features of the head of its host phrase, then DEF cannot be an element whose position is defined in terms of a phrasal unit. In all the languages discussed here, the shape of DEF does depend on the grammatical features of the host in this way. Hence all the DEFs discussed here are not clitics. On the other hand, the more conventional view of selectivity, where selectivity refers to the syntactic category of the

Table 3.2 Schematic representation of the behaviour of DEF in the Scandinavian and Balkan languages with respect to criteria for clitic status

	Clitic vs. Affix				Syntactic	
Language	Phrasal host	Selectivity	Order	Irregularities	Co-occurrence	Co-ordination
Swedish	–	–	±	±	–	±
Norwegian	–	–	±	±	–	±
Danish	–	–	±	±	**√**	±
Faroese	–	–	√	±	–	±
Icelandic	–	–	√	±	√	±
Albanian	√	√	±	±	–	±
Romanian	√	√	±	±	√	±
Macedonian	**√**	**√**	±	±	**√**	±
Bulgarian	**√**	**√**	±		**√**	±

host word, creates a clear dichotomy between the Balkan languages and the Scandinavian ones. In these languages, DEF appears to have developed either directly from demonstrative determiners, or from definite articles, which in turn developed from demonstrative determiners. In languages that have some form of gender distinction, this distinction is commonly reflected in the determiner system. The demonstratives (and the determiners that developed from them) even play a crucial role in the origin and development of gender (Corbett 1991: 310–12). It is not surprising therefore to find that the gender distinctions are also central to the bound forms that developed from these determiners. I cannot see a reason why the fact that gender distinctions are preserved when these determining elements become bound forms should mean that they could not be analysed as clitics if they share a convincing number of characteristics with other types of clitics, as is the case in the Balkan languages. Hence I will assume that these elements may still be clitics.

Linear theories of grammar, such as those envisaged by, for instance, Klavans (1983, 1985) and Zwicky and Pullum (1983), predict that morphological irregularities cannot be the result of cliticization. Cliticisation takes place in the syntax, and the units of the syntax do not have access to information about the internal structure of other syntactic units. This means that such an approach predicts that the addition of a clitic to a host word could not bring about a change in the shape of that host unless the change could be attributed to general phonological rules. Such irregularities do, however, occur in all the languages discussed here. There appear to be fewer examples in the Balkan languages than, for instance, in Swedish, but the differences are small and difficult to quantify. To my mind, this does not indicate that DEF in, for instance, Macedonian is not a typical clitic. Instead, it points to a weakness in the linear approach. As indicated in table 3.2, I do not consider this criterion to provide evidence either way. If instead a parallel view of the modules of grammar is assumed, then an analysis can be provided which accounts for these facts. In such an analysis, the notion of a clitic as a 'phrasal affix' can be represented. To the syntactic module, DEF has all the characteristics of a clitic; particularly in that its position is defined with respect to a phrasal unit and that it is not selective with respect to its host word. In the morphological module, on the other hand, the actual liaison between DEF and its host word can be governed by the same morphological rules that govern affixation proper. This follows from the two parameters used in Börjars and Vincent (1993).

Of the syntactic criteria in table 3.2, the co-ordination criterion appears to be irrelevant as an indicator of syntactic status. In none of the languages under discussion is it possible for DEF to determine a co-ordinated nominal, not even when the conjuncts form a close unit. However, this cannot be taken as an indication that DEF does not have syntactic status. The issue of the determination of conjoined nominals is a complex one in many languages. Welsh (W) provides a further example of a language where the determination of a co-ordinated nominal is not possible, see (3.89) and (3.90).[35]

(3.89) a. **y** fam **a'r** ferch — W
the mother and.the daughter

b. *y fam a merch
the mother and daughter
'the mother and daughter'

(3.90) a. **y** pysgodyn **a'r** sglodion — W
the fish and.the chips

b. *y pysgodyn a sglodion
the fish and chips
'the fish and chips'

I have no explanation for why determiners should be more restrictive with respect to co-ordination than other elements, but it does mean that the data relating to co-ordination are irrelevant to the discussion of the morphological and syntactic status of DEFS.

I turn now to the correlation between the morphological criteria and the syntactic criteria, of which only co-occurrence remains. There does not appear to be any relation between the morphological status of DEF and whether or not it can co-occur with a syntactic determiner. Languages which do not have co-occurring determiners are found both in the Scandinavian and in the Balkan language groups. Both the Scandinavian and Balkan languages provide examples where there is optional co-occurrence of semantic determiners. Examples of double determination constructions involving an independent syntactic determiner are found in both groups. This means that the morphological status of DEF, that is, as affix or clitic, is unrelated to whether or not the element can co-occur with a syntactic determiner. We can say then that the status of DEF elements varies in two dimensions.

In the introduction to section 3.3, I stated that a distinction between morphology and syntax is only justified if the rules which govern the construction of words are sufficiently different from those that govern the construction of larger units. When the distinction between morphology and syntax is made, it is usually assumed that there is one special type of bound element whose conduct is governed not (entirely) by morphological but (at least partly) by syntactic rules, namely, the category clitic. In this chapter, I hope to have provided convincing evidence that the criteria that have been put forward for a distinction between the two types of bound morphemes – affixes and clitics – is justified. The rules that govern the behaviour of Swedish DEF and Macedonian DEF are sufficiently distinct to warrant a division into two types of rules. This means that I see no reason to assume that a morphological component is superfluous in our theory of grammar (for further arguments, see Börjars, Vincent and Chapman 1997 and Vincent and Börjars 1997 as opposed to, for instance, Déchaine 1996). Instead, if we assume that there are two types of rules, morphological and syntactic ones, the distinction between DEFs in different languages with respect to the morphological criteria in table 3.2 can be captured.

One further conclusion that I have drawn on the basis of the data discussed in this chapter is that a division of bound morphemes into two discrete categories – clitics and affixes – is not sufficient to capture all aspects of the behaviour of DEFs in these languages. For any analysis to do justice to the facts it must be able to express variation in at least one other dimension. Autolexical Syntax provides tools which allow us to represent this variation in more than one dimension. Sadock (1991: 112–20) provides an analysis of Scandinavian and Balkan noun phrases containing DEF and Börjars (1997) offers a slightly different analysis.

I will not dwell further on how to analyse all these languages here. My main concern here is with the Swedish DEF. I have drawn two main conclusions on the basis of the data discussed in this chapter. Firstly, a distinction between two dimensions must be made. These two dimensions can be satisfactorily described in the traditional terms morphology and syntax. Secondly, given this distinction, I have not found evidence that the Swedish DEF has any independent syntactic status. It exists in the syntax only as a feature on a noun.

These conclusions have consequences for the choice of theoretical framework. Since I do not have an *a priori* reason to prefer one framework above another, I will choose one within which the distinction between these two dimensions can be represented straightforwardly. Even though Autolexical Syntax (Sadock 1991) provides a convenient way of representing discrepancies between the morphological and the syntactic analysis, it does not contain a well-developed theory of syntax as such. A context free phrase structure grammar using a number of assumptions from Generalized Phrase Structure Grammar (Gazdar, et al. 1985) is assumed (Sadock 1991: 21–3). The Autolexical framework could be used with any non-transformational phrase structure grammar, though. Due to this vagueness, I will not formulate my analysis with an Autolexical framework here.

The requirement that a theory should contain a convenient way of representing the syntax–morphology distinction makes modern transformational grammar an unlikely choice. In standard versions of transformational theory as developed from, for example, Chomsky (1986b, 1992, 1995) morphologically bound elements like DEF are given virtually the same analysis. Furthermore, these elements are distinguished from morphologically independent elements only by being bound. The Swedish *-en*, the Macedonian *-ot* and the English *the* would all be found under the syntactic node D in standard analyses (for similar analyses of Scandinavian and Balkan languages, see Delsing 1988, 1989, 1992, 1993, Taraldsen 1990, 1991, Sigurðsson 1992 and Dobrovie-Sorin 1987).[36] To me, therefore, transformational grammar is not the obvious choice of theoretical framework.

4

THE HEAD OF THE NOUN PHRASE

4.1. Introduction

Throughout this book, I will assume the proverbial 'some version of X-bar theory' (Pullum 1985). The scope of the book does not permit a detailed discussion of the principles of X-bar theory. I refer to Pullum (1985), Kornai and Pullum (1990) and the articles in Baltin and Kroch (1989) for thorough discussions of the issues involved.

Jackendoff (1977) assumes that a category X projects up to the level of X‴. For noun phrases this means that complements attach at N° level to form an N′ constituent, restrictive modification attaches at N′ level and non-restrictive modification at N″. Articles, finally, turn an N″ constituent into a full N‴.

In more recent analyses, a phrase is usually assumed to project to X″ level only. Even though this is the structure assumed standardly in major frameworks such as Generalized Phrase Structure Grammar (GPSG), Head-driven Phrase Structure Grammar (HPSG), Lexical-Functional Grammar (LFG) and most versions of transformational grammar, compelling arguments for this assumption are rarely given.[1] Still, as long as the present assumptions connected with X-bar theory are not taken to be irrefutable facts, I believe the system offers a helpful way of restricting the number of possible analyses for any given data. Therefore, in order to focus my examination of the phrase structure of Swedish noun phrases, I will assume as a starting point a representation of the syntactic structure of phrases as in (4.1).[2]

(4.1)

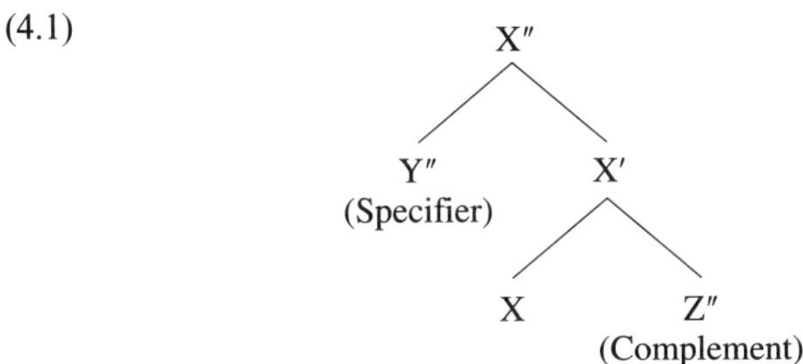

In (4.1), X, Y and Z are variables over syntactic categories. X, Y and Z need not be different categories. The X′ node is assumed to be recursive. Adjunct modifiers will be represented as sisters of an X′ node, but also daughters of an X′ node.[3] 'Complement' refers to elements subcategorized by the head X.[4] The status of the position labelled 'Specifier' is less clear. I refer to Stowell (1989, 1991), Bouma (1988) and Ernst (1991) for different views on the nature of the specifier.

A number of assumptions follow from the tree in (4.1). In this chapter I will consider the most significant one of these, namely the fact that in any phrase, one lexical element has a very special status: it is the head. The tree shows that the phrase as a whole will always be of the same syntactic category as its head, though it will differ in bar level.[5] The assumption that one element is the head has a number of significant consequences relating to subcategorization and feature percolation, for instance. This means that in any theory that assumes a tree structure like (4.1), or an equivalent structure, the choice of the head of a phrase will influence in important ways many other issues. Therefore, before I can develop an analysis of the Swedish noun phrases, I need to consider the issue of the head status within the noun phrase.

For a long time, the head status of major category phrases like noun phrases and verb phrases was not discussed to any great extent. The head of the phrase was assumed to be the noun and the verb respectively.[6] There are noteworthy counterexamples, like J. Lyons (1977) and Vennemann and Harlow (1977), to which I will return in section 4.3.4. However, in the 1980s an intensive debate on the headedness of phrases took place. This debate was driven mainly by an increased interest in so-called functional categories within transformational theory, and for the noun phrase it was greatly accelerated by Abney (1987). However, a number of linguists not working within this theory have arrived at similar conclusions, e.g. Hudson (1984) and Hellan (1986). Their arguments will be discussed in section 4.3.2. There is no room here for a full account of all the arguments that have been put forward in this debate, and I will therefore have to limit my discussion in several ways.

Firstly, I will discuss the notion of head almost exclusively with reference to noun phrases. Furthermore, I will focus on the NP vs. DP debate, that is, I will contrast the assumption that the noun phrase is headed by the noun with the so-called DP hypothesis, which states that the determiner heads the noun phrase. I will only briefly mention some other proposals, referring to other functional heads in the noun phrase, like Q(uantifier)P and Num(eral)P. I will also largely ignore the DP–AP–NP hypothesis, which to my knowledge was first proposed by Abney (1987). This is a version of the DP hypothesis which embraces the idea that the head of *stupid dog*, as in the phrase *that stupid dog*, is *stupid*. A number of serious shortcomings in the approach have been pointed out by, among others, Radford (1989), but the DP–AP–NP hypothesis has been adopted in many analyses of noun phrases, for example Delsing (1988, 1989). In fact, the account proposed by Radford (1993) clearly is a version of the DP–AP–NP hypothesis. A variant of this analysis is also proposed by Delsing (1992, 1993) where A heads a nominal like *stupid dog*, but where the NP *dog* is the specifier of that A rather than its complement.

There are in principle two closely related ways of using the notion 'head'. The head of any phrase can be considered always to be a terminal node, a lexical element. In this sense, the head of X″ in (4.1) is X. On the other hand, every level in the representation can be assumed to have a head. This is the way the notion is used in HPSG. Viewed this way, the head of X″ is X′ and the head of X′ is X. Here, I will focus on the first of these interpretations of 'head'. I will discuss the issue almost exclusively as a relation between a phrase and a lexical element. This means that I am concerned with what should be positioned under X in (4.1) in a correct representation of Swedish noun phrases.

Another important issue which I will leave out of my discussion here is whether or not headedness is a primitive. Even though most current theories make use of the notion head, very few of them actually permit explicit reference to the head status of one element (for an overview, see Hudson 1993: 266–9). A theory that relies heavily on the headedness of one element is GPSG (Gazdar et al. 1985). Still, even in this theory, headedness is not a primitive and heads cannot be referred to directly. Problems with the GPSG approach to heads have been discussed by Zwicky (1988) and Fenchel (1989). In HPSG (Pollard and Sag 1987, 1994), on the other hand, at every level of a constituent structure, there are attributes indicating the status of each daughter. One of these attributes is HEAD-DTR which refers explicitly to the head daughter of any non-co-ordinated structure (see Pollard and Sag 1987: 55–6). Dependency Grammar, exemplified for instance by Word Grammar (Hudson 1984, 1990) is another framework that allows direct reference to heads at every level of the phrase.

As a starting point for my investigation of the headedness of noun phrases, I will take the general criteria for head status used in the debate between Zwicky (1985a) and Hudson (1987). These will be discussed in section 4.2. In sections 4.3 and 4.4, I will discuss a number of other headedness criteria that have been used specifically in relation to noun phrases. In section 4.3 I will consider those that have been used to argue in favour of a DP analysis and in 4.4 those that have been used to support a traditional NP analysis. In section 4.5, I consider what conclusions can be drawn on the basis of these criteria with reference to Swedish noun phrases.

4.2. The Zwicky–Hudson criteria

4.2.1. *Functor and argument*

The first criterion for head status discussed by Zwicky (1985a: 4–5) is a semantic one. The semantic head of X+Y is considered to be X if X+Y is 'a kind of X'. Zwicky applies this criterion at an intuitive level and it means that the noun is the head, since *denna mus* 'this mouse' is a kind of *mus*.

At a less intuitive, more theoretical level, we can say that a noun phrase like *denna gråa mus* 'this grey mouse' is semantically different from *gråa mus* in that a determiner has applied to the nominal. This determiner represents a function from properties to a set of properties, and has hence changed the semantic nature of the phrase from being predicative to being referential. Under this interpretation of the 'kind of' argument, it is the determiner which contributes to the special semantic nature of a full noun phrase, and therefore it should be considered the head.

Zwicky then proposes 'a sharpening (and extension)' (1985a: 4) of the notion 'kind of', where the terms FUNCTOR and ARGUMENT are used. The semantic criterion can then be reformulated to say that X is the semantic head of X+Y if 'in the semantic interpretation of X+Y, Y represents a functor on an argument represented by X.' In theories of formal semantics, such as Montague semantics (Dowty et al. 1981, Montague 1973) or Boolean algebra (Keenan and Faltz 1985), the determiner represents a functor which applies to the argument represented by the noun. So, under this interpretation, as under the more obvious interpretation of the 'kind of' argument, the noun would be the semantic head of a Det+N phrase. In a note of caution, Zwicky warns that no system of formal semantics will actually force us to consider the noun the argument or to analyse the determiner as the functor: 'with a certain amount of formal ingenuity, a Montague style semantics that treats Det as a functor on the argument N can be redone as a system treating N as a functor on the argument Det.' (1985a: 4, note 3)

The prime example of how the interpretation of the notions of functor and argument has been loosened in Montague semantics is type raising. When type raising is applied, the argument of a functor can be 'raised' to functor status. As a functor, it takes the old functor as its argument. In this way, a proper noun, of the category 'names' (*e*) can be raised to the status of a generalized quantifier (*t*/(*t*/*e*)). This is done as follows; we have a functor *t*/*e* which can apply to an argument *e* to form a *t*. That element *e* can now be raised to become a functor which takes as its argument its old functor *t*/*e*, to form a *t*. Thus the old *e* is a functor of the category *t*/(*t*/*e*). This is illustrated in (4.2), where FA stands for functional application, the process by which the functor and the argument are joined. In (4.2a), *Andrew* has the status of argument, and in (4.2b) it has been raised to functor.

(4.2) a. Andrew giggles

$$\frac{\frac{\text{Andrew}}{e} \quad \frac{\text{giggles}}{t/e}}{t}\ \text{FA}$$

b. Andrew giggles

$$\frac{\frac{\text{Andrew}}{t/(t/e)} \quad \frac{\text{giggles}}{t/e}}{t}\ \text{FA}$$

As can be seen in (4.2), the type raising has no consequences for the syntactic or semantic structure of this particular sentence. However, this is not necessarily the case when type raising applies. Partee and Rooth (1983) use type raising to allow their grammar to provide readings of sentences that the semantics would not otherwise allow. It is used by Steedman (1985) and by Dowty (1988) to analyse different types of co-ordination, such as right node raising and non-constituent co-ordination. An example of a further extension of the use of type raising can be found in Roberts (1992), where it accounts for adverbial scope ambiguities in English.

There are, then, a number of difficulties with applying this test for head status. Firstly, in its simplest, 'kind of' version, it could be interpreted at different levels and therefore give different results. Secondly, even in its more formal interpretation in terms of functor and argument, this test is not absolutely clear cut, since there is no unambiguous way of establishing argument status. Furthermore, mechanisms exist in the formal theories which make reference to functor and argument to transform an argument into a functor. Other problems with relating syntactic headedness to semantic argument status have been pointed out by Hudson (1987: 113–16). Furthermore, Hudson finds that the syntactic tests for headedness yield a head that more often than not corresponds to the functor rather than the argument, as his final table shows (1987: 125). Cann (1989: 4–6) also argues against the validity of the functor-argument criterion as a means of establishing headedness.

The fact still remains that, at least in some intuitive 'kind of' sense, we would like to consider the noun as the semantic head of a Det+N combination. Furthermore, the selection frame of a transitive verb will often need to make reference to the semantic characteristics of the noun, but rarely to those of the determiner. Abney (1987) proposes to capture the intuition that the noun is the semantic head within his DP analysis by introducing two types of projections: C-PROJECTION (constituent projection) and S-PROJECTION (semantic projection). Radford (1993) captures the same idea in terms of a distinction between IMMEDIATE HEAD and ULTIMATE HEAD.[7] In a different type of approach, Netter (1994) proposes an analysis of German noun phrases in which the determiner is the head (noun phrases are referred to as *dp*s) with respect to subcategorization and also in the sense that certain crucial features (MINOR features) of the noun phrase are inherited from the determiner. On the other hand, the so-called MAJOR features are all inherited from the nominal daughter. Netter's (1994) approach will be discussed in sections 5.2.3.3, 5.3.3.3 and 5.4.3.3.

4.2.2. *Subcategorizand*

With respect to noun phrases, two aspects of subcategorization should be discussed. Firstly, subcategorization **of** the noun phrase, and secondly, subcategorization **within** the noun phrase. An example of the first kind is how a verb can subcategorize for a particular type of noun phrase. This aspect of subcategorization has been used as an argument in favour of functional heads in clausal elements. Bresnan (1970), for instance, showed that there are English verbs which subcategorize for clauses according to their complementizers. The verb *declare* takes a clausal complement with *that*, whereas *wait* takes the complementiser *for* (*to*). Baltin (1989: 3–5) also uses such facts together with the assumption that subcategorization may only refer to the head of the complement – rather than, say, to the specifier of the complement – as an argument in favour of C being the (functional) head of the clause.

With respect to noun phrases, however, this type of 'external' subcategorization has been largely ignored in the literature referred to here.[8] There are exceptions, however. Ernst (1991) and Payne (1993a), for instance, both point out that noun phrases are not selected, in English at least, on the basis of what determiner or quantifier they contain. 'We do not have a set of verbs x which only permit objects beginning with, for example, the quantifier *every*, and another set y which only permit objects beginning with *each*' (Payne 1993a: 130). Furthermore, in the theories which advocate functional categories as heads of clausal elements, a verb may subcategorize according to the category status of its complement, namely, CP, IP or 'small clause'. According to Payne, it is difficult to imagine a similar situation for verbs selecting nominal complements: 'there are no two different verbs x and y such that, for example, x only occurs with noun phrases which contain determiners and y only occurs with noun phrases which contain quantifiers' Payne (1993a: 130).

It could, however, be argued for Swedish that there are verbs which select for a noun phrase containing a determiner, and other verbs that select for a noun phrase with or without a determiner. In a DP analysis, this distinction would be expressed in terms of subcategorization of DP or of DP and NP. This has also been suggested for other languages by Dryer (1989) (see section 4.3.4). Swedish examples, partly borrowed from Cooper (1984: 118) are provided in (4.3).

(4.3) a. Det är jobbigt att inte kunna ha **bil** / **en bil**.
it is awkward not to be.able have car a car
'It is awkward not to be able have a car.'

b. Det är jobbigt att inte kunna se *bil / **en bil**.
it is awkward not to be.able see car a car
'It is awkward not to be able to see a car.'

c. Det är jobbigt att inte kunna ha *skurborste / **en skurborste**.
it is awkward not to be.able have scrubbing-brusha scrubbing-brush
'It is awkward not to be able to have a scrubbing-brush.'

d. Det är jobbigt att inte kunna se *skurborste / **en skurborste**.
it is awkward not to be.able see scrubbing-brush a scrubbing-brush
'It is awkward not to be able to see a scrubbing-brush.'

From (4.3a) and (4.3b), we may conclude that the difference between *ha* and *se* lies in the fact that *ha* subcategorizes for both DP and NP, whereas *se* only selects DP. However, as the examples in (4.3c) and (4.3d) show, whether or not the construction without a determiner is allowed also depends strongly on the semantics of the noun and of the verb+noun combination. Cooper (1984: 118–19) concludes that examples like *ha bil* are best analysed as complex verbs of some sort. It seems to me therefore that constructions like (4.3) do not provide a strong argument in favour of a DP analysis for Swedish noun phrases. I will return to this type of construction in section 6.4.3.

Verbs do select their complements with respect to semantic features which are typically associated with nouns. The verb *eat*, for instance, can only select a complement that is [+EDIBLE].[9] Since it can be assumed that nouns and not determiners are specified for this type of feature, this can be viewed as evidence that the noun is the head of the noun phrase with respect to external subcategorization. However, Abney (1987: 57–8) maintains that there are two types of projections: C(ONSTITUENT)-PROJECTIONS and S(EMANTIC)-PROJECTIONS. A c-projection is a projection in its most commonly used sense: XP is the c-projection of X, both for lexical categories such as V and functional categories such as I. An s-projection, on the other hand, is the semantic projection and must always have as its head a lexical category. 'A node's s-projection path is the path of nodes along which its descriptive content is "passed along"' (1987: 57). For a simple DP, this is illustrated in (4.4).

(4.4)

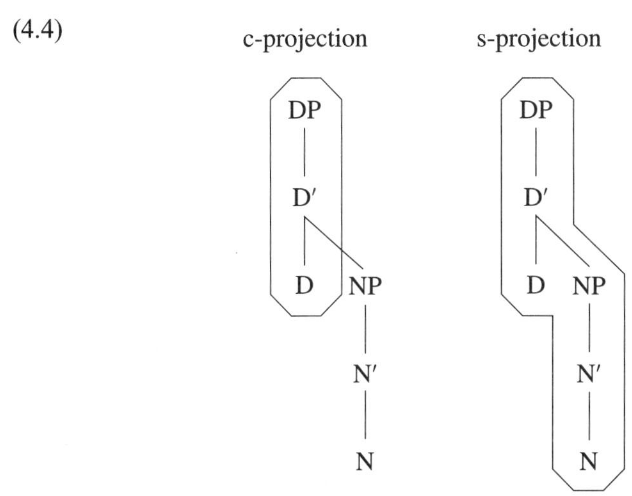

A verb can then select both according to c-projection and s-projection. Thus, under Abney's analysis, the fact that verbs select their complements with respect to the semantic features of the noun phrase cannot be used as an argument in favour of the head status of the noun. Radford's (1993) use of immediate head and ultimate head gives a similar result.

I will turn now to the type of subcategorization which is more commonly used as a criterion for head status, namely, subcategorization within the noun phrase. In most modern syntactic theories, subcategorization is understood to be a relation between a lexical element and its sister.[10] In GPSG, for instance, there are feature co-occurrence restrictions which state that an element of bar-level 0 must have a value for the feature SUBCAT and that elements of bar-level 1 or 2 must not be defined for SUBCAT. In most versions of transformational theory, subcategorization is a property defined in the lexicon and hence it must involve a lexical element which is the head of the phrase. The sister is its complement. This means that under these assumptions about subcategorization, subcategorization facts can be used as a criterion for head status. Cann (1993: 50) puts it more succinctly: 'subcategorization is a necessary and sufficient condition for determining the phrasal head of a construction.' In spite of the agreement about the importance of the notion of subcategorization, it is not clear exactly what it entails.[11]

Zwicky (1985a: 5) states it informally as one slot of a construction having to be listed in the lexicon while its sister constituents are not so constrained. From this it follows that only a lexical element can be the subcategorizand. In four of the six constructions which Zwicky considers, there is one lexical and one phrasal sister, and therefore he concludes without much discussion that the lexical sister must be the subcategorizand. For NP+VP combinations, since neither of the sisters is lexical, there cannot be any subcategorization. For the construction of main interest to me here, Det+N, Zwicky makes the obvious revision of the exact shape of the combination: Det is assumed to combine with a phrasal category Nom, which may in turn consist of just a single N. After this revision, there is only one genuinely lexical sister, Det, and therefore this must be the head. To Zwicky, this is correct, since determiners are lexically subcategorized according to whether they can combine with a singular, a plural or a non-count nominal.

Hudson (1987: 121–2) agrees with Zwicky's conclusions regarding subcategorization and determiners. He adds that treating the determiner as the subcategorizand can explain why some determiners, but not others, can occur in elliptical constructions. The determiners, like *this*, which can occur without a following noun phrase can then be defined in the lexicon as, in some sense, intransitive determiners.

Even though Zwicky and Hudson agree on this point, neither of them has offered more than intuitions about what exactly a subcategorizand is. Cann (1993, see also Cann 1989: 7–11 and 26–7) does propose a more formal definition of the notion. His definition is repeated here as (4.5).

(4.5) Subcategorizand
X subcategorizes for Y in a construction X+Y iff. the ability of members of X to appear with expressions in Y properly partitions the expressions in X into two disjoint non-null subsets
(Cann 1993: 44)

On the basis of this definition, Cann concludes that in English, neither Det nor N is the subcategorizand in a Det+N construction. The data that pointed Hudson in the direction of Det subcategorizing for N (or Nom) are accounted for differently by Cann. The selection restrictions between determiners and the following noun with respect to number and countability fall under Cann's notion FORM GOVERNMENT, which I will deal with in section 4.2.5. The fact that some determiners are 'transitive' and others are not is discussed by Cann only in relation to the articles and the demonstrative determiners. A covert element must be licensed by coindexing with a node that dominates phonetic material (the PF-Licensing Principle, Cann 1993: 54, see Chomsky's 1986a: 98 Principle of Full Interpretation). The demonstrative determiners are found in the specifier position of the noun phrase, where they are coindexed with the noun complement. It is this coindexing with a node dominating phonetic material that licenses an empty noun. The articles in English, on the other hand, are heads which subcategorize their nominal complement.[12] A complement must not be coindexed with the head that selects it. Hence in these constructions, an empty nominal cannot be licensed. This means that whereas the intransitive use of some determiners is seen by Hudson as an argument in favour of the head status of these determiners, Cann (1993: 66–7) explains the same behaviour by assuming that these determiners are **not** heads, but specifiers.[13]

This explanation seems to work satisfactorily for articles and demonstratives, but Hudson (1987: 121) also refers to the difference in behaviour between *each* and *every* with respect to 'intransitivity': *The winners lined up and each / *every was given a standing ovation.* In Cann's account, whether or not a determiner stands in a specifier–head or a head–complement relationship to the following noun depends on whether or not it agrees with the noun in number and on whether it allows only a subset of nouns to follow it (for example, only singular count nouns). This accounts for the different positions of articles and demonstratives (see section 4.2.5.). *Each* and *every* behave in the same way with respect to both these criteria though; that is, neither of them agrees with the noun and both of them can occur only with a subset of nouns (singular count nouns). Therefore we would expect to find both *each* and *every* in the same position (the head position, with the nominal as its complement) and thus the theory predicts that they should behave in the same way with respect to ellipsis: neither of them should allow a non-overt nominal. Still, *each* does allow an empty nominal and *every* does not, as Hudson's example showed. It is not clear to me how this problem can be solved within Cann's approach. He might prefer not to consider *each* and *every* as determiners, but rather as quantifiers. Presumably, though, Cann's definitions of form government and concord control and his condition on allowing empty heads are intended to apply not only to DP and NP, but to all nominal categories. Therefore the problem with *each* and *every* would remain in a QP analysis, though it would have been moved to a different level in the tree.

These tests give the same results for Swedish as for English. According to Hudson's arguments, most Swedish determiners are subcategorizands since they can occur intransitively as in (4.6).

(4.6) Jag tycker inte om **detta** / **den** / **den där**.
I don't like this it/that that

Under Cann's (1993) definitions, the same data lead to the conclusion that these elements are not heads. Since these determiners agree with the noun in gender and number, Cann must place them in the specifier position, where they can be coindexed with the noun. This would then also account for the 'intransitivity' in his theory, but would not assign head status to the determiners. If *varje* 'every, each' is assumed to be a determiner, its behaviour would support Cann's analysis. *Varje* cannot occur intransitively and Cann's analysis therefore predicts that it cannot be found in specifier position. If it is not in the specifier position, it is not expected to agree with the noun, and indeed *varje* does not agree with the noun. As will be shown in section 4.2.5, Cann's definitions of form governor and concord controller on the other hand, give contradictory results when applied to some of the Swedish determiners.

4.2.3. *Morphosyntactic locus*

The notion of morphosyntactic locus as a criterion for head status is closely associated with assumptions about feature percolation within a phrase. The inflectional marking is seen as the instantiation of some feature, and the features which are instantiated in this way are assumed to percolate via heads.[14] One of the most explicit statements of the percolation mechanisms underlying this assumption is formulated within GPSG as the Head Feature Convention (HFC). For a formal definition of the HFC, see Gazdar et al. (1985: 97). For constructions where the mother has only one head daughter (that is, non-co-ordinated constructions), the HFC can be simplified as in (4.7). (Gazdar, et al. 1985: 95).

(4.7) (i) $(\varphi\ (C_0)\ \cap\ \psi\ (C_h\ ,\ \Phi_r))|\ \textsc{head}\ \subseteq\ \varphi\ (C_h)|\ \textsc{head}$

(ii) $(\varphi\ (C_h)\ \cap\ \psi\ (C_0\ ,\ \Phi_r))|\ \textsc{head}\ \subseteq\ \varphi\ (C_0)|\ \textsc{head}$

In (4.7), $\varphi(C_0)$ and $\varphi(C_h)$ are those projections of the mother and the head daughter, respectively, that meet with other principles restricting the occurrence of features. $\psi(C_h, \Phi_r)$ and $\psi(C_0, \Phi_r)$ represent the set of free feature specifications on the head daughter and the mother, respectively. Free features are those which are not required by other feature principles to be present or absent on a particular category. Restriction (i) in (4.7) then states that the head feature specifications of the head ($\varphi(C_h)|$HEAD) are an extension of the intersection of the mother ($\varphi(C_0)$) and the free feature specification of the head ($\psi(C_h, \Phi_r)$). Part (ii) of (4.7) states that the head feature specifications of the mother ($\varphi(C_0)|$HEAD)) are an extension of the intersection of the head daughter ($\varphi(C_h)$) and the free feature specification of the mother ($\psi(C_0, \varphi_r)$).The HFC thus allows the feature specifications of the mother and head daughter to be identical, but it also allows for either the mother or the head daughter to have additional feature specifications which are required by some other principle of the grammar. In this way, features "percolate" from mother to daughter or the other way around.[15] A similar result is achieved by unification as used in HPSG and in some versions of Categorial Grammar (CG) (Shieber 1986, Zeevat 1988).

Within GPSG, the HFC restricts the occurrence of features in conjunction with three other mechanisms; FEATURE CO-OCCURRENCE RESTRICTIONS (FCR, Gazdar, et al. 1985: 27–9), the FOOT FEATURE PRINCIPLE (FFP, pp. 79–83) and the CONTROL AGREEMENT PRINCIPLE (CAP, (pp. 83–94). FCRs prevent certain feature specifications from co-occurring on a particular node, or they force such co-occurrence. The FFP deals with a different set of features from the HFC and is not relevant here. The CAP regulates feature specifications between sisters, where one is the controller and the other(s) the target(s). This principle only applies to a subset of features: the control features. The CAP then allows (control) features which have percolated by HFC to spread from the head to a non-head constituent, but there is no principle which allows features to spread from a mother directly to a non-head.

In a qualified statement, Zwicky (1985a: 10) decides on the morphosyntactic locus as the most reliable criterion for head status: 'I conclude that unless there is very good reason for doing otherwise, the morphosyntactic locus should be identified as the head in syntactic percolation.' This means that the morphosyntactic locus is regarded as the head for the purpose of feature percolation, not necessarily for other purposes.[16] According to Zwicky (1985a), when applied to English noun phrases, the morphological locus criterion indicates that N is the head of Det+N combinations. As evidence, he puts forward the fact that number is more regularly marked on nouns than on Dets. This result is disputed by Hudson (1987: 122). He comes to the opposite result and concludes that Det is the head. He points out that number can be marked on the determiner (e.g. *this/these*), and that the noun may lack number marking (e.g. *sheep, fish*). Furthermore, Hudson considers *you* and *we* to be the determiners of constructions like *you Americans* and *we linguists* (see Postal 1969 and Sommerstein 1972). Under such an analysis, there are features that can only be carried by the determiner, namely, person (*we linguists* vs. *you linguists*) and case (*we linguists* vs. *us linguists*). This analysis of the data makes the determiner the most plausible morphosyntactic locus of a Det+N combination.

Many linguists have been critical of the use of the morphosyntactic locus criterion, for example, Miller (1992b) and Payne (1993a: 135–8). Miller discusses a number of cases where a particular feature is instantiated not on what would be assumed to be the head by other criteria, but where feature instantiation is instead governed by what he terms the Edge Feature Principle (EFP, 1992b: 3).[17] This principle ensures that the features to which it applies are instantiated on either the first or the last constituent of the phrase to which the feature belongs. In conjunction, the HFC, the CAP and the EFP allow features to be instantiated on a head. If a feature is found on the head it may appear by agreement on certain non-head constituents, and finally, it may also now appear on the first or last lexical item of a phrase. In this system, though a feature may appear on non-head constituents, the head still plays an important role for feature spreading, and to some extent the notion of morphosyntactic locus is still relevant as a criterion for head status.

Payne (1993a: 135) has a bleaker outlook on the prospect of morphosyntactic locus as a test for headedness: 'virtually any feature can be marked on any constituent or combination of constituents (see Lehmann 1982 for a survey), so it is not obvious how the head of the noun phrase might be identified on a "morpho-syntactic locus" basis.'

A look at the Swedish data supports the view that the morphosyntactic locus criterion is not likely to yield one unique head. I will disregard here the purely semantic features that are of importance for subcategorization, such as for instance [±abstract] (*Oscar ate the pigeon/carpet/?idea/?independence*) which is associated with the noun and would in this context point to N as the head of noun phrases.

The most striking feature that will have to be shared between the head and its phrasal projection is the categorial feature.[18] If the phrase is an NP, then the head must be the N, if it is a DP, then the D is the head. There is, however, no obvious independent criterion for establishing the categorial status of the phrase. The tests seem to work 'the other way around' so to speak, that is, they establish which lexical element is the head, and the phrase is then assumed to be of the same category, but a different bar level. The implication above is therefore turned around: if N is the head, then the phrase is an NP, if D is the head, then it is a DP. For this reason, I cannot see how the percolation of the category feature can be used as evidence of headedness, except possibly in relation to distributional tests, to which I will return in section 4.2.6.

The features referred to most often in relation to noun phrases in the literature discussed here are number and gender. The only gender distinction made in modern Swedish is between neuter and common gender. In plural, this distinction is cancelled. The gender feature is relevant not only within the noun phrase, but certain predicates show gender agreement with a subject noun phrase.[19] The gender is inherent in the noun, and there may or may not be a morphological marking in the form of the definite suffix on the noun revealing its gender. A noun with a definite ending can also function as a full noun phrase without a determiner. Most determiners in Swedish are marked for gender in the singular. This means that there can be explicit morphological marking for gender on the noun only (4.8a), the determiner only (4.8b), both (4.8c) or neither (4.8d).

(4.8)	a.	gris-**en** pig-DEF.COM	murmeldjur-**et** marmot-DEF.NT
	b.	**denna** gris this.COM pig	**detta** murmeldjur this.NT marmot
	c.	**den** gris-**en** that.COM pig-DEF.COM	**det** murmeldjur-**et** that.NT marmot-DEF.NT
	d.	varje gris every pig	varje murmeldjur every marmot

However, since gender is inherent in nouns in Swedish, one can assume that a noun will always carry a feature for gender, regardless of whether or not there is an explicit morphological manifestation of it. This means that even in examples like (4.8b) – where there is no morphological reflection of gender on the noun, but there is on the determiner – we can assume that the marking on the determiner is due to some agreement principle which requires the noun to be the governor. Facts relating to gender in Swedish would therefore point towards the noun as the head.

Number, which for Zwicky (1985a) was the major argument in favour of considering the noun the morphosyntactic locus of the noun phrase in English, is relevant also in Swedish. Just as in the case of gender, number is of importance for agreement with certain VPs (see footnote 19). As in English, there are a number of nouns in Swedish which do not have any overt plural marking. Swedish differs from English, however, in that its articles and demonstratives all carry morphological marking for number. Quantifiers which can be used with both singular and plural indefinite nouns also always carry marking for number. This means that only when there is no determiner can the noun be the sole element with overt number marking (4.9a). Number can also be overtly present on the determiner only (4.9b) or on both the determiner and the noun (4.9c).[20] In the translations of (4.9), I have ignored gender.

(4.9)	a.	gris-**en** pig-DEF.SG	gris-**ar-na** gris-PL-DEF.PL

b. **detta** murmeldjur **dessa** murmeldjur
this.SG marmot this.PL marmot

c. **den** gris-**en** **de** gris-**ar-na**
that.SG pig-DEF.SG those.PL pig-PL-DEF.PL

With respect to Swedish and the HFC, if one wanted to follow Zwicky's (1985a: 10) example for English and 'take it as a rock-bottom, uncontestable requirement on the selection of heads for the purposes of this principle that Det+N should belong to an N-type category (that N should be its head)', then one could claim that there is an example of ∅-marking for plurality in (4.9b).[21] If this is the case the noun is still the morphological locus here, and the number feature spreads to the determiner by CAP. However, looking at the Swedish data from the perspective of Hudson (1987), one could conclude that the data in (4.9) forms evidence that the determiner is the morpho-syntactic locus in the Swedish noun phrase.

Definiteness is another feature that is of importance for the possible distribution of noun phrases and which must therefore be part of the feature specification. In a sentence like (4.10), the gap can only be filled by a non-definite noun phrase, parallel to the English *There is/are* context.

(4.10) Det står — i kylskåpet.
there stand in refrigerator.DEF
'There is/are . . . in the fridge.'

Determiners can be said to inherently carry a definiteness feature, in the same way that gender was considered an inherent feature of nouns above. From this it follows that if the data relating to gender led us to conclude that the noun is the head for the purpose of the HFC, then our conclusion here must be that the determiner is the head of the noun phrase in Swedish. However, the distribution of overt definiteness marking is as complex as the distribution of gender marking.

On the basis of the evidence presented in chapter 3, I concluded that the element that I refer to as DEF is best considered a definite affix, rather than a syntactic determiner. This means that under my analysis, Swedish nouns can be inflected for definiteness. Since a definite noun can function as a full noun phrase without a determiner, there are noun phrases in Swedish where definiteness is marked on the noun only, as in (4.11a). However, as (4.11b) shows, a definite adjective and a definite noun cannot occur in combination without the presence of a definite determiner.[22] In (4.11c) an example is found where the determiner is definite, but the noun carries no marking and in (4.11d) where the determiner is definite and the noun does carry a definiteness marking. So, definiteness can be marked on the noun only, the determiner only, or on both elements. In these examples, gender and number have been ignored in the translations.

(4.11) a. gris-**en**
pig-DEF

b. *hungrig-a gris-en
hungry-DEF pig-DEF

c. **denna** gris
this(DEF) pig

d. **den** gris-**en**
that(DEF) pig-DEF

If the prenominal elements in (4.12a) are given the same analysis as those in (4.12b) – regardless of whether they are all assumed to be determiners (as in Postal 1969, Abney 1987 and Radford 1993) or pronouns, that is, basically nominal elements (as in Sommerstein 1972 and Hudson 1987) – then these examples provide evidence that the determiner slot is the morphosyntactic locus of the noun phrase with respect to the features person and case.[23]

(4.12) a. vi hundägare / ni ekonomer
we dog.owners you economists

b. dessa hundägare / enekonom
these dog.owners aneconomist

The examples in (4.13) show that the person and case features of these determiners are relevant to the distribution of the noun phrase of which they are a part.

(4.13) a. [**Vi hundägare**]$_i$ vill att folk gillar **oss**$_i$ / ***dem**$_i$
we dog.owners want that people like us them
'We dog owners want people to like us.'

b. **Vi**$_i$ vill att folk gillar [**oss** / ***vi** **ekonomer**]$_i$.
we want that people like we.OBJ we.SUBJ economists
'We want people to like us economists.'

These examples then indicate that with respect to the person and case features, the determiner should be the head for the purpose of feature percolation.

There are two more noun phrase features in Swedish that are significant for the syntactic distribution of the phrase as a whole and which are only found on the determiner. These are [±WH] and [±REFL]. In an embedded *wh*-question in Swedish, the noun phrase carrying a [+WH] feature must be fronted (see (4.14a and b)) and in a main clause question it may be fronted. This means that the [WH] feature of a determiner is relevant for the syntactic behaviour of the noun phrase as a whole.

(4.14) a. Jag undrar [vilken mus] han såg?
I wonder which mouse he saw

b. *Jag undrar han såg [vilken mus] ?
I wonder he saw which mouse
'I wonder which mouse he saw.'

In Swedish, the possessive pronouns which can function as determiners have a reflexive and a non-reflexive form. The reflexive form of the determiner must occur when the noun phrase as a whole fills a position which, if filled by a pronoun would have required this pronoun to occur in its reflexive form. These noun phrases must be marked [+REFL] and this feature value is manifested on the determiner. An example of this is provided in (4.15).

(4.15) Musen_i tvättar [**sin**$_i$ svans] / *[hans_i svans].
the.mouse washes his.REFL tail his.NON-REFL tai
'The mouse cleans his own tail.'

The distribution of these features also points toward the determiner as the head of the noun phrase with respect to the HFC.[24]

The data presented in this section do not lead to an obvious conclusion about the morphosyntactic locus of the Swedish noun phrase, not even when the notion has been narrowed down to refer only to feature percolation according to the Head Feature Convention. I have looked at the following seven features: [NT/COM], [SG/PL], [±DEF], [1/2/3 PERS], [SUBJ/OBJ], [WH], and [REFL]. Four of these (person, case, *wh*-features and reflexivity) cannot be marked on the noun, nor can they be claimed to be inherent in the noun and therefore they clearly select D as the head of the noun phrase. One of the features (gender) is inherent in the noun, but can be marked on the determiner, and one (definiteness) is inherent in the determiner, but can be marked on the noun. These two features then point in opposite directions. The evidence based on number finally can be interpreted either way, depending on whether we take Zwicky's (1985a) or Hudson's (1987) view of the data. I am more inclined to agree with Zwicky that the number is semantically determined on the noun and is found on the determiner by agreement. However, I do not consider this a particularly strong argument.

The arguments favouring the determiner as the head of the Swedish noun phrase for the purpose of the Head Feature Convention thus outnumber those favouring the noun. Still, this discussion has made clear that whichever constituent is selected as the head, there will be cases where some feature percolation rule is necessary which allows non-head inheritance. This includes cases of non-head feature percolation which a rule like the Edge Feature Principle cannot cater for, since the features are not necessarily manifested on the first or last element of the noun phrase. The example in

(4.15), for instance could have contained *hela sin svans* 'his whole tail', where the word carrying the [+REFL] feature is preceded by *hela* 'whole'.

A principle of non-head percolation is thus necessary. Such a principle has been proposed for morphology by, for example, Lieber (1980, adopted by Marantz 1984: 122) and Di Sciullo and Williams (1987: 26). The principles were formulated to account for cases where a word inherits features not from an affix, which is considered the head, but from the non-head root. These proposals have been adapted for syntactic percolation by, for example, Holmberg (1986: 60) and Cowper (1987).[25] Under all these proposals, feature inheritance from a non-head can only take place if the head is not specified for the feature in question. Holmberg's formulation of a non-head inheritance principle, Feature Percolation 2, is given in (4.16).

(4.16) Percolation Convention 2: If a head α is neutral with respect to some feature (F), and a (non-head) sister β of α is specified (F), the specified feature value of (F) may percolate to the first branching node dominating α and β.

(Holmberg 1986: 60)

Holmberg's convention thus ensures that the first branching node gets the feature value from the non-head. From there, his Percolation Convention 1 will ensure that it percolates up to the maximal projection, as long as 'head' in this definition is not only taken to refer to lexical heads. Under Cowper's formulation of a virtually identical principle a feature may percolate directly from the non-head to the maximal projection of its head sister:

(4.17) In a structure $[_\alpha\ \beta\ \gamma]$ or $[_\alpha\ \gamma\ \beta]$, α a projection of β, features from γ will percolate to α iff β is not specified for those features.

(Cowper 1987: 324)

Once a principle has been introduced which allows for feature percolation to proceed not only along the heads of an X-bar projection, but also from a non-head to its mother, albeit under special circumstances, then the power of the morphosyntactic locus argument is substantially weakened. In principle, the non-head percolation rules discussed here could apply to all the features discussed.[26] So, even though there appear to be more features relevant to the distribution of noun phrases which originate on the determiner than on the noun, this is no longer a strong argument in favour of a DP analysis, since some features will have to be inherited from a non-head.

4.2.4. *Governor*

Zwicky (1985a: 7) informally distinguishes between government and subcategorization as follows: 'subcategorization concerns the very possibility of one constituent's combining with some other co-constituent(s), while government concerns the form that a co-constituent has in such a combination.'

However, in many accounts, this distinction is not formally made, and subcategorization frames make reference to form features. Government and concord are also easily confused since both notions refer to morphosyntactic features of one constituent influencing those of a co-constituent. However, as Zwicky (1985a: 7) puts it: 'in concord the same features are involved in the determining and the determined constituent, while in government different features are involved.' Subcategorization as a test for headedness and the problems relating to it were discussed in section 4.2.2, and the notion of concord will be dealt with in 4.2.5.

Zwicky (1985a) does not discuss the English Det+N constructions in relation to the governor criterion. The inapplicability of this criterion to English Det+N constructions is also represented in Hudson's final table (1987: 125). As one part of form control, Cann (1993: 44) defines FORM GOVERNMENT, a notion which is close to Zwicky's notion of governor. With this criterion Cann does achieve some interesting results with respect to Det+N combinations. This will be discussed in relation to concord in section 4.2.5.

Not much needs to be said about this criterion here, since I am exclusively interested in Det+N constructions. I will just briefly mention some data from Swedish which may be seen as evidence that the determiner is the head of the Swedish noun phrase according to Zwicky's governor criterion. In other accounts, the same data have been dealt with as subcategorization. Consider the examples in (4.18).

(4.18) a. det murmeldjuret
that(DEF) marmot.DEF

b. det här murmeldjuret
this(DEF) marmot.DEF

c. ett murmeldjur
a(INDEF) marmot.INDEF

d. något murmeldjur
some(INDEF) marmot.INDEF

If the data in (4.18) formed an exclusive representation of how definiteness can be distributed within Det+N combinations in Swedish, then this would be dealt with quite straightforwardly by concord or agreement rules. However, the data in (4.19) complicates the matter.

(4.19) detta murmeldjur
this(DEF) marmot.INDEF

Since in this case the feature values differ between the determiner and the noun, it cannot be a matter of concord or agreement. Instead we could conclude that the determiner governs the morphological form of the noun, and hence according to Zwicky's criterion, the determiner is the head of the construction. I will return to data such as (4.19) in section 4.2.5. and in section 5.3.3.2, I will provide an analysis of these constructions.

4.2.5. *Determinant of concord*

Zwicky (1985a) intuitively distinguishes determinant of concord from governor in the following way: 'in both phenomena morphosyntactic features of one constituent can determine the morphosyntactic features of a sister constituent, but in concord the same features are involved in the determining and the determined constituents.' Examples of features which are distributed within the Swedish noun phrase by concord are therefore gender and number. Gender is not usually marked on the noun, but is inherent in the noun. According to Zwicky's interpretation of this notion, the noun is considered the determinant of concord in both cases.

Hudson (1987: 116–117) re-examines the notion of concord and comes to the conclusion that the notion of determinant of concord is not relevant to the notion of headedness. In constructions involving one element which is a noun and one which is not, the relevant features – number, gender, etc. – will be fixed independently, for example, by the semantics, for the noun. This means that the features will always spread from the noun, regardless of whether it is the head of the construction in question or not. He therefore disregards this criterion in his own discussion of headedness.

Cann (1989, 1993) provides a more formal definition of a notion he terms FORM CONTROL. It consists of two parts, both of which are found in (4.20). The two parts capture the distinction Zwicky makes between form governor (4.20i) and determinant of concord (4.20ii).

(4.20) (i) Form Government
X is a governor in X+Y if there is some group of inflectional variants, $x_1, \ldots, x_n$ in X that all induce the same proper binary partition on the expression-forms of Y according to their morphological form

(ii) Concord controller
X is a concord controller in X+Y if there is some group of inflectional variants, $x_1, \ldots, x_n$ in X which induce different binary partitions on expression-forms of Y according to their morphological form

(Cann 1993: 44–45)

The difference captured by (4.20i) and (4.20ii) has consequences for the tree structure that should be chosen to represent the relationship (this was also referred to in section 4.2.2). If X is a form governor of Y, then with standard assumptions of government within X-bar syntax, a structure in which X is the head and Y its complement is correct. The notion of concord controller, on the other hand, captures the relationship of agreement which typically holds between a noun and an adjective, and therefore it does not indicate a head complement relationship.[27] This is pointed out by Payne (1993a: 135–8), who applies it to noun phrases containing Russian numerals and uses the result as an argument in favour of an NP, rather than DP, analysis of such noun phrases. (For a discussion of Payne's arguments, see section 4.4.)

Cann (1993) also relates the difference defined in (4.20) to differences in phrase structure. According to (4.20), in English noun phrases consisting of an article and a noun, the article is the form governor. Articles like *a* and unstressed *some* partition the set of possible Ns into singular versus plural nouns and plural and mass versus singular nouns, respectively. Cann (1993: 51–2) concludes that this is not a case of shared features, since there is no formal resemblance between the article and the noun. Idiosyncratic information of this kind must, according to Cann, be encoded in the lexicon. He combines the relations proper subcategorization, form-government and Θ-marking into one property: L-selection. This relation is represented in the lexicon as a relation between a lexical head and its sister. Thus Cann's analysis of the articles in combination with his assumptions regarding phrase structure and L-selection point towards an analysis of the articles as the heads of noun phrases.

Interestingly, however, Cann (1993: 59–65) comes to a different conclusion for the structure of noun phrases containing demonstrative determiners in English. The English demonstratives do not partition the set of possible following Ns the way the articles do. Instead, they co-vary with respect to number with the noun. This type of behaviour falls under (4.20ii) rather than (4.20i), and the noun functions as the concord controller. Co-variation as it holds between the concord controller and the controllee is captured by Cann in terms of coindexing. Coindexing is assumed to hold between heads and their specifiers, the head being the controller of concord. Coindexing allows the head to control the morphosyntactic properties of the specifier: coindexed elements must be category compatible, where the notion of category compatibility (c-compatibility) is understood in terms of category unification, for which Cann refers to Gazdar et al. (1985). Even though Cann does not want to reduce all concord relations to specifier–head coindexing, he does conclude from the fact that the noun concord controls the demonstrative that the two elements stand in a specifier–head relationship. The two different underlying structures assumed for *the penguin* and *that penguin* are provided in (4.21). The fact that the definite article does not agree in English, but the demonstrative does, is probably best described as a historical morphological accident. It is therefore not clear to me that it is justified to represent this as a major syntactic structural difference between the two types of noun phrases. Still, this is the consequence of Cann's definitions and assumptions about phrase structure and the relations between parts of syntactic trees. It should be pointed out that the difference in surface structure is smaller, since Cann assumes that the demonstrative in (4.21b) is moved into a higher Det position of which the N″ is a complement. The fact that English transitive verbs select D″s rather than N″s ensures that the N″ is contained under a D″ structure. This D″ is headed by an empty D position which is illegal. The element filling the Dem slot can, however, move up to Det and provide a lexical filler for this position. It does mean, however, that an element moves from a specifier position to a head position. As discussed in section 4.2.2, in Cann's analysis of agreement, the fact that an element is found in a specifier (rather than head) position is linked to its ability to occur intransitively. Since the Dem element can occur intransitively, but moves to a head position, the criterion for intransitivity must refer to the element's base position. In section 4.2.2, I pointed to some other problems that this analysis may raise with respect to *each* and *every* in English.

(4.21)

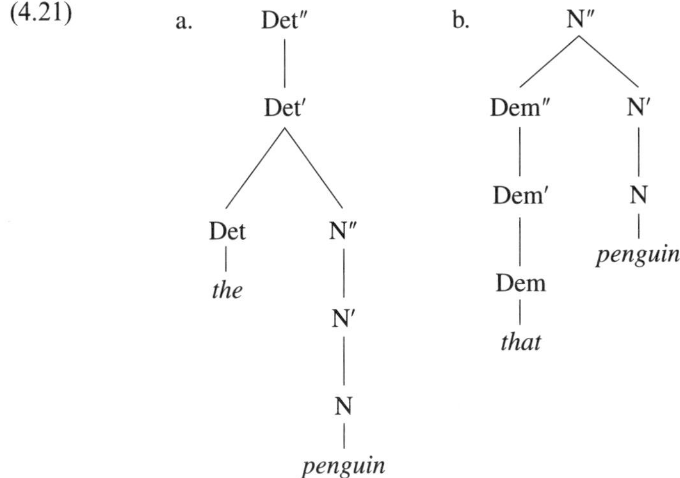

More generally, the consequences of Cann's discussion is that if a Det+N combination behaves in accordance with the definition in (4.20i), then the governor must be the head and the governed element the complement. If, on the other hand, the Det+N combination fulfils (4.20ii), then the controller of concord should be represented as the head of the phrase and the controllee should be found in the specifier (or some other non-complement) position. If we now consider the Swedish noun phrases in the light of this, we find that the distinction is less clear cut. Both the definite and indefinite articles *den* and *en* agree with the following noun in number and gender in the way that the English demonstrative agrees in number with the noun, and so do the Swedish demonstratives *denna* and *den*. This is shown for the indefinite article in (4.22).

(4.22) a. en / *ett mus
a.COM a.NT mouse(COM)

b. ett / *en murmeldjur
a.NT a.COM marmot(NT)

Since the gender and number distinction is inherent, or semantically determined, in the noun, this means that all these determiners are concord-controlled by the following noun in Cann's terms. The evidence thus far therefore points towards a tree structure in which the noun is the head and the determiner is in the specifier position. This would ensure that the determiner is coindexed with the following noun and as a consequence is c-compatible with it.

However, in a Det+N construction, the Swedish indefinite article *en*, and some other determiners, also partition the set of possible Ns according to their number or countability. Some examples are provided in (4.23) (see Cann's (6) 1993: 52).

(4.23) a. en mus / *möss
a mouse mice

b. varje mus / *möss
every mouse mice

For Cann, this type of behaviour is a reason to assume that the corresponding English determiners *a* and *every* form-govern their complements. This points towards a DP analysis of Swedish noun phrases in which a determiner like *en* or *varje* is the head. This argument could also be used for some of the Swedish determiners with respect to the morphological marking for definiteness. As pointed out in section 4.2.4, this relation cannot be accounted for in terms of agreement, since the feature of the determiner need not be the same as that of the noun. This is illustrated in (4.24). I will return to this problem in section 5.3.

(4.24) a. en mus / *musen
a mouse.INDEF mouse.DEF

b. den musen / *mus
that mouse.DEF mouse.INDEF

c. denna mus / *musen
this mouse.INDEF mouse.DEF

It seems then that at least for some of the Swedish determiners, arguments can be found in favour of both a form–government relationship and a concord–controller association. Since this would lead to two different phrase structure representations, the ambiguity has to be resolved. It might appear possible to resolve the discrepancy within a transformational approach by allowing the two elements to have different relations at different levels.

However, such a solution is disallowed by Cann. If two elements stand in a specifier–head relationship, they **must be co-indexed**. The relation between a head and its complement is one of L-selection and if an element L-selects another element, then they **cannot be coindexed** (Cann 1993: 54). I therefore conclude that this criterion for head status cannot be applied to Swedish noun phrases, neither in Zwicky's (1985a) informal version nor in Cann's (1993) more formal definition.

4.2.6. *Distributional equivalence*

There is a long-standing tradition of viewing distributional equivalence as a test for establishing which element is central in a phrase, though the word 'head' has not always been used for this notion. Zwicky (1985a: 11), for instance, quotes Bloomfield (1933: 194) and Hockett (1958: 184) on the importance of distributional similarity, and he refers to Harris (1951: chapter 16) and Wells (1947) for a discussion of the same notions. Zwicky himself is, however, critical of the value of the test. He regards the noun as the head according to this criterion, but also refers to J. Lyons (1977) (see section 4.3.2) and concludes that 'the criterion can be used to argue that N is the head, that neither constituent is, or that Det is, depending on which set of facts you look at' (Zwicky 1985a: 12, note 8). The familiar data from English relating to this issue are given in (4.25), where (4.25a) could be used as evidence that the noun is the distributional equivalent and (4.25b) points towards the determiner as the distributional equivalent.[28]

(4.25) a. The penguins / Penguins cannot fly.
       b. That boy / That / *Boy / cannot be right.

Hudson (1987: 122–4) also acknowledges this problem, but he follows in the tradition of Sommerstein (1972) and argues for an analysis in which the class of determiners is considered a subset of the set of pronouns, and therefore also of the category noun (further arguments in favour of this position are provided in Hudson 1984: 90–2). This means that what we have so far referred to as Det+N combinations are really N+N combinations, 'thus if the distributional equivalent of NP must be an N, then this could be a determiner as easily as the common noun'. The difficulties of establishing the head of the noun phrase on the basis of the distributional equivalence have also been discussed by Cann (1993: 65–8), among others.

The criterion yields ambiguous results also when applied to Swedish. However, there are two facts about Swedish that make the situation even more complex. Firstly, in Swedish not only plural count nouns, but also definite count nouns can function as full referential noun phrases. So, in a sense, this argument favouring the noun as the head of the phrase is stronger for Swedish. This is illustrated in (4.26a) and (4.26b).

(4.26) a. Dessa pingviner / Pingviner kan inte flyga.
these penguins penguins can not fly
'These penguins/Penguins cannot fly.'

b. De pingvinerna / Pingvinerna kan inte flyga.
those penguins.DEF penguins.DEF can not fly
'Those penguins/The penguins cannot fly.'

Secondly, however, more determiners can occur 'intransitively' in Swedish than in English. We could therefore claim that there is also a stronger distributional argument in favour of the determiner as the head of a noun phrase in Swedish than in English. Not only demonstratives, but also the definite and the indefinite article, for instance, can occur without a following noun, as in (4.27a) and (4.27b).

(4.27) a. Oscar har aldrig sett { denna pingvin. / en pingvin. / denna. / en. }
Oscar has never seen { this penguin / a penguin / this / a }
'Oscar has never seen this penguin / a penguin / this one / one.'

b. Oscar har sett den flygande pingvinen / den.
Oscar has seen the flying penguin.DEF the
'Oscar has seen the flying penguin/it.'

Furthermore, when a demonstrative is used without a following noun, the interpretation varies from that possible in a parallel English construction. This is illustrated by the difference between (4.28) and (4.25b). In English, *that* is not really a distributional equivalent of *that*+N combinations in the sense that in (4.25b) *That cannot be right* cannot mean *That boy cannot be right*. Hence something like ?*That cannot read*, sounds odd. To get this meaning, *one* must be used. All the Swedish noun phrases in (4.28), however, can be used to mean the same.

(4.28) a. Den där killen
that boy
b. Den killen
that boy
c. Den där
that
d. Den
that
} kan inte läsa.
can not read
'That boy/That one cannot read.'

The application of the distributional equivalence argument to English noun phrases proved unsatisfactory. Even though more arguments can be found for Swedish, the evidence is no less inconclusive, since it can be said to point more strongly both in the direction of the noun as the head and towards the determiner as the head.

One neglected aspect of true distributional equivalence, pointed out by J. Lyons (1977: 391) – albeit as a parenthesis – in his discussion of endocentric constructions, is that if a constituent X has the same distribution as the phrase XY in which it occurs, then this construction must allow recursion. Under this interpretation, X cannot be the distributional equivalence of XY unless XYY is also a possible construction. When distributional equivalence is defined in this way, neither Det nor N would be the head of the phrase. According to Lyons's criterion, Det+N combinations in Swedish are endocentric constructions.

4.2.7. *Obligatory constituent*

'If the head of a construct truly CHARACTERIZES it, then we should expect the head to be the part that is present in all its occurrences – that is, we should expect the head to be obligatory (and non-heads to be optional)', claims Zwicky (1985a). This criterion is closely related to the distributional equivalence criterion discussed in section 4.2.6. However, in order to make this criterion more applicable than the distributional equivalence test, Zwicky narrows down the meaning of optionality. Optionality that is due to ellipsis is excluded; thus if the meaning of the optional phrase must be derived from the linguistic or non-linguistic context, then this does not count as optionality for the purposes of this criterion. The Swedish noun phrases in (4.29) exemplify the importance of this restriction.

(4.29) a. Dessa gamla kvinnor
these old women

b. Dessa
these

c. Gamla
old

d. Kvinnor
women

} har det svårt
have it difficult.

'These old women/These ones/Old people/Women have a difficult time.'

Under the narrow interpretation of the criterion, only (4.29c) and (4.29d) show true optionality. In (4.29b), we find an elliptical construction. According to Zwicky's definition the noun is not optional here and hence this construction cannot be seen as an argument in favour of D as head of the

Swedish noun phrase. *Gamla* in (4.29c) is probably best analysed as a fully nominalized adjective, it has the narrow meaning typical of fully nominalized adjectives in Swedish (see *vänster* in section 3.3.2). This means that the obligatoriness criterion applied to the data in (4.29) supports an analysis in which the noun is the head of the noun phrase.

Having narrowed down the meaning of 'obligatory constituent' in this way, Zwicky concludes that the result of applying this criterion will be the same as when the distributional equivalence test is applied. However, for Swedish this is not the case, unless reference to non-ellipsis is built into that criterion as well. As was shown in the previous section, that criterion yielded an ambiguous result for Swedish, whereas the non-elliptical obligatoriness criterion points towards the noun as the head.

Hudson (1987: 118–19) argues that the non-ellipsis addition to the obligatory constituent criterion is unmotivated. He agrees that gapping constructions (e.g. *I ate sushi, and Kiyoko a hamburger*) should be excluded, but assumes that a sentence such as *I can swallow goldfish, but you can't* can be used to argue that Aux is the head of an Aux+VP combination. This is because the ellipsis in this construction is made possible by the subcategorization properties of the auxiliary. This argument is also used for determiners in sentences like *I borrowed both books from Oscar, but I didn't read either*. Again it is the subcategorization properties of *either* that permits the elliptical construction. It should be noted here that if obligatoriness is related to subcategorization, then only the constituent that is a head according to the subcategorization criterion can be the head according to this test. In this sense, the obligatoriness is not only related to the distributional equivalence test, but it is also dependent on the subcategorization criterion. The elements that are heads according to this criterion would be a subset of the elements that are heads according to the subcategorization criterion, namely those elements that are intransitive, that is, subcategorize for a zero element. This makes this version of the criterion superfluous, since it can only pick out elements that can be assigned head status on the basis of another criterion.

Hudson (1987: 124) states that it is 'as easy to omit a common noun as it is to omit a determiner'. Still, on the basis of his version of this criterion, Hudson concludes that the determiner is the obligatory constituent of the noun phrase in English. My conclusion is, however, that the obligatoriness criterion does not help in establishing the headedness of Swedish noun phrases.

4.2.8. *Ruler*

The term 'ruler' as used by Zwicky (1985a) refers to the head-like notion in dependency grammars. In the French and German literature, the same notion is referred to as *RÉGISSANT and REGENS*, respectively. Dependency grammarians writing in English prefer to use HEAD for the same notion (see, for example, Robinson 1970 and Hudson 1984, 1990). Dependency grammar differs from constituency based grammars, of course, in that the head–modifier relation holds between words, and not between constituents. Still, their notion of head is as multi-faceted as that used by constituency grammarians. This means that one would not expect there to be one test for 'ruler status', any more than one would expect a constituency grammar to use a head notion based on one aspect of headedness only. Therefore, just as the constituency-grammar notion of head is based on several, though rarely all, of the tests discussed in sections 4.2.1 to 4.2.7, so also is the dependency-grammar notion 'ruler'. And just as there is disagreement between constituency grammarians about which constituent is the head of certain constructions, so dependency grammarians are not in total agreement about which word in each construction should be considered the head. Hudson (1984: 77–8) informally states a number of characteristics of heads as he uses the notion. These are given below:

- the head provides the link between the modifier and the rest of the sentence, for example, the position of the modifier within the sentence or phrase is fixed in relation to the head;[29]
- the possibility of occurrence of the modifier is determined by the head;
- the head determines the inflectional form of the modifier;
- lexical selection ('collocation') is determined by the head;
- the head provides the semantic structure into which the modifier fits.

The characteristics described here agree fairly closely with criteria discussed in sections 4.2.1. to 4.2.7. From this, then, it becomes obvious that the dependency notion of head, or ruler, is not distinct from the headedness criteria discussed previously, but is based on a corollary of these criteria, just like most other uses of the notion head. Since the aspects that make up the dependency notion 'head' have been discussed in previous subsections, there is little to add here, except to note that for Hudson (1984, 1987, 1990) the determiner is the head in this sense.

4.2.9. *Conclusions*

Discussing a set of possible criteria for defining categories that have been part of the vocabulary of linguistics for so long that their validity and importance is hardly ever questioned strikes me as a worthwhile activity. Such terms often end up being used to refer to quite different phenomena depending on the particular theoretical framework within which they are used. This makes terminological spring cleaning like that attempted by Zwicky (1985a) and Hudson (1987) a really valuable contribution to the field, since it may help improve communication between linguists of different persuasions.

Problems arise, however, when these criteria are assumed to be watertight definitions of clearly distinguishable sets of elements. The discussion in this chapter has shown that this is certainly not the case with respect to the notion of head in Swedish noun phrases. Still, there are a number of examples in the literature, where a couple of headedness criteria are selected and applied to a limited set of data for which the selected criteria point in the same direction. This is then assumed to 'prove' which element is the head of that construction.

However, if used properly, criteria of this type can be used to shed new light on old issues. Corbett (1993) is a good example of how this can be done. He applies the headedness criteria to Russian noun phrases containing numerals and concludes that there is an argument for assuming that these numerals are in fact heads rather than modifiers.[30] His discussion is prefaced by words of caution, however: 'We shall see that there are two consequences. The first is that we still need to recognize that headedness is a gradient notion: a particular element may have head-like characteristics to a greater or lesser degree, and that these may vary according to external factors (notably, case assignment). The second is that the logic of the analysis requires re-assessment of the head-dependent relation elsewhere, namely in adjective-noun constructions, and the price to be paid may be unacceptably high' (Corbett 1993: 11).

4.3. Arguments for D as the head of the noun phrase

4.3.1. *Types of arguments*

Within transformational grammar, the credit for the introduction of D as the head of the noun phrase (the so-called DP hypothesis) is often attributed to Abney (1987). However, the idea that the determiner rather than the noun should be considered the head of the noun phrase had been voiced in the literature by linguists from varying backgrounds, working within different frameworks.[31] In this section, I will give a brief overview of some of these arguments. Since Abney's proposal gained ground in current transformational grammar, the literature has been flooded with pro-DP arguments and this is not the place to go through all of these. Therefore, I will only discuss Abney's (1987) arguments and those proposed by others before then. In section 4.3.2, I review arguments based on the criteria discussed in section 4.2. Arguments which, like Abney's, are based on assumed similarities between noun phrases and clauses are found in section 4.3.3.

I will, however, briefly outline one line of argument in favour of a DP analysis which has been formulated since 1987. Most of the arguments discussed here and in the previous section have been based on a small number of (European) languages. Dryer (1989) provides support for an analysis in which D is the head of the noun phrase from a typological perspective. Since typological arguments in favour of a DP analysis are quite rare, I find it worth including a short account of Dryer's arguments in section section 4.3.4, where I will also mention some earlier typological discussions, like Vennemann and Harlow (1977). It should be pointed out here, though, that Dryer's arguments are in fact based on a number of theory-dependent assumptions.

4.3.2. *Arguments based on headedness criteria*

An early example of an argument against the traditionally assumed headedness of noun phrases is provided by J. Lyons (1977). Lyons refers to distributional criteria and to the semantic nature of determiners, nouns and noun phrases when he points out that it is not obviously correct to analyse the noun as the head of the noun phrase. Lyons defines endocentricity in terms of distributional equivalence (see the discussion in 4.2.6): 'a phrase is said to be endocentric if it is syntactically equivalent to one of its immediate constituents' (1977: 391). For noun phrases, this means that it is not necessarily the noun which should be considered the head: 'such noun phrases as *the boy* or *my friend* are distributionally equivalent to proper names and personal pronouns.' (p. 392). Since personal pronouns can be analysed as determiners (see Postal 1969 and also Sommerstein 1972) the step is not great to treating this as evidence in favour of D as the head of the noun phrase. Lyons (1977: 464) makes this explicit: 'For determiners, despite their conventional treatment as modifiers of the noun with which they occur, may often be regarded, from a syntactic point of view, as heads rather than modifiers'.

Within Word Grammar, Hudson (1984: 90–2) argues for D as the head of the noun phrase.[32] Like Lyons (1977), Hudson refers to the distributional equivalence between noun phrases and certain determiners (such as *some*, *this* and *which*) for one of his arguments. Others of Hudson's arguments are related to the analysis of personal pronouns as determiners. On this view, *the* can be considered an allomorph of *they*; *we linguists* but *the/*they linguists*. In section 4.2.3 I have already discussed how this assumption can form the basis of an argument in favour of the head status of D. Hudson also points to the fact that some determiners can be followed by an optional *of*-phrase, as in *which of the boys*. In such constructions the noun does not behave like the head of the noun phrase. It is instead found in what Hudson (1984: 91) calls 'a clearly modifying position', and the determiner is assumed to be the head. The final argument provided by Hudson refers to the order of determiners and adjectival modifiers within the noun phrase. This argument is, however, based on one of Hudson's theory-specific assumptions and, in a way, it can be said that he is forced by his own assumptions to view D as the head. One of the fundamental assumptions of Hudson's Word Grammar is the Adjacency Principle. The part of this principle which is relevant to this argument is formulated as follows:

(4.30) The Simple Adjacency Principle
A modifier must not be separated from its head by anything except other modifiers of the same head.
(Hudson 1984: 99)

If D is assumed to be the head of the noun phrase, this principle can be used to explain the word order within the noun phrase. A sequence like **big the boy* is ungrammatical because *boy* is a modifier of D, but it is separated from its own modifier *big* by the determiner.

As already discussed in some detail in section 4.2, a more recent article by Hudson (1987) extends the list of arguments in favour of the head status of D. In this article, he argues that all applicable criteria for headedness point to D as the head of the noun phrase.

Hellan (1986), in a characteristically unorthodox analysis, relies on noun-phrase internal and external (dis)agreement and on facts relating to government for evidence in favour of the headedness of D. However, Hellan does not call the resulting phrase DP, but T.[33]

In Norwegian, and some of the other Scandinavian languages, a noun phrase can "disagree" in gender with a predicative adjective. An example from Hellan (1986: 95) is provided in (4.31).

(4.31) Tran er sunt. N
cod.liver.oil(M) is healthy.NT
'Cod liver oil is good for you.'

Hellan assumes that the subject noun phrase in examples like (4.31) does agree with the adjective, so that the disagreement is not external, but internal to the noun phrase. The noun phrase as a whole is neuter, but the noun it contains is masculine. This type of disagreement is not permitted between a phrase and its head, but Hellan assumes that a phrase can disagree with a non-head daughter. [34] Hence, if the determiner is assumed to be the head of the noun phrase, the subject of (4.31) could be assumed to be [NT]. I will return to a more detailed discussion of this type of non-agreement and also propose an alternative account in section 6.4.2.

Hellan's (1986: 100–2) second argument is based on facts already discussed for Swedish in section 4.2.4. The fact that some definite determiners can only be followed by a definite noun, whereas others require a non-definite noun is seen as evidence that the determiner governs the nominal. Only heads of phrases are assumed to be capable of exerting this kind of government.

4.3.3. *Arguments based on similarities with clauses*

The arguments presented in section 4.3.2 rely to a certain extent on the relatively theory-neutral criteria discussed in section 4.2. Even though such arguments have been put forward also within transformational approaches, these analyses tend to rely largely on a different type of argument.

Within modern transformational theory, the 1980s saw the development of functional categories like I(nflection) and C(omplementizer) as heads of clausal elements. The previous S and S′ were reanalysed as I″ and C″, respectively (Chomsky 1986b). Following this development, a number of linguists working within the transformational tradition focused on the similarities between clausal elements and noun phrases. From this follows naturally the introduction of functional categories as heads of the noun phrase. The base-generated lexical fillers of C and I are complementizers such as *that* and modal verbs, respectively. The obvious lexical fillers of at least one functional category within the noun phrase are the determiners. Hence noun phrases become Determiner Phrases (DPs). There is still argument as to whether D is parallel to C or I in the clause, and also as to what other functional categories there are in the noun phrase.[35] There is agreement though as far as the main issue goes, namely that the noun phrase, like the clause, has at least one functional head and that the lexical fillers of this slot are determiners. The DP analysis has become a standard assumption of Government and Binding theory and Minimalism.

In order to explain differences in the possibility of extracting from noun phrases in Greek and English, Horrocks and Stavrou (1987) posit a difference in noun-phrase structure between the two languages. Consider the sentences in (4.32) (Horrocks and Stavrou 1987: 83).

(4.32) a. *[$_{S'1}$ whom$_i$ [$_S$ did you hear [$_{NP}$ the story [$_{S'2}$**t**$_i$ that [$_S$ they dismissed **t**$_i$]]]]]

b. ^{OK}[$_{S'1}$ *pyon$_i$* [$_S$ *akuses* [$_{NP}$ *ti fimi* [$_{S'2}$**t**$_i$ *oti* [$_S$ *apelisan* **t**$_i$]]]]]
whom heard.2SG the story that dismissed.3PL

The standard assumption is that NP and S′ are barriers. In both examples in (4.32) this means that the moved *wh*-element has crossed two barriers, hence both examples ought to be ungrammatical. However, since (4.32b) is grammatical, this movement cannot have violated subjacency conditions. One solution to this problem would be to posit a parametric variation in barrierhood; either the NP or the S′$_2$ in (4.32b) is not a barrier. Horrocks and Stavrou, however, argue for a more substantive and, they claim, explanatory solution. They note that in Greek, noun phrases appear to contain a position parallel to the initial non-argument position of clausal elements. The noun phrases and sentences in (4.33) and (4.34) provide examples of one type of analogous behaviour, namely *wh*-movement (Horrocks and Stavrou 1987: 89).

(4.33) a. to vivlio tinos — Greek
the book who.GEN
'Whose book?!'

b. tinos to vivlio
who.GEN the book
'Whose book?'

(4.34) a. ekane ti — Greek
did.3SG what
'He did what?!'

b. tie kane
what did.3SG
'What did he do?'

In (4.34), the *wh*-element is assumed to move from its position as the complement of V to a clause-initial non-argument position, specifier of C (Spec–CP). The effect of this movement is to convert an echo question into a non-echo question. The movement of *tinos* to a noun-phrase initial position in (4.33) has the same effect of converting an echo question (4.33a) into a non-echo one (4.33b). This similarity in behaviour is used by Horrocks and Stavrou to argue that, in Greek, noun phrases contain an initial non-argument position, just like clauses. A further correspondence between clauses and noun phrases, namely focus movement, is also described by Horrocks and Stavrou (1987: 86–8).

Horrocks and Stavrou then assume that NPs, just like VPs, must be embedded under a functional category before they can be subcategorized by a lexical head. In this structure, the specifier position is a non-argument position into which a maximal projection of any category may be moved by *wh*-movement or focus movement. This means that, in Greek, the Spec–DP position in the noun phrase is analogous to the Spec–CP in the clause. With this revised structure of the noun phrase, the theory correctly predicts that (4.32b) should be grammatical. The new structure is given in (4.35).

(4.35) $^{OK}[_{S'1}$ *pyon*$_i$ $[_S$ *akuses* $[_{D''}$**t**$_i$ $[_{D'}$ *ti fimi* $[_{S'2}$**t**$_i$ *oti* $[_S$ *apelisan* **t**$_i]]]]]$
whom heard.2SG the story that dismissed.3PL

According to Horrocks and Stavrou's analysis, the reason the parallel English example (4.32a) is ungrammatical is that the English noun phrase lacks this non-argument position. Instead an English noun phrase resembles I″ in that its specifier is an argument position, with subject-like properties. This analysis not only explains why *wh*-movement is disallowed in English DPs, but also why NP movement like passive movement is allowed (Horrocks and Stavrou 1987: 93–4). As predicted by the fact that the specifier position in Greek DPs is a non-argument position, NP movement is not allowed in Greek DPs.

Parallels between clauses and noun phrases in Hungarian have been pointed out by Szabolcsi (1981, 1984). In a more recent paper, Szabolcsi (1987) suggests a formal analysis of the data which emphasises the clausal similarities of the noun phrase and also makes the determiner the head of the noun phrase.

In Hungarian there is agreement between a possessor, the assumed subject of the noun phrase, and the possessed element, in the same way that there is between a subject and a verb at the clausal level. Furthermore, the possessor appears in nominative case like a clausal subject. Relevant data from Szabolcsi (1987: 171) are given in (4.36).

(4.36) a. az én kalap-om — Hungarian
the I.NOM hat-POSS.1SG
'my hat'

b. a te kalap-od
the you.NOM hat-POSS.2SG
'your hat'

c. a Péter kalap-ja
the Peter.NOM hat-POSS.3SG
'Peter's hat'

From such data, Szabolcsi concludes that noun phrases have a position NI, projecting to NI″, parallel to the clausal INFL position. The agreement marker heads the phrase and the possessor is found in its specifier position. All Hungarian determiners except the definite article occur between the possessor and the possessed, as this analysis predicts. The definite article, on the other hand, precedes the possessor element, assumed to fill the specifier position of the IN″. Szabolcsi argues that the definite article *a*(*z*) heads another projection, namely CN″ (corresponding to clausal COMP), and takes IN″ as its complement. This extends the similarities between noun phrases and clauses; both contain not only an INFL head, but also a COMP head.

This analysis is supported by further data from Hungarian. Apart from possessors in the nominative case, as exemplified in (4.36), Hungarian also permits a possessor in the dative case. This dative possessor must precede rather than follow *a*(*z*) and it can also be extracted from the noun phrase. Examples are provided in (4.37) and (4.38) (from Szabolcsi 1987: 172, in (4.38), a is a subject trace).

(4.37) a. én-nek-em a kalap-om — Hungarian
I-DAT-1SG the hat-POSS.1SG
'my hat'

b. te-nek-ed a kalap-od
you-DAT-2SG the hat-POSS.2SG
'your hat'

c. Péter-nek a kalap-ja
Peter-DAT the hat-POSS.3SG
'Peter's hat'

(4.38) a. Péter-nek$_i$ láttam [t$_i$ a α kalap-já-t]. Hungarian
Peter-DAT saw.1SG the hat-POSS.3SG-ACC
'It was **Peter**'s hat that I saw.'

b. Ki-nek$_i$ láttam [t$_i$ a α kalap-já-t].
who-DAT saw.1SG the hat-POSS.3SG-ACC
'It was **whose** hat that I saw?!'[36]

If *a*(*z*) licenses a CN″ projection, parallel to the clausal complementizer, the dative possessor can be assumed to be found in its specifier position in (4.38). This would account for its linear position in the surface structure, and also for the extractability. Under this analysis, the Spec–CN″ position is analogous to the Spec–C″ position of clauses in that it is a non-argument position which can function as a landing site for *wh*- or focus movement.

The structure that Szabolcsi arrives at for the noun phrase is as in (4.39) (Szabolcsi 1987: 185).

(4.39)

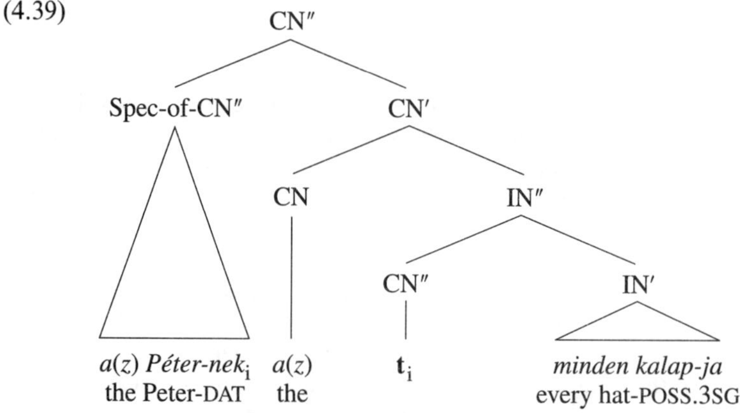

In Abney (1987) the most crucial argument in favour of a DP analysis is based on the so-called 'Poss V-*ing* construction' in English. An example of such a construction is provided in (4.40).

(4.40) John's building a spaceship.

Constructions of this type are more like clauses than derived nouns. Any verb can appear in the V-*ing* construction and the affix -*ing* is fully productive. The object of the verb occurs in its normal object form rather than with *of* as in nominalizations. Furthermore, a number of processes, such as subject raising, object raising and particle movement, usually associated with verbal elements can be found also in Poss V-*ing* constructions, but not with derived nominals. (See Abney 1987: 17 and 107–48 for a further discussion of similarities and differences between noun phrases and clausal elements.) On the other hand, the Poss V-*ing* constructions have many characteristics in common with noun phrases. The external distribution of Poss V-*ing* constructions is similar to that of the noun phrase. They can occur in noun phrase positions, where, for instance, *that*-clauses cannot. Internally, there are also a number of similarities. The fact that the subject in (4.40) is like the 'subject' of a noun phrase in that it occurs in the genitive rather than nominative case is emphasized by Abney (1987: 15) as the most important of these. Similarities between noun phrases and sentences in general are also discussed by Abney (Abney 1987: 30–106), not only for English, but also for some other languages.

In order to capture these similarities, Abney posits a structure for the noun phrase which contains an INFL node like the one assumed for clausal constituents in transformational theory. This is also supported by evidence from other languages where the noun phrase actually contains an agreement element similar to a clausal subject-verb agreement marker (Abney 1987: 37–43).[37] Abney argues that this nominal INFL(ection) or AGR(eement) node is the head of the noun phrase. He also provides evidence that the lexical fillers of this node, corresponding to modal verbs for the clausal INFL, are the determiners (Abney 1987: 265–97). The result is a DP analysis, where certain elements which may fill the D position may select a VP complement. The structure is given in (4.41).[38]

(4.41)

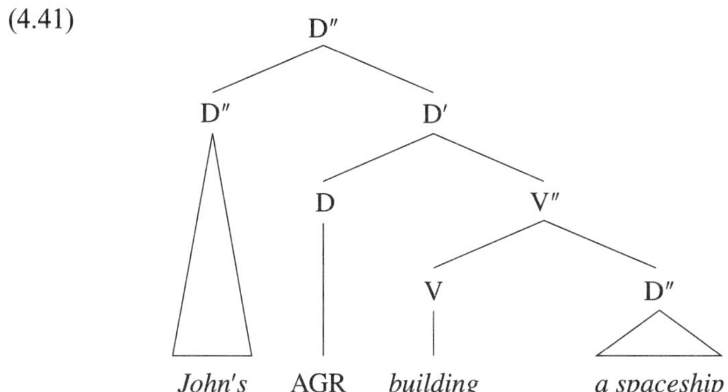

4.3.4. *Typological arguments*

Within a Categorial Grammar framework, Vennemann and Harlow (1977: 235) provide a formal definition of the notion head. According to their definition, the head is 'that constituent which determines the category of the resulting combination in the sense that its category is either identical to that of the combination or differs from it only by a "denominator".' The 'denominator' is then the category of the non-head constituent. This is illustrated in (4.42).

(4.42) a. old book — The category of the head 'book' is equal to that of the combination

old	book
c/c	*c*
c	

b. the old book — The category of the head 'the' differs from that of the combination by a denominator c, which is the category of the non-head

the	old book
n/c	*c*
n	

From this definition of head it follows that the noun is the head in (4.42a) and that the determiner heads the noun phrase in (4.42b). In this analysis, the fact that the determiner heads the noun phrase follows not from independent criteria for headedness, but from definitions within a formal system. Within the system, the head status of the determiner can actually be proven (Vennemann and Harlow 1977: 237), but this proof rests on two axiomatic definitions, namely on the definition of n and c as the only relevant basic categories and on their definition of head. However, Vennemann and Harlow find justification for their assumptions in the fact that the resulting formalism can capture generalizations and formulate predictions about languages with consistent basic serialization. This argument for the head status of determiners is therefore indirectly supported by typological data.

Dryer (1989) sets out to test two claims that have frequently been made in the typological literature, namely (1) articles are modifiers of nouns and (2) OV languages tend to place modifiers before nouns, whereas VO languages tend to place modifiers after nouns. On the basis of a sample of 125 languages, Dryer finds that, at least as far as articles are concerned, the opposite correlation between VO order and DetN order to the one predicted by (1) and (2) is actually found. This means that either one or both of these claims must be abandoned. On the basis of the position of modifiers in general, Dryer refutes (2). However, this only explains a lack of correlation; it cannot explain why the opposite correlation is found. Dryer (1989: 93–4) proposes two possible explanations for this, one in terms of left branching versus right branching and one in which (1) is reconsidered and the article is assumed to be the head. Dryer does not propose to adopt a DP analysis, but points out that there is some typological evidence in favour of such an analysis.

For instance, a DP analysis offers the possibility of expressing the difference between determiners and pronouns in the same terms as that between transitive and intransitive verbs. This is advantageous since many languages use the same words for determiners and pronouns. Dryer (1989: 93) provides an example from Jicaltepec Mixtec, and as the data in section

4.2.2 showed, the same can be claimed for Swedish. The fact that determiner and pronominal functions are, in many languages, filled by the same elements can, however, be accounted for in other ways. In section 4.2.2, I showed how Cann (1993) proposes to express this in terms of a coindexing relation which licenses an empty category. Another way still is to follow Sommerstein (1972) and assume that all determiners are in fact pronouns.

Dryer also refers to the fact that many languages require a noun phrase that functions as the argument of a verb to occur with an article. At the same time they allow predicative noun phrases to occur without determiners. In a traditional view, the predicative noun phrases would be non-maximal projections (N′). Dryer (1989: 94) considers it an undesirable situation for non-maximal projections to occur in positions where they are not constituents of other maximal projections. In a DP analysis the distinction can be made in terms of two maximal categories: DP and NP. This is, of course, not really a typological argument, but an argument based on theoretical assumptions about phrase structure for which it is difficult to find true empirical motivation.

Dryer (1989: 94) also points out that articles change the category of the nominal element in a way that modifiers generally do not; N′ is semantically a predicate, but NP is a referring expression. If one relies on a two-way distinction between heads and modifiers, then if determiners are not modifiers they are heads. However, with a more subtle distinction between heads, modifiers and specifiers, the specifier position could be argued to be the correct position for elements that change the semantic nature of the phrase in this way (see Bouma 1988).

If a DP analysis is adopted, then the correlation between ArtN and VO order on the one hand, and NArt and OV order on the other, can be accounted for. This is the manifestation of a tendency for heads to precede dependents in VO languages and heads to follow dependents in VO languages. As Dryer (1989: 94) points out, this tendency only holds when the dependent is a phrasal category, but this would, of course, be true in the case of D.

4.4. Arguments against D as the head of the noun phrase

In the transformational literature since 1987 the DP analysis has become a standard assumption.[39] Until then, the common view was that the noun was the head. This was such a generally accepted assumption that arguments were rarely provided in support of it. In the more recent literature, arguments have been provided against the DP hypothesis and in favour of the head status of the noun. In this section, I will discuss some of these arguments.

Within HPSG, the standard assumption is that noun phrases are headed by nouns rather than determiners.[40] Pollard and Sag (1994: 363–71) argue against assigning head status to determiners. However, their arguments are based on elements like *many*, *a few* and *more*, which are not usually assumed to belong to the category D in DP analyses, but rather to Q. In chapter 2 I claimed that the corresponding elements in Swedish are adjectival syntactically. This means that these arguments are actually against the head status of Q or A elements and not against the head status of D elements. As such the arguments are interesting and valid, but I will not discuss them here since my present concern is to decide between a DP and an NP analysis of Swedish noun phrases.

In a discussion of the distinction between specifiers and subjects within an HPSG framework, Borsley (1988) puts forward one argument against a DP analysis.[41] With reference to data from Corbett (1979), he points out that a DP analysis would make the wrong predictions for co-ordinated noun phrases like the subject of (4.43).

(4.43) **This man and woman** were squatting in the castle.

In this example, the nominal *man and woman* can reasonably be assumed to be plural, since the noun phrase as a whole has the distribution of a plural noun phrase. In a DP analysis, the determiner would subcategorize for the nominal, and there would be no mechanism whereby the nominal could select the determiner. However, a solution in which *this* can subcategorize for a plural nominal in English would make the wrong predictions in the majority of cases involving *this*. In an HPSG-type NP analysis, on the other hand, this type of construction would not be problematic since the co-ordinated nominal could be specified as a plural nominal selecting a singular determiner through its SPEC feature (see example (73) in Borsley 1988).

Payne (1993a) argues against the head status of D, but also more generally against the idea that a noun phrase has more than one head. Payne's criticism is based on examples from a wide variety of languages and on five types of argument: incorporation, subcategorization, the position of possessor phrases and, finally, agreement and government. I will give only a very brief account of his arguments here.

According to recent transformational theory, the incorporation of an object into a verb involves head-to-head movement (Baker 1988). As the object is moved, a trace is left behind which must be antecedent-governed. If the object noun phrase is assumed to be headed by the determiner or any element other than the noun, then antecedent-government will be blocked by the Minimality Principle, and the theory wrongly predicts that this type of incorporation should be ungrammatical. A solution to this problem has been proposed by Baker and Hale (1990) who assume that a functional category is not a potential antecedent and therefore the trace within the DP can still be governed. However, Payne shows that even with this modification, the theory makes the wrong predictions in cases where nominal modifiers are incorporated into a noun. Payne (1993a: 125–8) gives examples from Chukchi and Koryak for which the correct predictions will only be made if the noun phrase is assumed to be headed by the noun.

Payne's second argument is that a DP analysis would lead us to expect that verbs would subcategorize for different determiners, and also that some verbs would subcategorize for a DP, some for an NP and some for, for example, a Q(uantifier)P. According to Payne (1993a: 129–30) this is not attested in language. I refer to section 4.2.2, where I discussed the possibility that some verbs in Swedish could be said to subcategorize for NP as opposed to DP. This was also suggested by Dryer (1989) as an argument in favour of a DP analysis (see section 4.3.4).

As the overview in section 4.3.3 showed, the position of the possessor phrase in the languages discussed plays an important role in the argumentation in favour of the DP hypothesis. The possessor is assumed to fill either the specifier position of the functional category or the complement position following the noun. Payne (1993a: 131–2) shows that there are languages (such as Farsi) where the position of the possessor phrase cannot be accounted for by these analyses. This then weakens one of the arguments in favour of the DP hypothesis.

Payne's fourth argument is based on the behaviour of Dama noun phrases. In this language, prenominal modifiers behave differently from post-nominal ones with respect to order and person/number/gender marking. The Dama data can be accounted for in a simple way if the noun is assumed to be the pivotal element. If the determiner is assumed to be the head, the obvious generalization cannot easily be stated.

Noun-phrase internal agreement provides the data for Payne's final argument. In Russian, certain numerals change the expected agreement patterns within the noun phrase. In a nominative or accusative noun phrase, the noun and the modifiers following these numerals receive genitive case. Such data have been used to argue in favour of an analysis in which the numeral is the functional head of the noun phrase (see Corbett 1993). Under such an analysis, the numeral would govern the constituent which follows and genitive case could be assumed to be assigned under government. However, as Payne (1993a: 135–8) shows, the relation between these numerals and the elements which follow them within the noun phrase is not typical of government, but rather of concord or agreement. For instance, some numerals agree with their noun in gender. Also, in oblique noun phrases, the numeral fails to assign genitive case to the following constituent. This is not the behaviour of a typical governor. In terms of Cann's (1993) definitions, this is characteristic of a concord relationship rather than of government. An account of the Russian data in terms of agreement points towards a structure where the noun is the head with which the numeral modifier agrees.

Ernst (1991) is the only example I know of a post-Abney (1987) defence of an NP rather than DP analysis for noun phrases articulated within a transformational framework. Ernst's evidence is based partly on specific English constructions, partly on theory-internal assumptions and partly on word order typology arguments.

Ernst (1991) claims that adverbs like *even*, *mostly* and *only* may attach to the left of any maximal projection. He refers to Ernst (1984) for a discussion of these adverbs. Ernst's (1991: 195) examples are provided in (4.44).

(4.44) a. Vern likes [$_{NP}$ even the flowers his mother planted]
b. Vern may [$_{VP}$ even like the flowers his mother planted]
c. Vern seems [$_{AP}$ even ecstatic over his mother's flowers]
d. *Vern likes the [$_{N'}$ even flowers his mother planted]

The ungrammaticality of (4.44d) is then taken as evidence that the string following the definite article cannot be a maximal projection. This is a counter-argument to the DP hypothesis, since under a DP analysis, this constituent would be an NP.

The distribution of *bara* 'only' in Swedish corresponds to that of *even* in (4.44). The relevant data are found in (4.45), where the labelling in (4.45a) and (4.45e) reflects the standard assumption in a DP analysis. Ernst's (1991) claim would be that the ungrammaticality of (4.45e) shows that this labelling is wrong. Instead it should be N′.[42]

(4.45) a. Oscar äter bara [$_{DP}$ den bananen]
Oscar eats only that banana
b. Oscar vill bara [$_{VP}$ äta den bananen]
Oscar wants only eat that banana
c. Oscar verkar bara [$_{AP}$ arg på henne]
Oscar seems only angry with her
d. Oscar verkar arg bara [$_{PP}$ på henne]
Oscar seems angry only with her
e. *Oscar äter den bara [$_{NP}$ bananen]
Oscar eats that only banana

If we accepts Ernst's argument, and the idea that a complement must be a maximal projection, then the data in (4.45) can be viewed as an argument against a DP hypothesis for Swedish. Fukui and Speas (1986) have, however, proposed an analysis in which all lexical categories, including N, are assumed to be complements of a functional category and to project only to X′ level. Following Fukui and Speas's assumptions, (4.45) could be viewed not as evidence against the head status of D, but rather as evidence that the complement of D here is not maximal. However, Fukui and Speas claim that **all** lexical categories project up to X′ only. If it is the case that *even* in English (and *bara* in Swedish) may not precede a non-maximal projection, then the grammaticality of at least (4.44b) and (4.45b) is unexpected since *even* would here presumably precede a lexical and hence non-maximal projection. The generalization captured by Ernst (1991) therefore seems to make a distinction between the strings following modals (verbal) or verbs (nominal or adjectival) on the one hand and the strings following determiners on the other. Under Ernst's analysis, this can be expressed in terms of a distinction between maximal and non-maximal projections. Under Fukui and Speas's (1986) analysis, this generalization cannot be expressed.

As the review of arguments in section 4.3 showed, the advocates of the DP hypothesis in transformational grammar base their arguments to a great extent on assumed similarities between nominal elements and clausal elements, that is, between D and I or C. Ernst (1991: 195) points out a number of ways in which the parallelism does not hold true. Like Payne (1993a), Ernst refers to the fact that a verb may select with respect to a particular C or I in a clausal complement, but that it does not select for a particular D in a nominal complement. Ernst (p. 195) also claims that whereas there is 'widely accepted evidence' for V-to-I and I-to-C movement, the examples of movement of D to a higher head are not convincing. He refers to suggestions that the French *au* is an example of *le* having raised to incorporate with a preposition *à* and claims that the explanation of this phenomenon is more likely to lie in the phonetic than the syntactic component (see also Longobardi 1994). Ernst proposes the same type of explanation for Galician data put forward by Uriagereka (1988) in support of a DP analysis. The two examples that Ernst challenges are both of movement from a functional category, which means it is parallel to I-to-C movement. Ernst does not discuss the parallel of V-to-I movement, that is, movement from a lexical category to a functional one. For the noun phrase, this would be N-to-D movement, which has been proposed for the Scandinavian languages by, for instance, Delsing (1988, 1992, 1993), Taraldsen (1990, 1991) and Sigurðsson (1992). Clearly these examples could not be explained in terms of phonetics.[43] The argument that determiners are heads because some of the elements belonging to this category select their complements by means of subcategorization or government is not valid according to Ernst. He extends the notion of SPEC–head agreement to a licensing relationship.[44] In his analysis, SPEC–Head selection could account for what others assume to be a matter of subcategorization.

Ernst (1991) also refers to word order typology for arguments against the DP hypothesis. In section 4.3.4, I showed how word-order facts led Dryer (1989) to suggest that seeming irregularities might be turned into an expected pattern if determiners were assumed to be heads rather than modifiers. Ernst (pp. 196–97), on the other hand, claims that even though the DP hypothesis makes the right predictions for a consistently head-first SVO language, namely, that D precedes its nominal complement, this cannot be extended to consistently head-last SOV languages. These would be expected to have the nominal complement preceding the D head. However, Ernst (p. 196) claims that this is not the order generally found in SOV languages.

Finally, Ernst discusses what he refers to as ClPs (Classifier Phrases). He assumes that in a DP analysis these elements would also be considered heads with nominal complements. He argues that this would make the wrong predictions both with respect to order and co-occurrence of determiner-like elements. It seems to me, however, that the data presented by Ernst could be accounted for within a transformational DP account. The data could, for instance, be viewed as evidence that these languages have two functional nodes within the noun phrase. This is not to say I would wish to propose such an account.

4.5. Conclusions

The only obvious conclusion that can be drawn from the arguments and data discussed so far in this chapter is that determining the headedness of noun phrases in general, and that of Swedish noun phrases in particular, is no easy matter. Considering how important the notion of headedness is to the type of structure I have adopted in this book, this is a very disappointing result. The structure in (4.1) will be spelled out as (4.46a) or (4.46b) depending on which element is assumed to be the head.

(4.46)

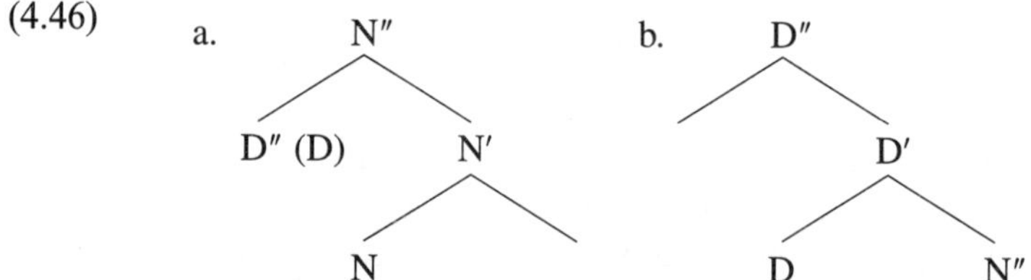

The results of applying the criteria from the debate between Zwicky (1985a) and Hudson (1987) to Swedish noun phrases can be summarized as in table 4.1. In this table, ∅ indicates that, in my opinion, the criterion does not give any evidence either way, for instance, because it does not apply, or because the result is ambiguous. A question mark after the category indicates that the criterion could be applied to yield this category as head but that the result is open to some doubt. Since I found that the notion 'ruler' did not add anything to the discussion, I have omitted this from the table. The discussion in section 4.2 made clear that Cann's (1993) more formal criteria did not yield an unambiguous result either. Since the choice between the two structures in (4.46) will have far-reaching consequences for the analysis, for example, with respect to subcategorization, government and feature percolation, it would have been more satisfying if I had been able to

Table 4.1 Headedness criteria applied to Swedish noun phrases

Criterion			Head
1	'Kind of'		N
2	Semantic	Argument (Zwicky)	N?
		Functor (Hudson)	D?
3	Subcategorization	a. External	N
		b. Internal[45]	D
4	Morpho-syntacticlocus		∅
5	Governor[45]		D
6	Determinant of concord (irrelevant to Hudson)		∅
7	Obligatory constituent[46]		∅ (N)
8	Distributional equivalence[46]		∅ (N)

establish an unambiguous head of the Swedish noun phrase. However, at the present state of knowledge, a choice between (4.46a) and (4.46b) will always be based on just a selection of the criteria or of the data or the choice will be made on theory internal-grounds.

In an attempt to resolve problems like those captured by table 4.1, Zwicky (1993) argues that the notion 'head' is used in syntax to refer to three distinct aspects of headedness. The head of a phrase for each of these purposes will often coincide, but need not do so. He therefore proposes to distinguish three notions which all cover some aspects of headedness: FUNCTOR, BASE and HEAD. The FUNCTOR, obviously, is the semantic functor, as discussed in section 4.2.1, but the element singled out by this criterion is, according to Zwicky, also the agreement target (AGR), the government trigger (GOV) and the lexically subcategorized element (LEX). With reference to a generalization by Keenan (1974), Zwicky (1993: 295) assumes that functors are always agreement targets and government triggers, so that these are not independent criteria. The BASE is the required part of a phrase (REQ), the external representative (REP), and the classifying element (CLS, related to the 'kind of' criterion). The HEAD, finally, is the element which is the morphosyntactic locus of the phrase (LOC), it is of word rank (WRD) and it is the category determinant (CAT).

If Zwicky's notions FUNCTOR and BASE are adopted, some of the contradictory results in table 4.1 can probably be resolved. One might take the data discussed here as evidence that the determiner is the FUNCTOR and the noun is the BASE. In Zwicky's (1993: 302–7) terms, this means that the Swedish determiner is an instance of a split. It can be described as SPECIFIER, more specifically, a specifier whose BASE constituent is an argument (see (10) in Zwicky 1993: 308). According to Zwicky this is an instance of the split behaviour typical of determiners.

So, Zwicky's development of the notion head can help us understand why D has some head-like qualities in Swedish noun phrases whereas other headedness characteristics are carried by the noun. However, the main purpose of my investigation into the headedness of Swedish noun phrases is related to the head-like properties referred to as HEAD by Zwicky. With respect to this notion, the matter has not become any clearer; none of the criteria LOC, WRD or CAT singles out unambiguously either D or N as the head of the Swedish noun phrase. (LOC is 4 in table 4.1, both N and D are WRD and either of them could be CAT. For a discussion of the inheritance of categorial features, see note 18 in section 4.2.3.) Unless we find a way of establishing which category is the morphosyntactic locus, we cannot tell which category is the HEAD. In section 4.2.3, I claimed that it is impossible to establish which of the two elements is the morphosyntactic locus, that is, the head with respect to feature percolation. No matter which category is represented as the head, some features will have to be inherited by a rule of non-head-feature inheritance. In general, I agree with the scepticism of Payne (1993a) as regards the criterion of morphosyntactic locus. This scepticism is strengthened by the fact that even with respect to the small number of construction types in English that Zwicky (1985a) and Hudson (1987) discuss, on the basis of this criterion they come to opposite conclusions.

The arguments in favour of the DP hypothesis which I discussed in section 4.3.3 do not apply to Swedish. Swedish does not have *wh*-movement out of noun phrases of the type referred to for Greek in the arguments put forward by Horrocks and Stavrou (1987).[47] Szabolcsi's (1987) arguments are not applicable to Swedish either, since Swedish lacks (overt) case except on pronouns, and it also lacks agreement, both between subject and verb and between possessor and possessum. The English construction type which Abney (1987) uses to argue in favour of the DP hypothesis does not have a parallel in Swedish. The corresponding constructions in Swedish are completely nominalized forms, which, for instance, are modified by adjectives and take oblique objects, as in (4.47) (see Abney's example quoted in (4.40) in section 4.3.3).

(4.47) a. Hans hemliga skrivande av billiga romaner avslöjades.
his secret writing of cheap novels reveal.PASS
'His secret writing of cheap novels was revealed.'

b. *Hans hemligt skrivande av billiga romaner avslöjades.
his secretly writing of cheap novels reveal.PASS

c. *Hans hemliga skrivande billiga romaner avslöjades.
his secret writing cheap novels reveal.PASS

Only if we assume that the headedness of noun phrases is universal can these arguments be extended to Swedish. Whether or not the head of the noun phrase, or indeed of any other phrase, can vary between languages is a big issue which I will avoid here. In terms of modern transformational theory, the question is whether or not headedness is subject to parametric variation. Cann (1993), for instance, assumes that it is. Indeed if his criteria are applied strictly, they are bound to yield different results for different languages with respect to noun phrases. However, most linguists advocating a DP analysis within a transformational framework seem implicitly to assume that headedness is universal. The Hungarian data from Szabolcsi (1987) are quoted to strengthen the argument in favour of a DP analysis even for languages which have neither subject-verb agreement nor possessor-possessum agreement (for example, for Swedish by Delsing 1988, 1993).

In the more theory-independent typological discussions, the underlying assumption seems to be that headedness should be the same universally. The examples of such approaches that I have referred to here (Dryer 1989, Ernst 1991, Payne 1993a, Vennemann and Harlow 1977) do make use of data from a wide variety of unrelated languages, and in both cases the result is assumed to have wider validity. However, the problem with the typologically based articles is that they do not arrive at the same conclusion; Vennemann and Harlow (1977) and Dryer (1989), for instance, conclude that D is the head, whereas Ernst (1991) and Payne (1993a) come to the opposite conclusion.

I conclude, then, that the issue of the headedness of noun phrases is still open. Since the typological evidence is inconclusive, I will focus here on the Swedish data. On the basis of the discussion in this chapter as summarized in table 4.1, two facts can be established:

(4.48) • semantically, the noun is the head
• there is some sense in which a determiner selects its nominal sister

The first fact in (4.48) is obvious in terms of the 'kind of' criterion, but it also shows up in the external subcategorization and in the narrower interpretation of the obligatory constituent and distributional equivalence criteria. In a DP analysis, this must be dealt with through some formal mechanism which allows the D to inherit certain properties from its nominal sister (see Abney's 1987 c-projection and s-projection, Radford's 1993 immediate head and ultimate head and Netter's 1994 distinction between the inheritance of MINOR and MAJOR features). In any such solution, the noun phrase can therefore be said to have two heads. The second fact in (4.48) is usually explained in terms of subcategorization or government by the determiner. Only heads are assumed to subcategorize or be a governor, hence this is taken as evidence that the determiner is the head of the noun phrase. In a noun phrase analysis, this selectional relation would have to be accounted for in some other way.

My conclusion on the basis of this chapter is, then, that the criteria that have been proposed for head status clearly yield contradictory results. Until further evidence is found, I believe that the choice can only depend on one's specific theoretical assumptions and how they, in effect, render irrelevant a subset of the headedness criteria. For me, the first fact in (4.48) is more basic. The second fact I see as a product of the kind of theoretical assumptions linguists tend to make. In chapters 5 and 6 I will therefore attempt to develop an NP analysis of Swedish noun phrases. However, this must be done within a framework in which the type of selectional restrictions which the determiner puts on the nominal can be accounted for without necessarily assuming that the determiner is the head. A theory which does permit this relation between a specifier and its sister to be expressed is HPSG (Pollard and Sag 1987, 1994). In chapters 5 and 6 I will therefore use HPSG and show that with the assumptions made within this theory, an NP analysis of Swedish noun phrases is possible. In fact, I will claim that there are reasons to prefer an NP analysis tp one in which D is assumed to be the head.

5

FEATURES IN DEFINITE NOUN PHRASES

5.1. Introduction

5.1.1. *The approach*

With respect to Swedish definite noun phrases, there are a number of basic issues that any analysis must be able to account for. In this chapter, for each of these issues I will provide an overview of previously suggested solutions and then propose my own analysis. Since a number of the difficulties that confront an analysis of Swedish are also relevant for Norwegian, I will consider analyses that have been proposed for Norwegian as well.

Two general properties relevant to an analysis of Swedish noun phrases have already been discussed: the status of the definite ending (DEF) and the headedness of noun phrases. In chapter 3 I discussed data which led me to conclude that, in order to capture the behaviour of DEF correctly, it should be analysed as a morphological element; DEF forms a word with the noun to which it is attached. If we observe a principle of lexical integrity, this means that DEF should not be found under a syntactic node of its own. This is the approach I will take in my analysis. Instead DEF will be represented in the syntax as a feature of nouns which is manifested as morphological marking. In section 3.7, this led me to exclude recent versions of transformational grammar from the potential frameworks to be used to formulate my analysis of Swedish noun phrases.

In chapter 4, I found that there is no conclusive evidence in favour of either N or D as the head of the noun phrase. In section 4.5 I concluded that the only (reasonably) unambiguous argument in favour of a DP analysis which applies to Swedish is based on subcategorization, or feature assignment under government, depending on how one chooses to express the fact that certain definite determiners may only occur with nouns which are not marked for definiteness (see sections 4.2.2 and 4.2.4). Under standard assumptions about government and subcategorization this can only be expressed if D is the head and the nominal its complement sister.

The major argument in favour of an NP analysis, on the other hand, is less theory dependent and more intuitively general. This is the fact that, categorially and distributionally, the phrase shares important properties with the noun. This is reflected in a number of DP analyses in the form of a dual head analysis (see discussion in sections 4.2.1 and 4.5).

There appear to be two ways of reconciling these conclusions about headedness. One is that most commonly taken in recent accounts, namely, to analyse noun phrases as DPs, but to assume that there is a mechanism for assigning some sort of secondary head status within the DP to the noun. The other option is to assign the status of head of the phrase to the noun but to introduce a more flexible mechanism for selection, such that an element can select another element without having to stand in a head–complement relation to that element.

I will take the latter option and explore an NP analysis of Swedish noun phrases using the tools of a theory in which an element is not required to be the head of the phrase in order to select its sister. The theory I will be using is Head-driven Phrase Structure Grammar (HPSG) (Pollard and Sag 1987, 1994). In order to establish not only whether an NP analysis is possible, but whether it might, in fact, have certain advantages over a DP analysis, I will contrast my NP analysis of definite noun phrases with a basic DP analysis at each stage. I have concluded that the major theory-independent argument for a DP analysis is valid only if subcategorization (or feature assignment) is restricted to head–complement relations. Therefore, when I discuss a DP analysis, I will incorporate this assumption, but otherwise I will formulate it in a general phrase-structure format. My goal is not to develop the DP analysis in any detail, but to respond to the fairly common claim that subcategorization facts force us to consider D the head of a noun phrase. The idea behind my dual strategy is then to establish two things: firstly, whether or not an NP analysis of Swedish noun phrases can be offered with the more powerful assumptions about selection, and secondly, whether or not a DP analysis of Swedish noun phrases is plausible without the more elaborate view of selection. If it turns out to be the case that a correct NP analysis in these terms is possible, then the force of the subcategorization argument is weakened. If it also turns out to be the case that a DP analysis cannot easily make the correct predictions without additional assumptions, the strength of the argument is further weakened.

It should be pointed out here that an analysis in which D heads the noun phrase has been proposed within HPSG by, for instance, Netter (1994) (for German) and Kolliakou (1994) (for Greek). However, it seems to me that, at least for the Swedish data, if a satisfactory NP account can be formulated within HPSG, then there is no reason to adopt any version of the DP hypothesis. If further evidence comes to light which supports the head status of D, then this possibility should be explored.

5.1.2. *Head-driven Phrase Structure Grammar basics*

Head-driven Phrase Structure Grammar (HPSG) is often referred to as an information-based theory (though this term is vague and could in principle be applied to almost any syntactic theory). Associated with any string – be it lexical or syntactically complex – is an INFORMATION STRUCTURE, expressed in terms of ATTRIBUTES and their VALUES. These structures are referred to as Attribute-Value Matrices (AVMs).

Each sign has two types of features associated with it, PHON and SYNSEM.[1] Of these, only the SYNSEM features will be of interest to us. The value of the SYNSEM attribute can be referred to as a *synsem* object, and it has attributes and values of its own. The two highest attributes within the *synsem* object are LOCAL and NONLOCAL. Only the LOCAL information is relevant to my analysis. LOCAL has as its value the attributes CATEGORY, CONTENT and CONTEXT, each of which is an attribute with its own (complex) value. This gives the basic AVM structure in (5.1) for a sign:

(5.1)

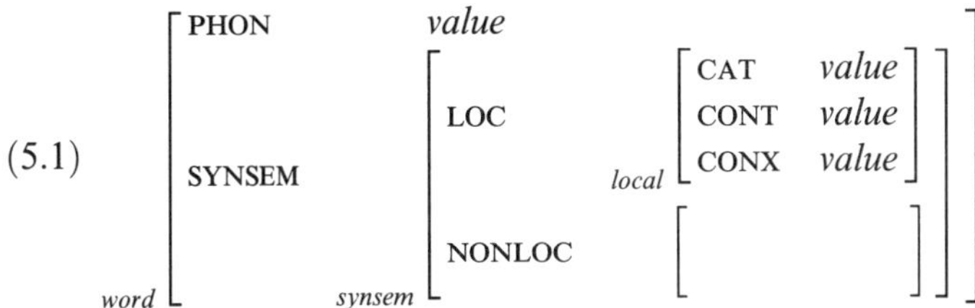

The value of the CAT attribute can consist of two types of attribute and their values: HEAD and features representing the valency of the element, that is, all the elements required for the head to be saturated. The HEAD value is roughly the part of speech, and different parts of speech may have attributes of their own (head features), for example, nouns may have CASE. In Pollard and Sag (1987, and 1994 up to chapter 9), there is assumed to be only one valence feature: SUBCAT. In chapter 9, however, Pollard and Sag (1994) adopt a proposal made by Borsley (for example 1987, 1998) to the effect that this list needs to be divided into two parts: SUBJ for the subject argument and COMPS for other arguments. A third valence attribute, SPR, for specifiers is then introduced. Since determiners are assumed to be specifiers, and since the nouns which I am dealing with here cannot be said to have subjects, it is SPR that will be of interest to us. The value of all the valency attributes are lists of *synsem* objects, that is, the elements on the list can make reference to any information available within the *synsem* object in (5.1).

SUBJ, COMPS and SPR are the features which allow heads to select their sisters, but they are not the only selectional feature in HPSG. There are two other features which allow elements to select their sisters – SPEC and MOD, whose values are also *synsem* objects. These two features differ from the valence features discussed above in that they are HEAD features. The SPEC attribute is associated with specifiers, like for instance a determiner, hence a determiner and its head sister mutually select each other. MOD is associated with modifiers, like adjectives, and these can then mono-directionally select their nominal sisters. Illustrations of AVMs for a noun and a determiner are given in (5.2). Note that a value like Det on a valency list is really an abbreviation of an AVM.

(5.2) a. *sheep*: SYNSEM| LOC| CAT $\begin{bmatrix} \text{HEAD} & \textit{noun} \\ \text{SPR} & \langle \textit{det} \rangle \end{bmatrix}$

b. *a*: SYNSEM| LOC| CAT [HEAD *det*[SPEC *noun*]]

The abbreviated AVMs in (5.2) show that *sheep* is a noun which requires a determiner to become a saturated noun phrase. *A*, on the other hand, is a determiner which obligatorily combines with a *noun*; this is captured by the SPEC feature.

CONTENT, together with CONTEXT (see (5.1)), specifies the sign's contribution to semantic interpretation. For nominal objects, CONTENT has an attribute INDEX, with a value of the kind *index*, where information to do with reference is indicated. The CONTENT attribute is slightly more complex for a determiner, but also contains the INDEX attribute. Indices have three agreement features: PERSON, NUMBER and GENDER. For a more detailed account of particularly the semantic features of HPSG I refer to Pollard and Sag (1994).

When strings (such as lexical elements) merge to form new strings, information associated with each of the elements – as captured in the AVMs – also combines. The initial information structures may be partial, and may cumulatively become more specific as elements are combined. There are no destructive operations on information structures (monotonicity is maintained). The information structures may involve structure sharing, where one information structure may form the value of two distinct attributes. The main operation on feature structures is UNIFICATION, which yields a new information structure from two (or more) compatible (unifiable) information structures. This will be illustrated by an example shortly.

Of the principles which guide the way in which the information associated with the resulting phrase depends on the information associated with the merging objects, the most important ones for our purposes are (all references are to Pollard and Sag 1994):

The ID Principle
Every headed phrase must satisfy exactly one of the ID schemata. (p. 399)

The Valence Principle
In a headed phrase (i.e. a phrasal sign whose DTRS value is of sort *head-struc*), for each valence feature F, the F value of the head daughter is the concatenation of the phrase's F value with the list (in order of increasing obliqueness) of SYNSEM values of the F-DTRS value. (p. 348)

The SPEC Principle
If a non-head daughter in a headed structure bears a SPEC value, it is token-identical to the SYNSEM value of the head daughter. (p. 51)

The HEAD Feature Principle
The HEAD value of any headed phrase is structure-shared with the HEAD value of the head daughter. (p. 399)

The ID schemata basically do the same job as X-bar rules and do not indicate the order in which elements occur. This is done by separate LINEAR PRECEDENCE RULES. Examples of ID schemata are:

ID schema 1 A phrase with DTRS value of sort *head-subj-str* in which the HEAD-DTR value is a phrasal sign.

ID schema 2 A phrase with DTRS value of sort *head-comp-struc* in which the HEAD-DTR value is a lexical sign.

ID schema 1 allows a subtree which has a head daughter and a subject daughter; the head daughter must be phrasal. This is then roughly equivalent to X″ → Y″, X′. The subtree permitted by ID schema 2 has one head daughter which is lexical and an unspecified number of complement daughters. This can then be compared with an X-bar rule like X′ → X, Y″.

An ID schema will then allow a subtree in which *a* and *sheep* in (5.2) are the daughters, but it does not instruct the resulting phrase to 'stop looking for a determiner', that is, it says nothing about the SPR list of the resulting mother.[2] This is done by the Valence Principle which makes sure that the valency list of the head daughter (*sheep*) is a concatenation of the SYNSEM value of the daughter(s) (*a*) and that of the mother phrase. This has two consequences: firstly, it means that the SPR attribute of the mother must have as its value an empty list, that is, it is saturated; the concatenation of the empty list (of the mother) and the SYNSEM value of the daughter (abbreviated as *det*) is a list of one element, *det*, which indeed is the SPR value which we find on the head daughter. Secondly, it makes sure that the element with which the head combines has the appropriate features: the object on the SPR list of the head must be unifiable with the SYNSEM value of the determiner. In the same way, the SPEC Principle will ensure that the SPEC value of the determiner is token-identical to the SYNSEM value of the head sister. Since this involves structure sharing, it means that incompatible elements cannot combine: if a head noun required an element through its SPR list which had the specification [NUM *sg*], the valency principle would stop it from combining with a [NUM *pl*] determiner. It also means that the information associated with one or both of the elements may become more specific. This can be illustrated if we provide a more detailed AVM for the determiner *a* and use numbers to indicate structure sharing imposed by the Valence Principle ([1]) and the SPEC Principle ([2]). The two AVMs are found in

(5.3), the subscript *sg* after the noun which is the value of SPEC for *a* is an abbreviation for the required INDEX value for that noun.

(5.3) a. *sheep*: [2] SYNSEM| LOC| CAT $\begin{bmatrix} \text{HEAD} & \textit{noun} \\ \text{SPR} & \langle [1]\ \textit{det} \rangle \end{bmatrix}$

b. *a*: [1] $\begin{bmatrix} \text{CAT} & [\text{HEAD}\ \textit{det}\ [\text{SPEC}\ [2]\ \textit{noun}_{\text{sg}}]] \\ \text{CONT} & [\text{RESTIND}\ [\text{INDEX}\ [\text{NUM}\ \textit{sg}]]] \end{bmatrix}$

The structure-sharing indicated by [2] means that the SYNSEM value for *sheep* and the SPEC value of *a* must now refer to the same object. Since *sheep* does not have an incompatible attribute value like [NUM *pl*] this is possible and hence *sheep* will have a singular feature after the combination.

The Valence Principle will make sure that the mother's SPR list is empty. The Head Feature Principle, finally, makes sure that mothers and head daughters structure-share their HEAD features. Hence the mother node will inherit the HEAD value *noun* from its head daughter.

5.1.3. *The issues*

The most obvious problem for an analysis of Swedish noun phrases is how to account for the fact that a definite singular noun can function as a full referential noun phrase without requiring the presence of a syntactic determiner, as in (5.4). This is dealt with in section 5.2.

(5.4) Mus-en åt ost-en.
mouse-DEF ate cheese-DEF
'The mouse ate the cheese.'

In examples like (5.4), DEF appears to be able to do duty as a determiner in the sense that it fills the same semantic function as the English *the*. In a number of the analyses reviewed in section 5.2, some level of syntactic determiner status is indeed assigned to the definite ending. This then gives rise to two problems.

Firstly, if DEF does in some sense function as a syntactic determiner, then the fact that it can co-occur with other determiners, as the examples in (5.5) show, must be accounted for.[3]

(5.5) a. den musen
that mouse.DEF
'that mouse'

b. det där murmeldjuret
that marmot.DEF
'that marmot'

Secondly, if the presence of DEF on a singular count noun can permit that noun to function as a full referential noun phrase, why can it not do so when the noun is preceded by an adjective? This is not possible even when the adjective carries marking specific to definite noun phrases. Adjectives in definite noun phrases must be preceded by a syntactic determiner, as (5.6) shows.[4] This constraint is discussed in section 5.4.

(5.6) a. *Glad-a mus-en åt ost-en.
happy-DEF mouse-DEF ate cheese-DEF

b. Den glad-a mus-en åt ost-en.
the happy-DEF mouse-DEF ate cheese-DEF
'The happy mouse ate the cheese.'

This issue is further complicated by the fact that there are certain adjective+noun.DEF combinations in Swedish which do not appear to require the presence of a syntactic determiner. Examples of such constructions are provided in (5.7). These seeming exceptions to the general principle will be discussed in section 5.5.[5]

(5.7) a. Svenska Dagbladet har bra kultursidor.
Swedish daily has good arts pages
'*Svenska Dagbladet* has a good arts section.'

b. Sista försök-et misslyckades.
last attempt-DEF failed
'The last attempt failed.'

c. Högra sida-n av vägen är sämre.
right side-DEF of road.DEF is worse
'The right side of the road is worse.'

d. Båda ostbitarna var borta.
both pieces-of-cheese.DEF were gone
'Both the pieces of cheese were gone.'

If DEF is assumed to be a feature instead, a solution in terms of definiteness agreement might suggest itself, but the issue is complicated by the fact that not all definite determiners can co-occur with a definite noun. As we have seen, some determiners require that the noun does not carry the definite ending. Examples of this are provided in (5.8). The co-occurrence restrictions that apply to syntactic determiners and DEF will be dealt with in section 5.3.

(5.8) a. samma mus(*-en)
same mouse(-DEF)
'the same mouse'

b. vilket murmeldjur(*-et)
which marmot(-DEF)
'which marmot'

One issue which I will not deal with in this book since I have limited myself to prenominal modification, but which should at least be mentioned here, is relative clauses. Restrictive relative clauses pose special problems for an analysis of Swedish noun phrases. A restrictive relative clause can occur with a definite noun, as in (5.9a). It can however also occur with a noun lacking the definite ending preceded by the syntactic definite article, as in (5.9c). This in spite of the fact that the syntactic definite article usually requires a definite noun, as in (5.9b). A third possibility is that the restrictive relative clause is preceded by a syntactic definite article and a definite noun, as in (5.9c). This example is unexpected since the syntactic article is normally only possible when there are premodifiers to the noun, otherwise *den* can only be interpreted as a demonstrative, as in (5.5a).

(5.9) a. Mus-en
mouse-DEF
b. Den mus
the mouse
c. Den mus-en
the mouse-DEF
} som vi såg hade inte ätit osten
which we saw had not eaten cheese.DEF

I refer to Holmberg (1987) and van der Auwera (1990) for discussions of relative clauses in Swedish. Payne and Börjars (1994) provide a detailed analysis of Swedish noun phrases containing restrictive relative clauses in terms of Categorial Grammar (CG).

5.2. Nouns without syntactic determiners

5.2.1. *The data*

Semantically, noun phrases like *musen* and *denna mus* are of the same kind. They can each function as a full referential noun phrase. They have argument status rather than the status of predicatives. Their internal syntactic structure, on the other hand, appears to be quite different; a nominal without a syntactic determiner would normally be assumed to be of the category N′ (in an NP analysis) or of the category NP (in a DP analysis). Since the two types of noun phrases in Swedish have the same syntactic distribution they are often assumed to be of the same syntactic category. This avoids a number of complications, for example with respect to the selection frames of elements selecting a noun phrase (see section 5.2.3.1), which would arise if *musen* and *denna mus* were assigned to different syntactic categories. In this chapter I will look at different ways of resolving these issues.

5.2.2. *Previous analyses*

5.2.2.1. *Analyses in which* DEF *has independent syntactic status*

Examples of analyses in which DEF is assumed to have independent syntactic status are found for example in Delsing (1988, 1989, 1992) and Taraldsen (1990, 1991). In these analyses, DEF has the same status as a syntactic determiner like English *the* or Swedish *en* 'a(n)', so that the structure of the noun phrase *musen* is virtually identical to that of *the mouse* and *en mus* 'a mouse'. The representation that results is found in (5.10).[6]

(5.10)

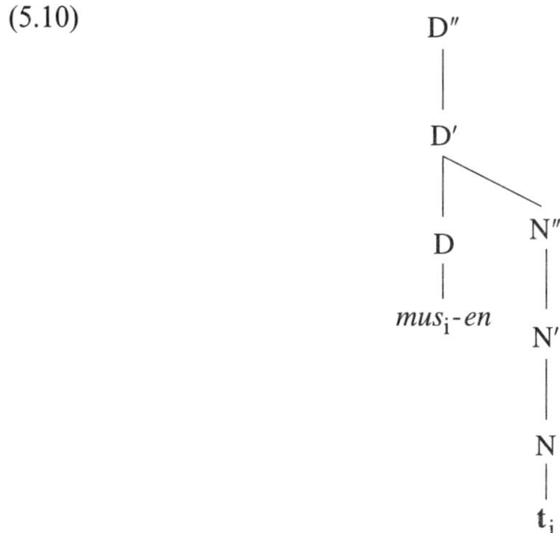

In such analyses, then, the determiner slot is filled at the syntactic level, and therefore it is expected that the phrase should be able to function as a full referential noun phrase.

Delsing (1993) does assume that the definiteness is base-generated on the noun in N, at least in noun phrases where DEF co-occurs with syntactic elements like *den* 'the/that' or *den här* 'this'. For noun phrases like *musen* 'the mouse', Delsing (1993: 130) states: 'in such cases, it is of course impossible to judge whether the article is base-generated on the noun or generated in D and attached to the noun by N-raising, but I assume that raising applies in any case, in order to lexicalize the D position.'

One point to note here is the way in which Delsing accounts for the absence of noun movement in noun phrases like *en mus* or *denna mus.* Delsing (1988: 63; 1989) assumes that the movement from N to a higher functional projection D takes place only when D can govern the N position.[7] This is possible only when D contains a [+DEF] feature. This is the reason why the noun cannot raise when D is filled by the indefinite article *en.* A further assumption is that a referential element in the D position blocks movement. This accounts for why the noun may not raise in noun phrases like *denna mus* in spite of the fact that *denna* is [+DEF] and hence a potential governor. I fail to understand why the difference is not ascribed to the fact that *-en* is a bound element, and therefore needs a host word. *Denna* and *en*, on the other hand, are not bound. Assuming that movement only takes place when necessary, this would explain why *-en* does not move in these cases. This seems to me to be the most straightforward account. In Delsing (1993) I cannot find any explicit discussion of how this movement is blocked. In a discussion of demonstratives he simply states that the movement is blocked, without reference to further discussion (p. 136). I will return to Delsing's (1989, 1992, 1993) analyses of definite noun phrases containing attributive adjectives in section 5.4.2.1, and to his treatment of demonstratives in section 5.3.2.1.

An analysis which is related in that DEF is assumed to have syntactic status, but differs in that DEF is not assumed to fill the same slot as prenominal determiners, has been proposed by Santelmann (1992). Since *-en* and the prenominal determiners do not occur in complementary distribution, she assumes that they cannot both be D^0 elements. The D node in Santelmann's analysis is filled by the prenominal definite determiner *den* (or some other prenominal determiner), to be dealt with in sections 5.3 and 5.4. She claims that there are several arguments which support this assumption, but mentions only two. Firstly, Swedish is in general left headed, so that the determiner that occurs to the left of the noun is the most likely head. Of course, in an analysis which assumes movement – as Santelmann's does – this is not a very strong argument. In (5.10) the structure is left headed even though *-en* is assumed to be the head. Santelmann's second argument is 'furthermore, positing *den* as the head of D^0 [*sic*] still allows us to place *-en* in a position lower in the structure, and makes it possible to account for the distribution of these elements' (Santelmann 1992: 105)

According to Santelmann, there is broad typological evidence for an extra functional node between D and N within the noun phrase (she refers to Carstens 1990, Giusti 1992, Ritter 1991, Valois 1990), and, therefore, *-en* can be analysed as a syntactic element without being placed in D. She thus posits a functional node between DP and NP under which DEF is found. She follows Ritter in labelling it NumP. She assumes (pp. 106–7) that what she terms the enclitic article (in Num^0) is selected by 'a definite noun phrase'.[8] This gives the structure in (5.11) (Santelmann (1992: 109). In (5.11) the noun moves from N to Num^0 because the element in Num^0 is bound and therefore requires a host. Santelmann furthermore assumes that definiteness features are found under D in Swedish and that they are 'strong' in the sense of Chomsky (1992, 1995) so that they need to be supported by a lexical element. This means that DEF with its noun host must move into D^0 to support these features. So, the noun phrase *musen* is the result of the definite ending (with the attached noun) raising via head movement to the D node. This is not the only possibility of movement for DEF. As we will see in section 5.4.2.1, the bound element may also lower to the N node to find a host.

(5.11)

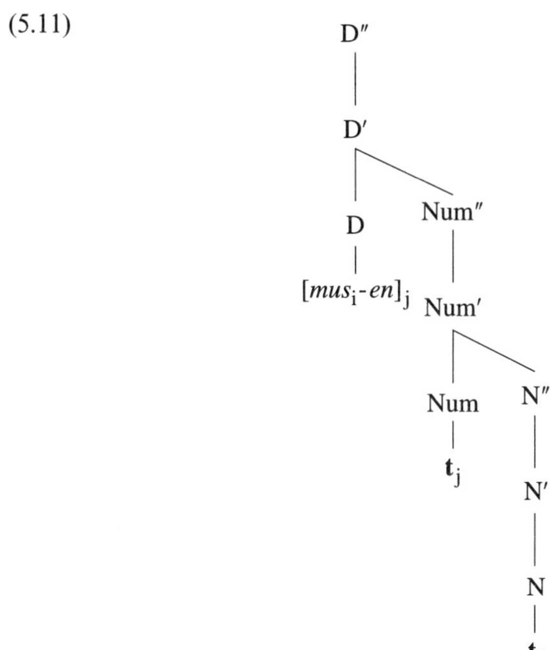

Santelmann's analysis then differs from the one represented in (5.10) in that DEF is not a syntactic determiner – that is, D^0 – underlyingly, but it is similar to (5.10) in that DEF with its noun host does fill the D^0 position in the surface structure. I will return to Santelmann's arguments in favour of this more complex analysis in sections 5.3.2.1 and 5.4.2.1.

5.2.2.2. *Analyses in which* DEF *does not have independent syntactic status*

Cooper (1984, 1986) assumes that DEF does not have independent syntactic status. In his analysis, DEF is the morphological realization of a feature [+DEF] on the head noun of a noun phrase. Thus his analysis must explain why these noun phrases need not contain a syntactic determiner. For every issue relating to Swedish noun phrases, Cooper (1984) suggests two solutions, one syntactic and one semantic in nature. In this chapter, I will give an account of both, even though the semantic solution is the most elegant and appears to be the one Cooper favours. I will do so because Cooper's (1984) is the only detailed example of a traditional phrase-structure approach to Swedish noun phrases and it is of interest because it shows that a syntactic solution is possible within a context-free grammar.

In the syntactic solution, the grammar of Swedish is assumed to contain a number of quite specific phrase-structure rules referring to noun phrase-structure. The rule relevant to the type of noun phrase dealt with in this section is found in (5.12) (Cooper 1984: 134).[9]

(5.12) $N^2 \rightarrow \underset{\begin{bmatrix} +\text{DEF} \\ \alpha \end{bmatrix}}{N}$

This rule is one of the seven needed under this solution to generate all Swedish noun phrases. A number of the rules are formulated in terms of a disjunction and require the categories involved to have specific feature values. Cooper points out that under such a solution a number of syntactic generalizations are lost. He also shows that in order to assign the correct semantic interpretation to some of the Swedish noun phrases, this system of rules would have to be made even more complex.

Instead, Cooper (1984: 138–42) proposes a solution in which all Swedish noun phrases are generated by two very general phrase-structure rules. These are found in (5.13).

(5.13) a. $N^2 \rightarrow (\text{Det}) \quad N^1$

b. $N^1 \rightarrow \begin{Bmatrix} \text{Adj} \quad N^1 \\ N \end{Bmatrix}$

These rules generate a large number of feature combinations which are not possible Swedish noun phrases. For instance, the rule in (5.13a) does not impose any restrictions on when the determiner is optional. The illicit structures are then filtered out by semantic interpretation rules. The rule relevant to the interpretation of noun phrases consisting of just one definite noun can be found in (5.14). In these rules, ⟦X⟧ stands for 'the interpretation of X'.[10]

(5.14) $[\![[[\underset{\substack{+\text{DEF} \\ \alpha}}{N}]_{\underset{\alpha}{N^1}}]_{\underset{\alpha}{N^2}}]\!] \rightarrow \text{THE}([\![N^1]\!])$

Another of the interpretation rules states that if there is no syntactic determiner and the noun is [–DEF], then a special 'propositional' semantic interpretation is forced if the noun is also [SG]. If the noun is [PL] then the propositional reading is possible, but not forced. For a discussion of these cases, see section 6.4.2.

The essence of Cooper's solution is then that the feature instantiated by DEF on a Swedish noun can trigger a semantic interpretation equivalent to that of an independent syntactic determiner, like English *the*. DEF is a semantic determiner in this sense, but not a syntactic one.

Unlike Cooper (1984, 1986), Hellan (1986) assumes that the determiner is the head of a noun phrase. However, as already discussed in section 4.3.2, he does not term the resulting phrase a DP, but refers to it as a T, which is headed by a DET, which in turn takes as its complement an N^{max}. For Norwegian noun phrases corresponding to *musen*, Hellan (p. 102) discusses the possibility of introducing an empty determiner governing N^0 from DET. He rejects this solution, because he claims that the only way to predict correctly the ungrammaticality of noun phrases like (5.15) would be by an *ad hoc* restriction on the distribution of this empty DET.

(5.15) *gamle skoen N
old shoe.DEF

Instead, Hellan (pp. 102–3) proposes that the DET merges with the N^0 and after the merger gets realized on the noun as DEF. Under this solution, the nature of the element contained under the DET node before merger is unclear. Hellan (p. 100) defines four uses of the term ‘definiteness’ with respect to Norwegian (and by extension, Swedish) noun phrases.

(5.16) (i) A T as a whole is *definite*$_1$ if it is unable to occur after a main verb in a presentational construction.

(ii) The suffix *-en* (*-et*/*-a*/*-ene*) on a noun is the *definite*$_2$ article.

(iii) A noun is *definite*$_3$ when it has the *definite*$_2$ article as suffix.

(iv) A DET is *definite*$_4$ when it induces either *definite*$_3$-ness on the noun, or the weak form of the adjective.

Hellan states that the merger of DET and N^0 may only happen to DET[+definite$_4$]. The definite$_2$ article which results appears in two roles: it is the realization of DET[+definite$_4$] and it is a property induced under government by DET [+definite$_4$]. It is unclear to me whether DET before the merger contains a DET [+definite$_4$] determiner like the independent definite article *den*, or whether the DET node contains a feature matrix consisting of just [+definite$_4$]. The first option would be unusual in that one lexical element, *den*, would turn into another lexical element, *-en*, when the nodes merge. The second option, on the other hand, gets close to the empty determiner which Hellan rejects. The principle of Hellan's solution is still quite clear; a syntactic determiner is not necessary in noun phrases like *skoen* because the definite ending represents the property that the determiner would otherwise have to carry.

Svenonius (1992a, 1992b) considers a number of analyses of definite nouns in Scandinavian in which DEF is not assigned the status of a syntactic determiner. In all of them, noun phrases are assumed to be DPs. One of these is based on an idea proposed by Haider (1988a, 1988b) in an account of some aspects of the structure of German noun phrases, but which shares certain characteristics with Hellan's (1986) solution. The analysis is based on the notion of MERGER of 'congruent projections'.[11] The assumption is that empty heads are not permitted because an empty head will not be able to project. It is clear from the analysis that this restriction holds only for the later stage of a derivation, or surface structure. At an earlier stage, an empty head may be present. As Haider (1988b: 47) puts it: 'where an empty head seems to appear, we have a case of a congruent projection.'[12] If the correct conditions pertain, a merger may take place, as illustrated in (5.17)[13] and the projection of the empty head (X^{max}) can be collapsed with the projection of its complement (Z^{max}), so that the specifier of the empty head (SP-X) is mapped onto the specifier of the complement (SP-Z), the head of the complement (Z) onto the empty head (X), etc.

(5.17)

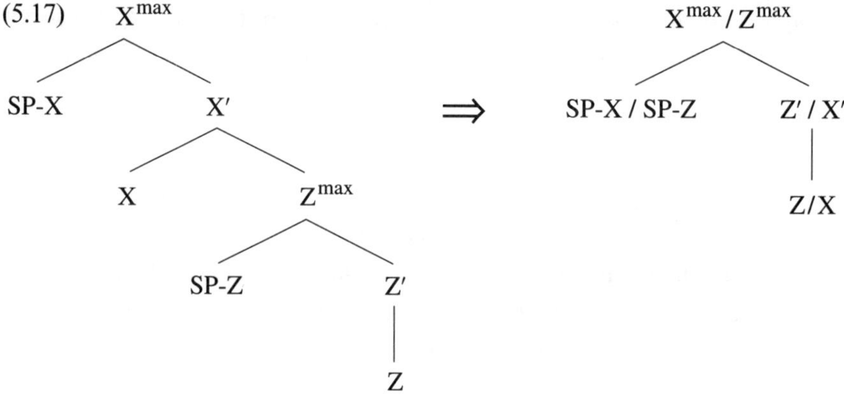

If it is assumed that Swedish has a ∅-determiner which selects a definite noun, then this analysis can be applied to noun phrases like *musen.* The ∅-determiner is found under X and the definite noun under Z. Restrictions on this process will be discussed in sections 5.3.2.2 and sections 5.4.2.2.

Svenonius discusses another analysis which is similar to that of Haider in that the definite ending does not have syntactic status, but the definite noun ends up filling the D position. In this case, the explanation for why a definite noun can function as a full referential noun phrase – in these analyses a DP – is that the N+DEF combination itself functions as a determiner. Under this solution, it is assumed that two things happen when DEF is attached to N in the lexicon. Firstly, by inflection, a noun is formed which has all the features of the original noun plus definiteness. Secondly, there is a derivational rule at work which changes the category of the element from N to D. This is actually a plausible analysis for Danish, since DEF is only present when the definite noun functions as a full noun phrase on its own. The Danish DEF cannot co-occur with any independent syntactic determiner (see section 3.6.3.1). In Norwegian and Swedish, on the other hand, DEF can co-occur with independent syntactic determiners. The derivational rule for these languages would therefore have to be a null derivation which may, but need not, take place when the inflectional rule has added DEF to a noun. As Svenonius (p. 158) points out, this is a drawback with applying this solution to Swedish and Norwegian. Svenonius (1992c: 158) also refers to theoretical problems with this solution relating to the preservation of selectional properties through the derivation.

Svenonius's (1992a, 1992c) most original solution builds on work done by Miller (1992a) on French function words within a phrase-structure grammar framework. Halpern (1992b) also uses the same mechanism for analysing the distribution of DEF within Bulgarian noun phrases. It is based on the Edge Feature Principle (EFP; see section 4.2.3). This principle is similar in its working to the Head Feature Convention (HFC), in that it accounts for the percolation and realization of features relevant at the phrasal level. However, whereas features governed by the HFC percolate to the head of the phrase, the features to which EFP applies will be manifested on the left-most or right-most element of the phrase. In the case of the Norwegian [+DEF] feature (and that of Swedish) it appears to occur on the left-most element. The constraint which applies to Norwegian (and Swedish) noun phrases under this solution is then that the left-most element in a noun phrase must be marked [+DEF]. Obviously, this is a requirement for definite noun phrases only. Svenonius (1992a, 1992c) does not discuss indefinite noun phrases in this respect, and offers no explanation for why *mus* is not a grammatical referential noun phrase (see section 6.2.2).

Svenonius's EFP analysis of Swedish noun phrases is most impressive when applied to noun phrases containing prenominal elements of different kinds. I will discuss this aspect of the analysis in sections 5.3.2.2 and 5.4.2.2. It also turns out that, for certain of these examples, a refinement of the notion of left-most element is required.

The analysis proposed by Payne and Börjars (1994) is based on an idea developed by Payne (1993b). Payne shows that a number of the problems relating to headedness and bar levels which are associated with an analysis in terms of X-bar phrase structure can be avoided. In his alternative solution, Payne makes use of a CG framework augmented by features (see Bach 1983). With reference to a wide variety of languages, Payne shows that their noun phrase structure can be accounted for if noun phrases are assumed to be neither NPs nor DPs. Instead, noun phrases are of the same basic category as a noun, namely N. In order to be able to function as a full noun phrase, a nominal needs to be specified for a feature [DEF], but the value for this feature need not originate from a determiner. No features indicating bar level or a category change are required. Payne and Börjars (1994) show that a more subtle solution is required for Swedish noun phrases. Swedish noun phrases need to be specified as + or – for two features: [DEF] and [INDEF]. However, the basic idea is the same: a noun phrase is a nominal which carries specific values for features related to definiteness. In the case of noun phrases like *musen*, the feature values originate from the noun, and not from a determiner as in the English equivalent *the mouse.* The specification for *musen* is then as in (5.18).[14]

(5.18) *musen*: $\underset{\left[\begin{array}{c}+\text{DEF}\\ -\text{INDEF}\end{array}\right]}{\text{N}}$

As with Svenonius's solution, the advantages of this analysis show up most clearly when noun phrases containing prenominal elements are considered. I will return to this in sections 5.3.2.2 and 5.4.2.2.

In a paper which deals mainly with predicative noun phrases, Holmberg (1992) also provides an analysis of definite argument noun phrases. The analysis is of special interest to me because even though it is formulated within the then current version of transformational theory, DEF is still not assumed to be a syntactic element.[15] Holmberg assumes a distinction between predicative and argument noun phrases in terms of open and closed categories. A predicative noun phrase is an open expression containing a variable in its specifier position which must be bound from outside the phrase. This is similar to the way in which the subject of a sentence binds its VP-internal trace. In the case of predicative noun phrases, the element outside the phrase which binds the variable can be thought of as the subject of that noun phrase. I will return to Holmberg's account of predicative noun phrases in section 6.4.4. An argument noun phrase, on the other hand, is a closed category in the sense that it does not contain a variable which must be bound from outside. Instead, the highest specifier of an argument noun phrase must be licensed internally. This can be done in two ways; either it contains a lexical filler, or it contains an empty pronominal element *pro* which is licensed by specifier–head (Spec–Head) agreement. The element *pro* can be licensed either by a syntactic determiner or by a definite noun. Holmberg follows the principle of minimal structure, so that a noun phrase like *musen* has the structure in (5.19).

(5.19)

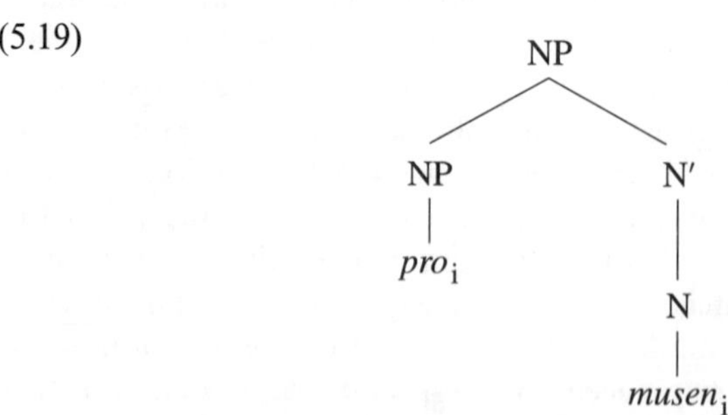

This solution has interesting implications for noun phrases which contain adjectival prenominal modifiers. I will return to this in section 5.4.2.2.

5.2.3. *Proposed analysis and comparisons*

5.2.3.1. *The issues*

In chapter 3, I presented evidence against assigning syntactic status to the Swedish DEF. Hence, to capture the difference in behaviour between elements like *-en* and *denna* simply in terms of a distinction between bound and non-bound syntactic elements, as in the solutions discussed in section 5.2.2.1, is unsatisfactory in my opinion. This means that I will be looking for a solution more akin to those discussed in section 5.2.2.2.

In principle, determination is a matter of semantics, rather than syntax or morphology. A determiner is a function from properties to a set of properties, or in terms of Boolean Semantics, from P to P* (Keenan and Faltz 1985). English is a language where this semantic function must be manifested as a syntactic element, for example, *the.* In Swedish, on the other hand, it can be represented either in the syntax, for example, by *denna*, or in the morphology, by *-en.* It should be pointed out here that, in a typological perspective, the semantic notion of determiner need not be reflected either in the syntax or the morphology. Russian is an example of a language which lacks a definite article.

For Swedish, we can then say that the morphological marking for definiteness does the same job semantically as a syntactic determiner. Therefore, a syntactic determiner need only be present if it is required for independent reasons (see sections 5.3 and 5.4). This means that semantically, *musen* is identical to *the mouse.* Of the analyses discussed in section 5.2.2, it is Cooper's (1984) and Payne and Börjars's (1994) which most closely capture this notion of semantic determination.

However, the selection mechanisms in most major theories refer to syntactic rather than semantic categories.[16] If we assume that *musen* and *denna mus* are similar only in semantic structure, and if we assume that verbs select for syntactic categories, then the subcategorization frame of all verbs which select a noun phrase in Swedish would have to contain a disjunction. In an NP analysis, the distinction would presumably be in terms of NP and N′[+DEF], and in a DP analysis between DP and NP[+DEF]. The selectional properties of a verb like *kittla* 'to tickle' could then be represented as in (5.20).

(5.20) *kittla*:	__ NP	or	*kittla*:	__ DP
	__ N′[+DEF]			__ NP[+DEF]

It strikes me as undesirable to let the subcategorization specification of every single element in the Swedish grammar which can select a full noun phrase contain a disjunction between two types of elements. In each case, the disjunction would contain the same two elements, NP and N′ [+DEF], or, in a DP analysis, DP and NP[+DEF]. In all positions where NP/DP can occur, so can N' [+DEF]/NP[+DEF]. Instead, I conclude from this that since they have exactly the same distribution, as far as the syntactic component is concerned, they really are the same kind of syntactic animal, and should be represented as the same category.

5.2.3.2. *NP analysis*

HPSG offers a convenient formalism for expressing the fact that definite noun phrases may appear without a syntactic determiner. For the details of this HPSG analysis it is crucial that noun phrases are considered NPs rather than DPs. However, it seems plausible that the analysis could be recast as a DP analysis if convincing evidence in favour of D as the head of the noun phrase came to light. For the time being, for reasons given in section 4.5, I will follow standard HPSG assumptions (Pollard and Sag 1994 *pace* Netter 1994, Svenonius 1992a, 1992c and Kolliakou 1994) and provide an NP analysis of Swedish noun phrases.

In standard HPSG, a noun subcategorizes for its determiner through the SPR feature (see section 5.1.2).[17] A definite noun like *musen* can then be specified as 'optionally transitive', in the sense that it has one element on its SPR list, but that this element is optional.[18] I give the relevant SPR values in an abbreviated form for the nouns *mus* and *musen* in (5.21), the parenthesis in (5.21b) indicating the optionality of the determiner with definite nouns.[19]

(5.21) a. *mus*: $\text{SYNSEM}|\ \text{LOC}|\ \text{CAT} \begin{bmatrix} \text{HEAD} & \textit{noun} \\ \text{SPR} & \langle \textit{det} \rangle \end{bmatrix}$

b. *musen*: $\text{SYNSEM}|\ \text{LOC}|\ \text{CAT} \begin{bmatrix} \text{HEAD} & \textit{noun}\,[\text{DEF}\ +] \\ \text{SPR} & \langle (\textit{det}) \rangle \end{bmatrix}$

Naturally, this would not have to be specified for each definite and non-definite noun. Instead, it would be captured in a multiple inheritance hierarchy as something that all definite nouns have in common. Both *mus* and *musen* are of category N, which by combining with a determiner can become phrasal: NP. Since *musen* without a determiner may also function as a full NP, we would have to specify that a noun with an optional *det* on its SUBCAT list will become phrasal even when it does not actually combine with a determiner. Presumably such a rule is independently necessary to capture other cases of optional subcategorization, for example *eaten* and *eaten the last biscuit* should be of the same syntactic category in *Andrew has* ***eaten*** and *Andrew has* ***eaten the last biscuit***, respectively.

A brief discussion of the notion of optional arguments is in order here. If, for the sake of simplicity, we look at all the arguments of an element as one list, including subjects and specifiers (that is, in terms of the SUBCAT list, rather than the three separate lists) then we can think of the core notion of (in)transitivity as that manifested on verbs. If we consider how intransitivity works in this case, we find that the element most similar in behaviour to the verb is the determiner, rather than the noun. In the case of verbs, optional transitivity is an unpredictable property of certain elements of this particular class. For instance, both *eat* and *devour* are activities which involve two participants, the eater/devourer and that which is eaten/devoured. Both these participants are ontologically necessary in Pollard and Sag's terms (1987: 132–3). Furthermore, the relationship between the two participants is quite similar in both cases. Still, *eat* permits one semantic role to be unexpressed, but *devour* does not.[20] This is similar to the behaviour of determiners, where elements which are semantically quite close behave differently with respect to optionality of their SUBCAT elements. The example of *each* and *every* has already been mentioned (see section 4.2.2), where *each* can occur intransitively, whereas *every* cannot. If instead we assume that all definite singular nouns, but no non-definite singular nouns, have an optional element on their SUBCAT list, then this would be like, say, all past tense verbs being optionally intransitive, but all verbs in the present tense having only obligatory elements on their COMPS list. However, I believe that the introduction of the SUBJ, SPEC and COMPS lists provides a different way of looking at this. In the case of optionally transitive verbs, it is an element on the COMPS list which is optional. The nouns, on the other hand, have an optional element on their SPR list, the optionality of which is related to morphological marking on the noun. This is then more closely related to the kind of 'optionality' with respect to the subject that verbs in so-called pro-drop languages exhibit. In some of these cases, the possibility of omitting the subject may be related to the morphological marking on the verb.[21] It seems to me then that optionality on a COMPS list has some different characteristics from optionality on a SUBJ or SPR list.

5.2.3.3. *Netter (1994)*

Netter (1994), working within a modified HPSG framework, does, in effect, make the noun phrase dual-headed.[22] Netter introduces two kinds of HEAD feature: MAJOR and MINOR. The two features encode properties normally associated with lexical categories (N, V, A, Adv) and functional categories (such as Det, Comp), respectively. However, the features are not exclusively associated with categories in this way: a lexical category may be specified for some MINOR feature and vice versa. A noun phrase, in his terms a *dp*, inherits its MINOR features from the determiner – if there is one – but inherits its MAJOR features from the nominal daughter. If there is no determiner present, the MINOR features can be inherited from the nominal. The MINOR features crucially used by Netter are three binary-valued features: [FCOMPL], [SPEC] and [DECL *we/st*]. I will return to the last two features in section 5.4.3.3. For the moment, only FCOMPL is relevant.

Netter (pp. 310–12) introduces the notion of FUNCTIONAL COMPLETENESS, which, in conjunction with SATURATION, defines maximal projections. A singular count noun, for instance, is saturated when it has combined with all elements required by its SUBCAT list (if any).[23] It is then, however, not functionally complete, since it cannot function as a full referential noun phrase. A noun phrase can inherit the crucial [FCOMPL +] either from a determiner, or from certain nouns. In section 5.3.3.3 I will return to noun phrases which contain determiners.

Netter proposes that non-count nouns and plural nouns be unspecified in the lexicon for FCOMPL. In Swedish, definite nouns would also naturally fall into this category. The lack of specification for this feature means that they can take either value, depending on the context. The discussion in this section refers to the contexts in which definite nouns are [FCOMPL +]. Cases where the context induces the value [FCOMPL –] will be dealt with in sections 5.3.3.3 and 5.4.3.3.

If we take an intransitive verb as an example, then in this approach it has one element on its SUBCAT list, namely a *dp*, which is any nominal category specified as saturated: [SUBCAT⟨ ⟩], that is, it has an empty SUBCAT list, and as functionally complete: [FCOMPL +]. This means that an intransitive verb like *nyser* 'sneezes' can unify with a saturated nominal unspecified for FCOMPL, like *musen* 'mouse.DEF', and in doing so it induces the feature value [FCOMPL +] on the noun through the requirement of token identity between the element on the verb's SUBCAT list and the *dp* itself as stated in the Valence Principle (see section 5.1.2). A non-definite singular count noun like *mus* 'mouse', on the other hand, is explicitly specified as [FCOMPL –] and can therefore not be the subject of *nyser*. In order to form a *dp*, *mus* has to combine with a determiner.

For the noun phrases dealt with so far, Netter's (1994) solution does not appear to give strikingly different results from the one I propose in this section: definite nouns are specified in the lexicon for a certain feature in such a way that they may function as full noun phrases. In favour of the pure NP account it can be said that the feature DEF is required independently on the noun. Presumably this feature will also have to be present in Netter's account to distinguish definite and indefinite noun phrases. The advantage of Netter's account, on the other hand, is that it does not require any stipulations about how the noun expands to N′ and NP through unary branching projections. On the other hand, as I have already pointed out, some such mechanism is likely to be required in other constructions, for instance, verb phrases containing optionally transitive verbs without an object, though optionally transitive verbs may also be unspecified with respect to [FCOMPL]. Even though the analyses seem roughly equivalent so far, in section 5.4.3.3, I will show that Netter's (1994) account does not extend easily to all Swedish noun phrases dealt with in this book.

5.2.3.4. *DP analysis*

If we assume that *denna mus* and *musen* should be of the same syntactic category, and also that the category of a full noun phrase is DP, then a definite noun, N[+DEF], should also be a DP. There appear to be two types of DP solution. Firstly, it is possible to introduce a phrase-structure rule like (5.22a) into the grammar, which would yield the tree in (5.22b). I assume here that standard rules about the optionality of modifiers permit the N[+DEF] to project up to NP[+DEF]. A version of this solution is to follow Bresnan (1995) and assume that all elements in a phrase-structure rule are optional unless required by some other principle.

(5.22) a. DP → NP[+DEF]

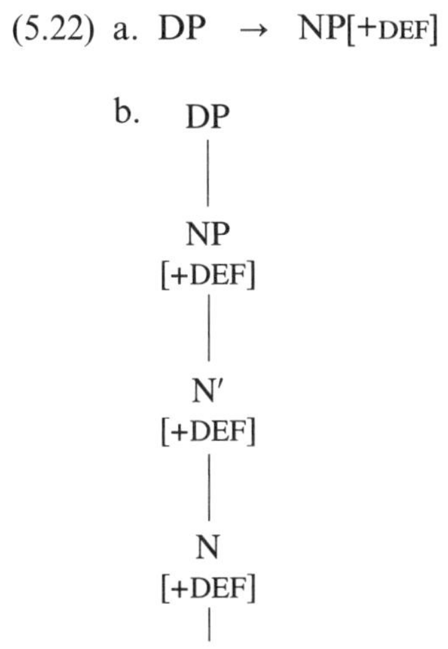

This solution is similar in nature to the syntactic solution proposed by Cooper (1984) (see section 5.2.2.2). Following Cooper, an alternative solution where the semantic interpretation rules do the work is also possible. Under such a solution, any kind of noun phrase lacking a syntactic determiner could be generated by the syntactic component, but only if the noun was definite would such a noun phrase be interpreted by the semantic rules. I will not discuss the semantic solution in more detail here, but focus on the syntactic analyses.

The DP in (5.22b) lacks a head, since there is no lexical node with the same category value as the phrase. A standard assumption within most versions of the X-bar formalism requires that (almost) all phrases must have a head which is lexical and of the same major category as the phrase (though compare discussion in section 4.2.1).[24] This means that the tree in (5.22b) violates one of the basic principles of X-bar syntax.

In order to preserve the assumption that a DP must be headed by a D, a zero determiner must be posited. In order to enure that this element does not occur with non-definite nouns to yield illicit DPs like *[*mus*]$_{DP}$, the zero determiner must be specified as in (5.23a) in the lexicon. The resulting tree is provided in (5.23b).

(5.23) a. ∅: $\left[\text{---} \underset{[+\text{DEF}]}{\text{NP}} \right]_{\text{DP}}$

b. DP

```
DP
|
D'
|\
D   NP
|   [+DEF]
∅   musen
```

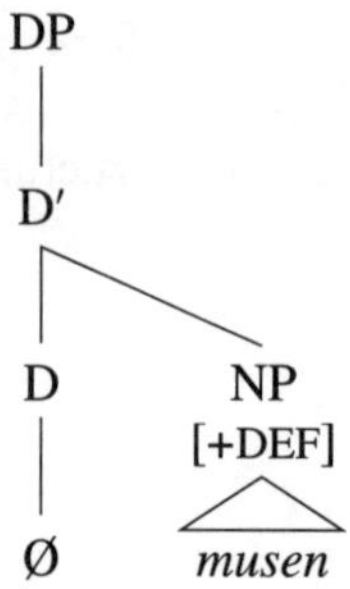

The precise status of the zero element is not clear. It seems unlikely that one would want to equate it with its common use in logic to mean the empty set. Rather it would have to be viewed as the null element of syntactic concatenation, so that a^∅→a. The standard view in transformational grammar is that a node containing a base generated ∅ element really contains a feature bundle, the phonological representation of which is null. In modern transformational theory, analyses involving zero elements are extremely common. Especially if there is morphological marking for some feature relating to the category of the zero element, the standard analysis will often involve a zero element, which is 'licensed' by the morphological marking. Most phrase-structure grammars have, however, been very careful about admitting zero elements into the lexicon. Pollard and Sag discuss the possibility of a phonologically unexpressed determiner in relation to bare plurals in English: 'the lack of any independent syntactic motivation for such a proposal argues strongly against it' (1987: 141). Even though it is not quite clear to me what would constitute independent syntactic motivation for a zero determiner, it seems desirable to avoid zero elements unless forced to adopt them (see Sag and Fodor 1995). In (5.23) the zero element could be related to the morphological definiteness marking on the noun. However, it seems clear that the relation between morphological marking and zero elements is not as direct as it has in general been considered in transformational accounts (see note 21 in this chapter).

5.2.3.5. *Conclusions*

In all three analyses discussed here, the role of the definite marking in allowing the nominal to function as a full referential is indirect. The fact that it is the morphological marking on the noun which does the semantic job of a determiner is not made obvious in any of the proposed solutions. However, I think it is difficult to achieve this in a syntactic solution. Firstly, I am critical of a general principle of morphological marking licensing empty categories. Secondly, the subcategorization frames of verbs refer to syntactic rather than semantic categories: thus elements which are of the same type semantically must be of the same category syntactically.[25] This means that I force an entirely syntactic resolution. It is therefore to be expected that semantic factors will be represented only in an indirect way.

All three proposed analyses involve slightly unorthodox assumptions about phrase structure or lexical elements. In the NP analysis, we must assume that the phrase projects from N′ to N″, even though it does not contain any specifier or subject. We can, however, assume that this will be a general principle of the grammar, which will be activated in all cases of optional selection. In the first of the two suggestions for a DP analysis, we must assume that a maximal phrase need not project normally under certain circumstances. Under the second DP proposal, we have to posit a zero determiner. In a restrictive phrase-structure analysis, the two assumptions associated with the DP analyses are undesirable. They are however, not totally ruled out, and if either of the analyses turns out to account neatly for the Swedish noun phrases, then the assumptions can be said to be motivated.

In this section, I have tried to account for the fact that certain Swedish nouns can function as full referential noun phrases without the presence of a syntactic determiner. There is however another aspect of optionality in relation to the Swedish noun phrases. Most of the Swedish determiners that I have discussed here may also function as full referential noun phrases, without the presence of any nominal element. This can be expressed in different ways. A number of linguists (see discussion in sections 4.2.2 and 4.2.4) have taken this as indirect evidence in favour of a DP analysis, because if we assume that D is the head, and thereby the element which subcategorizes for a complement, then we can capture the optionality of the nominal element in terms of intransitivity. This can then be claimed to be an advantage of the DP analysis in section 5.2.3.4 above the NP analysis in section 5.2.3.2.

Another way of describing these distributional facts of Swedish determiners is to label the determiners ‘pronominal’. This terminology is perfectly compatible with an NP analysis (as well as with a DP analysis, but there the notion of intransitive determiners is more attractive). We could then assume that the determiners which can occur without a noun have two lexical entries, one where its category is described as D, and one where it is described as NP_{PRON}. An alternative to this, suggested already by Sommerstein (1972) and followed up by, for example, Hudson (1984: 90f., 1987: 122–24), is to assume that these elements are not determiners functioning as pronouns – ‘intransitive’ determiners – but that they are pronouns functioning as determiners, – ‘transitive’ pronouns. In an NP analysis, we would assume that pronouns are unanalysable NPs, and we could then conclude that the specifiers (or subjects) of nouns are not of the category Det, but NP.

I will return to this briefly in section 5.5.2. So far, then, there is nothing to choose between the two types of analysis.

5.3. Nouns with syntactic determiners

5.3.1. *The data*

An analysis of the Swedish (or Norwegian) DEF is complicated by the fact that, unlike its correlate in Danish, it can co-occur with other elements which can be assumed to have syntactic determiner status. This phenomenon is often referred to as 'double determination' or 'double definiteness'.[26] Examples from Swedish are provided in (5.24). For corresponding Danish examples, I refer back to section 3.6.3.1. In all the examples 'double determination' is the only grammatical possibility in standard Swedish.

(5.24) a. den musen
that mouse

b. den där / den här musen
that this mouse

c. den gråa musen
the/that grey mouse

This means that analyses, like those discussed in section 5.2.2.1, which assign syntactic determiner status to DEF must explain why two determiners can co-occur in a language that otherwise does not allow determiners to co-occur.

On the other hand, it cannot be assumed that DEF is an agreement marker and that Swedish requires that head nouns agree in definiteness with their determiners. As the examples in (5.25) show, there are also definite determiners which cannot co-occur with a definite noun. *Denna* in (5.25a) is followed by a definite noun in a number of Swedish dialects, but in standard Swedish and my own dialect (5.25a) is the only possibility.

(5.25) a. denna mus
this mouse

b. vilken mus
which mouse

c. samma mus
same mouse

d. varje mus
each/every mouse

In section 5.3.2, I will look at how the analyses discussed in section 5.2.2 deal with this aspect of Swedish noun phrases. In section 5.3.3 I will present an alternative analysis.

5.3.2. *Previous analyses*

5.3.2.1. *Analyses in which* DEF *has independent syntactic status*

Since Delsing (1988, 1989: 14) provides an analysis in which DEF is a syntactic determiner, the phenomenon of double definiteness is in effect a case of co-occurring determiners and as such is unexpected. Most of the examples given by Delsing (1989: 14) involve an adjective intervening between the determiner and the noun, so that they require the solution which will be discussed in section 5.4.2.1. Delsing assumes that *här* and *där* in *den här/där* are equivalent to adjectives, so that he assigns virtually identical structure to *den här musen* 'this mouse' and *den gråa musen* 'the grey mouse'. This will also be discussed in section 5.4.2.1. However, in section 2.2.3 I argued against an analysis of *här* and *där* in *den här/där* as independent elements.

In later work, Delsing (1993: 113–14 and 134–7) claims that Swedish does not, in fact, display double definiteness. In constructions which appear to be instances of double definiteness, only one element is assumed to be definite. He discusses what he claims to be similarities between demonstratives and adjectives and concludes that demonstratives are in fact of the same category as adjectives.[27] The structure for a noun phrase like *den mannen* 'that man.DEF' is then as in (5.26) (see Delsing 1993: 97 and 136).

(5.26)

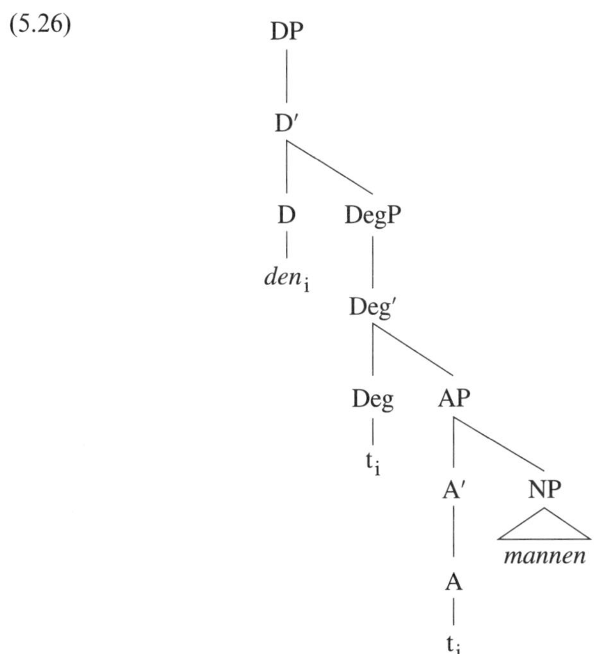

In (5.26) *den* has to raise to D to provide a lexical filler for this position. Delsing (1993: 136) claims that this is not a case of double definiteness since demonstratives are not definite in his analysis.[28] Since I assume that Delsing would not consider the demonstratives indefinite, (5.26) provides an example of a determiner which is neither definite nor indefinite. Hence the DP must inherit its definiteness from the noun.

In Delsing (1993) the demonstrative *denna* in standard Swedish (as in *denna man* 'this man') is assumed to be different from the other demonstratives in that it **is** definite and hence does not permit definiteness on the noun. Delsing does not provide any arguments for this distinction between definite and non-definite demonstratives.

With respect to the dialectal *denna mannen* 'this man.DEF', Delsing (1989, 1993) assumes that *denna* is a quantifier and is found in the same position as quantifiers like *hela* and *alla* (which I assume to be adjectival in nature, see section 2.4). This claim is based on two examples, given here as (5.27) (Delsing 1989: 14, 1993: 137–8).

(5.27) a. hela / detta det gamla huset
whole this the old house.DEF

b. alla / dessa/ *de hans många beundrare
all these the his many admirers

The example in (5.27a) assumes a dialect in which *denna* selects a definite noun. The example in (5.27b), on the other hand presumes a dialect in which *denna* combines with a non-definite noun. For each dialect it holds that the other example in (5.27) involving *denna* would be ungrammatical. This means that it is difficult to take the two examples as an argument in favour of the quantifier status of *denna* in a dialect where one of them can be presumed to be ungrammatical. The example in (5.27a) with *detta det gamla huset* is grossly ungrammatical in my dialect. Examples such as (5.27b) I have analysed in terms of the selectional properties of *denna*. I refer to Börjars (1990) for the details of this analysis. In Delsing's (1993) analysis, the quantifier *alla* 'all' is generated under a nominal node. Assuming an identical treatment of *denna*, the tree in (5.28) results (Delsing 1993: 199).[29]

To my mind, there are objections to the classification of *denna* as a quantifier. None of the other quantifiers referred to by Delsing puts any restrictions on the definiteness features of the noun. As the examples in (5.29) and (5.30) show, the definiteness of the noun is controlled by the determiner, not by the quantifier. In this respect, *denna* is like a determiner: it selects a noun with a particular value for the feature [±DEF], even though dialects vary as to the exact value of this feature. The examples in (5.29) are based on a dialect in which *denna* requires a noun without the definite ending.

(5.28)

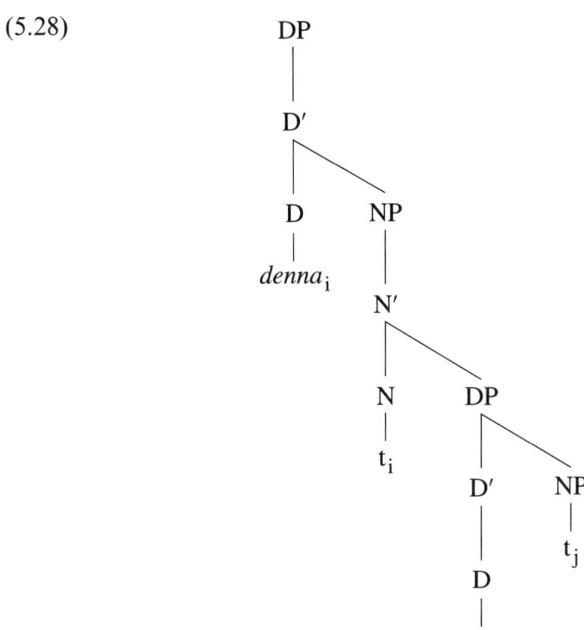

(5.29) a. alla dessa möss / *mössen
all these mice mice.DEF

b. alla de här mössen / *möss
all these mice.DEF mice

(5.30) a. alla möss
all mice
'all mice'

b. alla mössen
all mice.DEF
'all the mice'

Furthermore, if *denna* were a quantifier, it would be unique amongst quantifiers in being able to combine with an indefinite singular count noun to form a full referential noun phrase. This ability is rather a property of determiners like *vilken*, *samma* and *varje*.

In section 2.4 I showed that two categories of prenominal elements can be distinguished in Swedish, depending, for instance, on whether or not the element can carry the possessive ending *-s* when occurring in elliptical constructions in which the noun is not expressed. Adjectives can, but determiners cannot, carry this ending. I showed that elements like *båda* and *alla* behave like adjectives in this respect, but *denna* does not. *Denna* is also unlike the quantifiers and like the determiners in that it cannot be modified (see Payne 1993c). Finally, from a semantic point of view, *denna* is closely related to determiners such as demonstratives rather than to quantifiers.

Santelmann (1992: 102) makes the following claim about examples of double determination where there is no modifier present between the determiner and the adjective: 'In this environment, the noun phrase has emphatic or demonstrative meaning, and intonation and context require the noun to be contrasted with something else, as in example (6a).' Santelmann's example (6a) is repeated here as (5.31), with her emphasis, glossing and translation.

(5.31) **Den** film-en var rolig (men den här film-en var tråkig).
the film-the was funny but this here film-the was dull
'**That** film was funny, but this film was dull.'

In fact, a noun phrase like *den filmen* can always be translated into English as 'that film'. It does not require special emphasis (as the bold in the translation of (5.31) may imply) or a notion of contrast any more than English noun phrases containing *that* do. *Den* as used in (5.31) can occur with or without emphatic stress, but in either case it can only have a demonstrative interpretation. The use of a demonstrative may often involve contrast, but this is not a necessary requirement in Swedish or in English. Someone can utter (5.32a) even if they think that every film they have ever seen was funny, or indeed without ever having seen or heard of another film. (Though admittedly, knowledge of present-day cultural climate and cinematography makes both these alternatives unlikely.) This is shown by the fact that both (5.32b) and (5.32c) are possible follow-ups to (5.32a).

(5.32) a. Den filmen var rolig.
that film.DEF was funny
'That film was funny.'

b. Egentligen har alla filmer jag har sett varit roliga.
'Actually, all films that I have seen have been funny.' (No contrast with a boring film required.)

c. Det är synd att jag aldrig har haft tid att se någon annan film.
'It is a shame that I have never had the time to see another film.' (No contrast with any other film required.)

It seems misguided, therefore, to analyse an example like *den filmen* as an emphatic version of *filmen*. Instead, in a synchronic analysis, Swedish can be assumed to have two homophonous elements *den*: the definite article and the demonstrative. A noun phrase like *den roliga filmen* is thus ambiguous. It can mean 'the funny film' or 'that funny film'.

For Santelmann, however, the idea that *den filmen* is an emphatic construction, rather than a construction containing a demonstrative element *den*, is crucial. Her analysis is based on the idea that Swedish *den* is inserted for emphasis in the way that the English auxiliary *do* is. She terms this 'den-support'. Her claim is that in a definite noun phrase like *filmen*, 'neither the clitic *-en* nor a null D^0 can support the stress at PF.' (1992: 111). The prenominal *den* is therefore inserted under D^0 to support the stress. This means that the noun moves from N^0 to Num^0 since *-en* under Num^0 is a bound element which needs a host (see (5.11) in section 5.2.2.1). However, since the higher D^0 node is now filled by *den*, the noun-*en* combination does not move further. Santelmann is correct in pointing out that the definite ending cannot carry stress. Also, it is difficult to imagine how an empty determiner could carry stress. However, there is a third component in definite noun phrases such as *filmen*, namely, the root noun. As (5.33) shows, the noun in these cases is quite capable of carrying contrastive stress. In order to ensure *den*-insertion and to prevent the subject noun phrase in (5.33) from being derived instead of that in (5.31), Santelmann's analysis crucially involves ordering; *den* must be inserted before noun+DEF 'tries' to raise to D. If *den* is not inserted at this stage, the definite noun could raise and could carry the stress on the root.

(5.33) **Filmen** var rolig, men **boken** tyckte jag var skräp.
film.DEF was funny but book.DEF thought I was rubbish
'The film was funny, but I thought the book was rubbish.'

Santelmann's account also leaves unexplained the fact that *den* in this (in her view) emphatic structure is interpreted as a distal demonstrative rather than a proximal one. If it is just a dummy inserted to carry the stress of emphatic intonation, then might we not expect it to be neutral with respect to distal–proximal? It should also be noted that in Santelmann's analysis, the demonstrative interpretation in *den filmen* and *denna film* arises in two very different ways.

Like Delsing (1988, 1989), Santelmann (1992: 102) assumes that *här* and *där* in *den här/där* should be treated exactly like premodifying adjectives. I will return to her account for this type of double determination in section 5.4.2.1.

5.3.2.2. *Analyses in which DEF does not have independent syntactic status*

Most of the analyses which do not assign syntactic determiner status to DEF assume instead that it is the morphological manifestation of a feature [+DEF]. A noun lacking the definite ending would then naturally be considered to be of the category N[–DEF]. For such analyses, combinations such as *denna mus* have to be accounted for separately, since there is disagreement with respect to the value for [±DEF] between the noun, on the one hand, and the determiner and the noun phrase as a whole, on the other.

Cooper (1984: 129–30) suggests a syntactic solution to this which is based on selectional restrictions between the determiner and its sister constituent. He suggests a number of different solutions, but the main idea in all of them is that disagreement with respect to the value for [±DEF] is permitted between an N^0 and its mother. The different propositions are really equivalent, and I will just discuss one of them here. In this version, rather than introducing more features, Cooper makes use of a distinction in terms of category. Determiners are subcategorized as admitting one of the two rules in (5.34a) or (5.34b). The category $N^{1.1}$ is expanded as in (5.34c).

(5.34) a. $\underset{\alpha}{N^2} \rightarrow \underset{\begin{bmatrix} N^1 \\ \alpha \end{bmatrix}}{\text{Det}} \; \underset{\alpha}{N^1}$

b. $\underset{\alpha}{N^2} \rightarrow \underset{\begin{bmatrix} N^{1.1} \\ \alpha \end{bmatrix}}{\text{Det}} \; \underset{\alpha}{N^{1.1}}$

c. $\underset{\begin{bmatrix} +\text{DEF} \\ \alpha \end{bmatrix}}{N^{1.1}} \rightarrow \underset{\begin{bmatrix} -\text{DEF} \\ \alpha \end{bmatrix}}{N}$

As discussed in section 5.2.2.2, Cooper (1984: 138–42) also provides a semantically based solution which avoids a number of the problems associated with the syntactic proposal. The syntactic rules are the same as those quoted in (5.13). The relevant semantic rule is given in (5.35).

(5.35) $[\![[\underset{\substack{\text{poss} \\ \text{detta} \\ +\text{DEF} \\ \alpha}}{\text{Det}} \; [\ldots \underset{\substack{-\text{DEF} \\ \alpha}}{N} \ldots]_{\underset{\substack{+\text{DEF} \\ \alpha}}{N^1}}]\!]_{\underset{\substack{+\text{DEF} \\ \alpha}}{N^2}} \rightarrow \text{Det}\,([\![N^1]\!])$

In principle, all Cooper's solutions are based on the idea that a definite determiner like *denna* carries some feature which allows the following head noun to disagree with it in definiteness. The NP as a whole is definite. Note that this is done without assuming that the determiner is the head. The restriction is defined through legal sub-trees rather than a relation between a head and its complement.

Hellan (1986) also accounts for this phenomenon in Norwegian in terms of the determiner putting restrictions on the shape of the following noun. However, for Hellan this is an argument in favour of assuming that the determiner is the head. Hellan (pp. 90, 100) assumes that, for X to require the presence or absence of certain properties on Y, X must govern Y. Hellan (p. 90) further assumes that the element which can exert government within a constituent is the head of that constituent. Since certain definite determiners require the absence of the definiteness marker ([+definite$_2$] in Hellan's 1986: 100 terms) on the following noun (see (5.16) in section 5.2.2.2), Hellan assumes that the determiner must head the noun phrase. A Swedish determiner like *den* would then require the presence of the definiteness marker on the head noun of its complement, whereas *denna* would require its absence.

In the merger solution based on Haider (1988a, 1988b) which Svenonius (1992c: 155–6) discusses, the Swedish determiner *denna* would select an indefinite NP complement and *den* a definite one. Since the D position would have been filled in both cases, the functional projection and its lexical complement cannot be collapsed. Haider's analysis would therefore in this case yield a standard DP analysis.

For the radical lexical solution also discussed by Svenonius (1992c: 156–8), it is with noun phrases like *den musen* that the most serious drawback shows up. Under this solution it is assumed that the morphological rule adding DEF to the noun is both inflectional and derivational in nature. It changes an N element into an element of category D which has all the features (except category) of the original N plus definiteness. However, as Svenonius points out, because of examples like *den musen*, Swedish must be assumed to have two separate rules. One is an inflectional rule which turns an N into an N[+DEF]. The other rule is a derivational rule which changes the category from N to D. It is, however, always a null derivation. In examples like $[\textit{musen}]_{DP}$ both rules have applied, but only the first one has left a morphological mark. The second one has changed the category, but with no overt marking. In *den musen*, only the inflectional rule has applied. Noun phrases like *denna mus* are not discussed in the light of this approach.

In Svenonius's (1992c) EFP solution, the presence of DEF on a noun is accounted for by the EFP only when there is no syntactic determiner present. If EFP is the major mechanism for distributing the feature [+DEF], it is unexpected that this feature should be manifested on a noun when the noun phrase as a whole already contains a first element carrying [+DEF]. However, it is obvious from the Swedish and Norwegian data that if *-en* is always the manifestation of a feature [+DEF] then the EFP cannot account for all instances of it. Instead, Svenonius assumes that a determiner places selectional restrictions on its complement, so that in Swedish *den* selects an N[+DEF] and *denna* selects an N[–DEF]. Svenonius (1992a: 11) points out that the N[–DEF] 'does not make the noun phrases "indefinite"; +/–DEF is a morphologically realised feature (historically derived from a definite article) which is not directly semantically relevant.'

Svenonius, who formalizes his EFP solution in HPSG terms, does not seem to adopt the mechanism for selection proposed within this theory by Pollard and Sag (1994). Instead he follows standard assumptions about subcategorization, namely, that in order to select for features the selecting element must be the head. Since he assumes that determiners select for a [+DEF] noun or a [–DEF] one, determiners must head noun phrases. The [–DEF] feature on the noun in noun phrases like *denna mus* will not percolate through to the maximal projection of the whole noun phrase, since D is the head, and the phrase as a whole will always have the same value for [DEF] as the determiner.

The CG solution proposed by Payne and Börjars (1994) relies on lexical under-specification. The differences between *denna* and the demonstrative *den* are expressed in terms of a form of selectional restrictions. Nouns with a definite ending are of category N[–INDEF] and nouns lacking the definite ending are N[uINDEF]. Neither type of noun is specified for the feature [DEF] in the lexicon. *Den* and *denna* are specified as in (5.36).

(5.36) a. *den* (dem.) $\underset{[+\text{DEF}]}{\text{N}} \Big/ \underset{\begin{bmatrix}\text{uDEF} \\ -\text{INDEF}\end{bmatrix}}{\text{N}}$

b. *denna* $\underset{\begin{bmatrix}+\text{DEF} \\ -\text{INDEF}\end{bmatrix}}{\text{N}} \Big/ \underset{\begin{bmatrix}\text{uDEF} \\ \text{uINDEF}\end{bmatrix}}{\text{N}}$

Den can successfully unify with *musen* since this noun is N[–INDEF] and not specified for [DEF]. The result is a phrase of category N[+DEF, –INDEF]. *Den* cannot unify with *mus*, since *mus* is specified as [uINDEF] and *den* is looking for an element which is specified as [–INDEF]. *Denna*, on the other hand, can only unify with *mus* since it is looking for an element specified as [uINDEF]. In a dialect where *denna musen* is grammatical, *denna* would have the specification in (5.36a).

5.3.3. *Proposed analysis and comparisons*

5.3.3.1. *The issues*

The difference in behaviour between the two classes of definite determiners in (5.24) and (5.25) – those which combine with a definite nominal and those which combine with a non-definite one – does not appear to be linked to any other possible classification. The examples are repeated here for convenience as (5.37) and (5.38).

(5.37) a. den musen
that mouse.DEF

b. den där / den här musen
that this mouse.DEF

c. den gråa musen
the/that grey mouse.DEF

(5.38) a. denna mus
this mouse

b. vilken mus
which mouse

c. samma mus
same mouse

d. varje mus
each/every mouse

Both classes contain demonstratives and neither class contains only demonstratives. The difference seems to be idiosyncratic and not derivable from any other feature, at least not in a synchronic analysis. This means that it is best described in terms of feature subcategorization specified in the lexicon or assignment under government. As discussed in section 4.2.4, this type of subcategorization is often taken as evidence that the selecting head must be the head of the phrase. This is the conclusion that both Hellan (1986) and Svenonius (1992c) come to, using quite different frameworks (see section 5.3.2.2). However, in section 5.3.3.2, I will show that an NP analysis of this phenomenon is possible using the tools of HPSG.

The question of headedness is not the only one which is urgent here. It is also necessary to establish what feature, and more controversially, what value is relevant to the selection. I propose that the feature value for which determiners like *denna* select is not [−DEF], but [uDEF]. This means that I consider nouns like *mus* unmarked for definiteness rather than indefinite. The fact that non-definite nouns do not carry overt marking for definiteness, makes this a plausible analysis. This view follows from my conclusion that [DEF] is a semantic feature, in the sense that the value [+DEF] fulfils the function of a semantic determiner. Maintaining this view, I could not claim that the same feature with another value does not have any semantic content and say that in this case it is purely morphological. Hence [–DEF] must be assumed to have semantic consequences, just like [+DEF] does. This semantic view of [DEF] implies that we would not expect a [+DEF] determiner to select a [–DEF] noun. This is contrary to Svenonius (1992c), who defines the criterion for full noun-phrase status in terms of marking by [+DEF] (via the EFP), but who still does not consider it impossible for a [+DEF] determiner to combine with a [–DEF] noun, since this feature value does not make the noun semantically indefinite.

The definite ending, that is, the manifestation of [+DEF], functions as a semantic determiner, and a syntactic determiner does not have to be present unless this is required for independent reasons. This section deals with one case where a syntactic determiner is required, namely, when a more subtle semantic distinction needs to be expressed, such as a demonstrative meaning. Swedish only has morphological marking for simple definiteness; any further distinctions must be made in the syntax.[30] This view is supported by the behaviour of *den* when it combines with a noun without premodification. *Den* is in principle ambiguous between a 'the-reading' and a 'that-reading'. However, when it combines with just a definite noun, only the 'that-reading' is available. Since the definiteness captured by the 'the-reading' is already expressed on a noun like *musen*, there is no independent reason for adding the definite article *den*. The fact that some of the syntactic determiners require that the noun with which they combine retain the definite ending even though it is semantically redundant can be viewed as a historical accident. In section 5.4 I will discuss another type of structure which requires the presence of a syntactic determiner, even if the noun is marked as [+DEF]. In chapter 6 I will show that the analysis of [DEF] as a semantic feature and *mus* as a noun with the feature value [uDEF] can actually help explain certain facts about indefinite noun phrases as well.

5.3.3.2. *NP analysis*

I am assuming here that DEF is a HEAD feature, which applies to both *det* and *noun* elements. It is also possible to envisage a much more semantically oriented analysis of definiteness, but I will not explore this further here. A determiner and its nominal sister will stand in a specifier–head relationship to each other. Since this relationship involves mutual selection, through SPEC and SPR, respectively, there are in principle two ways of expressing the patterns of co-occurence between the two elements: either the determiner selects for a definite (or non-definite) nominal, or the noun selects a definite (or indefinite) determiner. The latter of these possibilities is uneconomical to say the least. In such an account, non-definite nouns like *mus* would be able to select for either a definite or an indefinite determiner. We would then have to specify further exactly which definite determiners these nouns could select, to ensure that noun phrases like **den mus* were not accepted. This could take the shape either of a second feature on the noun, or a special feature on the determiner. This solution would then require two features, whereas if we allow the determiner to select for its noun, only one feature is required. I conclude therefore that it is the determiner which selects for the value of DEF on the noun. Within HPSG, this does not, however, mean that the determiner must be the head, *pace* Svenonius (1992c: 147–8)).

In the HPSG solution which I propose, Swedish definite determiners have as their value for the SPEC feature either N′ [DEF +] or N′ [DEF *u*]. In (5.39) I provide sample entries for the demonstratives *denna* and *den*, where I have abbreviated the path, to start at LOC. The value for SPEC has also been simplified. The value of SPEC is actually an element of the type *synsem*, that is, a whole sign except its phonological value. In (5.40). I provide a more expanded description of N′ [DEF +]. The structure sharing which ensures agreement for INDEX features is indicated by subscripts. This means that the information contained must be able to describe the same element, that is, the feature matrices must be unifiable.

(5.39) a. *den*:

$$\begin{bmatrix} \text{CAT} & \begin{bmatrix} \text{HEAD} & det \begin{bmatrix} \text{DEF} & + \\ \text{SPEC} & \text{N}' \ [\text{DEF} +]\ [1] \end{bmatrix} \end{bmatrix} \\ \text{CONT} & \begin{bmatrix} \text{RESTIND}\ [1] & \begin{bmatrix} \text{INDEX} & \begin{bmatrix} \text{PER} & 3 \\ \text{NUM} & sg \\ \text{GEND} & com \end{bmatrix} \end{bmatrix} \end{bmatrix} \end{bmatrix}$$

b. *denna*:

$$\begin{bmatrix} \text{CAT} & \begin{bmatrix} \text{HEAD} & det \begin{bmatrix} \text{DEF} & + \\ \text{SPEC} & \text{N}' \ [\text{DEF}\ u]\ [1] \end{bmatrix} \end{bmatrix} \\ \text{CONT} & \begin{bmatrix} \text{RESTIND}\ [1] & \begin{bmatrix} \text{INDEX} & \begin{bmatrix} \text{PER} & 3 \\ \text{NUM} & sg \\ \text{GEND} & com \end{bmatrix} \end{bmatrix} \end{bmatrix} \end{bmatrix}$$

(5.40)

$$\text{SYNSEM} \begin{bmatrix} \text{LOC} \begin{bmatrix} \text{CAT} & \begin{bmatrix} \text{HEAD} & noun\ [\text{DEF} +] \\ \text{SPR} & \langle det\ [1] \rangle \\ \text{LEX} & - \end{bmatrix} \\ \text{CONT} & \begin{bmatrix} \text{INDEX}\ [1] & \begin{bmatrix} \text{PER} & 3 \\ \text{NUM} & sg \\ \text{GEND} & com \end{bmatrix} \end{bmatrix} \end{bmatrix} \end{bmatrix}$$

The AVMs in (5.39) state that *den* and *denna* are both of the (functional) category Det and that they are both definite.[31] They are specifiers, and can therefore put restrictions on the element with which they combine through the SPEC feature. Both elements combine with an N′ element, but *den* requires that the N′ have the head feature value [DEF +], whereas *denna* requires that the N′ carry the feature value [DEF *u*].

The nouns with which the determiners may combine will have the specifications in (5.41). The determiners do not strictly speaking combine directly with nouns, but rather with projections of nouns, which may or may not contain modifiers such as adjectives (see section 5.4.3.2). All relevant features will, however, percolate from lexical elements such as those in (5.41) to their mothers.[32]

(5.41) a. *mus*:

$$\begin{bmatrix} \text{CAT} & \begin{bmatrix} \text{HEAD} & noun\ [\text{DEF}\ u] \\ \text{SUBJ} & \langle\ \rangle \\ \text{COMPS} & \langle\ \rangle \\ \text{SPR} & \langle det\ [1]\rangle \end{bmatrix} \\ \text{CONT} & \begin{bmatrix} \text{INDEX}\ [1] & \begin{bmatrix} \text{NUM} & sg \\ \text{GEND} & com \end{bmatrix} \end{bmatrix} \end{bmatrix}$$

b. *musen*:

$$\begin{bmatrix} \text{CAT} & \begin{bmatrix} \text{HEAD} & noun\ [\text{DEF}\ +] \\ \text{SUBJ} & \langle\ \rangle \\ \text{COMPS} & \langle\ \rangle \\ \text{SPR} & \langle (det\ [1])\rangle \end{bmatrix} \\ \text{CONT} & \begin{bmatrix} \text{INDEX}\ [1] & \begin{bmatrix} \text{NUM} & sg \\ \text{GEND} & com \end{bmatrix} \end{bmatrix} \end{bmatrix}$$

Both elements are of category noun, *mus* is [DEF *u*] and *musen* is [DEF +]. Neither selects a subject or any complements, but both select a specifier of the category *det*. In the case of the definite noun, the specifier is optional (see (5.21) in section 5.2.3.2). The basic rule for this optionality can be said to be that a determiner is only present if it is required for independent reasons. One reason might be that a semantically more specific determiner, say a demonstrative, is required to express the desired meaning. In such cases, definite nouns may co-occur with the determiners which select a definite noun, through their SPEC feature.[33] The SPR value of the nouns need not be further defined in terms of definiteness, since the SPEC values of the determiners themselves will ensure that only the legal combinations are accepted. In the case of the noun with the value [DEF *u*] this is, of course, a desirable result, since, if we had to specify the selected determiner in (5.41a) as [DEF +], we would need a second entry for every non-definite noun. In this second entry, the determiner on the SPR list would have to be specified as [DEF –], since *mus* can also combine with determiners like *en* 'a'. In the entry in (5.41b), the determiner will in effect always be definite, but since this selectional restriction is specified on the determiner, there is no need to specify it on the noun as well. Their INDEX values are identical, which ensures, for instance, that noun phrases projected from these nouns will be able to co-index with the same set of pronouns.

Given these lexical entries, the ID schemata in co-operation with the other principles governing feature distribution (see section 5.1.2) will generate phrase structures. Given the lexical entries for *denna* and *mus*, the schemata and principles could generate the sub-tree in (5.42) with structure sharing as indicated.

(5.42)

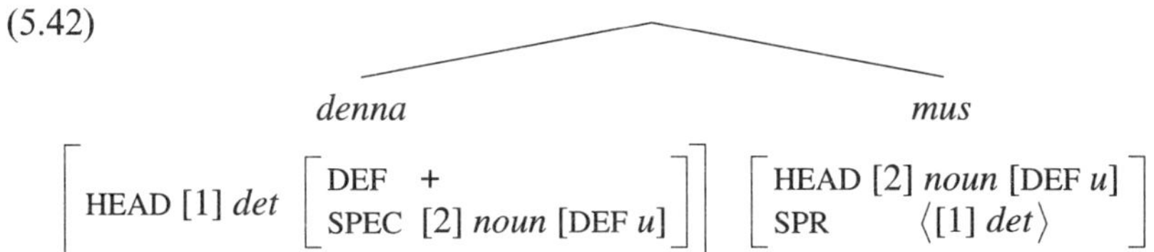

In (5.42), the determiner's SPEC feature is satisfied by the N′ sister and its value for DEF. The Valence Principle (see section 5.1.2) will ensure that the mother's SPR value is ⟨ ⟩, that is, that the mother is saturated. There is a remaining problem which I touched on in section 4.2.3, namely, that the mother's value for DEF must be inherited not from the head, but from the non-head. Much against the spirit of HPSG, I will assume some form of non-head inheritance. I firmly believe that, given the facts and discussion in section 4.2.3, non-head inheritance is a necessary part of feature distribution. I shall assume that if the head is not marked for a particular feature and the non-head daughter is, then the mother will receive that feature value if it is compatible with its category feature (and any other feature specifications it carries). The resulting noun phrase, assuming non-head inheritance is then (5.43).

(5.43)

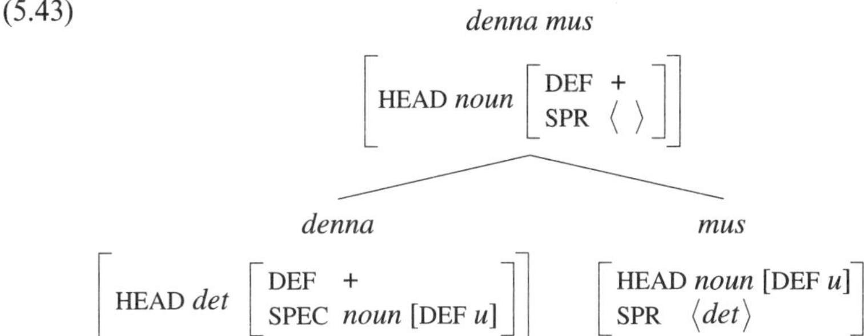

5.3.3.3. *Netter (1994)*

The HPSG analysis proposed by Netter (1994) extends straightforwardly to the determiner+noun combinations discussed here. In Netter's approach, a determiner is a functional element which subcategorizes for a saturated nominal, specified as [FCOMPL –]. Its own value for the feature is [FCOMPL +]. Since determiners are functional elements, they pass on their feature values for all MINOR features – of which FCOMPL is one – to their mother node. With respect to subcategorization and MINOR feature inheritance, the determiner is then the head of a noun phrase. The values for the MAJOR features are inherited from the nominal element. Netter's distinction between MAJOR and MINOR HEAD features is then, in effect, another way of approaching the problem of non-head inheritance, in that the determiner is made the head for the purpose of some features. However, I do not exclude the possibility that features which are not HEAD features may need to be inherited from a non-head, for example, some of the INDEX features.

A noun which is unspecified for the feature FCOMPL can assume the value [FCOMPL +] and hence function as a full noun phrase (see section 5.2.3.3). This includes plural count nouns and non-count nouns in German, and also definite nouns in Swedish. On the other hand, such a noun can also combine with a determiner and then its feature value is set as [FCOMPL –] through unification with the value of the element on the determiner's SUBCAT list. In the latter case, the noun combines with the determiner to form a *dp* which is headed by the determiner. Nouns, like singular count nouns, which are specified as [FCOMPL –] in the lexicon can, of course, also combine with these determiners.

There still do not seem to be any strong arguments for or against Netter's analysis as applied to the Swedish data, as opposed to the NP analysis I have proposed here. It should be pointed out that the feature DEF would have to be present also in an account in terms of FCOMPL. Determiners always select for an [FCOMPL –] nominal. The distinction between *den* 'that' selecting a noun like *musen* 'mouse.DEF' and *denna* 'this', selecting a noun like *mus* 'mouse' would still have to be expressed in terms of a definiteness-related feature. With respect to the type of noun phrases to be discussed in section 5.4, clear differences between the two accounts will appear.

5.3.3.4. *DP analysis*

As discussed in section 5.3.3.1, the feature [DEF] which is morphologically marked on the noun, and semantically inherent in determiners, is not an agreement feature in Swedish; instead a determiner selects its nominal sister with respect to definiteness. The selectional restrictions which appear to hold between determiners and nominals in Swedish can be quite straightforwardly described if D is assumed to be the head of the noun phrase. In this analysis, D will subcategorize for a nominal sister which is specified either as [+DEF] or [–DEF] if we assume that a noun like *mus* is actually indefinite, and [uDEF] otherwise.

The selectional restrictions of *den* and *denna* can then be expressed as in (5.44).

(5.44) a. *den*: D[+DEF]
[__ NP[+DEF]]$_{DP}$

b. *denna*: D[+DEF]
[__ NP[uDEF]]$_{DP}$

In (5.44) I have assumed that D selects an NP as its sister. If we follow standard X-bar assumptions about phrase structure, then this NP could potentially have the structure in (5.45).

(5.45)

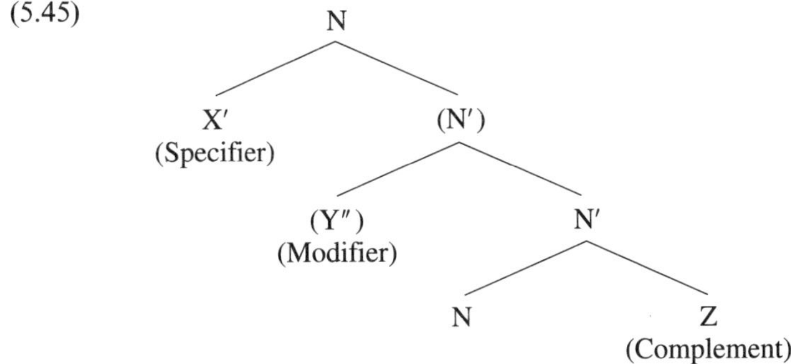

Certain nouns do indeed take a complement, like *bild* 'picture' which selects a PP[*av*] (PP[*of*]) as its complement. The N′ is recursive so that more than one modifier may be present; premodifying APs do indeed occur recursively in the noun phrase. It is, however, difficult to imagine what could fill the specifier position of the NP.[34] In NP analyses, the determiner is standardly assumed to be the specifier, but in a DP analysis this is not an option, since the determiner is the head that selects the NP. Note that the specifier is assumed to be unique, since it expands an N′ to an N″. This problem holds more generally when functional categories are introduced. If adjective phrases are assumed to be DegPs, for instance, then it is unclear whether the AP complement of Deg can really contain an overt specifier. In a phrase-structure solution, it is undesirable to permit structures containing nodes that cannot ever contain lexical material. In an analysis by Fukui and Speas (1986) it is argued that, if functional categories are assumed to be heads, their lexical category complements are of category X′, rather than X″. In Börjars (1990) this idea has been applied to Swedish noun phrases containing prenominal genitives. However, for the issues that I will deal with here, it is not crucial whether the complement of D is N″ or N′.

In Swedish noun phrases, it is the definiteness feature of the determiner which decides the definiteness feature of the noun phrase as a whole. In the structures produced by lexical entries such as (5.44), this is what is expected, since the D is the head of the structure and DEF is a head feature. This means that there is no need for a non-head inheritance rule to ensure correct distribution of DEF in this analysis. This does not, however, mean that a non-head inheritance rule as such is not required under this solution. There will be features that are only manifested on the noun which are relevant to the phrase as a whole, and such features would have to be distributed by a rule permitting mothers to inherit features from the complement rather than the head daughter. This confirms my view that some form of non-head inheritance must be allowed (see section 4.2.3). The same effect can, of course, be achieved by assigning partial head status to the constituent which is not the full head, as in Netter (1994).

In (5.44b) the head D selects a nominal complement which is specified for a feature for which the head is also specified, but the complement has a different value for that feature. This means that the D passes on a feature value to its head which is different from the value it requires its complement to have. Note that this is something which frequently occurs in the grammar of Swedish. For instance, in the sentence in (5.46a), each verb selects a verbal complement with a value for the feature VFORM which differs from that of the selecting head (see Svenonius (1992c: 146–7). In order to account for the distribution of each individual VP, we must assume that its VFORM feature percolates from the head to its mother. This is illustrated in (5.46b), where PST, SUP and INF are all values of the feature VFORM.

(5.46) a. Musen hade velat äta osten.
mouse.DEF have.PST want.SUP eat.INF cheese.DEF
'The mouse had wanted to eat the cheese.'

b. *hade*: V [PST]
[__ VP [SUP]] $_{\text{VP [PST]}}$
velat: V [SUP]
[__ VP [INF]] $_{\text{VP [SUP]}}$
äta: V [INF]
[__ NP] $_{\text{VP [INF]}}$

5.3.3.5. *Conclusions*

In section 5.2.3.5 I concluded that, even though the NP analysis and the DP analysis dealt with noun phrases like *musen* in different ways, there was no reason to prefer one to the other. In sections 5.3.3.2 and 5.3.3.4, the two analyses have been applied to slightly more complex noun phrases, where selectional restrictions hold between the determiner and the noun. I argued that it is the determiner, rather than the noun, which imposes selectional restrictions, but I also showed that, with the mechanisms contained in HPSG, this does not mean that the determiner must be the head. I have also argued for an analysis of nouns not carrying the definite ending as [uDEF], rather than [–DEF]; further evidence for this assumption will be provided in chapter 6. This assumption has been introduced in both the NP and the DP analysis.

With respect to the feature [±DEF], I have found that the data discussed in this section can be captured in a slightly simpler way within a DP analysis. The DP analysis involves a head D selecting an NP or an N′ specified for the feature [uDEF]. The value for the head feature DEF is inherited from the head D to the DP, to make the phrase as a whole [+DEF]. The NP analysis does not, however, involve any mechanisms which are not assumed to be part of the theory for independent reasons. In the NP analysis, the head noun selects the determiner through its SPR feature, but it does not impose any further restrictions on the D which it selects. In HPSG, the specifier–head relation is one of mutual selection, and the specifier, in this case D, can therefore restrict the types of N′ with which it combines. This is done through the specifier's HEAD feature SPEC, which has the value N′ [DEF +] for *den* and N′ [DEF *u*] for *denna*. The mother node NP may get the correct feature specification either from the head noun or, when this head is unspecified for the feature, through inheritance from a non-head daughter.

The conclusion is that both analyses can deal with the data adequately, though the DP analysis does so with less machinery than the NP analysis. However, the mechanisms required in the NP analysis are of the kind present in the HPSG framework for independent reasons. The discussion in this chapter has therefore not forced a choice between the two approaches. On the basis of the discussion in Chapter 4, I concluded that an NP analysis is preferable as long as a way of specifying the selectional restrictions between determiners and nouns can be found. If this is taken into account the discussion so far can be said to favour the NP analysis.

5.4. Nouns with adjectives and determiners

5.4.1. *The data*

In Swedish, and the other Mainland Scandinavian languages, a noun phrase consisting of a definite noun preceded by an adjectival modifier is ungrammatical.[35, 36] In such noun phrases, the independent syntactic definite article must precede the adjectival modifier. The adjective occurs in a special form, referred to as 'weak' in the traditional literature. Examples are provided in (5.47). The corresponding form in indefinite noun phrases is 'strong'; I will return to these in chapter 6.

(5.47) a. *hungriga musen
hungry.WK mouse.DEF

b. den hungriga musen
the hungry.WK mouse.DEF

c. *sömniga murmeldjuren
sleepy.WK marmot.PL.DEF

d. de sömniga murmeldjuren
the sleepy.WK marmot.PL.DEF

If the noun phrase contains one of the other syntactic determiners, such as a demonstrative or a *wh*-determiner, then the independent definite article is not required. As the examples in (5.48) and (5.49) show, the adjective following these definite determiners will be weak regardless of whether the determiner selects a definite noun or not.

(5.48) a. den här hungriga musen
this hungry.WK mouse.DEF

b. den hungriga musen
that hungry.WK mouse.DEF

(5.49) a. denna hungriga / *hungrig mus
this hungry.WK hungry.STR mouse

b. samma hungriga / *hungrig mus
same hungry.WK hungry.STR mouse

The same holds true for perfect participles when they function as prenominal modifiers, as demonstrated by (5.50a). Since these elements inflect similarly to adjectives (5.50b–d), the two types of prenominal modifiers can be treated as one category for these purposes.

(5.50) a. *(det) skrivna brevet
the written.WK letter.DEF

b. ett skrivet / gammalt brev
a written.STR.NT old.STR.NT letter(NT)

c. en skriven / gammal dikt
a written.STR.COM old.STR.COM poem(COM)

d. några skrivna / gamla brev
some written.STR.PL old.STR.PL letter.PL

Postmodifiers differ from premodifiers in that they do not require the presence of an independent syntactic determiner. In fact, they do not permit the syntactic definite article unless its presence is required for independent reasons. Examples with a preposition phrase, an adverb (or intransitively used preposition), and an infinitival phrase, respectively, are provided in (5.51). Relative clauses, which always follow the noun in Swedish, pose special problems for an analysis of both definite and indefinite noun phrases and I will not discuss them at all here. I refer to Payne and Börjars (1994) for a discussion of relative clauses and an analysis in terms of CG. I will not discuss post modifiers in any more detail here.

(5.51) a. musen i fällan
mouse.DEF in trap.DEF

b. *den mus(en) i fällan
the mouse(DEF) in trap.DEF

c. musen framför
mouse.DEF in front

d. *den mus(en) framför
the mouse(DEF) in front

e. förmågan att misslyckas
ability.DEF to fail

f. *den förmåga(n) att misslyckas
the ability(DEF) to fail

5.4.2. *Previous analyses*

5.4.2.1. *Analyses in which* DEF *has independent syntactic status*

In Delsing (1988), the weak morphology on attributive adjectives in definite noun phrases is accounted for in terms of Case.[37] Since I have not found an account in his later work of how these adjectives receive their weak morphology, I will discuss Delsing's (1988) solution even though aspects of his analysis have changed quite radically since then. The underlying structure of a definite noun phrase with a prenominal adjective according to Delsing (1988) is provided in (5.52) (see note 6 in this chapter).

(5.52)

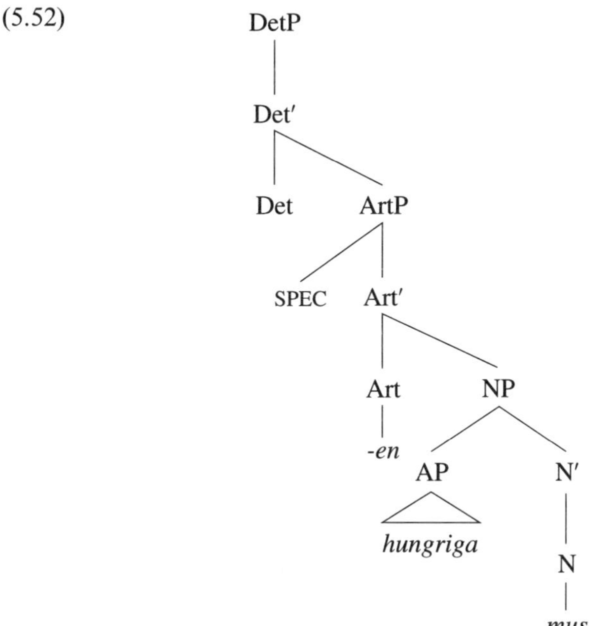

The noun moves into the Art position and attaches to *-en* because the bound element in Art needs a host, and a definite Art can govern the N node. Since adjectives are prenominal in Swedish, there must be something which forces the adjective to move into a prenominal position. It moves from the Spec–NP position to the Spec–ArtP. The trigger of this movement, according to Delsing (1988: 66) is Case assignment. He assumes that a definite, or weak,

AP must be assigned Case. According to Delsing, Case is assigned to the definite AP by Art through the specifier–head relationship. Art can assign case since it is [+definite], and therefore a governor. Note that in this account a weak AP does not require the presence of a syntactic determiner. This is because nominals like *Vita Huset* 'the White House' (see discussion in section 5.5.1.2) are grammatical in Swedish, and Delsing (1988) does not consider this type of phrase to be lexicalized. He assumes that definite noun phrases must be full DPs, and therefore, the independent definite article *den* must be inserted to fill the head of this projection (1988: 70). There are a number of problems with this analysis, but since Delsing appears to have abandoned it in later work, I will just briefly mention some of them here.

There are technical problems, like the exact nature of *den* insertion, and how noun phrases like *Vita huset* can be represented as definite when they lack a Det element. The assumption that the weak morphology is a manifestation of DP-internal Case, which is crucial to this analysis, is motivated by the claim that weak adjectives are 'more noun-like' than strong ones.[38] I am not convinced by Delsing's arguments in support of this claim. Historically, there is a relation between the inflectional morphology on weak adjectives and that on weak nouns. Delsing (1988: 65) claims that weak adjectives are still more nominal in that 'they may constitute a noun phrase together with the definite article'. However, as Thorell (1973: 72) points out: 'an independent adjective can, both in non-neuter and neuter, occur without an article or be preceded by an indefinite article or definite prenominal article.' In the cases where they are preceded by an indefinite article, the adjectives occur in the strong form. The strong form of the adjective can also occur without the indefinite article. In (5.53) examples are given of independently used adjectives which function as indefinite noun phrases and occur in their strong form. Examples (5.53d) and (5.53e) are taken from Thorell (1973: 71–2).

(5.53) a. Jag valde en blå.
I chose a blue.STR
'I chose a blue one.'

b. Rika skall betala mer skatt än fattiga.[39]
rich.STR shall pay more tax than poor.STR
'Rich people ought to pay more tax than poor people.'

c. Det står några kalla i kylskåpet.[40]
there stand some cold.STR in refrigerator.DEF
'There are some cold ones in the refrigerator.'

d. På hela resan träffade jag inte en enda svensk.
during whole journey.DEF met I not a single Swedish.STR
'During the journey, I did not meet a single Swede.'

e. De har fått en liten.
they have received a little.STR
'They have had a baby.'

A further problem with the analysis, as Delsing (1988: 70, note 18) points out himself, is that there is nothing in his analysis that stops *mus-en* in (5.52) from moving from Art to Det, to yield **musen hungriga*. Delsing remarks that the AP appears to have some blocking effect on the movement, but does not develop this idea.

In his more recent articles, it is exactly the idea of the blocking effect of the AP that Delsing explores in an attempt to account for the obligatoriness of *den* with attributive adjectives. As pointed out in section 5.2.2.1, Delsing (1989, 1992) assumes a structure for Scandinavian DPs in which a D subcategorizes for two types of complements: NP, when no attributive adjective is present, and AP otherwise. In the latter case, the NP is found in the (right-hand) specifier position of AP. This gives the structure in (5.54) for *den hungriga musen*.

(5.54)

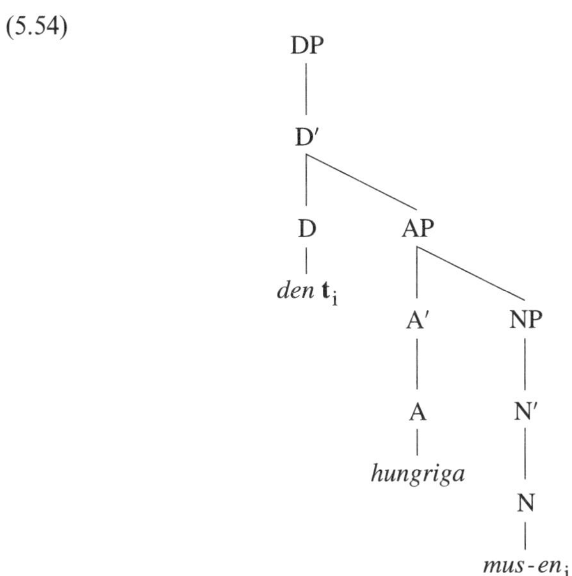

In (5.54), the noun *mus* cannot raise to D because it would not be able to antecedent-govern its trace from the D position, since another potential antecedent governor, A, would intervene (see Relativized Minimality Principle, Rizzi 1990). Delsing (1989: 15) assumes that, instead, the DEF must be lowered to N, leaving a trace behind in D.[41] However, a lexically filled D position is required to properly govern, and assign weak morphology to, the A. He therefore assumes that an article, namely the syntactic *den*, has to be inserted to assign weak morphology to the AP. Delsing claims support for the insertion process in data that I will deal with in section 5.5.1. As I will point out there, it is not clear to me that Delsing's interpretation of the data is the most obvious one.

This analysis of definite APs is maintained in Delsing (1992), where the blocking effects of APs are mentioned as an argument in favour of the Spec–AP analysis advocated there. Delsing refers to his previous article (1989) for a detailed discussion. As mentioned in section 5.2.2.1, in more recent work (1993), he claims that, in this type of construction, DEF is base-generated on the noun, in N. The adjective blocks movement of the definite noun into D. The basic structure of the noun phrase is the same as in (5.54). Since the D position requires a lexical filler, *den* has to be inserted. *Den* is considered an expletive determiner in this analysis and is not assumed to carry any definiteness (like the demonstratives, see section 5.3.2.1). This is in line with Delsing's (1993) assumption that Swedish noun phrases do not in general show double definiteness.[42]

(5.55)

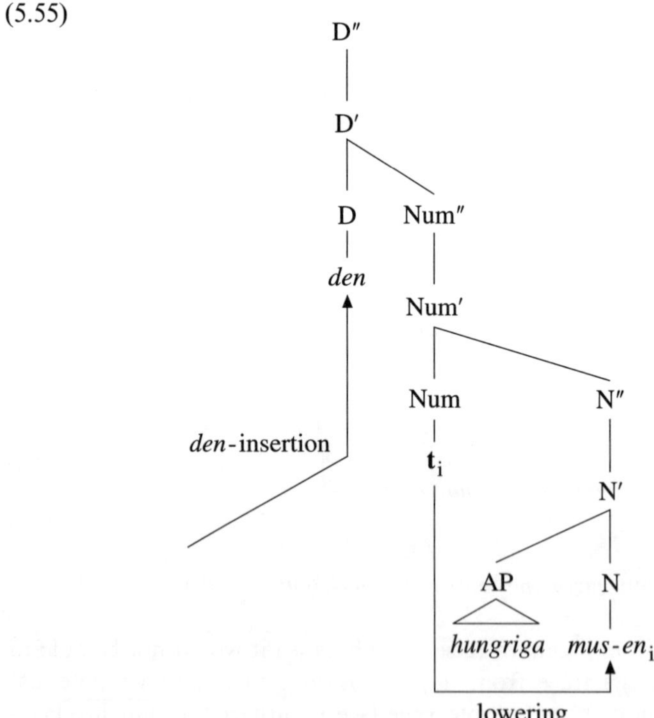

With regard to prenominal adjectives, and also *här* and *där* in the demonstratives *den här/där*, Santelmann (1992: 108) makes a number of specific assumptions. The adjective must receive gender and definiteness features from the noun and the determiner respectively. These features must be received from an m-commanding element. For the licensing of gender by the noun, there is an additional condition, namely, that the relationship between the N and the A be local and lexical. The trace left behind by a noun after head movement (as described in section 5.2.2.1) is not sufficient to license the gender feature on the adjective, and hence the noun may not move when the DP contains an adjective. This means that the bound element *-en* is left without a host in Num^0, and that the strong definiteness features in D are unsupported. Santelmann assumes that *den* is inserted into D^0 to support the strong features found there. The DEF, which cannot find a host by raising, may instead lower to the N node and attach to the noun. This is represented in (5.55).

There are no details about the insertion of *den*, nor is there any indication about where in the derivation this takes place. However, Santelmann compares the nominal *den*-support with the English *do*-support, and presumably the insertion would take place in the same way. In the case of *do*-support, negation is assumed to prevent the verb from moving up to the INFL node, and instead *do* is inserted to support the features found under that node.

5.4.2.2. *Analyses in which* DEF *does not have independent syntactic status*

As in the case of the noun phrases discussed in sections 5.2 and 5.3, Cooper (1984) offers one syntactic and one semantic solution. In the discussion of the syntactic solution, he focuses on the distribution of definiteness features within a noun phrase consisting of a determiner, an adjective and a noun. The problems with this type of noun phrase are similar to those involved in Det+N combinations, namely, that we appear to get a definite determiner combining with an indefinite noun. However, here the problem is made worse by the fact that the adjective has the same marking in all definite noun phrases, regardless of the morphological shape of the noun. Cooper (pp. 123–30) concludes that, in a syntactic solution, introducing two distinct features, [±DEF] and [±WK] is not sufficient. A determiner would then have to be specified for both features, so that *denna* would be [−DEF, +WK]. With these two features, the noun in *denna hungriga mus* 'this hungry.WK mouse.INDEF' would carry the feature [−DEF] but the adjective could still be [+WK]. However, by inheritance, this would mean that the noun phrase as a whole would be [−DEF] which does not make the correct predictions about its distribution. Instead, Cooper (1984: 130) suggests a solution similar to the one he proposes for noun phrases like *denna mus* 'this mouse' (see discussion in section 5.3.2.2). This solution is based on the introduction of a separate node, $N^{1.1}$, which permits disagreement in definiteness between this level and N. There are therefore two different rules introducing adjectives into Swedish noun phrases. These are given in (5.56) (Cooper 1984: 134).

Under this solution, the reason why an adjective must be preceded by a determiner is that all rules introducing N^1 and $N^{1.1}$ also introduce a syntactic determiner.[43]

$$\text{(5.56)}\quad N^1 \rightarrow \left\{ \begin{matrix} \begin{matrix} \text{Adj} & N^1 \\ [\alpha] & [\alpha] \end{matrix} \\ \begin{matrix} \text{N} \\ [\alpha] \end{matrix} \end{matrix} \right\} \quad \text{and} \quad \begin{matrix} N^{1.1} \\ \begin{bmatrix} +\text{DEF} \\ \alpha \end{bmatrix} \end{matrix} \rightarrow \left\{ \begin{matrix} \begin{matrix} \text{Adj} & N^{1.1} \\ \begin{bmatrix} +\text{DEF} \\ \alpha \end{bmatrix} & \begin{bmatrix} +\text{DEF} \\ \alpha \end{bmatrix} \end{matrix} \\ \begin{matrix} \text{N} \\ \begin{bmatrix} -\text{DEF} \\ \alpha \end{bmatrix} \end{matrix} \end{matrix} \right\}$$

In the semantic solution offered by Cooper (1984) there are only two syntactic rules, namely those represented in (5.13), repeated here as (5.57).

$$\text{(5.57)}\quad N^2 \rightarrow (\text{Det})\quad N^1$$

$$N^1 \rightarrow \left\{ \begin{matrix} \text{Adj} & N^1 \\ & \text{N} \end{matrix} \right\}$$

These two rules drastically over-generate, but interpretation rules are more restrictive and can process only the correct noun phrases. The interpretation rules relevant for noun phrases containing adjectives are given in (5.58) (Cooper 1984: 139). Noun phrases containing adjectives not preceded by a syntactic determiner cannot be interpreted by the rules, since there is no rule that interprets an N^2 containing an Adj but no Det.

$$\text{(5.58) a.}\quad [\![\, [\underset{\alpha}{\overset{}{\begin{matrix}\text{Det}\\ \text{de}\end{matrix}}}\quad [\underset{\alpha}{\text{Adj}}\quad \underset{\alpha}{N^1}\quad]_{\underset{\alpha}{N^1}}]\quad {}_{\underset{\alpha}{N^2}}]\!] \rightarrow \text{THE}\,([\![N^1]\!])$$

$$\text{b.}\quad [\![\, [\underset{\alpha}{\text{Adj}}\quad \underset{\alpha}{N^1}\quad]_{\underset{\alpha}{N1}}]\!] \rightarrow [\![\ \text{Adj}\ ]\!]\,([\![N^1]\!])$$

Hellan (1986) assumes that the weak form of an adjective and the relevant form of the noun is assigned under government by a definite determiner. The adjective cannot receive its correct morphology by means of feature assignment to the sister of the determiner, since different features will have to be assigned to the two daughters of the sister in certain noun phrases. Hellan's analysis, adapted to relevant Swedish examples, is illustrated in (5.59) (see (25) in Hellan 1986: 101).

According to Hellan's (1986: 90) proposed criteria for headedness, an element which exerts government within a phrase is the head of that phrase. Following this line of reasoning, the fact that the weak morphology of the adjective appears to be dependent on the determiner becomes an argument in favour of the determiner heading the noun phrase, hence DET is the head of T in (5.59).

(5.59)

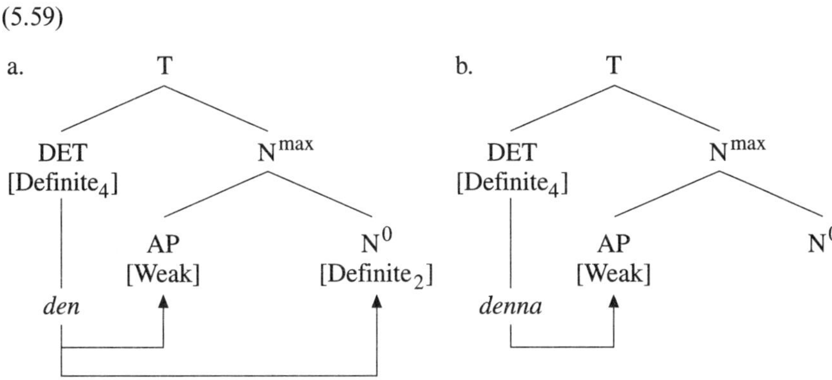

I turn now to Svenonius's (1992c) discussion of Haider's (1988a, 1988b) 'merger analysis'. In this analysis, a definite noun can function as a full DP because the functional projection may collapse with its complement when the head of the functional projection is empty. However, a further restriction on this merger is that the resulting structure should be legal. This analysis applied to a definite noun preceded by an adjective would yield the result in (5.60) (see (5.17)).

(5.60)

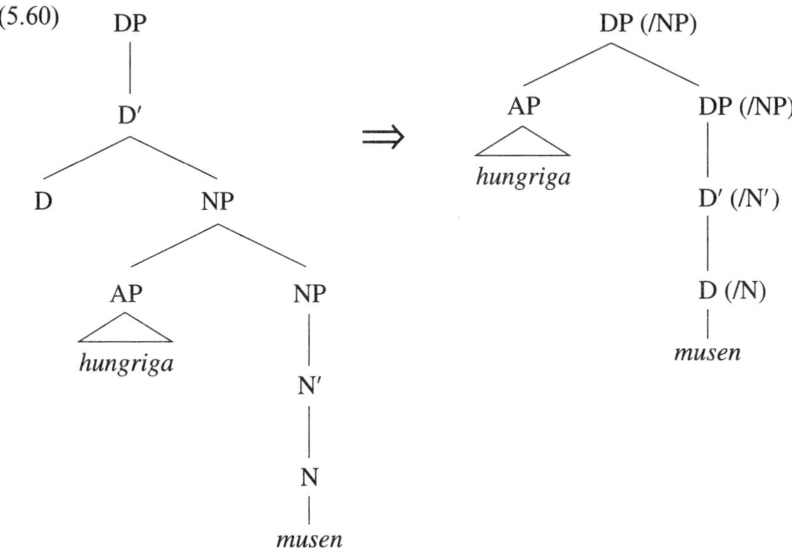

The collapsed tree must be of category DP, since its distribution would be that of any other noun phrase, but I have indicated, in parentheses, the category of the complement at each level. The functional node D is indeed empty in the left tree, so one criterion for merger is fulfilled. However, the other restriction on merger is not satisfied, since, in the merged tree, an AP is adjoined to a DP. Since AP may otherwise only modify NP, the collapsed tree is an illicit structure. Instead, *den* must fill the D slot in the non-merged tree, to yield the grammatical *den hungriga musen*.

The 'radical lexical solution' discussed by Svenonius (1992c: 156–8) provides a very similar mechanism for ruling out *hungriga musen* as a full DP. *Musen* is assumed to become a D in two steps, firstly by application of an inflectional rule, which changes an N to an N[+DEF], then a null derivational rule applies which changes the category from N to D. If *musen* is of category D, an AP may not adjoin to it, since APs adjoin only to NP. It is exactly because of examples like these that the Swedish (and Norwegian) derivational rule must take place in two steps, the second being a null derivation. In the case of *den hungriga musen* 'the hungry.WK mouse.DEF' we can then assume that only the first step has applied: N has been inflected to became N[+DEF], but no derivation to make it a D has taken place. As Svenonius (p. 158) points out, the fact that a null derivation must be assumed for Swedish (and Norwegian) makes this solution unlikely for these languages.

In Svenonius's (1992c: 158–62) EFP solution, a definite noun phrase must bear the feature [+DEF] on its left edge. A definite determiner carries the feature, and is therefore a legal left element (5.61a), and so is a definite noun (5.61b). Adjectives, on the other hand, are assumed not to be specified for [+DEF] (presumably another feature such as [WK] will be used for adjectives), and therefore a noun phrase with an initial adjective may not function as a full noun phrase. Hence (5.61c) is an illicit noun phrase. (All examples in (5.61) are from Svenonius 1992a: 19–20.)

(5.61) a. den nære vennen — Norwegian
the close friend

b. vennen
friend.DEF

c. *nære vennen
close friend.DEF

Svenonius distinguishes between the EDGE feature posited by Miller (1992a) for French and the Swedish [+DEF] EDGE feature. The French feature is a FIRST feature, which must be instantiated on the first element in a French noun phrase. The data from Swedish complicate the situation slightly. A prenominal modifying AP may in Swedish have within it a premodifying noun. This noun occurs in its definite form, that is, there is a manifestation of the feature [+DEF] on it. As (5.62a) shows, this definite noun could then be the first element of a noun phrase. Still, (5.62a) is ungrammatical as a full noun phrase, which is unexpected if [+DEF] is an EDGE feature which must be manifested on the first element of the noun phrase. The grammatical construction requires an independent syntactic determiner in these cases as in (5.62b). (Svenonius' examples are taken from Platzack 1982: 49.)

(5.62) a. *fienden överlägsna armén
enemy.DEF superior army.DEF
b. den fienden överlägsna armén
the enemy.DEF superior army.DEF
'the army superior to the enemy'

Instead, Svenonius (1992a: 20) dubs Swedish [+DEF] a LEFT feature. A LEFT feature is manifested not on the first element of a phrase, but on the head of the left-most phrasal constituent of the phrase. In (5.62a) the adjective is the head of the first phrase, but, as already mentioned, Svenonius assumes that adjectives cannot be specified for [+DEF]. Therefore, the independent definite article is required as in (5.62b) to provide an instantiation of [+DEF]. Svenonius (1992a, 1992b) does not provide any explicit discussion of why the adjectives require weak morphology in these cases.

It should be pointed out here that the intuition behind the EFP has also been expressed by van der Auwera (1990: 207–8). He proposes 'periphery placement' as a possible principle accounting for the positioning of determiners within noun phrases in languages like English, Swedish and Romanian. Van der Auwera's ideas are formulated within a FG framework (see for example Dik 1980, 1989 or Siewierska 1991). Using FG terminology, definiteness is a term operator, and as such can be taken to have scope over the whole term. Since scope often correlates with linear order, it is to be expected that the scope-bearing element is placed at the periphery of the phrase. Syntactic determiners and DEF can then be assumed to be manifestations of this term operator whereas the marking on an adjective is not.

In section 5.2.2.2 I discussed Holmberg's (1992) analysis of argument noun phrases. His analysis rests on the assumption that the specifier of an argument noun phrase must be licensed and that this can be done in either of two ways: the specifier can contain a lexical filler, or it can contain *pro* which must be licensed through Spec–Head agreement. As we saw in section 5.2.2.2, in a noun phrase such as *musen*, the definite noun licenses *pro*, which is found in Spec–NP. With respect to noun phrases like *den hungriga musen*, Holmberg assumes that the adjectival premodifier occurs in the specifier position of the NP. This means that *pro* cannot occur in this position. Instead a functional projection must be created to provide a specifier position for *pro*. This nominal functional projection which Holmberg refers to as nP can be created with the help of an overt determiner in the n position. This means that, whenever a definite noun is preceded by an adjective, it must be preceded by a determiner which heads a functional category nP. The resulting tree is found in (5.63). A comparison with the tree in (5.19) (in section 5.2.2.2) shows that the two noun phrases *musen* and *den hungriga musen* are of distinct categories in this analysis, NP (lexical) and nP (functional), respectively.

(5.63)

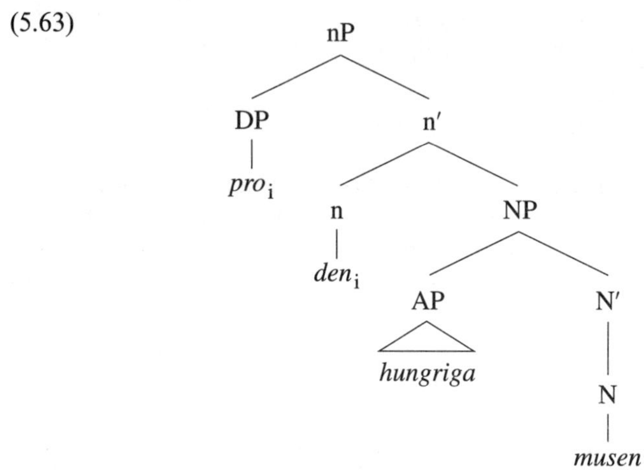

In this section, we have seen examples of three analyses of noun phrases containing a determiner, an adjective phrase and a noun which rely on feature distribution. One of the solutions is based on fairly standard assumptions as far as feature percolation goes (Cooper 1984). One solution claims that the facts of Norwegian (and by analogy, Swedish) show that feature percolation is not sufficient to predict the morphological form of the adjective and the noun in such noun phrases (Hellan 1986). In both these solutions, certain non-standard assumptions must be made. Cooper's syntactic solution assumes an intermediate node $N^{1.1}$, the status of which is unclear. Hellan has to assume that the determiner can assign a feature to the specifier of its complement that it does not assign to the complement itself. In the third approach, a different principle for feature distribution is introduced, namely the Edge Feature Principle (Svenonius 1992a, 1992c).

Finally, I have discussed one solution which does not involve feature percolation to any great extent, but which evolves from assumptions about the semantic differences between argument noun phrases (closed expressions) and predicative noun phrases (open expressions). The semantic distinction, in conjunction with a number of theoretical assumptions, requires an empty element *pro* to be present in the noun phrase. The presence of this element necessitates a functional projection in the syntax. This projection must be headed and this forces the introduction of a syntactic determiner *den*.

5.4.3. *Proposed analysis and comparisons*

5.4.3.1. *The issues*

The weak morphology on the adjective is evidently related to the presence of a syntactic (definite) determiner. It cannot be made dependent on the definiteness of the noun phrase as a whole, since there are definite noun phrases which cannot contain an adjective with weak morphology. Examples of this have been mentioned previously: *musen* is a legal definite noun phrase, yet **hungriga musen* is not. Nor can it be explained in terms of specifier–head agreement, even if the AP is assumed to occur in the specifier position of the noun, or as in Delsing (1992, 1993) the other way around, with the noun phrase in the specifier position of the AP.

Firstly, I think there is evidence that the feature manifested on the adjective in a definite noun phrase is not the same as that on definite nouns. When weak adjectives are used nominally, without a head noun, they must be preceded by a determiner. If the weak form of the adjective was really a manifestation of [+DEF], the feature which also occurs on the nouns, then we might expect that an A[+DEF] would be able to function as a full noun phrase, in the same way that N[+DEF] may. However this is not true, as the examples in (5.64) illustrate.[44]

(5.64) a. *Hungriga åt osten.
hungry.WK ate cheese.DEF

b. Den hungriga åt osten.
the hungry.WK ate cheese.DEF
'The hungry one ate the cheese.'

I will therefore assume that the feature for which adjectives are marked is not the [DEF] feature which marks nouns. Since the feature is obviously related to definiteness, in that weak adjectives only occur in definite noun phrases, we could term it [ADEF] for adjectival definiteness. However, I will follow traditional terminology here, and refer to the features as WK and STR.[45] In the NP solution which I propose, this feature will become redundant, at least for the purpose of selection within the noun phrase.

Secondly, weak adjectives may occur with both definite and non-definite nouns, as (5.65) shows.

(5.65) a. den hungriga musen
the hungry.WK mouse.DEF

b. denna hungriga mus
this hungry.WK mouse

An indication of the connection between adjectives and syntactic determiners is the fact that weak forms cannot occur in predicative positions, where they cannot be preceded by a definite determiner since definite determiners are ruled out in predicative positions. This is in spite of the fact that adjectives in this position are sensitive to the gender and number features of the subject. Examples are provided in (5.66) and (5.67).

(5.66) a. En mus är hungrig.
a.COM mouse(COM) is hungry.STR.COM.SG

b. Musen är hungrig / *hungriga.
mouse.DEF.COM.SG is hungry.STR.COM.SG hungry.WK

(5.67) a. Ett murmeldjur är hungrigt.
a.NT marmot(NT) is hungry.STR.NT.SG

b. Murmeldjuret är hungrigt / *hungriga.
marmot.DEF.NT.SG is hungry.STR.NT.SG hungry.WK

In poetic and old-fashioned Swedish, one can sometimes find examples of adjectives which occur after the noun in definite noun phrases. The crucial fact for my argument here is that the adjective must then always be accompanied by a syntactic determiner. Examples can be found in (5.68).

(5.68) a. solen *(den) varma
sun.DEF the warm.WK

b. livet *(det) outgrundliga
life.DEF the unfathomable.WK

Since a weak adjective appears always to be accompanied by a syntactic determiner, I will assume that the WK feature – and therefore also the weak morphology on the adjective – is directly dependent on a syntactic definite determiner. It is not, however, the case that the adjective needs to be adjacent to the determiner. In a noun phrase where the adjective phrase contains premodification, so that the adjective is actually not adjacent to the determiner, the adjective is still marked for WK. As an illustration, compare (5.69a) and (5.69b). Furthermore, in a noun phrase where more than one AP occurs between a definite determiner and the noun, all adjectives receive the feature WK (5.69c). There are a number of adjectives in Swedish which cannot occur with the morphological marking for WK; these include present participles.[46] However, adjectives which are separated from the determiner by such an adjective are still marked for WK. This point is illustrated in (5.69d) and (5.69e), where *spännande* is not marked.

(5.69) a. den av häxan förtrollade musen
the by witch.DEF bewitched.WK mouse.DEF

b. en av häxan förtrollad mus
a by witch.DEF bewitched.STR mouse

c. den törstiga, hungriga, nästan utmattade musen
the thirsty.WK hungry.WK almost exhausted.WK mouse

d.	den	spännande	billiga	moderna	thrillern
	the	exciting	cheap.WK	modern.WK	thriller.DEF
e.	en	spännande	billig	modern	thriller
	a	exciting	cheap.STR	modern.STR	thriller

Even though I will not discuss postmodification here, it should be pointed out that, with the exception of certain types of restrictive relative clauses, postmodification can occur in noun phrases which do not contain any syntactic determiner.

5.4.3.2. *NP analysis*

As described in section 5.1.2, in HPSG as it is laid out in Pollard and Sag (1994), modifiers select their heads through a head feature MOD. The value of the MOD feature, as that of SPEC, is a *synsem* object, which is structure-shared with the SYNSEM value of the (head) element with which it combines. This means that the sister of the modifier must have such feature values that it can unify with the modifier's value for MOD.

Since the value of the MOD feature is a *synsem* object, it can not only contain information about the syntactic category, such as N′, with which the modifier combines, but also specify the HEAD, valence and INDEX features of its sister. In the case of the Swedish weak adjectives, we can specify that they combine with an element of category N′, but specifically with an N′ which obligatorily selects a definite determiner via its SPR list. In this way, we can ensure that weak adjectives are always preceded by a determiner. This is similar to the analysis initially suggested for German by Pollard and Sag (1994: 88–91). I will return to their revised analysis of German later in this subsection. The suggested specification for a weak adjective like *hungriga* is given in (5.70). I have simplified the MOD value to make the AVM easier to read, but I provide a more detailed description of the MOD value in (5.71).

$$(5.70)\quad \begin{bmatrix} \text{CAT} & \begin{bmatrix} \text{HEAD} & \textit{adjective} \begin{bmatrix} \text{MOD} & \text{N}' \; [\text{SPR} \; \langle \textit{det}\,[\text{DEF} +] \rangle]\,[1] \\ \text{PRD} & - \end{bmatrix} \\ \text{SUBJ} & \langle\ \rangle \\ \text{SPR} & \langle\ \rangle \\ \text{COMPS} & \langle\ \rangle \end{bmatrix} \\ \text{CONT} & [\text{INDEX}\ [1]] \end{bmatrix}$$

$$(5.71)\quad \text{SYNSEM} \begin{bmatrix} \text{LOC} \begin{bmatrix} \text{CAT} & \begin{bmatrix} \text{HEAD} & \textit{noun} \\ \text{SPR} & \langle \textit{det}\,[\text{DEF} +]\,[1] \rangle \end{bmatrix} \\ \text{CONT} & [\text{INDEX}\ [1]] \end{bmatrix} \end{bmatrix}$$

A number of comments are in order. I will first explain the matrices in (5.70) and (5.71). The adjective does not select any other elements; the SUBJ, SPEC and COMPS lists are all empty. This is peculiar to the adjective *hungriga*. An adjective like *förtjust* 'delighted', for instance, may take a PP[*i*] (PP[*in*]) complement and would therefore have one (optional) element on its COMPS list. The adjective specifies, through its MOD feature, that it combines with a nominal element, specifically a nominal element of the kind that obligatorily selects a definite determiner through its SPR feature. As discussed in section 5.3.3.2 (especially (5.41)), nouns in Swedish are specified through their SPR feature as selecting a determiner. This determiner may, however, be unspecified for definiteness. Furthermore, for definite nouns, the determiner on the SPR list is optional. In (5.72) I give simplified definitions of nouns, where I disregard number and gender features (see (5.21) in section 5.2.3.2).

(5.72) a. *mus*: $\begin{bmatrix} \text{HEAD} & \textit{noun} \\ \text{SPR} & \langle \textit{det} \rangle \end{bmatrix}$ as in *denna hungriga mus*

b. *musen*: $\begin{bmatrix} \text{HEAD} & \textit{noun}\ [\text{DEF} +] \\ \text{SPR} & \langle (\textit{det}) \rangle \end{bmatrix}$ as in *den hungriga musen*

This means that the value for definiteness of the element on the SPR list of AP[DECL WK]+N′ combinations arises through unification. In the case of *musen* 'mouse.DEF', this also cancels the optionality of the determiner. This is exactly the desired result – a noun like *mus* is free to combine with a definite or an indefinite determiner; however, when it has combined with an adjective, this freedom is restricted by unification with the information structure associated with the form of the adjective. Similarly, *musen* may occur without a determiner until it combines with an adjective, when the presence of a syntactic determiner is obligatory. The relevant immediate dominance schema requires that the MOD value of the adjective be token-identical to the SYNSEM value of the nominal with which it combines. This means that the two feature matrices must be unifiable. The resulting unification can be represented as in (5.73) and (5.74).

In order to make the correct predictions about the necessity for a determiner in such phrases, we must assume that SPR⟨*det* [DEF +]⟩ unifies with SPR⟨(*det*)⟩ to yield SPR⟨*det* [DEF +]⟩. This means that, when a modifier requiring a nominal sister which requires a determiner comes across a nominal which optionally selects a determiner, then it may unify with that nominal, but in doing so it forces the nominal to make the optional element obligatory. It seems a reasonable assumption that something containing an optional element in a valency list may unify with an element obligatorily requiring an identical element and that the result of the unification is that the element is obligatory.

The adjective in (5.70) is further specified as [PRD –]; it cannot occur in predicative positions. The feature PRD applies to all major (substantive in Pollard and Sag's 1994 terms) categories: nouns, adjectives, verbs and prepositions. For an element to occur in a predicative position, it must have the value + for PRD. The fact that *hungriga* is [PRD –] captures the fact that weak adjectives cannot occur predicatively.

(5.73) *hungriga musen* as in *den hungriga musen* '(the) hungry mouse'

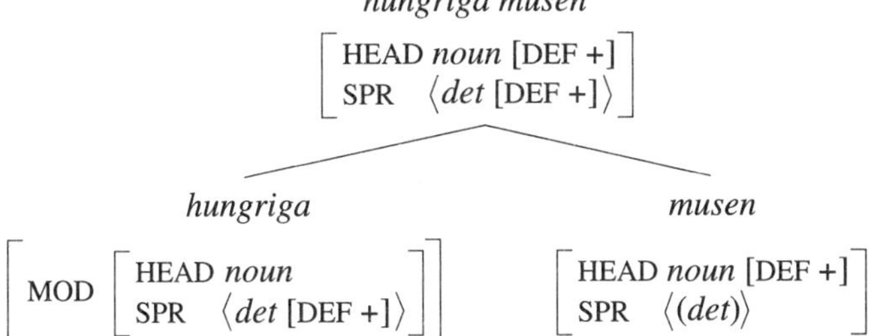

(5.74) *hungriga mus* as in *denna hungriga mus* '(this) hungry mouse'

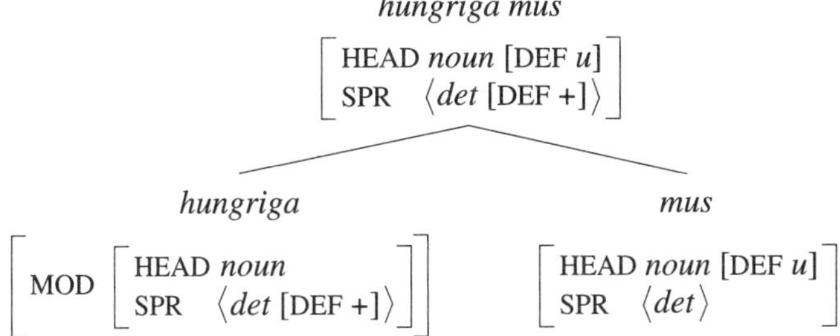

The index [1] on the noun and under the INDEX feature of the adjective in (5.70) indicates that the noun and the adjective must share their INDEX features, in the sense that the two sets of features and values must be unifiable. Note that the adjective is not specified for person, number and gender. According to this lexical entry, *hungriga* can combine with any noun which (after unification) selects a definite determiner. It does not matter whether the noun is definite or non-definite, or what values it has for person, number and gender. Of course, adjectives will occur most often in noun phrases specified as third person. However, weak adjectives can also occur in first and second person contexts as the examples in (5.75) show. In section 2.2.2, I showed that the elements *vi* and *ni* behave like determiners in certain crucial ways.

(5.75) a. **Vi hungriga studenter** kräver högre studiebidrag.
we hungry.WK students demand higher grant
'We hungry students demand a higher grant.'

b. **Ni ansvarslösa hundägare** borde få böta dyrt.
you irresponsible.WK dog owners ought may pay fine expensively
'You irresponsible dog owners ought to get large fines.'

These constructions are more restricted, but this need not be specified on the adjectives. The restrictions will follow from the AVMs of first and second pronouns functioning as determiners.

One of the major advantages that the tools of HPSG offer is related to the sharing of INDEX features and the under-specification of adjectives. The fact that adjectives can be under-specified means that identical forms which would occur in different slots in a traditional paradigm can be captured by one lexical entry. It is not only in traditional paradigms that this multiplication of identical forms occurs. In a system where agreement is viewed as features being assigned by one element to another, the agreement controller (in this case the noun) would have to assign all its features to the adjective. This means that an A[3, SG, COM, WK] is considered to be distinct from an A[3, SG, NT, WK] and an A[3, PL, COM, WK], even if these distinctions are not visible in the linguistic shape. This point is discussed by Pollard and Sag (1994: 64–7) in relation to German. Even though there are similarities between the German and the Swedish system, there are also significant differences, to which I will return later. The paradigm for adjective inflection in Swedish is listed in table 5.1. The paradigm has eight slots, but only three distinct forms. At least, there appear to be only three distinct forms. I will, however, claim that there are actually four distinct forms. The weak forms are different from the strong forms ending in *-a* even though their shapes are identical. My argument for making this distinction is that the strong-*a* forms differ from the weak ones in that they do not depend on a determiner. Consider the data in (5.76).

Table 5.1 Paradigm for adjectival inflection in Swedish

Gender	Number	Strong	Weak
common	singular	*hungrig*	*hungriga*
	plural	*hungriga*	*hungriga*
neuter	singular	*hungrigt*	*hungriga*
	plural	*hungriga*	*hungriga*

(5.76) a. Hungriga möss äter mycket ost.
hungry.STR mice eat much cheese
'Hungry mice eat a lot of cheese.'

b. *Hungriga mössen äter mycket ost.
hungry.WK mice.DEF eat much cheese

c. De hungriga mössen äter mycket ost.
the hungry.WK mice.DEF eat much cheese
'The hungry mice eat a lot of cheese.'

d. Mössen äter mycket ost.
mice.DEF eat much cheese
'The mice ate a lot of cheese'

The adjective *hungriga* which occurs in an indefinite noun phrase in (5.76a) does not require a determiner to be present.[47] The adjective *hungriga* which occurs in a definite noun phrase in (5.76c), on the other hand, cannot occur without a determiner, as (5.76b) shows. That this requirement is not due to the noun is shown in (5.76d), where the same noun occurs without any syntactic determiner. The *hungriga* which occurs in definite noun phrases is then the kind of adjective which selects a nominal which selects a determiner. *Hungriga* in (5.76a), on the other hand, does not put these restrictions on the nominal with which it combines. This means that the strong *hungriga* and the weak *hungriga* are really different forms of the adjective, which happen to have the same ending. Hence there are really four forms in table 5.1, as illustrated in (5.77).

(5.77) *hungrig* strong singular common
hungrigt strong singular neuter
hungriga strong plural
hungriga weak

HPSG allows these facts about Swedish to be captured neatly, as in the feature matrix for *hungriga*(WK) in (5.70): only one lexical entry is needed, the adjective requires its sister to be of category noun and it must select a determiner. No further constraints are put on the features of the noun.

Note also that we do not need the feature [DECL *wk/str*]. The adjectives are equipped to sort out their own distribution and neither determiners nor nouns need to refer to the two types of adjectives. This means that the discussion in section 5.4.3.1 regarding the distinction between a nominal definiteness feature DEF and an adjectival definiteness feature [DECL *wk*] is not relevant for this solution.

Pollard and Sag (1994: 88–91) outline an analysis for German which is similar to the one proposed here for Swedish. German is more complicated than Swedish, as their overview of adjective forms shows. Still, their analysis of German is similar to the one presented for Swedish here in that declension classes for adjectives need not be made explicit. A weak adjective is one which through its MOD feature selects a 'strong' determiner (which in the terms I use for Swedish would be a definite determiner). I will refer to this as the 'modifier selects' analysis. At a later stage, however, Pollard and Sag (pp. 371–6), with reference to work done by Maier and Steffens (1989) and Kathol (1994), revise this analysis. In the revised analysis, 'weak' and 'strong' are made values of a feature DECL which is relevant to both adjectives and nouns. Determiners need then not be classified as weak or strong; instead they select through their SPEC feature an N′ whose value for DECL is either weak or strong. I will refer to this solution as the 'determiner selects' analysis.

There is some evidence in favour of making [DECL *wk*] and [DECL *str*] features of nouns as well as of adjectives in German (see Kathol 1991). There are certain nouns, like *Beamt-* and *Verwandt-* which are actually inflected for weak and strong declension. However, the consequence of this solution is that all nouns, the majority of which are not inflected for weak and strong, have the feature DECL with either of the values *wk* or *str*. Nouns on which there is no morphological reflection of the feature, will not be specified in the lexicon for DECL but will receive their values from context, through unification. There is a further undesirable consequence of this solution, as Pollard and Sag (1994: 373) point out. Just as in English, German plural and mass nouns can occur without a syntactic determiner. There is, however, an overriding principle: any noun phrase containing a weak element needs a determiner. This means that plural and mass Ns must combine with a (strong) determiner when they contain either a weak noun or a weak adjective. Hence weak forms of variable nouns must obligatorily select a determiner through their SPR feature. This lexical specification must then override the more general rule that plural forms of nouns and mass nouns do not require a specifier. In the case of plural and mass noun phrases containing weak adjectives, Pollard and Sag (1994: 373) propose that the adjective through its MOD feature specifies that it can only occur in noun phrases containing a (strong) determiner. As far as I can understand, this means that any weak adjective in German must have the MOD specification referring to the SPR feature of its sister, just as it did in the 'modifier selects' solution. The 'determiner selects' solution then seems to have two problematic consequences: the fact that all nouns in German must be marked as [DECL *wk/str*], and the fact that a certain amount of modifier selection must still be assumed to take place.

I will look now at Swedish in the light of Pollard and Sag's (1994) second proposal. There are a few elements in Swedish which are similar to the variable nouns in German. One example is *anställd* 'employed, employee', which is illustrated in (5.78).

(5.78) a. Vi har en **anställd** som alltid ställer till besvär.
we have an employed.STR COMP always causes difficulties
'We have an employee who always causes trouble.'

b. Den **anställda** har alltid rätt att försvara sig.
the employed.WK has always right COMP defend REFL
'The employee always has the right to defend him/herself.'

I do not, however, find this sufficient evidence to adopt the 'determiner selects' analysis. Instead, I propose to maintain the 'modifier selects' analysis and analyse noun phrases containing 'variable nouns' (as in (5.78)) as elliptical constructions. As discussed in section 5.4.2.1, both weak and strong adjectives can occur in elliptical constructions lacking a head noun. The adjective then retains its weak/strong morphology, and it is only when the adjective has been fully nominalized that it can carry the nominal definite ending.[48] One reason for preferring the 'modifier selects' solution is that I find the 'determiner selects' analysis implausible. It is uneconomical to let all Swedish nouns receive a value for an attribute which always has null realization on that element because Swedish has a small number of seemingly nominal elements which are inflected for the attribute. I believe that such proliferation of unrealized features should be avoided. As far as possible, a 'wholewheat' syntax should be maintained (see Cooper 1982). Furthermore, since weak adjectives require a determiner even when they combine with a noun that does not obligatorily require a determiner, the weak adjectives would still have to be specified through their MOD feature as selecting a nominal which requires a definite determiner. Finally, I think there are reasons to analyse elements like *anställda* as adjectives.

Firstly, these elements do not take the definite ending that normally attaches to nouns. Hence the examples in (5.79) are not possible versions of the subject of (5.78b) (compare this with the discussion of nominalized adjectives in section 3.3.2).

(5.79) *Anställd-en / *Anställda-n
employed-DEF employed.WK-DEF

Secondly, such elements may combine with elements which normally only occur with adjectives. In standard Swedish, an element like *ny* 'new' may form a compound with adjectival elements (often a participial in an adjectival function, with adjectival inflection), but not with nominal elements.[49] An example is provided in (5.80a). As (5.80c) and (5.80d) show, *ny* can combine with *anställd*, and I take this as an indication that *anställd* is best analysed as an adjective, so that there is no strong argument to adopt the 'determiner selects' analysis for Swedish.

(5.80) a. Pojken har **nykammat** hår.
boy.DEF has new.combed hair
'The boy has recently combed hair.'

b. Har ni sett *nyhuset / det nya huset.
have you seen new.house.DEF the new house.DEF
'Have you seen the new house.'

c. Vi har en **nyanställd** som verkar lite lat.
we have a new.employed.STR COMP seems little lazy
'We have a new employee who seems to be a bit lazy.'

d. Den **nyanställda** verkar lite lat.
the new.employed.WK seems little lazy
'The new employee seems to be a bit lazy.'

I cannot find any evidence in Swedish which points towards a 'determiner selects' analysis. I will therefore maintain an analysis in which only adjectives are involved in the weak/strong distinction, but where the declension need not occur as a feature in the specification of adjectives. Instead, the distribution of adjectives is determined through the MOD feature of the adjectives themselves. For weak adjectives, we only need one entry, namely the one in (5.70), repeated here as (5.81).

$$(5.81)\quad \begin{bmatrix} \text{CAT} & \begin{bmatrix} \text{HEAD} & \textit{adjective} \begin{bmatrix} \text{MOD} & \text{N}' \ \langle \textit{det}\,[+\text{DEF}]\rangle]\,[1] \\ \text{PRD} & - \end{bmatrix} \\ \text{SUBJ} & \langle\ \rangle \\ \text{COMPS} & \langle\ \rangle \\ \text{SPR} & \langle\ \rangle \end{bmatrix} \\ \text{CONT} & [\text{INDEX}\ [1]] \end{bmatrix}$$

5.4.3.3. *Netter (1994)*

Two of the three issues where Netter (1994: 333–9) claims that his approach is superior relate to noun phrases containing attributive adjectives. As already discussed in section 5.2.3.3, Netter assumes a feature FCOMPL which indicates whether a constituent can function as a maximal projection or not. There I showed that definite nouns in Swedish could be unspecified for this feature, as Netter proposes for non-count and plural nouns in German, and hence could function as a maximal projection on their own – in which case they would become [FCOMPL +] through unification with the specification on the valence list of some element – or combine with a determiner – in which case they would become [FCOMPL −] through unification with the SPEC requirement of the determiner. Let us consider now how this proposal could be extended to account for the obligatoriness of a syntactic determiner when definite nouns combine with attributive adjectives.

One solution would be if there was a way of indicating that the underspecification of the noun was limited when it combined with an AP. This would be very similar to the CG solution proposed in Payne and Börjars (1994) (see section 5.4.2.2). In such a solution, the AP would somehow impose the value [FCOMPL –] on its sister. This is, however, explicitly ruled out by Netter (1994: 322): 'thus, functional completeness encodes whether or not a constituent still has to combine with a functional head to qualify as a maximal projection. Clearly, if we treat this property as a (lexically determined) HEAD feature, it must not be affected by adjunction but remain invariant within a head domain.' This is then not a possible account of Swedish noun phrases.

One of the advantages which Netter claims for his account as compared to that of Pollard and Sag (1994) is related to the categorial status of the nominal element to which attributive adjectives adjoin. The issue really is how to refer to the category N′ as opposed to N and NP. I refer to Netter (1994: 335–9) for a discussion of the problems he claims are present in Pollard and Sag's approach. Netter (pp. 322–4) introduces a binary-valued MINOR feature [SPEC ±] for this purpose, indicating whether or not the constituent carrying the feature has yet combined with a specifier. Adjectives may then adjoin to elements which have the value [SPEC –], that is, which have not yet combined with a determiner. This feature gives no indication of whether or not the nominal will have to combine with a specifier. Hence it permits the adjunction in the German noun phrases in (5.82a) and (5.82b), but correctly rules out (5.82c).

(5.82) a. der gute Wein — German
the good.WK wine

b. guter Wein
good.STR wine

c. *gute / *guter der Wein
good.WK good.STR the wine

It should be pointed out here that the feature value for SPEC has nothing to say about whether the nominal is a full noun phrase, in Netter's terms a *dp*. This is indicated by the value for FCOMPL.

The feature SPEC is a MINOR feature for which all nouns are specified. Determiners are specified as [SPEC +], and since it is a minor feature, this value is inherited to the level of *dp*. An adjective is then specified as adjoining only to a nominal specified as [SPEC –]. The nominal which results from this adjunction will also be [SPEC –] since the feature value will be inherited from the head noun in this case. This is, of course, the desired result: since attributive adjectives occur recursively, an attributive adjective must be allowed to adjoin to this resulting category. This feature cannot help us account for the Swedish data, since it only expresses the fact that the nominal has not attached to a specifier. A negative value does not mean that the nominal still has to combine with a specifier. A definite noun like *musen* could be specified as [FCOMPL +, SPEC –], correctly predicting that the noun on its own may function as a full *dp*, and also that an adjective may occur with it. However, if *musen* combines with an adjective like *hungriga*, the resulting nominal will have the same value for SPEC. There is then nothing in its feature specification to predict that this nominal does, in fact, require a determiner because of the presence of the adjective.

Another advantage which Netter claims for his account is related to adjectival declensions in German. I will not go through the details of his proposal here, but only touch upon the aspects which are relevant to my analysis of Swedish noun phrases. Netter (p. 324) assumes that not only adjectives, but also nouns and determiners, are defined for the feature DECL. This is also a binary-valued MINOR feature which has two values: *we* (weak) and *st* (strong).[50] He (p. 326) further assumes that the type definition of *dp* requires it to have the value [DECL *st*]. The only element that can change a nominal's value for DECL is a determiner (p. 327). An AP will always agree with the nominal to which it adjoins for this feature (p. 326). It is thus predicted that a nominal marked [DECL *st*] can occur without a determiner as long as it is also [FCOMPL +]. Any nominal marked as [DECL *we*] would require a determiner. At first sight, these assumptions might appear to provide the tools for a satisfactory account of the Swedish facts. The adjectives under discussion here, like *hungriga*, are weak. Since APs agree for DECL with the phrase they modify, their nominal sisters must also be [DECL *we*]. The resulting nominal will have the value [DECL *we*], since only determiners can change the value of this feature. This means that if the adjective combines with a nominal which can have the value [FCOMPL +], say *musen*, the resulting category will be N′ [DECL *we*, FCOMPL +]. This means that it will still need [DECL *st*] which it can only receive from a determiner. Determiners like *den* would then be specified as requiring a [DECL *we*] sister, but yielding a [DECL *st*] constituent.[51]

However, there are some problems associated with applying Netter's analysis to Swedish. In this argument, the definite noun with which a weak adjective may combine must be assumed to be [DECL *we*] since adjectives agree for the DECL value with the nominal they modify. On the other hand, since definite nouns can function as full *dps* without a determiner they must be [DECL *st*]. Note that this conflict cannot be solved by assuming that definite nouns are under-specified for DECL. If they were, then we would predict that strong adjectives could combine with definite nouns. However, this would be incorrect, as the ungrammaticality of **hungrig musen* 'hungry.STR mouse.DEF' shows.

A further objection to this account as applied to Swedish relates to strong adjectives in indefinite noun phrases. Under this account, the requirement for a determiner in an indefinite noun phrase containing an adjective would be accounted for differently from the requirement in a definite noun phrase. The determiner would be required to supply the value [FCOMPL +] but would not be needed for the DECL value. This is illustrated in (5.83). In (5.83a) the determiner is required because the nominal has inherited the feature value [FCOMPL –] from the non-definite noun. In (5.83b), it is the feature value [DECL *we*] which requires the determiner to be present. In section 6.3.3 I will argue that the requirement for a determiner is actually related to the presence of an adjective in indefinite noun phrases, just as in definite ones. This cannot be captured in this analysis.

(5.83) a. *(en) hungrig mus
a hungry mouse
[DECL *st*] [DECL *st*, FCOMPL –]

b. *(den) hungriga musen
the hungry mouse
[DECL *we*] [DECL *we*, FCOMPL –]

Finally, my objections to treating nouns in general, or even nouns like *anställd* 'employee', as specified for DECL remain (see the discussion of examples (5.78–80)). The arguments which Netter (1994: 325–6) uses to support the assumption that determiners are specified for DECL in German do not apply in Swedish. So, even though Netter's account for German might claim advantages over that proposed by Pollard and Sag (1994), the account, as it stands, is not straightforwardly applicable to the Swedish data. So, in spite of the relative elegance of Netter's account of German, the fact that it cannot easily be extended even to a closely related language like Swedish strikes me as quite a serious disadvantage. As I hope to have shown, the slightly more complex mechanisms proposed by Pollard and Sag (1994) can provide an account of the Swedish data.

5.4.3.4. *DP analysis*

In the DP analysis which I have discussed in sections 5.2.3.4 and 5.3.3.4, the head D selects its nominal complement, which I assume to be of level N′, rather than N″, but nothing in this section hinges on this distinction. This head can select its sister with respect to a certain feature, or in a different terminology, it can assign features to its sister. If these features are head features in the sense of Gazdar et al. (1985), they can percolate from there to the head of the complement.[52] Any grammar must then also have some means of accounting for agreement between a modifier and its head. In GPSG, the Control Agreement Principle (CAP) (Gazdar et al. 1985: 89) regulates the spread of agreement features. Provided the features are also so-called control features, the CAP ensures that they spread from the head to modifying sisters. In other approaches Spec–Head Agreement is assumed to be the major (or maybe only) principle governing this type of feature distribution. In such an analysis, the adjective would fill the specifier position of the noun phrase, and hence agreement is ensured.[53] In HPSG these features would spread by the requirement for unifiability of the MOD feature of a modifying adjective with its head sister. The principles which guide this feature percolation in GPSG, namely the HFC and the CAP, were discussed in section 4.2.3. I have concluded that DEF is not a feature which is distributed by agreement principles. The reason for this is that not all definite determiners select definite nouns and that therefore not all definite noun phrases contain a definite noun. The feature that is marked on the adjective, on the other hand, does, in some sense, agree with the determiner. A weak adjective will always co-occur with a definite determiner, and a strong adjective will always co-occur with an indefinite determiner. However, this 'agreement' between modifier and head cannot be defined in terms of the DEF feature, since not all definite determiners select a [+DEF] complement. Instead, the feature which is manifested on adjectives in definite noun phrases is a separate feature, WK/STR.[54] These are, of course, really two values of one adjectival head feature, but to simplify the representations here, I will simply refer to them as [WK] and [STR].

The conclusion so far is that there is a feature value WK which a weak adjective receives from the definite determiner which must precede it. In Hellan's (1986) analysis, which was discussed in section 5.4.2.2, he describes this relation as the determiner deciding the shape of the adjective under government. However, in standard phrase-structure grammars, there is no way in which a head can 'reach' a non-head daughter within its complement (in this case its 'niece') except via (the head of) the complement itself. This means that under standard assumptions about phrase-structure grammar, a definite determiner cannot assign a feature to the AP without also assigning it to its complement N′ (or NP).[55] We will have to assume therefore that a definite determiner assigns the feature WK to its complement, regardless of whether it also assigns [+DEF] or [uDEF].

To ensure a close relation between the determiner and the feature value WK on an adjective, I will assume that this is a feature assigned by the determiner through its selectional restrictions. The resulting subcategorization frames for *den* and *denna* are given in (5.84). All definite determiners assign the feature WK to their complements. The feature value [+DEF] can then be said to be the feature which triggers the assignment of WK.

(5.84) a. *den*: $[\_\_\ \mathrm{NP}_{[+\mathrm{DEF},\mathrm{WK}]}]_{\mathrm{DP}}$

b. *denna*: $[\_\_\ \mathrm{NP}_{[\mathrm{uDEF},\ \mathrm{WK}]}]_{\mathrm{DP}}$

These rules and lexical entries make sure that the feature WK is assigned to the N′ (or NP) complement of the determiner. From there it will percolate to all levels of the nominal. The agreement mechanism of the grammar ensures that the feature spreads to the AP modifier.

Under different assumptions about feature percolation, where feature distribution is governed by specifier–head agreement, a slightly different structure would have to be assigned to noun phrases containing APs. The AP is commonly assumed to be the specifier of the NP which the D selects, so that agreement between the AP and the N can be ensured through specifier–head agreement. The result under this analysis, with respect to the data discussed, would be identical to that illustrated in (5.84) and I will not consider this solution in detail here, especially since it is, as far as I am aware, exclusively presented within a framework that presupposes movement. In section 3.7 I motivated my decision not to attempt an analysis in terms of transformational theory with reference to the difficulties of distinguishing between morphological and syntactic elements within standard versions of this theory.

The standard phrase-structure solution discussed above can correctly predict that all adjectives must be marked for WK or STR and that the presence of this feature depends on the presence of a syntactic determiner. However, the analysis has a couple of less desirable consequences. Firstly, all nouns heading the complement of a determiner will be marked as WK or STR. In section 5.4.3.2 I argued that these feature values are never instantiated on Swedish nouns. This could mean that the lexicon must contain two entries for a noun like *mus*: one with a feature matrix containing the feature value WK and one with an identical feature matrix except for the value STR instead of WK. If one permits under-specified lexical entries, this redundancy need not occur in the lexicon, but each noun would receive a value when inserted into the syntax.

Secondly, under this solution, the principles governing agreement will pass on not only the feature value WK, but also values for the features person, number and gender. This means that in a noun phrase containing a definite determiner and an attributive adjective phrase and a noun, the head of the AP can receive any of the feature specifications in (5.85).

$$
(5.85)\quad
\begin{bmatrix} \text{AFORM} & \text{WK} \\ \text{PER} & 3 \\ \text{NUM} & \text{SG} \\ \text{GEND} & \text{COM} \end{bmatrix}
\quad
\begin{bmatrix} \text{AFORM} & \text{WK} \\ \text{PER} & 3 \\ \text{NUM} & \text{PL} \\ \text{GEND} & \text{COM} \end{bmatrix}
$$

$$
\begin{bmatrix} \text{AFORM} & \text{WK} \\ \text{PER} & 3 \\ \text{NUM} & \text{SG} \\ \text{GEND} & \text{NT} \end{bmatrix}
\quad
\begin{bmatrix} \text{AFORM} & \text{WK} \\ \text{PER} & 3 \\ \text{NUM} & \text{PL} \\ \text{GEND} & \text{NT} \end{bmatrix}
$$

All entries in (5.85) correspond to one form, namely the one ending in the weak *-a*, as in *hungriga*. This means that we get one specification for each slot in the paradigm even though they all correspond to one form (see table 5.1 in section 5.4.3.2). This leads to an even greater redundancy than the one resulting from the marking for WK on the noun. As in that case, the redundancy need not be carried over into the lexicon, if under-specified forms are permitted. In that case there is one entry, *hungriga*, which is specified as WK, but which does not contain any values for the features PER, NUM and GEND. All entries in (5.85) are then legal extensions of this feature matrix. However, the lexical elements would receive the redundant specifications when inserted into the syntax.

Finally, the features WK and STR will also be present on prenominal elements which are not morphologically marked for the features. For instance, the participle *spännande* 'exciting' will carry the feature WK in (5.86a) and STR in (5.86b).

(5.86) a. den här spännande boken
this exciting book.DEF
'this exciting book'

b. en spännande bok
an exciting book
'an exciting book'

5.4.3.5. *Conclusions*

In sections 5.4.3.2 and section 5.4.3.4 we have seen that adequate accounts of the feature spreading in Swedish noun phrases consisting of a definite determiner, a prenominal AP and a noun can be provided in both an NP and a DP analysis. In section 5.4.3.2, I showed that the notion of modifier selection, which has been introduced for independent reasons, provides an economical way of predicting the correct feature distribution in Swedish noun phrases. It is economical in two ways. Firstly it does not require a separate feature like [DECL *we/str*] for adjectives, and secondly, no redundant feature marking is required on nouns. There will be one under-specified feature matrix for each form, rather than one for each slot in the paradigm.

In the DP analysis in section 5.4.3.4 the major problem is to define the relation between the definite determiner and the weak ending on the adjective. In more standardly assumed versions of phrase-structure grammar a head cannot 'reach' the modifier (or specifier) of its complement except through that complement. In terms of the Swedish noun phrases, this means that the determiner can only assign a feature to the AP in an indirect way. It must assign it to the N′ (or NP) complement, from where feature distribution rules take it to the modifier. In this analysis, a separate feature for adjectives [WK/STR] is required. Furthermore, this feature will also percolate to the head noun, so that the N node will carry redundant marking for a feature that can only be instantiated on adjectives.

In these more complex noun phrases I can still not find any evidence that necessitates the assumption that D is the head. With the tools of HPSG, a satisfactory account of adjectival definiteness marking can be provided. In fact, this account is more economical in a number of ways than the DP account provided here.

5.5. Some residual issues

5.5.1. *Types of Adj+N combinations seemingly without a determiner*

5.5.1.1. *The issues*

In section 5.4, I claimed that weak morphology on adjectives is directly related to the presence of a definite determiner. I consider this to be one of the most striking aspects of noun phrases containing adjectives, and something that any analysis must account for. There are, however, certain types of element which may appear to be weak adjectives, but which do not require the presence of a determiner. In sections 5.5.1.2, 5.5.1.3 and 5.5.1.4, I will consider three such types. I will conclude that none of them is a counterexample to the generalization about the relation between weak adjectives and determiners.

5.5.1.2. *Lexical phrases*

In (5.87) I provide some examples of Swedish noun phrases which contain a weak adjective, but no preceding determiner.

(5.87) a. Svenska Dagbladet
Swedish daily.DEF
the name of a newspaper

b. Vita huset
white.WK house.DEF
'the White House' (not 'the white house')

c. Svarta havet
black.WK sea.DEF
'the Black Sea' (not 'the black sea')

Delsing (1988) assumes that such phrases are generated in the syntax, like all other noun phrases (see section 5.4.2.1). It is indeed because of such noun phrases that Delsing allows the feature [+DEF] of the syntactic node to assign Case to an AP, rather than requiring a syntactic determiner to do so.

Contrary to Delsing (1988), I do not believe that the phrases in (5.87) have the same status as other noun phrases in Swedish. There are a large number of constraints that apply to this type of noun phrase which do not apply to syntactically generated noun phrases, the most striking one being the fact that a syntactic determiner is not required. There are also some such lexicalized phrases which do not even require the definite ending. Examples are given in (5.88) (see Anward and Linell 1976: 90).

(5.88) a. röda hund
red.WK dog
'rubella'

b. Röda Kvarn
red.WK mill
'Moulin Rouge'

If we assume that the noun phrases in (5.87) and (5.88) are generated in the syntax by the same rules that permit *den hungriga musen*, then some mechanism will have to be introduced into the syntactic rules which makes sure that **hungriga musen* and **hungriga mus* are disallowed noun phrases. This seems not only uneconomical, but also unintuitive, since it is actually noun phrases like *Vita huset* and *röda hund* which show an irregular pattern in that the semantics of such phrases is irregular. Instead, I will follow for instance Anward and Linell (1976) and Cooper (1984) in assuming that such phrases are lexicalized, and therefore subject to lexical rules and not to the same constraints as syntactically generated noun phrases.

Anward and Linell present a large number of arguments in support of analysing certain phrase types in Swedish as lexical rather than syntactic elements. Not all of these apply to the noun phrases illustrated in (5.87) and (5.88), but when they do they place them alongside the lexicalized phrases.

Lexical units, like compounds and lexicalized phrases show what Anward and Linell (1976: 77–9) term connective prosody: that is, such elements are connected prosodically by de-accentuation of certain elements. In the case of a lexicalized phrase it is a de-accentuation of the left-most element, resulting in prominence on the right edge of the phrase. This is illustrated in (5.89), where a syllable carrying main stress is preceded by ˈ and where ˌ precedes a syllable with secondary stress. In (5.89b) the article is necessary for the nominal to function as a full noun phrase.

(5.89) a. ˌVita ˈhuset
white.WK house.DEF
'the White House'

b. *(det) ˈvita ˈhuset
the white.WK house.DEF
'the white house'

Lexicalized phrases have in common that their meaning is not directly derived from the meaning of the parts. As Anward and Linell (p. 86) point out, lexicalized 'A[WK] N[+DEF]' strings refer only to specific objects. *Vita huset* cannot be used to refer to any house which is white. This sort of semantic opacity is characteristic of lexicalized phrases.

Lexicalized phrases do not permit any internal modification. In the case of lexicalized 'A[WK] N[+DEF]' phrases, any modification of the nominal element must precede the adjective, and must, in turn, be preceded by a determiner, as shown in (5.90). The examples in (5.91) and (5.92) illustrate that this is not due to general rules regarding the placement of adjectives in Swedish.

(5.90) a. *ˌVita fallfärdiga ˈhuset
white.WK ramshackle.WK house.DEF

b. *ˌSvenska vältryckta ˈDagbladet
Swedish well-printed daily

(5.91) a. *(det) fallfärdiga ˌVita ˈhuset
the ramshackle.WK white.WK house.DEF

b. *(det) vältryckta ˌSvenska ˈdagbladet
the well-printed Swedish Daily

(5.92) a. ˈvita ˈfallfärdiga ˈhus
white ramshackle houses
'white ramshackle houses'

b. ˈsvenska ˈvältryckta ˈböcker
Swedish well-printed books
'well-printed Swedish books'

Parts of a lexicalized phrase cannot be co-ordinated with an equivalent part of a syntactic phrase, as illustrated by (5.93). Note that this is ungrammatical with the connective accent regardless of whether or not the phrase as a whole is preceded by a syntactic determiner.

(5.93) *(*det) ˈstora och ˌVita ˈhuset
the big and white house.DEF

All these characteristics receive a simple explanation if we assume that these phrases are not actually formed by the normal syntactic component. Anward and Linell (1976: 111) do assign internal structure to the lexicalized phrase, a structure similar to that of syntactic noun phrases, but which the element receives in the lexicon. It is not clear how the rules generating this structure would work within a general theory of grammar. However, we can assume that they are different in nature from the syntactic rules. For one thing, they must apply within the lexicon. Anward and Linell compare the rules which create lexical phrases with inflectional and compound rules. Alternatively, one could assume that these elements have some degree of pre-specification which does not follow from any general rules.

Cooper (1984: 131–3) also concludes that phrases such as *Vita huset* should not be generated freely by the syntactic rules. Instead, these phrases are proper nouns, whose structure is ruled by lexical processes. One piece of evidence in favour of a proper-noun analysis of this type of lexicalized phrase relates to the use of restrictive relative clauses in Swedish. A proper noun can be used with a restrictive relative clause, but only if a syntactic determiner is also introduced (see section 3.3.4). This is illustrated in (5.94a). As (5.94b) and (5.94c) show, this holds also for the noun phrase type under discussion here. Definite nouns like *musen,* on the other hand, can be followed by restrictive relative clauses without a syntactic determiner being required.

(5.94) a. *(Den) Anders jag känner gillar pizza.
the Anders I know likes pizza
'The Anders that I know likes pizza.'

b. *(Det) Vita huset vi läser om i tidningarna
the white house we read about in newspapers.DEF
verkar alltid förknippat med skandaler.
seems always associated with scandals
'The White House that we read about in the newspapers always seems to be associated with scandals.'

c. *(Det) Svenska Dagbladet jag läste som student
the Swedish daily I read as student
hade intressanta kultursidor.
had interesting culture pages
'The Svenska Dagbladet that I read as a student had interesting sections on the arts.'

I conclude from this discussion that noun phrases such as *Vita huset* and *röda hund* are not generated by syntactic rules. They are found in the lexicon as one entry. Like proper nouns they are inserted under a full noun-phrase node in the syntax. I will not provide any further discussion of the lexical processes which guide the formation of such lexical phrases. My main concern here is with the syntactic structure of Swedish noun phrases, and I think the evidence presented in this chapter (mainly from Anward and Linell 1976 and Cooper 1984) shows that the structure of these phrases is not governed by syntactic rules.

5.5.1.3. *Adjectival determiners*

Another type of definite adjective not requiring the presence of an independent syntactic determiner is illustrated in (5.95). Some of these elements have already been discussed briefly in section 2.2.2.

(5.95) a. **sista** försöket
last attempt.DEF

b. **högra** sidan
right side.DEF

c. **ovannämnda** institution
above-mentioned department

d. **ena** ostbiten
one out of the two piece of cheese.DEF

e. **tredje** ostbiten
third piece of cheese.DEF

All examples in (5.95) are full noun phrases, but in all cases, a definite determiner could have preceded the adjectival elements. Some of the bold elements appear to be weak adjectives in that they end in *-a*, which could be assumed to be a manifestation of WK, or definiteness, or case, depending on how one analyses the adjectival feature. This feature is normally associated with the presence of a definite determiner and it is therefore unexpected to find it on an adjective in a noun phrase lacking a determiner.

Delsing (1988) suggests that these elements can occur without a preceding definite article because they are themselves inherently definite (this has also been suggested by van der Auwera 1995). In Delsing's analysis, an adjective in a definite noun phrase must be assigned Case by the determiner. The assumption is then that if an adjective is inherently definite, it does not need to be assigned Case.[56]

Delsing's basic idea can be reformulated in my approach, especially since I have linked the ability of a noun like *musen* to appear as a full referential noun phrase without a determiner to the fact that it carries the feature [+DEF]. If we consider the bold elements in (5.95), there is something intuitively definite about them. The use of *sista försöket* 'last attempt.DEF' would imply that there is one specific attempt in the discourse domain which the speaker expects the hearer to be able to identify as the last attempt. In an ordered set of pieces of cheese, one unique element is the third piece of cheese, and the noun phrase in (5.95e) assumes that this referent is known by the hearer.

In spite of the initial appeal of an analysis relying on the inherent definiteness of these elements, I do not think it is tenable. Firstly, in section 5.2.3 I defended DEF as a feature with semantic implications. That is, [+DEF] is equivalent semantically to the English syntactic determiner *the*. In section 5.4.3.1 I claimed that the *-a* marking on adjectives is an instantiation of a different feature, which I referred to as WK. This feature is not a semantic feature in the sense described above for [+DEF]. If it were, we would expect *hungriga* 'hungry.WK' to be able to function as a full noun phrase for the same reasons that *musen* 'mouse.DEF' can. The feature WK marks some form of agreement rather than definiteness *per se*.

A more concrete argument against inherent definiteness analysis is the fact that some of the elements in (5.95) can occur in indefinite noun phrases.

Consider the data in (5.96). As (5.96b) shows, they can even carry the marking associated with an indefinite noun phrase.

(5.96) a. ett sista försök
a last attempt

b. en ovannämnd institution
an above-mentioned.STR institution

If the explanation for noun phrases such as those in (5.95) is defined in terms of the inherent definiteness, then the bold elements are basically adjectives. The only difference is that these particular adjectives do not need to be preceded by a determiner. This is another reason to reject this analysis; there are more differences between the bold elements in (5.95) and ordinary adjectives like *hungriga*. In fact, these special adjectives turn out to share certain characteristics with determiners. Firstly, they behave like syntactic determiners in that they can 'license' an adjective. This means that elements like *sista* and *ovannämnda* may be followed by adjectives that would otherwise require a preceding determiner.[57] This is shown in (5.97) and (5.98).

(5.97) a. sista misslyckade försöket
last failed.WK attempt
'the last failed attempt'

b. *misslyckade försöket
failed.WK attempt

(5.98) a. ovannämnda ärevördiga institution
above-mentioned venerable.WK institution
'the above-mentioned venerable institution'

b. *ärevördiga institution
venerable institution

Secondly, these elements show the same type of selectional behaviour with respect to the morphological shape of the following head noun as is characteristic of syntactic definite determiners in Swedish. As discussed in section 5.3.3, some definite determiners in Swedish require that the noun be definite, whereas others only co-occur with nouns lacking the definite ending. As the examples in (5.99) show, this selectional behaviour is shared by the adjectival elements exemplified in (5.95).

(5.99) a. sista försöket / *sista försök
last attempt.DEF last attempt

b. ovannämnda institution / *ovannämnda institutionen
above-mentioned institution above-mentioned institution.DEF

From the data discussed in this section, I conclude that these special adjectives should be viewed as adjectival determiners, rather than adjectives which do not require a preceding determiner. This means that I will assume that these elements have two specifications in the lexicon, one as an adjective and one as an adjectival determiner. I refer to these elements as 'adjectival determiners' because they are exceptional in that some of their adjectival properties remain, for instance, in that they can take modifications as in (5.100).

(5.100) alldeles sista försöket
completely last attempt.DEF
'the very last attempt'

The fact that some of them occur only in definite noun phrases can be captured in their selectional restriction, the MOD feature in their adjectival function, and the SPEC feature when they function as determiners. I provide the simplified HPSG entries for *sista* and *ovannämnda* in (5.101). This could also be expressed within the DP analysis including more conventional phrase structure assumptions which was sketched in sections 5.2.3.4, 5.3.3.4 and 5.4.3.4, with the same advantages and drawbacks as are described in those sections.

(5.101) a. **sista** försöket

$$\begin{bmatrix} \text{CAT} & \begin{bmatrix} \text{HEAD } \textit{det} \begin{bmatrix} \text{DEF} & + \\ \text{SPEC} & \text{N}' \; [\text{DEF} +] \; [1] \end{bmatrix} \end{bmatrix} \\ \text{CONTENT} & [\text{RESTIND } [1] \; [\text{INDEX } [\text{PER} \;\; 3]]] \end{bmatrix}$$

b. det **sista** försöket

ett **sista** försök

$$\begin{bmatrix} \text{CAT} & \begin{bmatrix} \text{HEAD } \textit{adjective} \begin{bmatrix} \text{MOD} & \text{N}' \; [\text{SPR } \langle \textit{det} \rangle] \; [1] \\ \text{PRD} & \end{bmatrix} \end{bmatrix} \\ \text{CONT} & [\text{INDEX } [1]] \end{bmatrix}$$

c. **ovannämnda** beslut

$$\begin{bmatrix} \text{CAT} & \begin{bmatrix} \text{HEAD } \textit{det} \begin{bmatrix} \text{DEF} & + \\ \text{SPEC} & \text{N}' \; [\text{DEF } \textit{u}] \; [1] \end{bmatrix} \end{bmatrix} \\ \text{CONTENT} & [\text{RESTIND } [1] \; [\text{INDEX } [\text{PER} \;\; 3]]] \end{bmatrix}$$

d. det **ovannämnda** beslutet

$$\begin{bmatrix} \text{CAT} & \begin{bmatrix} \text{HEAD } \textit{adjective} \begin{bmatrix} \text{MOD} & \text{N}' \; [\text{SPR } \langle \textit{det} \; [\text{DEF} +] \rangle] \; [1] \\ \text{PRD} & - \end{bmatrix} \end{bmatrix} \\ \text{CONT} & [\text{INDEX } [1]] \end{bmatrix}$$

This type of adjective then has two lexical entries, one in which it functions as a determiner, (5.101a) and (5.101c), and one in which it is specified in the same way as any other adjective, (5.101b) and (5.101d). It should be pointed out that *sista* as a determiner has a similar specification to *den*, with the exception that it is not restricted for number and gender. The adjectival entry for *sista* differs from most other adjectives in that the value of its SPEC feature is an N′ which selects a determiner, but this determiner is not further specified for definiteness. This means that the adjectival use of *sista* requires a determiner, but that it can occur both with either a definite or an indefinite determiner. *Ovannämnda* in its determiner use is similar to *denna* except that the gender and number of the N′ with which it combines need not be specified. In its adjectival use, *ovannämnda* resembles other adjectives, in that this is a weak form, which requires the specifier of its sister to be a definite determiner. Like other adjectives, *ovannämnd* requires two more entries for the forms that the adjective takes in indefinite noun phrases, different forms depending on whether the noun is common gender or neuter.

5.5.1.4. *Predeterminers*

In (5.102) I provide examples of a third type of adjective which does not appear to require a preceding syntactic determiner. All the elements of this category may (but need not) be followed by a determiner, and they are therefore traditionally called predeterminers.[58]

(5.102) a. Halva (den gamla) ostbiten var borta.
half the old piece of cheese was gone
'Half the (old) piece of cheese was gone.'

b. Alla (de gamla) ostbitarna var borta.
all the old pieces of cheese were gone
'All the (old) pieces of cheese were gone.'

As with the special types of adjectives discussed in section 5.5.1.3, it seems implausible that the explanation lies in the inherent definiteness of these adjectives. The same arguments that were used in that section apply here. Firstly, the feature which adjectives carry in a definite noun phrase is not a semantic feature, and is therefore not expected to function semantically as a determiner. Secondly, the fact that these elements can occur in indefinite noun phrases argues against an explanation in terms of inherent definiteness. Examples of this are given in (5.103).

(5.103) a. En halv ostbit var kvar.
a half piece of cheese was left
'Half a piece of cheese was left.'

b. Alla ostbitar är mögliga.
all pieces of cheese are mouldy
'All of the pieces of cheese are mouldy.'

Instead, I will propose a solution in which these elements are modifiers, not of N′ like other adjectives, but of NP. This would give the specification in (5.104) for *halva* and *alla*, respectively.

(5.104) a. **halva** (den gamla) ostbiten

$$\begin{bmatrix} \text{CAT} & \begin{bmatrix} \text{HEAD} & \textit{adjective} \begin{bmatrix} \text{MOD} & \text{NP} \, [\text{DEF} +] \, [1] \\ \text{PRD} & - \end{bmatrix} \end{bmatrix} \\ \text{CONT} & [\text{INDEX} \, [1] \, [\text{NUM } \textit{sg}]] \end{bmatrix}$$

b. **alla** (de gamla) ostbitar(na)

$$\begin{bmatrix} \text{CAT} & \begin{bmatrix} \text{HEAD} & \textit{adjective} \begin{bmatrix} \text{MOD} & \text{NP} \, [1] \\ \text{PRD} & - \end{bmatrix} \end{bmatrix} \\ \text{CONT} & [\text{INDEX} \, [1] \, [\text{NUM } \textit{pl}]] \end{bmatrix}$$

A number of things follow from these specifications. Firstly, determiners attach below NP level, which means that in this function these modifiers must precede the determiner if there is one. The only other restriction these two elements put on their sisters is that the noun phrase must have the right feature values for the INDEX features. *Halva* also requires its sister to be definite. Note furthermore that *alla* puts no restrictions on the PER value, since *alla vi hundägare* 'all of us dog owners' is acceptable. This may also be true for *halva*, though given its semantics and its NUM value, it is difficult to imagine what an example would look like. There are two major types of singular definite noun phrases, namely, those which do not have a syntactic determiner, such as *ostbiten* 'piece-of-cheese.DEF', and those which do, like *den gamla ostbiten* 'the piece-of-cheese.DEF'. This then explains why *halva* in this usage can occur with or without a syntactic determiner following it. *Alla* in (5.104b) does not require the sister NP to be definite. Since it does require it to be specified as plural, there are three types of noun phrases with which it can combine: NPs which contain a syntactic determiner, like *de gamla ostbitarna* 'the old piece-of-cheese.PL.DEF'; definite NPs without a determiner, like *ostbitarna* 'piece-of-cheese.PL.DEF'; or indefinite plural NPs without a determiner, like *ostbitar* 'piece-of-cheese.PL'. In this way, the specifications in (5.104) correctly predict the behaviour of the so-called predeterminers with respect to their co-occurrence with determiners and determinerless noun phrases.

One possible objection to this solution might be that if they are modifiers, we would expect them to occur recursively, but they do not. I do not, however, find this a serious objection, since there are only a few adjectives in Swedish which can be specified as NP modifiers and combinations of these are either semantically incompatible or redundant.

5.5.1.5. *Conclusions*

In this section, I have discussed three types of elements, all of which have been claimed to be counterexamples to the generalization that weak adjectives require a preceding definite determiner. This means that they have been used to argue that the syntactic rules, or whatever equivalent mechanism is used, should permit definite noun phrases which contain an adjective but not a syntactic determiner. I have argued against this conclusion, claiming that none of these three types is a genuine counterexample. For the first type of adjective–noun combinations, I claimed that we are actually dealing with lexical units, which are not generated by the syntax. In the second case, I argued that the so-called adjectives function as determiners in certain constructions. Finally, predeterminers cannot be expected to be preceded by a determiner, since they are modifiers of NPs, rather than N′s and there are no determiners which select for an NP.

5.5.2. *Subjects and specifiers in HPSG*

Pollard and Sag (1994: 358ff.) follow Borsley (1988) in assuming that determiners are specifiers rather than subjects. There is a semantic motivation for making a distinction between determiners and subjects. For instance, subjects are semantic arguments, whereas determiners (with the possible exception of possessives) are not. Problems also arise at the syntactic level if determiners are considered subjects. Pollard and Sag (pp. 359–62) discuss the examples in (5.105) in the light of arguments put forward by Borsley.

(5.105) a. [John] is *an* idiot.
b. We consider [Sandy] *an* idiot.
c. [His father] *a* lifelong Elk, John was assured admission to the brotherhood.

In these examples, the element in square brackets is assumed to be the subject of the predicative noun (see the GB notion ‘small clause’). One fundamental assumption about the SUBJ list is that it can contain at most one element, that is, any element can have at most one subject. If determiners are considered subjects, then the noun phrases in (5.105) contain two subjects. Borsley (1988: 16–19) proposes to solve this by reconsidering the status of determiners; they are specifiers rather than subjects. This means that nouns may select both a subject and a specifier, and hence the noun phrases in (5.105) are predicted to be correct. With Borsley’s revision, an argument noun would have the category in (5.106a) and a predicative noun would be specified as in (5.106b) (Borsley 1988: 17).

(5.106) a. N $\begin{bmatrix} \text{SUBCAT} & \langle\ \rangle \\ \text{SPEC} & \langle \textit{det} \rangle \end{bmatrix}$

b. N $\begin{bmatrix} \text{SUBCAT} & \langle\ \rangle \\ \text{SPEC} & \langle \textit{det}\ [\text{DEF} -] \rangle \\ \text{SUBJ} & \langle \text{NP} \rangle \end{bmatrix}$

One consequence of this assumption is that determiners in noun phrases are given the same analysis as the bold elements in (5.107) which are also specifiers: of adjectives (5.107), prepositions (5.107b) and adverbs (5.107c) (all examples are from Pollard and Sag 1994: section 9.4, but similar examples are discussed by Borsley 1988). Pollard and Sag (pp. 364–6) also include complex elements in the set of determiners. These are exemplified in (5.108).

(5.107) a. John is **very / too / six feet** tall.
b. Mary's office is **just / right** around the corner.
c. Kim ran **so / too** fast.

(5.108) a. **many fewer** students
b. **much more** beer

Two issues arise here: first, how similar are elements like the bold ones in (5.107) and (5.108) to determiners, and, second, how different are determiners and subjects?

In section 2.4 I argued that Swedish elements corresponding to those in bold in (5.108) are most appropriately analysed as adjectives, rather than determiners. I also follow Payne's characterization of determiners as elements which do not permit modification (1993c) (though certain minor problems with this characteristic were discussed in section 2.2.2). The specifiers (in Borsley's and Pollard and Sag's terms) in (5.107) are, as far as I am aware, always optional. I do not know of any adjective, preposition or adverb which obligatorily selects a specifier. This means that there is quite a difference between this type of specifier and those elements which I call determiners. In the sense that they are almost always obligatory, determiners resemble subjects more than the type of specifier illustrated in (5.107) and (5.108).[59] The solution to the problem exemplified in (5.107) and (5.108) may then lie in reconsidering the status of the bold elements in those examples as adjectives, rather than specifiers.

If determiners are treated like subjects rather than specifiers, we could describe determinerless definite noun phrases in Swedish as showing a form of 'pro drop'. The inflection on the noun can be said to serve the same function as a syntactic determiner and therefore to permit the determiner to be unexpressed syntactically in the same way as the verbal inflections are said to do this in languages like Italian.[60]

A problem with assigning determiners the status of specifiers and assuming that a noun may take both a specifier and a subject relates to possessives. It seems quite reasonable to assume that possessives function as the subjects of nouns, especially in noun phrases such as those in (5.109).

(5.109) a. **Johans försök** misslyckades.
Johan's attempt failed
'Johan's attempt failed.'

b. **Den lille pojkens gråtande** irriterade hans mamma.
the little boy's crying irritated his mother
'The little boy's crying irritated his mother.'

Still, as the examples in (5.110) show, such noun phrases do not accept determiners in general, as might be expected if determiners were specifiers and possessives were subjects.[61]

(5.110) a. *vilket / *samma Johans försök
which same Johan's attempt

b. *det här / *samma den lille pojkens gråtande
this same the little boy's crying

If we follow Sommerstein's (1972) line of argument and analyse determiners as pronouns, that is NPs, then we can say that this position within the noun phrase can be filled by NP_{PRON} or NP_{GEN}. This would, of course, not mean that all pronouns must be able to occur in this position. Any pronouns which cannot fill the position would be marked in the lexicon as not being able to occur as specifiers, that is, they would be [SPEC ⟨ ⟩].

Even though I accept Borsley's arguments with respect to examples like those in (5.105), I would favour a solution in which determiners (as defined in section 2.2.2) are analysed in a different way from the entirely optional specifiers in (5.107) and (5.108). It should be noticed that it is only predicative noun phrases that permit this co-occurrence of determiners and subjects. In these cases, there are a very limited number of determiners which can occur, probably only the indefinite articles. It also appears that the status of a determiner in a predicative noun phrase is different from that in an argument noun phrase, the most striking difference being that in Swedish (and most other Germanic languages) the determiner is not obligatory in a predicative noun phrase, whereas the subject is. This is shown in (5.111).[62]

(5.111) a. Torun blev journalist.
Torun become journalist
'Torun became a journalist.'

b. Sture är lärare i kemi.
Sture is teacher in chemistry
'Sture is a teacher of chemistry.'

In this sense the determiner of a predicative noun phrase appears to function in a different way from ordinary determiners. The optionality is more reminiscent of elements like the bold words in (5.107) and (5.108).

I believe that this is a topic which requires further research involving a much wider language sample. Issues like what the assumed implications are of assigning subject status to an element need to be considered carefully. This links in with a broader discussion of what is entailed by all the notions referred to in standard X-bar syntax; if we permit specifiers to select their sisters in the way done here, then how should the distinction between specifier and head be defined? I will not deal with these complex issues here. For the purpose of my present analysis, I will tentatively propose that Swedish determiners, as defined by the criteria proposed in section 2.2.2, are selected by the same features as subjects of verbs and subjects of predicative noun phrases, that is, the SUBJ feature. I would, however, be happy to give this feature a different name in order to avoid the connotations with a particular grammatical function, subject. A broader term, parallel to 'complement' (as opposed to 'object') would be preferable. In fact, I think the term 'specifier' would be suitable to capture elements like subjects of clauses and determiners (see Bouma 1988).The bold elements in (5.107) and (5.108) which are referred to as 'specifiers' by Borsley (1988) and Pollard and Sag (1994) are, in my view, closer to modifiers in their nature. The major difference between specifiers and modifiers in HPSG lies in their selectional behaviour; with specifiers, there is mutual selection, whereas modifiers unidirectionally select their sister. This distinction seems to be appropriate in distinguishing between subjects and determiners on the one hand, and elements like the bold ones in (5.107) and (5.108) on the other. In section 6.4.4 I will discuss further the role of the determiner in predicative noun phrases.

5.6. CONCLUSIONS

What I hope to have demonstrated in this chapter is that an NP analysis can satisfactorily account for the distribution of features in Swedish definite noun phrases. Such an analysis can account for the fact that definite nouns can function as full noun phrases. Furthermore, it can account for the distribution of syntactic determiners, both in noun phrases lacking adjectival modifiers and in those containing such modifiers. In section 5.5 I showed that the analysis developed can account for a number of exceptional constructions as well.

The analysis developed depends on the assumptions made about selection in HPSG – namely that specifiers and their head sisters bi-directionally select each other, that modifiers may select their sisters, and that lexical heads select their complements. Crucially, this selection is expressed in terms of SYNSEM values, that is, complex feature matrices which can contain quite detailed information about the selected elements. The SYNSEM values must be token identical, that is, unifiable, with those of the sister.

With respect to the features involved, I have concluded that the feature DEF needs to have three values: +, – and u(nspecified).[63] I have shown that in this analysis, a separate feature for adjectives, such as [DECL *wk*/*str*] is not required. Furthermore, the feature matrices which specify lexical elements can be optimally under-specified. The advantages of this are especially obvious with respect to adjectives.

I have also provided evidence that this NP analysis is better than a DP analysis with more traditional assumptions about selection. What I have not demonstrated is that the present NP account is superior to a DP analysis within the same theoretical framework. This is, however, something I did not set out to do. Simplified, the premises which arose from chapter 4 were:

(i) Most so-called headedness criteria when applied to Swedish noun phrases do not actually provide any clear evidence as to the headedness of the phrase.

(ii) there are, however, some criteria which indicate that the noun is the central part of the noun phrase (semantic arguments, external selection, obligatory constituent and distributional equivalence, the last two in their narrow interpretation as described in sections 4.2.7 and 4.2.6).

(iii) Noun-phrase-internal selectional restrictions, under standard assumptions about head–complement relationships, require D to be the head.

In order to resolve (ii) and (iii), I set out to explore an analysis of Swedish noun phrases within a theoretical framework which has different assumptions about selection from those on which (iii) is founded. The central idea was that if an acceptable NP analysis can be formulated then this is preferable to a DP analysis. To my mind, I have shown that an NP analysis is feasible and furthermore that it has certain advantages over a DP analysis under more conventional assumptions about subcategorization. However, if convincing evidence to support the head status of D were to come to light, then I think a DP analysis could fruitfully be explored within this framework.

6
FEATURES IN INDEFINITE NOUN PHRASES

6.1. INTRODUCTION

In Swedish, non-predicative indefinite noun phrases whose head noun is a singular count noun must always contain a syntactic determiner. So whereas a definite noun like *musen* 'mouse.DEF' may function as a referential noun phrase, the corresponding non-definite form *mus* 'mouse' may not. This is exemplified in (6.1).[1] This difference between definite nouns and nouns lacking the definite ending must be accounted for here. In section 6.2, I will propose such an account.

(6.1) a. *(**En**) **mus** kom gående på köksbordet.
a mouse came walking on kitchen.table.DEF

b. Anders matade *(**ett**) **murmeldjur**.
Anders fed a marmot

There are cases in Swedish where indefinite nouns, both count and non-count, may function as a subject or as a complement of verbs or prepositions without being accompanied by a determiner. A number of examples of such nouns are provided in (6.2) to (6.5).

(6.2) a. **Möss** tycker om ost.
mice like cheese
'Mice like cheese.'

b. **Alkohol** fryser inte vid minus fem grader.
alcohol freezes not at minus five degrees
'Alcohol doesn't freeze at minus five degrees centigrade.'

(6.3) a. **Bil** är dyrt.
car is expensive
'Having a car is expensive.'

b. **Mjölk** är nyttigt.
milk is wholesome
'Drinking milk is good for you.'

(6.4) a. Karin fick **brev** från Anders.
Karin received letter from Anders
'Karin got a letter from Anders.'

b. Karin har **bil**.
Karin has car
'Karin has a car.' (in the sense of 'Karin owns a car.')

c. Anders äter **apelsin**.
Anders eats orange
'Anders is eating an orange.'

(6.5) a. Torun blev **journalist**.
Torun became journalist
'Torun became a journalist.'

b. De ansåg honom för **idiot**.
they considered him for idiot
'They considered him an idiot.'

The subjects of the sentences in (6.2a) and (6.2b) consist of a plural noun and a non-count noun respectively. The use of determinerless noun phrases with plural and non-count nouns is a notorious problem in all Germanic languages. I will provide a brief discussion of such examples in section 6.4.1.

Each of the types of determinerless noun phrases represented in (6.3) to (6.5) is severely restricted in its use. Noun phrases like those in (6.3) have some special characteristics that have been dealt with by a number of linguists. In section 6.4.2 I will give an overview of the literature and provide my own account of their properties. The very limited distribution of some of the examples in (6.4) makes them resemble collocations or idioms. In other cases they appear to depend on a very special use of the singular count noun in the object position. In section 6.4.3, I will consider these types of predicates. The type of predicative noun phrases exemplified in (6.5) will be discussed in more detail in section 6.4.4.

6.2. Nouns with determiners

6.2.1. *The issues*

With respect to argument positions, the analysis of indefinite noun phrases involves less complex issues than that of the definite ones. Obviously, an analysis has to be provided for indefinite noun phrases consisting of a non-definite noun and an indefinite determiner. This analysis must involve some way of distinguishing indefinite noun phrases from definite ones. In the majority of cases, this will be made in terms of a definiteness feature, but there are also proposals that the distinction be made in categorial terms.

Secondly, the analysis must account for the fact that, whereas definite nouns may function as full noun phrases without a determiner, the corresponding non-definite nouns may not. This is illustrated in (6.6).

(6.6) a. Musen / *Mus åt upp osten.
mouse.DEF mouse ate up cheese.DEF
'The mouse ate all the cheese.' Attempted reading as 'A mouse . . .' fails.

b. Murmeldjuret / *Murmeldjur sov alltid när vi såg det.
marmot.DEF marmot slept always when we saw it
'The marmot was always asleep when we saw it.' Attempted reading as 'A marmot . . .' fails.

6.2.2. *Previous analyses*

The focus of almost all the analyses of Swedish noun phrases discussed in sections 5.2.2, 5.3.2 and 5.4.2 is on definite noun phrases (notable exceptions are Holmberg 1992 and Delsing 1993). In such cases, since the authors set out to deal with Swedish (or Scandinavian) noun phrases in general, I assume that the proposed analysis is meant to extend straightforwardly to indefinite noun phrases.

In all the analyses to be discussed in more detail here, definite and indefinite noun phrases in argument positions will be of the same basic category (NP, DP or nP). The distinction between the two types will be defined in terms of some definiteness feature. In an early article, Delsing (1988) did, however, propose that the difference is categorial.[2]

Delsing (1993) provides an interesting account of a number of unexpected aspects of indefinite noun phrases. He does not discuss in detail ordinary indefinite singular nouns occurring with an indefinite determiner in an argument position. However, it is clear that their structure can be straightforwardly extrapolated from his analysis of the definite articles. Delsing's claim is that all noun phrases in argument position must contain a determiner in the surface structure. In singular indefinite noun phrases in argument position, the indefinite article *en* fills this function.[3] The reason a non-definite noun, like *mus*, cannot function as an argument noun phrase, whereas *musen* can, lies in the simple fact that *mus* does not contain a syntactic determiner, which makes it an illicit argument noun phrase.

The structure of indefinite noun phrases with an indefinite determiner is parallel to that of definite noun phrases. Delsing (1993) distinguishes between 'meaningful determiners' – like demonstratives – and articles. Of these, only the meaningful determiners are present in the underlying structure, hence they are BASE-GENERATED DETERMINERS in Delsing's terms. ARTICLES, on the other hand, are inserted into that surface structure in order to fill the D position, which must be filled in all argument noun phrases.

Presumably, indefinite determiners, like the definite ones, will select for at least three different complements: NP, AP and DegP. The different types are illustrated in (6.7), and the corresponding trees are found in (6.8) (see Delsing 1993: 69–100).

(6.7) a. en [mus]$_{NP}$
a mouse
b. en [hungrig mus]$_{AP}$
a hungry mouse
c. en [mycket hungrig mus]$_{DegP}$
a very hungry mouse

(6.8)

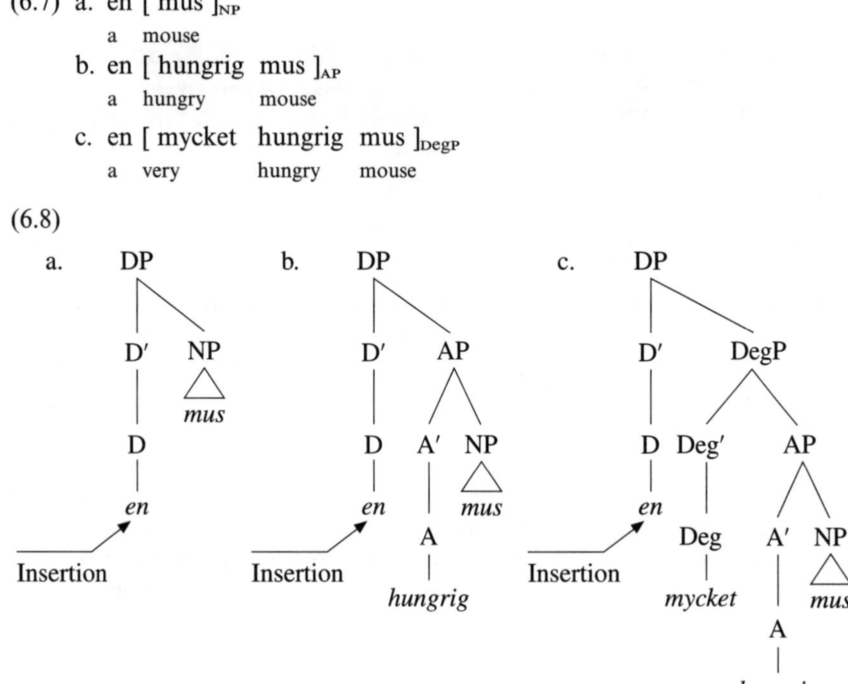

Santelmann (1992) does not explicitly state in which position *en* is generated. Definite determiners differ as to their position in the underlying structure: *den* is inserted in D, and *-en* is in Num (see (5.11 in section 5.2.2.1 and (5.56) in section 5.4.2.1). Santelmann appears to assume that other syntactic definite determiners are base-generated in D. Since the indefinite *en* occurs in complementary distribution with other determiners, we can assume that it is also generated in D. Her analysis of an indefinite noun phrase like *en* (*hungrig*) *mus* would presumably have the shape in (6.9). It is not clear to me whether or not Santelmann would assume an empty Num projection between the D and the N projections.

In (6.9) *en* supports the [–DEF] feature in D, it also m-commands the AP and can therefore license the strong morphology on the adjective. The gender features on the adjective are licensed by the noun. The reason why *mus* is not a legal DP on its own is then presumably that an indefinite noun cannot support the [–DEF] feature in D in the way that a definite noun can support [+DEF]. A definite noun can do this because of the special properties of the *-en* element.

In Svenonius's (1992c) Edge Feature solution, the principle governing the structure of definite noun phrases was defined in terms of the feature value [+DEF] which must be manifested on the head of the left-most element of each definite noun phrase. Whereas a noun like *musen* has the feature [+DEF], *mus* is specified as [–DEF]. As pointed out in section 5.3.2.2, Svenonius (1992c: 149) assumes that this is not a semantic feature, and therefore there is no problem with a definite determiner selecting an indefinite noun. So, the restriction that applies to definite noun phrases is morphosyntactic, rather than semantic, in nature. Still, the feature value [–DEF] seems to have a different status from its positive counterpart [+DEF], and the structure of indefinite noun phrases cannot be accounted for in terms of the Edge Feature Principle. A noun like *mus* carries the feature [–DEF] in Svenonius's analysis. This means that a noun phrase consisting of *mus* on its own has an element carrying the feature value [–DEF] as its left-most element. If the same principles applied to indefinite noun phrases as to definite noun phrases, Svenonius's analysis would lead us to expect that *mus* may be a full DP. However, since this not the case, I assume that Svenonius would account for these facts in a different way.

(6.9)

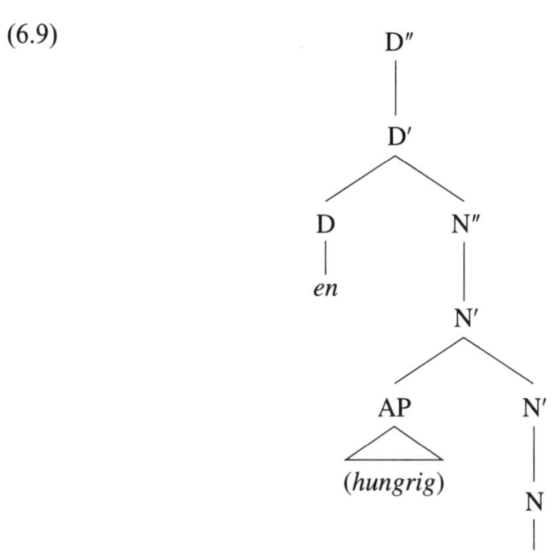

In Cooper (1984), the rule that permits *musen* to function as a full noun phrase refers specifically to the feature value [+DEF]. This is the case in both the syntactic and the semantic solutions which he proposes. The grammar would not therefore be expected to permit an indefinite noun, which is marked [–DEF], to project up to phrasal level without the presence of a determiner. Indefinite noun phrases containing a determiner are generated by the standard phrase structure rule NP → Det N′.

Holmberg (1992) does explicitly discuss indefinite referential noun phrases and contrasts them both with definite referential noun phrases and predicative noun phrases. As outlined in section 5.2.2.2, Holmberg assumes that, in an argument noun phrase, the highest specifier of the noun phrase must be licensed internally. In most noun phrases, the specifier position will contain *pro* which is licensed by Spec–Head agreement. In the case of indefinite singular noun phrases, we get the structure in (6.10), where n is the functional head of the noun phrase.

(6.10)

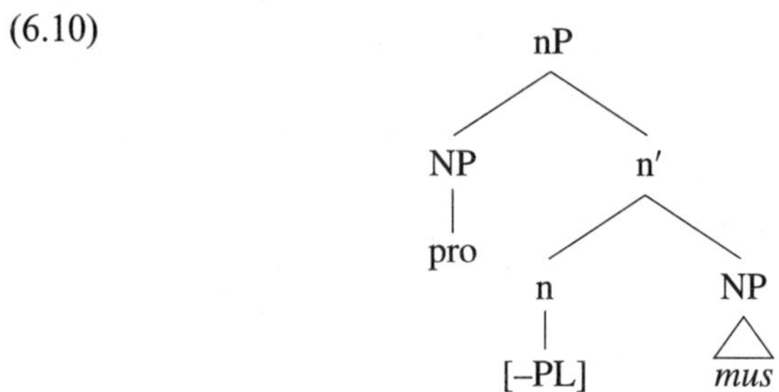

In (6.10), the noun moves to n to have its features checked. The feature value [–PL] is assumed to be an instance of 'weak agreement' in the sense of Chomsky (1992), and therefore movement is triggered only at LF. In the syntax, the position is instead filled by the indefinite article *en* which licenses the n position and its specifier. In argument positions, the specifier position will be filled by *pro*. In non-argument positions, certain nouns may license a subject in the specifier position. I will return to Holmberg's account of such cases in section 6.4.4. In section 6.4.1 I will discuss what happens when the n position contains the feature value [+PL].

6.2.3. *The proposed analysis*

In section 5.2.3, I claimed that the definite ending on nouns is the manifestation of a definiteness feature with semantic implications, which means that it can function as a determiner semantically. Hence, a noun like *musen* can function as a full referential noun phrase; the feature [DEF +] does the same job in the semantic component as a syntactic determiner like English *the* would do. This assumption entails that [DEF –] should also have the semantic function of a determiner, similar to English *a*. Therefore if *mus* is assumed to be characterized by the feature [DEF –], we would expect sentences such as (6.11) to be grammatical.

(6.11) a. ***Mus** kom gående på köksbordet.
mouse came walking on kitchen.table.DEF

b. *Anders matade **murmeldjur**.
Anders fed marmot

In section 5.3.3 I showed that certain definite determiners, like for instance *denna*, may select as their complement a nominal headed by a non-definite noun. This led me to assume that a noun like *mus* is actually unspecified for definiteness – it is [DEF *u*]. Having the feature value [DEF *u*] is not the same as lacking any possibility of specification for the feature DEF in the way that a verb like *kittla* 'tickle' does. An element which is specified as [DEF *u*] can become [DEF +] through unification with an element specified as [DEF +].

The consequence for indefinite noun phrases is that since a noun like *mus* is [DEF *u*], we do not expect that it can trigger the semantic interpretation of a determiner. In other words, we do not expect *mus* to be able to function as a full noun phrase. This is the correct prediction, as the examples in (6.11) showed. In terms of Boolean Algebra (Keenan and Faltz 1985), *mus* and *murmeldjur* require a determiner to trigger the semantic function necessary to take the element from P to P*. Within the NP analysis I discussed in section 5.2.3.2, this distinction has to be expressed in terms of syntactic differences.

In an NP solution the difference would be that an indefinite noun obligatorily selects a determiner through its SPR feature. A definite noun, on the other hand, has an optional DET element on its SPR list. This is illustrated in (6.12), repeated from (5.21).

(6.12) a. *mus*: SYNSEM| LOC| CAT $\begin{bmatrix} \text{HEAD} & \textit{noun} \\ \text{SPR} & \langle \textit{det} \rangle \end{bmatrix}$

b. *musen*: SYNSEM| LOC| CAT $\begin{bmatrix} \text{HEAD} & \textit{noun}[\text{DEF} +] \\ \text{SPR} & \langle (\textit{det}) \rangle \end{bmatrix}$

It should be noted that the determiner on the SPR list of a non-definite noun does not have to be further specified for definiteness. In fact, it should not be specified for definiteness, since it can combine either with a definite or an indefinite noun. As discussed in sections 4.3.2 and 5.3.3.2, I assume that the grammar must contain some principle which allows non-head inheritance regardless of whether an NP or a DP analysis is assumed. This principle will then ensure that the noun phrase as a whole inherits the feature value for DEF from the determiner. The optional determiner on the SPR list of definite nouns does not have to be specified for definiteness either, since the determiners with which they combine will be specified through their SPEC feature as selecting definite nominals only. Furthermore, in these cases, unification could not take place between a definite noun and an indefinite determiner, since they would carry contradictory values for the feature DEF.

The resulting representation for an indefinite determiner like *en* is then as in (6.13). In (6.13) the element on the SPR list is an abbreviation; the full sign is provided in (6.14). Unification of the feature values of a determiner with this specification and a noun specified as [DEF *u*] (as in (6.12a)) results in an N″ [DEF –].

$$(6.13)\ \textit{en}\ \left[\begin{array}{ll} \text{CAT} & \left[\text{HEAD}\ \textit{det}\ \left[\begin{array}{ll} \text{DEF} & - \\ \text{SPEC} & \text{N}'\ [\text{DEF}\ u]\,[1] \end{array}\right]\right] \\ \text{CONTENT} & \left[\text{RESTIND}\ [1]\ \left[\text{INDEX}\ \left[\begin{array}{ll} \text{PER} & \textit{3} \\ \text{NUM} & \textit{sg} \\ \text{GEND} & \textit{com} \end{array}\right]\right]\right] \end{array}\right]$$

$$(6.14)\ \textit{synsem}\ \left[\text{LOC}\ \left[\begin{array}{ll} \text{CAT} & \left[\begin{array}{ll} \text{HEAD} & \textit{noun}\ [\text{DEF}\ u] \\ \text{SPR} & \langle \textit{det}\ [1] \rangle \\ \text{LEX} & - \end{array}\right] \\ \text{CONT} & \left[\text{INDEX}\ [1]\ \left[\begin{array}{ll} \text{PER} & \textit{3} \\ \text{NUM} & \textit{sg} \\ \text{GEND} & \textit{com} \end{array}\right]\right] \end{array}\right]\right]$$

6.3. Noun phrases containing adjectives

6.3.1. *The issues*

If we restrict the discussion to noun phrases containing singular count nouns, we can say that the strong adjectives involved resemble the weak ones discussed in section 5.4 in that they need to be preceded by a determiner. Since the presence of a determiner is usually required for independent reasons in an indefinite noun phrase, this similarity is not obvious and rarely noted (though for an exception, see Holmberg 1992). However, if we look at a type of indefinite noun phrase where a determiner is not obligatory, then the similarity will become more obvious.

Certain nouns may occur without an indefinite determiner in predicative position. These kinds of nouns can be referred to as 'role nouns'. They will be discussed in more detail in section 6.4.4. Examples are provided in (6.15), where the version without the determiner is preferred.

(6.15) a. Torun är (en) **journalist**.
Torun is a journalist
'Torun is a journalist.'

b. Gazza är (ett) **fotbollsproffs**.
Gazza is a professional football player
'Gazza is a professional football player.'

If an adjective occurs in one of these predicative role noun phrases, an indefinite article becomes obligatory. This is illustrated in (6.16).

(6.16) a. Torun är *(en) **skicklig journalist**.
Torun is a skilful journalist
'Torun is a skilful journalist.'

b. Gazza är *(**ett**) **överbetalt fotbollsproffs**.
Gazza is a over-paid professional football player
'Gazza is an over-paid professional football player.'

I take this as evidence that strong adjectives as well as weak ones require the presence of a determiner.[4]

6.3.2. *Previous analyses*

Since the fact that strong adjectives require the presence of a determiner in much the same way as the weak ones often passes unnoticed, not many of the analyses I have dealt with in this book consider this issue. An exception is Holmberg (1992). In his account of indefinite noun phrases, all indefinite noun phrases have an element which must fill the specifier position of the projection. If the noun phrase is predicative, the filler is (the trace of) a subject. In an argument noun phrase it is an empty pronoun *pro*. Holmberg (pp. 64–5) argues that adjectives also occupy the specifier position of the noun phrase NP. In order to provide a new specifier position for the subject trace or *pro* when an adjective is present, a determiner must be inserted. This is illustrated in (6.17), where e_j is the subject trace and is bound outside the noun phrase. Note that this account is identical to the one Holmberg proposes of the requirement for determiners in definite noun phrases with adjectives (see section 5.4.2.2).

(6.17)

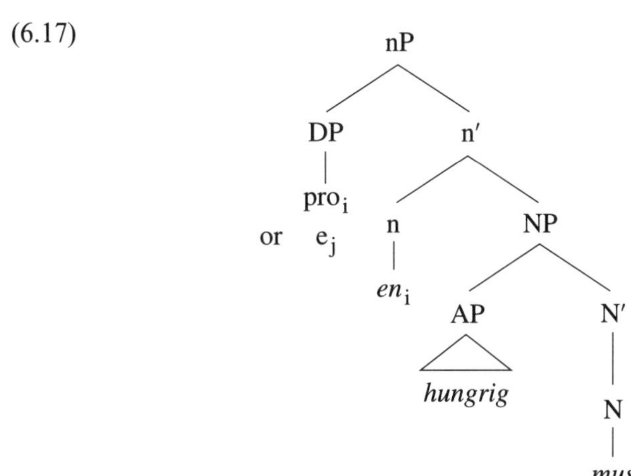

6.3.3. *Proposed analysis*

In section 5.4.3.2, I showed that one of the advantages of the NP analysis proposed in this book is the fact that the feature [DECL *wk/str*] becomes redundant. The two sets of adjectives which are usually distinguished by means of this feature can be distinguished by other means. A weak adjective is one which, through its MOD feature, selects a nominal selecting a definite determiner. The singular forms of strong adjectives can be defined as those which select a nominal selecting an indefinite determiner. The relevant specification for an adjective with neuter gender marking is given in (6.18). As in chapter 4, I give a more detailed version of the MOD feature separately, in (6.19).

(6.18)
$$\begin{bmatrix} \text{CAT} & \begin{bmatrix} \text{HEAD} & \mathit{adjective} \begin{bmatrix} \text{MOD} & \text{N}' \; [\text{SPR} \; \langle \mathit{det} \, [\text{DEF} -] \rangle] \; [1] \\ \text{PRD} & - \end{bmatrix} \\ \text{SUBJ} & \langle \; \rangle \\ \text{SPR} & \langle \; \rangle \\ \text{COMPS} & \langle \; \rangle \end{bmatrix} \\ \text{CONT} & \begin{bmatrix} \text{INDEX} \; [1] \begin{bmatrix} \text{NUM} & \mathit{sg} \\ \text{GEND} & \mathit{nt} \end{bmatrix} \end{bmatrix} \end{bmatrix}$$

(6.19)
$$\text{SYNSEM} \begin{bmatrix} \text{LOCAL} \begin{bmatrix} \text{CAT} & \begin{bmatrix} \text{HEAD} & \mathit{noun} \\ \text{SPR} & \langle \mathit{det} \, [\text{DEF} -] \; [1] \rangle \end{bmatrix} \\ \text{CONT} & [\text{INDEX} \; [1]] \end{bmatrix} \end{bmatrix}$$

Unlike the weak adjectives, the strong ones need to be specified for gender and number, since there are different forms for neuter singular, common singular and plural. I assume that they need not be specified for person. Since there are no indefinite first and second person determiners in Swedish, their distribution will be restricted to third person noun phrases anyway. The MOD value in (6.18) ensures that these adjectives are preceded by an indefinite determiner. Possibly, this specification could be different for a plural adjective. If we do not assume zero determiners for indefinite plural noun phrases, then plural strong adjectives do not require their sisters to select a determiner at all.

There is a further distributional difference between weak adjectives and strong ones. Weak adjectives cannot occur in predicative positions, whereas the corresponding strong forms can. This is reflected in their feature specifications. Weak adjectives have the feature value [PRD –] (see (5.70) in section 5.4.3.2), whereas strong adjectives are unspecified for PRD.

6.4. Nouns without determiners

6.4.1. *Plural and non-count nouns*

In section 5.2, I discussed one type of noun that may function as a full referential noun phrase without a syntactic determiner, namely definite nouns. For such noun phrases, I have claimed that the morphological definiteness marking functions semantically as a determiner and that this is why definite nouns can function as full noun phrases. In the syntactic analyses that I provided, this semantic argument was not always represented in an obvious way. Instead, the absence of a syntactic determiner was indirectly related to the morphologically manifested feature. In the NP analysis, definite nouns were specified as having different valency requirements from nouns lacking morphological marking for definiteness, that is, they do not select a specifier. In the DP analysis, the feature [DEF +] was assumed to license a zero determiner.

There are, however, two other major classes of nouns which do not obligatorily select a specifier: plural nouns and non-count nouns. In this book, I will have rather little to say about such noun phrases, since they involve extremely complex semantic issues. In what follows, I will, however, discuss some of the issues involved and consider some of the ways proposed for dealing with them in Swedish.

6.4.1.1. *The issues*

Some examples of noun phrases containing plural and non-count nouns are provided in (6.20). As (6.20b) and (6.20d) show, such nouns do not require a syntactic determiner even when they are preceded by an AP. Compare this with the examples in (6.21) where the corresponding definite forms do require a determiner (though see the discussion in section 5.5.1).

(6.20) a. **Katter** har ofta hängmage.
cats have often swag belly

b. **Gamla katter** har ofta hängmage.
old cats have often swag belly

c. **Gröt** är nyttigt.
porridge is wholesome

d. **Kall gröt** är läskigt.
cold porridge is horrible

(6.21) a. *(**De**) **gamla katterna** har hängmage.
the old cats.DEF have swag belly

b. *(**Den**) **kalla gröten** är läskig.
the cold porridge is horrible

The bold noun phrases in (6.20) have generic reference, whereas the ones in (6.21) have specific reference. One issue that must be dealt with before analysing the type of noun phrases illustrated in (6.20) is the status of generic noun phrases; are they full noun phrases: with the same structure as noun phrases used referentially? Predicative noun phrases, for instance, are often assumed to differ in structure from referential ones (see section 6.4.4.2). In a DP analysis, predicative noun phrases may be assumed to be NPs. For Swedish this assumption can be motivated by the fact that singular count nouns can occur without an article in predicative position (see discussion in section 6.4.4).

A similar distinction can be made between referential noun phrases and generic noun phrases, as proposed by Delsing (1988: 67–8). One problem with this approach is that generic noun phrases may also take other shapes, identical to referential noun phrases. Certain count nouns can occur with an indefinite article or in their definite form and still receive a generic reading. This is exemplified in (6.22), where a generic reading is certainly possible, and in the context it is the most plausible one. This option does not seem to be open to non-count nouns. We would, of course, not expect non-count nouns to occur with a determiner like *en* which requires a count noun. However, a non-count noun in its definite form appears not to be accessible to a generic reading, as (6.23) shows.

(6.22) a. **En katt** sover upp till tjugo timmar per dygn.
a cat sleeps up to twenty hours per 24 hours
'A cat sleeps up to twenty hours per day.'

b. **Katten** är egentligen ett nattdjur.
cat.DEF is actually a nocturnal animal
'The cat is actually a nocturnal animal.'

(6.23) **Gröten** är nyttig.
porridge.DEF is wholesome
'The (particular) porridge is good for you.' Not 'Porridge in general is good for you.'

This means that, if we assign a different structure to generic noun phrases because some of them do not require or do not permit a determiner, we must still be able to account for why some of them do have the structure of a full noun phrase and do contain a determiner.

When plural noun phrases such as the one in (6.20a) are used referentially, a determiner corresponding to the English unstressed *some* [sm̩] is used. Examples are provided in (6.24). The Swedish word *några* in these examples is assumed to be unstressed.[5]

(6.24) a. Hunden jagade **några katter**.
dog.DEF chased some cats
'The dog was chasing some [sm̩] cats.'

b. Jag såg **några katter** med hängmage.
I saw some cats with swag belly
'I saw some [sm̩] cats with swag bellies.'

If a plural noun such as *katter* is used without a determiner where a generic reading is not obvious it sounds odd, if not ungrammatical. The example in (6.25a) in the context given sounds distinctly odd to me; (6.25b) would have to be used. This seems to interact in complex ways with exactly how many elements one would normally expect *några* to refer to in each example. Consider the examples in (6.25c). This strikes me as entirely correct with a referential reading, unlike (6.25a), but like (6.25b).

(6.25) Jag öppnade dörren till sovrummet och . . .
'I opened the door to the bedroom and . . .

a. ? . . . jag såg **katter** på fönsterbrädan.
I saw cats on window.sill.DEF

b. . . . jag såg **några katter** på fönsterbrädan.
I saw some cats on window.sill.DEF
. . . I saw some [sm̩] cats on the window sill.'

c. . . . jag såg **myror** på fönsterbrädan.
I saw ants on window.sill.DEF
. . . I saw some ([sm̩]) ants on the window sill.'

In a major work on these issues, Carlson (1977) shows that the type of predicate that follows a plural noun phrase in subject position also influences the interpretation. Due to the extremely complex semantic issues involved here, I will not propose a solution. I will instead turn now to a discussion of a couple of proposals that have been put forward for this type of determinerless noun phrase in Swedish. The term 'determinerless' is not entirely appropriate here, since it is commonly assumed, especially in the transformational tradition, that this type of noun phrase contains a zero determiner.

6.4.1.2. *Previous analyses*

The analysis proposed by Cooper (1984) for bare plurals does not make reference to covert determiners. In the syntactic solution, there is a phrase structure rule which permits a plural indefinite N^1 to expand as a plural indefinite N^2. This rule, slightly adapted from Cooper (1984: 134), is found in (6.26a). In the analysis based on semantic filtering, the syntactic rules involved are instead those in (6.26b). The appropriate interpretation rule is provided in (6.26c).

(6.26) a. $\underset{\begin{bmatrix}-\text{DEF}\\+\text{PL}\end{bmatrix}}{N^2} \rightarrow \underset{\begin{bmatrix}-\text{DEF}\\+\text{PL}\end{bmatrix}}{N^1}$

b. $N^2 \rightarrow (\text{Det}) \quad N^1$

$N^1 \rightarrow \left\{\begin{matrix}\text{Adj} & N^1\\ & N\end{matrix}\right\}$

c. $\left\| \left[\underset{\begin{bmatrix}-\text{DEF}\\+\text{PL}\\ \alpha\end{bmatrix}}{N^1} \right] \quad \underset{\begin{bmatrix}-\text{DEF}\\+\text{PL}\\ \alpha\end{bmatrix}}{N^2} \right\| = \text{BARE} - \text{PL}\ (\|N^1\|)$

As mentioned in section 6.2.2, Holmberg (1992) assumes that an argument noun phrase must be a closed expression, in the sense that its specifier position may not contain a variable bound outside the noun phrase. Instead, the noun licenses a subject argument, or more commonly, a *pro* in its specifier position. In the case of indefinite plural nouns, Holmberg (p. 63) assumes the structure in (6.27) (see (6.10) in section 6.2.2), where n is a functional projection heading the noun phrase.

(6.27)

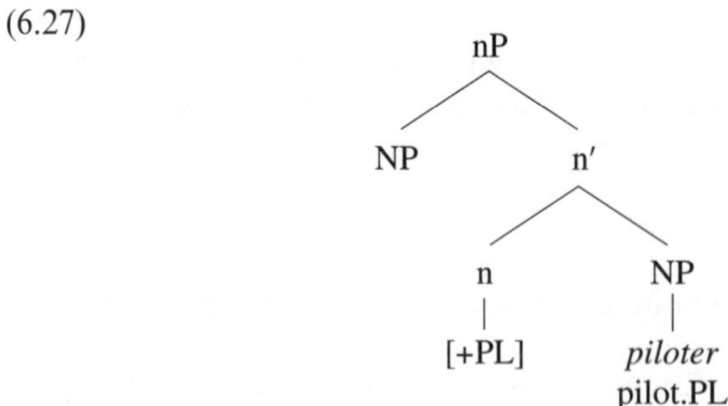

In (6.27), the feature value [+PL] differs from [–PL] in that it is a case of 'strong agreement' in terms of Chomsky (1992) (see (6.10)). The noun moves to the n position to have its number morphology checked. When the feature in n is [+PL], movement is triggered in overt syntax. Having moved there, the noun licenses the n node and its specifier position. In most cases, the specifier position will be filled by *pro*. Another possibility will be discussed in section 6.4.4.

None of the articles referred to so far discusses explicitly or in any detail the distinction between generic and non-generic use of bare plurals and non-count nouns. Delsing (1988: 67–8) does, however, provide a brief discussion. He claims that generic noun phrases are NPs rather than DPs, and as such they are not expected to contain a determiner. He does not provide detailed arguments, but refers to two facts about this type of noun phrase in support of the categorial distinction he makes. Firstly, he claims, generic noun phrases never contain determiners. As I showed in (6.22), both a noun in its definite form and a noun with an indefinite determiner may be interpreted generically. In Delsing's analysis, the definite ending of the noun is, in fact, a syntactic determiner. This means that both the examples in (6.22) would be evidence against the generalization that generic noun phrases may not contain determiners. It does probably hold true for non-count nouns, but Delsing's structural distinction is meant to have wider application. Secondly, the type of non-agreement that will be discussed in section 6.4.2 is used as an argument. However, Delsing himself points out that a problem with this is that non-agreeing noun phrases may in fact contain determiners. Despite the brevity of Delsing's argument, the possibility he introduces of making a categorial distinction between generic and non-generic noun phrases is an interesting one.

In his thesis, Delsing (1993) deals in more detail with bare plural and non-count noun phrases. He argues that noun phrases which consist of a bare plural or a non-count noun contain a syntactic determiner when they occur in an argument position, but that they do not in a predicative position. Delsing (p. 30) aims to maintain a strong claim about noun phrases and determiners (the claim was originally proposed by Stowell 1991):

(6.28) a. If a noun phrase is a non-argument, then it has no determiner.
b. If a noun phrase is an argument, then it has a determiner.

The claim in (6.28b) entails that, for all argument noun phrases which do not contain an overt determiner, Delsing must assume that there is a covert one. If the same type of noun phrase can also occur in a predicate position, it must be assumed not to contain a determiner in those instances.

Delsing (1993: 40–53) uses the term UNCOUNTABLE to refer to three classes of nouns: bare plurals, non-count nouns and 'bare singulars'. Bare singulars are nouns which do in principle have a plural form, but which may be used in their singular form in the same way as bare plural or non-count nouns. Examples are *potatis* 'potato' and *fisk* 'fish', which have the plural forms *potatisar* and *fiskar*, respectively. Examples of the 'uncountable' use of such nouns are given in (6.29) (see Delsing 1993: 43).

(6.29) Han köpte mycket fisk (*fiskar) / potatis (*potatisar).
he bought much fish potato
'He bought a lot of fish/potatoes.'

Delsing's argument for assuming that uncountable noun phrases do contain covert determiners (apart from his desire to maintain the claim in (6.28)) is based on facts from certain Northern Swedish dialects. In these dialects, a form identical to the definite form of the noun is commonly used with uncountables, where Standard Swedish would use a bare plural or bare non-count noun. Compare the two examples in (6.30) (the example in (6.30b) is from Delsing (1993: 49).

(6.30) a. De satt och drack **öl**. Standard Swedish
they sat and drank beer
b. Däm satt å drack **öl-e**. N. Swedish dialect
they sat and drank beer-DEF
'They were drinking beer.'

In these Northern Swedish dialects, this form of uncountable noun can also occur in existential constructions. This is illustrated in (6.31) (from Delsing 1993: 52).

(6.31) Hä finns **fisk-en** däri hinken. N. Swedish dialect
there exist fish-DEF there.in bucket.DEF
'There is fish in the bucket there.'

The fact that definite noun phrases are usually not permitted in this position leads Delsing to conclude that the ending *-en* is in this case actually an instance of an indefinite article. The dialects in question therefore have two homophonous bound articles, one definite and one indefinite. The latter of these two is used with uncountable nouns only. Delsing (1993: 52–3) concludes further that 'if uncountable noun phrases have the same structure in Standard and Northern Swedish, we must assume that the Standard Mainland Scandinavian languages have a null determiner with uncountables, and that [5.12] still holds.' This line of argument strikes me as a bit brittle, and I will return to Delsing's discussion of other potential counter-examples to the generalization in (6.28) in sections 6.4.3 and 6.4.4.

6.4.1.3. *Conclusions and proposed analysis*

The brief discussion of the relevant data (in section 6.4.1.1) and the account of the analyses of this type of noun phrase that have been proposed in the literature on Swedish (in section 6.4.1.2) have only served to emphasize the complexity of these issues. In order to establish whether or not a zero determiner is motivated in all or some of these cases, for instance, a detailed study of the subtle semantics of these noun phrases, and their interaction with different types of predicates, is required. Such a thorough investigation is well beyond the scope of this book.

For this reason, I will not even attempt a syntactic description of bare plurals and non-count nouns. Suffice it to say here that if the conclusion of a detailed study of such noun phrases was either that generic noun phrases should be assigned the same structure as referential ones, or that a plural or non-count noun without a determiner can function as a full referential noun phrase, then the analyses provided in sections 5.2.3.2 and 5.3.3.2 can be extended to cover plural and non-count nouns as well. One alternative would be to assume that plural and non-count nouns are preceded by a zero determiner, one that induces a generic reading and is also capable of 'covering' the adjective in the way that an overt determiner can.

6.4.2. *Non-agreeing noun phrases*

6.4.2.1. *The issues*

I turn now to cases where determinerless indefinite singular nouns function as the subjects of clauses. This type of construction has two main characteristics. Firstly, the subject is always indefinite and may consist of a non-definite singular count noun without a determiner. Secondly, there may be gender and number disagreement between the subject and a predicative adjective. Regardless of the gender and number features of the subject, a predicative adjective will occur in its singular neuter form. This means that it need not lead to disagreement; when the subject is neuter singular the two forms will actually agree. A more appropriate term is therefore 'non-agreement'.

The agreement distinction is only visible on the adjectival part of the predicate, since Swedish verbs show no number or gender distinctions.[6] In (6.32), I give examples where the adjective occurs in its singular neuter form, regardless of the number and gender features. This should be compared with (6.33), where the subject noun phrases are ordinary legal definite subjects and the predicative adjectives must agree. The examples in (6.34) show that there are similar examples with subjects containing indefinite articles. In such cases, agreeing examples can also always be found, as in (6.35).

(6.32) a. Bil är **dyrt** / ***dyr**.
car.COM.SG is expensive.NT.SG .COM.SG

b. Gröt är **nyttigt** / ***nyttig**.
porridge.COM.SG is wholesome.NT.SG .COM.SG

c. Nyrostade jordnötter är **gott** / ***goda**.
newly-roasted.PL peanut.COM.PL are tasty.NT.SG .PL

(6.33) a. Denna bil är **dyr** / ***dyrt**.
this car.COM.SG is expensive.COM.SG .NT.SG

b. Den här gröten är **nyttig** / ***nyttigt**.
this porridge.COM.SG is wholesome.COM.SG .NT.SG

c. Våra nyrostade jordnötter är **goda** / ***gott**.
our newly-roasted.PL peanut.COM.PL are tasty.PL .NT.SG

(6.34) a. En flaska vin om dagen är **nyttigt** / ***nyttig**.
a.COM bottle.COM wine a day is wholesome.NT.SG .COM.SG
'A bottle of wine a day is good for you.'

b. Några öl före maten är alltid **gott** / ***god**.
some.PL beer before food.DEF are always tasty.NT.SG .COM.SG
'A couple of beers before dinner always tastes good.'

(6.35) a. En flaska vin blir **god** / ***gott**
a.COM bottle.COM wine becomes tasty.COM.SG .NT.SG
om den värmes till rumstemperatur.
if it is warmed to room temperature
'A bottle of wine improves if you warm it to room temperature.'

b. Några öl som har stått i solen är inte **goda** / ***gott**.
some.PL beer that have stood in sun.DEF are not tasty.PL .NT.SG
'A few beers which have stood in the sunlight are not nice.'

As the examples in (6.36) show, there are semantic restrictions on the noun which occurs in the subject position. The examples in (6.37) illustrate the fact that restrictions also apply to the predicate part of the non-agreeing clauses.

(6.36) a. *Bok är intressant.
book.COM.SG is interesting.NT.SG

b. *Skurborste är dyrt.
scrubbing brush.COM.SG is expensive.NT.SG

(6.37) a. *Bil är rostigt.
car.COM.SG is rusty.NT.SG

b. *Gröt är hett.
porridge.COM.SG is hot.NT.SG

The semantic restrictions are probably related to the type of interpretation which these sentences give rise to. Sentences which have this type of non-agreement always generate some form of clausal reading, in which the non-agreeing subject functions as the object of the clause. The sentences in (6.32a) and (6.32b) would correspond to (6.38a) and (6.38c), respectively. Note that (6.38b) is not a possible reading of (6.32a). The attempted reading of (6.36) would be as in (6.39). Since scrubbing brushes do not tend to involve running costs, (6.36b) sounds odd even in its clausal version (6.39b).

(6.38) a. [Att äga en bil] är dyrt. [←(6.32a)]
to own a car.COM.SG is expensive.NT.SG
'To own a car is expensive.'

b. [Att köpa en bil] är dyrt. [↚(6.32a)]
to buy a car.COM.SG is expensive.NT.SG
'To buy a car is expensive.'

c. [Att äta gröt] är nyttigt. [←(6.32b)]
to eat porridge.COM.SG is wholesome.NT.SG
'To eat porridge is good for you.'

(6.39) a. [Att läsa en bok] är intressant.
to read a book.COM.SG is interesting.NT.SG

b. ??[Att äga en skurborste] är dyrt.
to own a scrubbing brush.COM.SG is expensive.NT.SG

If a speaker wants to convey the fact that the prices of cars – as opposed to the cost of actually owning and running one – are high, (6.32a) cannot be used. Instead, a normal legal subject with an agreeing predicative must be used, as in (6.40).

(6.40) Bilar är dyra.
car.PL are expensive.PL

Since these restrictions hold between the subject and the predicate, the only possible way of representing the fact in the lexicon would be by entering the whole clause as an idiom. The construction is too productive to make this a plausible solution. Viewed in the light of the clausal reading, the non-agreement becomes less mysterious. In Swedish, as in many languages, the neuter gender is selected for an adjective or a pronoun when it is linked to a clause. This is exemplified in (6.41).

(6.41) a. [Att man inte får köpa vin i mataffärer] är **dumt** / ***dum**.
that one not may buy wine in food.shops is stupid.NT.SG .COM.SG
'It is stupid that one is not allowed to buy wine in supermarkets.'

b. [Att inte få gå ut] är **tråkigt** / ***tråkig**.
to not may go out is boring.NT.SG .COM.SG
'It is boring not to be allowed to go outside.'

6.4.2.2. *Previous analyses*

The semantic relation between sentences with non-agreeing subjects and sentences with clausal subjects led Faarlund (1977) to assume that there is also a syntactic relation. Faarlund's uses data from Norwegian, but since the data correspond very closely to Swedish, his analysis can be transferred to Swedish. In his analysis, the subjects of sentences like (6.32) are really themselves clausal constructions containing an abstract verb called 'relation'.

This verb does not appear in the surface structure. The derivation of (6.32b) would proceed as in (6.42) in Faarlund's analysis.

(6.42) a. $[_{VP}$ $[_{S}$ Att X äter gröt]] är nyttigt för X

↓

Equi-NP Deletion
S-pruning

↓

b. $[_{VP}$ Att äta gröt] är nyttigt för X

↓

Unspecified NP Deletion

↓

c. $[_{VP}$ Att äta gröt] är nyttigt

↓

Abstract V Deletion
VP-pruning

↓

d. $[_{NP}$ Gröt] är nyttigt

The pruning and deletion rules of (6.42) would not be acceptable in more recent, more restrictive versions of transformational grammar. This solution is therefore interesting only because it relates the subject of sentences like those in (6.32) to clausal subjects. The explanation for the non-agreement lies in the fact that the subject is in fact a clausal element at the stage where agreement rules are assumed to apply (that is, before stage d). Apart from the unrestricted theory assumed in this solution, there are other problems. I refer to Hellan (1986: 96) for discussion of a number of drawbacks with Faarlund's analysis.

In Cooper's (1984) solution, the relation between the subject noun phrase and a clause is also present, but only at the interpretation level, not at a syntactic level. Within a GPSG type framework, Cooper posits an analysis in which the [–NT] feature of a noun like *gröt* in (6.32b) is not inherited to the N″ level. This is achieved by having a phrase structure rule which is specified for certain features. The rule given by Cooper (1984: 134) is reproduced in (6.43).

(6.43)
$$\begin{array}{l} N^2 \quad \rightarrow \quad N^1 \\ \begin{bmatrix} -\text{DEF} \\ \alpha \end{bmatrix} \quad \begin{bmatrix} -\text{DEF} \\ \beta \end{bmatrix} \quad \text{where} \\ \text{a. } [-\text{PL}] \in \beta \rightarrow \alpha = [+\text{NT}, -\text{PL}] \\ \text{b. } [+\text{PL}] \in \beta \rightarrow \alpha = [+\text{NT}, -\text{PL}] \\ \qquad \vee\ \alpha = \beta \end{array}$$

As Cooper points out, the rule in (6.43) only predicts the grammaticality of the non-agreement sentences in (6.32), it does not account for the interpretation that the non-agreement generates. Therefore he presents an alternative account, in which the syntactic rules are not specified for features. There are instead two very general phrase-structure rules which drastically over-generate syntactic structures. Interpretation rules then apply to rule out all non-agreeing sentences except those where a propositional reading is plausible. This account is captured by the interpretation rules in (6.44) (from Cooper 1984: 139).

(6.44)

a. $$\left\| \left[\begin{matrix} N^1 \\ \begin{bmatrix} -\text{DEF} \\ \alpha \end{bmatrix} \end{matrix} \right] \quad \begin{matrix} N^2 \\ \begin{bmatrix} +\text{NEUT} \\ -\text{PL} \\ -\text{DEF} \end{bmatrix} \end{matrix} \right\| = \text{PROP}\,(\| N^1 \|)$$

b. $$\left\| \left[\begin{matrix} N^1 \\ \begin{bmatrix} -\text{DEF} \\ +\text{PL} \\ \alpha \end{bmatrix} \end{matrix} \right] \quad \begin{matrix} N^2 \\ \begin{bmatrix} -\text{DEF} \\ +\text{PL} \\ \alpha \end{bmatrix} \end{matrix} \right\| = \text{BARE} - \text{PL}\,(\| N^1 \|)$$

These interpretation rules permit a definite N^1 to expand as a neuter singular indefinite N^2, but when it does, the resulting interpretation is a propositional one. The second part of the rule accounts for the fact that a plural nominal may also expand as an ordinary plural noun phrase, in which case the gender features remain the same. Cooper's solution then differs from Faarlund's in that the propositional interpretation is not represented by a clausal unit in the syntax. It involves non-agreement within the noun phrase and it is this noun-phrase-internal non-agreement which triggers the propositional reading.

The rules in (6.44) do not actually account for the examples where the non-agreeing noun phrase contains a determiner. In order for the rules to cover examples like (6.35a) and (6.35c), (6.44a) would have to be changed to include a possible determiner. The rule covering ordinary agreeing indefinite noun phrases is already present in Cooper's system of rules (1984: 139). As in the case of the bare plural, both rules would in principle apply to all indefinite noun phrases, but the propositional reading would only result when the other conditions were fulfilled.

The solution proposed by Hellan (1986) resembles that of Cooper (1984) in that the non-agreement is assumed to be internal to the noun phrase. In fact this type of non-agreement forms one of Hellan's arguments in favour of D as the head of the noun phrase. As already pointed out (section 5.3.2.2), Hellan assumes that noun phrases are of category T, but since this T is headed by the determiner, it is equivalent to a DP. If D is the head of the noun phrase, then the subjects exemplified in (6.32) can be described as non-headed noun phrases. Hellan's (1986) assumption is that a phrase may not disagree in its feature values with its head, but that it may disagree with a non-head daughter. Hence the fact that the noun phrases are not headed means that they can enter into these particular non-agreement relations.

As pointed out by Hellan, one problem for this account is the fact that the noun phrases which do not agree with their predicates may actually contain an indefinite determiner, as (6.35a) and (6.35c) showed. Such noun phrases may also show a normal agreement pattern (cf. (6.35b) and (6.35d)). Hellan therefore assumes that the indefinite determiners may occur in two different positions. In one case they head the T, and the T must agree with the determiner in number and gender. This means that the noun phrase as a whole must be of the same gender as the determiner and that the noun phrase may not disagree with the predicate. In the cases where the determiner is not a daughter of the T, the noun phrase need not agree with the determiner and hence it may carry the neuter gender feature to agree with the singular neuter predicate. Simplified tree structures for the subjects of (6.32a), (6.34a) and (6.35a) are given in (6.45a), (6.45b) and (6.45c), respectively.

(6.45)

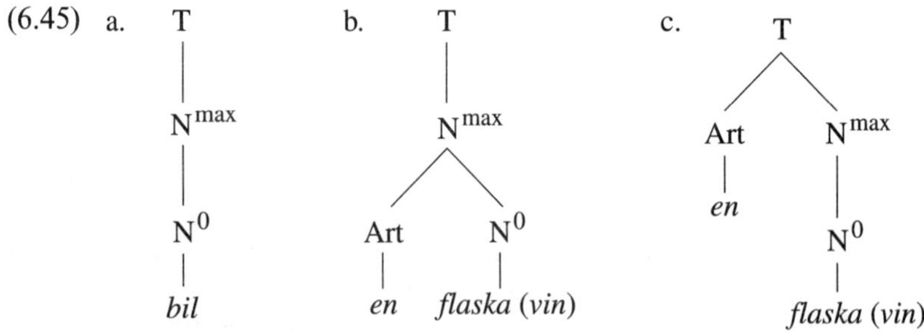

The noun phrases in (6.45a) and (6.45b), by virtue of being non-headed, induce a propositional reading ('event related' in Hellan's terms), whereas (6.45c) only permits an ordinary, 'matter related' reading.

6.4.2.3. *Conclusions and proposed analysis*

Within the approach to Swedish noun phrases that I have proposed here, a number of different analyses are possible of the facts discussed in section 6.4.2.1. The bare singular nouns which fill the subject position in sentences like (6.32a) are illegal noun phrases, in that they are not specified for DEF. The noun is [DEF *u*], and there is no determiner present to supply the value

[DEF +] or [DEF –]. Since I claim that DEF is a feature with semantic implications, its absence means that the expected semantic functions cannot apply. We can assume that when this is the case, alternative semantic functions yielding the propositional reading may come into play. These semantic functions are severely restricted in that they can only lead to interpretations like 'to own and run X' or 'to eat X', not 'to read X' or 'to bath X'. Naturally, X must not violate the selectional restrictions of the verb involved in each propositional reading. There are also restrictions on the predicate of non-agreeing subjects. We have seen examples like 'be expensive', but not 'be green', or 'be rusty'. However, these restrictions can be related to the propositional reading; if the subject is interpreted as 'to own a car', then we do not expect 'be rusty' to be a possible predicate. The mechanism which triggers the propositional reading can also be assumed to trigger the special form of the agreement, which can be said to be semantic in nature. This account is most akin to the interpretation-based solution proposed by Cooper (1984).

The cases, illustrated by (6.35a) and (6.35c), where the non-agreeing subject noun phrase contains an indefinite determiner, are more complex. These noun phrases are ambiguous in the sense that they permit either a nominal reading, in which case the predicate must agree, or a propositional reading, in which case there must be non-agreement.[7] Two basic types of solution seem possible: one in which the noun phrases are identical and interpretation rules apply freely, and one in which the noun phrases have different structure.

It should be pointed out here that we cannot rely on the non-agreeing predicate to trigger the propositional reading. Firstly, if the subject is singular neuter, then the non-agreement is not visible. Secondly, not all subjects which trigger a propositional reading are the subject of a predicate which can show agreement. One example is provided in (6.46a). Intuitively, this subject is interpreted as 'to drink a cup of black coffee', rather than 'buy' or 'see one'. Furthermore, the use of the neuter pronoun to refer to the subject noun phrase in the more emphatic (6.46b) indicates that the subject is interpreted as a proposition. The example in (6.46c) shows that a common gender form of the pronoun is used when a propositional interpretation of the subject is not plausible. For this reason, I will refer to examples resulting in a propositional interpretation in terms of non-agreement, even when there is no overt manifestation of the neuter gender.

(6.46) a. [En kopp svart kaffe] kan göra underverk när man är trött.
a.COM cup.COM black coffee can do wonders when one is tired

b. [En kopp svart kaffe], **det** kan göra underverk när man
a.COM cup.COM black coffee it.NT can do wonders when one
är trött.
is tired
'A cup of black coffee can do wonders when one is tired.'

c. Jag har just gjort [en kopps vart kaffe], **den** står på bordet.
I have just made a.COM cup.COM black coffe it.COM stands on table.DEF
'I have just made a cup of black coffee, it is on the table.'

In a solution where the noun phrases are assumed to be identical and the interpretational rules may apply freely, a propositional reading is always possible. If the subject is an indefinite noun phrase and there is an accessible propositional reading, a propositional interpretation may be triggered. This type of solution is proposed by Cooper (1984) and it is also discussed as an option by Hellan (1986: 113). In the description of noun phrases developed so far, no changes would have to be made to the syntactic component or the lexical specifications of nouns and determiners. A semantic rule would have to be added to the one producing standard indefinite nominal interpretations. The new rule would generate a clausal interpretation and trigger the non-agreement where this is applicable, possibly by assigning the feature value [GEND *nt*] to the noun phrase.

The other option is to make a syntactic distinction between indefinite noun phrases which allow a propositional reading and those which do not. This type of solution involves the assumption that there are really two versions of each indefinite determiner in Swedish. This is in fact what Delsing (1993) assumes for the indefinite article in argument and predicative noun phrases (see section 6.4.4.2). In the type of account proposed here, this distinction could be captured in two different ways. One would be to follow Hellan's (1986) proposal and assume that the indefinite determiners may occur in two different positions – one in which they function as a determiners and one in which they do not. Within the NP analysis proposed in chapter 5, this would involve adding one lexical entry for each indefinite determiner. The obvious thing is to assume that in these cases the indefinite determiners function like numerals. In section 2.4 I claimed that numerals in Swedish are basically adjectival in their syntactic behaviour. Like adjectives, the indefinite determiners could then be assumed to occur as modifiers within the noun phrase in these examples. This would mean that for the indefinite article *en*, which is specified as in (6.47a), the specification in (6.47b) would have to be introduced (both specifications are abbreviated).

(6.47)a. *en*:

$$\begin{bmatrix} \text{CAT} & \begin{bmatrix} \text{HEAD } det \begin{bmatrix} \text{DEF} & - \\ \text{SPEC} & \text{N}' \ [\text{DEF } u]\,[1] \end{bmatrix} \end{bmatrix} \\ \text{CONTENT} & \begin{bmatrix} \text{RESTIND } [1] & \begin{bmatrix} \text{INDEX} & \begin{bmatrix} \text{PER} & 3 \\ \text{NUM} & sg \\ \text{GEND} & com \end{bmatrix} \end{bmatrix} \end{bmatrix} \end{bmatrix}$$

$$\text{b. } en\text{:} \quad \begin{bmatrix} \text{CAT} & \begin{bmatrix}\text{HEAD } det \begin{bmatrix}\text{DEF} & - \\ \text{SPEC} & \text{N} \;\; [\text{DEF } u]\,[1]\end{bmatrix}\end{bmatrix} \\ \text{CONTENT} & \begin{bmatrix}\text{RESTIND } [1] \begin{bmatrix}\text{INDEX} \begin{bmatrix}\text{PER} & 3 \\ \text{NUM} & sg \\ \text{GEND} & com\end{bmatrix}\end{bmatrix}\end{bmatrix}\end{bmatrix}$$

In (6.47) the category of the determiner is assumed to be the same in both uses. Hence *en* really is assumed to be a determiner which may occur at a lower level within the noun phrase (cf. Hellan 1986). It can only do so when a special semantic reading is accessible. The modifying determiner in (6.47b) is assumed to combine with a third person singular common gender noun in its non-definite form. The result is an element of category N′ [DEF –]. Note that this means that we need not specify that this use of the determiner does not permit a determiner in the specifier position. There are no determiners in Swedish which combine with a N′ [DEF –]. They either select a N′ [DEF +] or a N′ [DEF *u*]. In this solution, the special semantic rules required for the propositional reading of the subject would be triggered by the presence of a N′ [DEF –] in the subject position.

Another possibility would be to assume that the indefinite determiner *en* has been reanalysed as a numeral adjective. This would mean that it cannot be specified as [DEF –], since this feature is not applicable to adjectives. In order to prevent determiners from selecting the N′, the adjectival *en* would have to be further specified with respect to the SPR value of its N′ sister. This N′ must be assumed not to accept any specifier; the value for SPR must be empty. This could give rise to a specification like the one in (6.48) for the adjectival *en*.

$$\text{(6.48) } en\text{:} \quad \begin{bmatrix} \text{CAT} & [\text{HEAD } adjective \; [\text{MOD N}' \; [\text{DEF } u]\,[\text{SPR } \langle\;\rangle]\,[1]]] \\ \text{CONT} & \begin{bmatrix}\text{INDEX } [1] \begin{bmatrix}\text{NUM} & sg \\ \text{GEND} & nt\end{bmatrix}\end{bmatrix}\end{bmatrix}$$

The problem with this specification is that all N[DEF *u*] which I have considered so far obligatorily select a determiner. In section 6.4.4, I will discuss a small class of nouns in Swedish which do not require a determiner in certain positions. However, this is not the same set as the ones which can occur as non-agreeing subjects. Furthermore, it is not clear that these nouns should even be specified as N[DEF *u*]. An analysis based on the feature specification in (6.48) for *en* and other indefinite determiners is therefore not plausible.

A distinction between the two uses of indefinite determiners can be made without assuming that they occur in different positions. Rather than assume that the *en* which may permit a propositional reading occurs in a modifier position, we can assume that it does occur in the specifier position but that it lacks the crucial feature which defines it as a determiner.

Holmberg (1986) does not explicitly discuss non-agreeing subjects in Swedish. However, his account of the distinction between predicative and argument noun phrases is interesting here in that it provides an account in terms of feature values of the fact that the English indefinite determiner *a* can occur in both argument and non-argument noun phrases. The features used for this purpose are the major category features [N] and [V]. Holmberg (1986) assumes that the major category feature [±V] is an argument-predicate feature. A category with the feature value [+V] may function as (the head of) a primary predicate. A category with [–V] may function as (the head of) an argument. There is also a neutral feature [%V], which is interpreted as ‘neither argument nor predicate’ (Holmberg 1986: 58). The feature value [+N] indicates that the item is capable of receiving Case (in terms of Chomsky 1982a) or carry other nominal features, and [–N] means that the unit may assign Case. The nominal feature also has a neutral value, [%N], which indicates that the item can neither receive nor assign Case. Holmberg (1986: 63) assumes that there are two varieties of the indefinite article in English. One has the features [–V, +N] and thus allows the noun phrase in which it occurs to function as an argument. The article which occurs in predicative noun phrases has the features [%V, +N]. Since a noun also has the feature value [%V], a noun phrase with this kind of indefinite determiner will not receive the value [–V] required for it to function as an argument.

In the account proposed here the feature characteristic of a determiner is not a major category feature, but the feature DEF. This means that we can distinguish the two uses of *en* by specifying one of them as [DEF *u*]. Since the determiner would combine with an N′ [DEF *u*], the resulting N″ would also be unspecified for DEF. The normal interpretational rules do not accept an N″ unspecified for definiteness and hence the special interpretation rule yielding a propositional reading would be triggered, along with the accompanying possible change of gender. The appropriate specification for the special use of the indefinite determiner *en* is provided in (6.49).

(6.49) *en*:

$$\left[\begin{array}{ll} \text{CAT} & \left[\text{HEAD}\ \textit{det} \begin{bmatrix}\text{DEF} & u \\ \text{SPEC} & \text{N}'\ \ [\text{DEF}\ u]\ [1]\end{bmatrix}\right] \\ \text{CONTENT} & \left[\text{RESTIND}\ [1]\ \left[\text{INDEX} \begin{bmatrix}\text{PER} & 3 \\ \text{NUM} & sg \\ \text{GEND} & com\end{bmatrix}\right]\right]\end{array}\right]$$

Note that the N′ element on the SPEC list must be specified as [DEF *u*]. Definite nouns may not combine with this predicative use of the indefinite determiner. This must be specified in the entry for the determiner, since the specifications for definite nouns do not carry this information. A definite noun is specified as in (6.50) (see section 5.2.3.2). The definite determiners which may combine with such nouns are specified as [SPEC N’ [DEF +]]. If the use of *en* represented in (6.49) was not specified as [SPEC N' [DEF *u*]], there would be nothing to stop it from unifying with a definite noun, to yield an ungrammatical noun phrase like **en musen*.

(6.50) *musen* : [SPR ⟨ (DET) ⟩]

If one follows Delsing's (1993) assumption (see section 6.4.4.2) that there is a plural form of *en*: *ena*, which may only occur in predicative noun phrases, then *ena* is specified as *en* in (6.49), with the exception of the index features, where NUM is *pl* and GEND can be omitted.

I will opt for this latter solution since the absence of a + or – value for DEF is crucial in my account of determinerless noun phrases. This will then make for a consistent use of the features. The subject noun phrases of non-agreeing constructions are then syntactically deviant in that they have the value [DEF *u*]. This deviance is assumed to trigger a semantic function giving the clausal interpretation, if such a reading is available. If no clausal reading is available, the sentence will be ruled ungrammatical, as in (6.36) and (6.37). I will not try to provide details of the exact nature of the semantic function here. I refer to Cooper (1984) (see (6.44)) for one possible version.

Note that the account I have provided here in terms of under-specification correctly predicts that definite noun phrases cannot function as the subject of these constructions.[8] All analyses discussed here permit only indefinite noun phrases, but none offers any form of explanation for this fact (Cooper 1984, Hellan 1986, Holmberg 1986). Note that the restriction cannot be due to the fact that definite noun phrases cannot occur in the corresponding clausal versions, since the examples in (6.51a) and (6.51c) are perfectly felicitous even though the non-agreeing versions of (6.51b) and (6.51d) are not acceptable.

(6.51) a. [Att äga den bilen] är **dyrt**.
to own that car.DEF is expensive.NT.SG
'To own that car is expensive.'

b. Den bilen är ***dyrt** / **dyr**.
that car.DEF is expensive.NT.SG .COM.SG

c. [Att äta de nötterna] vore **gott**.
to eat those nuts would.be tasty.NT.SG
'To eat those nuts would be tasty.'

d. De nötterna vore ***gott** / **goda**
those nuts would.be tasty.NT.SG .PL

6.4.3. *Bare singular nouns in object position*

Another type of singular non-definite noun which appears to be able to function as a full noun phrase in certain limited contexts was exemplified in

(6.4), repeated here as (6.52). In these cases, the noun is always the complement of a verb or a preposition.

(6.52) a. Karin fick **brev**.
Karin received letter
'Karin got a letter.'

b. Karin har **bil**.
Karin has car
'Karin has a car.' (in the sense of 'Karin owns a car.')

c. Anders äter **apelsin**.
Anders eats orange
'Anders is eating an orange.'

The examples in (6.53) show that there are severe restrictions on these combinations, both on the verb and on the noun (see data in Cooper 1984).[9]

(6.53) a. *Karin brände brev.
Karin burnt letter.SG
Intended reading: 'Karin burnt a letter.'

b. *Karin fick skurborste av Anders.
Karin received scrubbing brush.SG from Anders
Intended reading: 'Karin got a scrubbing brush from Anders.'

c. *Karin hittar bil.
Karin finds car.SG
Intended reading: 'Karin found a car.'

d. *Karin har skurborste.
Karin has scrubbing brush.SG
Intended reading: 'Karin owns a scrubbing brush.'

e. ??Anders kastar apelsin.
Anders throws orange
This could only be interpreted as some weird branch of athletics, on par with *Anders kastar spjut* 'Anders throws the javelin.'

For all the examples in (6.52), there is a corresponding example with the indefinite determiner, as (6.54) shows.

(6.54) a. Karin fick **ett brev**.
Karin received a letter
'Karin got a letter.'

b. Karin har **en bil**.
Karin has en car
'Karin has a car.'

c. Anders äter **en apelsin**.
Anders eats en orange
'Anders is eating an orange.'

It is interesting to note that the idiomatic translations used in (6.52) are, in fact, more appropriate for the sentences in (6.54) than for the corresponding ones in (6.52) without a determiner. The meaning of the sentences with determinerless objects is more general than the suggested English translations. The difference between *få brev* and *få ett brev* can be captured in terms of generic and specific. In (6.54) the reading is specific: Karin received a specific letter, Karin owns a specific car and Anders eats a specific orange. In (6.52) it is as if the verb has formed a semantic unit with the determinerless object. The meaning is best captured by translations like 'Karin was involved in letter-receiving', 'Karin is a car-owner' and 'Anders is involved in orange-eating'.

Further evidence that the object nominals in these constructions are generic and cannot have specific reference is illustrated by the infelicity of the sentences in (6.55)

(6.55) a. *Jag har köpt bil som jag skall laga och sälja.
I have bought car which I will mend and sell
'*I have done some car-buying which I am going to mend and sell.'

b. *Jag har köpt bil. Den skall jag laga och sälja.
I have bought car it will I mend and sell.
'*I have done some car-buying. I am going to mend it and sell it.'

This generic, almost idiom-like reading can be understood in two ways. It could lead to the assumption that each of these V+N combinations is, in fact, a lexical unit which should have a separate entry in the lexicon. The other approach is to focus on the similarities between this use of singular count nouns and the way in which non-count nouns function. Non-count nouns may occur without a determiner, and when they do, they are often interpreted as generic. In this case, we could claim that the determinerless nouns in (6.52) are in fact count nouns which have been reanalysed as non-count nouns. This would be a reanalysis in the opposite direction to examples like (6.56).

(6.56) a. Jag köpte **öl**.
I bought beer

b. Jag köpte **två öl**.
I bought two beers

In (6.56a) the object consists of a non-count noun which lacks a determiner and has a general interpretation. In (6.56b), on the other hand, the noun has been reanalysed as a count noun, and the meaning is more specific; something like 'two pints of beer' or 'two bottles of beer'. Viewed as reanalysed count nouns, the determinerless objects in (6.52) can be treated as any other non-count nouns.

In fact, within the analyses of Swedish noun phrases that I have considered here, accounts have been proposed along both these lines. Cooper (1984: 118–19) provides an overview of singular non-definite nouns which may occur without a determiner in object position. Since these combinations are so restricted and not productive, Cooper proposes that they are lexical units with the internal structure in (6.57).

(6.57) $[\text{få}]_V$ $[\text{brev}]_N$

Arguments of the kind proposed and discussed by Anward and Linell (1976) can be used in support of this analysis. I will not go through the arguments in detail here but refer to Anward and Linell and back to section 5.5.1.2, where these criteria were applied to another type of lexicalized phrase.

Delsing (1993: 57–60) also considers this type of construction. He draws a parallel with the type of noun phrases discussed in section 6.4.2. He gives the examples in (6.58) (Delsing's (101)).

(6.58) a. Han ska köpa **bil** / **lägenhet**.
he shall buy car flat
'He is going to buy a car / flat.'

b. Hon har **hund** / **svår lunginflammation**.
she has dog bad pneumonia
'She has got a dog / serious pneumonia.'

About these examples he says: 'the verb phrases in (101) above have connotations of getting a loan in the bank, paying the insurance, moving to the new apartment, having to go out with the dog every day, or being bound to bed' (1993: 58). This would parallel the propositional reading that we get in non-agreeing examples like (6.32) in section 6.4.2.1. He compares (6.58) with the examples in (6.59) (his (104)).

(6.59) *sälja bil / lägenhet
sell car flat

He then continues his argument: 'a verb like *sell* denotes an act without the special connotations that are connected with the verb *buy*' (1993: 58). Having considered these data, Delsing concludes that the bare nouns in these cases are really uncountables, and therefore in his analysis they form noun phrases containing a covert determiner (see my discussion of Delsing's account of bare plurals and non-count nouns in section 6.4.1.2).

In the analysis that I have presented, if I were to follow a parallel path to that suggested by Delsing and treat these noun phrases on a par with the non-agreeing subject, then they would be analysed as nominals of less than NP status which occur in argument positions where a full NP would be expected. This could then be assumed to trigger a special semantic interpretation. However, the argument in favour of a special semantic reading is substantially weaker than in the non-agreement cases. There is no syntactic evidence here for any form of clausal interpretation. Nor is the resulting semantic interpretation obviously clausal. The intuition that there are more connotations associated with the buying of a flat than with the selling of a flat is not strong enough for a special semantic interpretation.

I do not agree with Delsing's arguments relating to the claim that there are more connotations related to the buying of a flat than to the selling of a flat and that this is the motivating factor for the fact that the noun can occur without a determiner. Still, the solution he proposes in terms of count nouns used as non-count nouns is quite plausible. There is a semantic difference between sentences like those in (6.52) and their parallels in (6.54), and this could be captured by a distinction in terms of a generic use of the noun induced by a reanalysis as non-count nouns. However, such a distinction does not account for the difference in grammaticality between (6.58a) and (6.59). It seems to me, therefore, that in spite of the fact that there are quite a number of V+N combinations of this type, a solution in terms of lexical phrases (as in Cooper's 1984 account) is the most appropriate.

6.4.4. *Predicative 'role' nouns*

6.4.4.1. *The issues*

There is one type of non-definite singular nouns lacking a determiner, where a lexical solution seems inappropriate, because the construction type is too productive. In a predicative position, a non-definite singular noun can occur without a determiner. In (6.60), examples are provided which involve the verb *vara* 'be'.

(6.60) a. Torun är **journalist**.
Torun is journalist
'Torun is a journalist.'

b. Min syster är **lärare**.
my sister is teacher
'My sister is a teacher.'

c. Gazza är **fotbollsproffs**.
Gazza is professional football player
'Gazza is a professional football player.'

Not all nouns occurring in a predicative position may occur without a determiner. Examples of nouns which require a determiner in the same position are provided in (6.61).

(6.61) a. Nisse är *(**en**) **sötnos**.
Nisse is a sweetie pie
'Nisse is a sweetie pie.'

b. Oscar är *(**en**) **katt**.
Oscar is a cat
'Oscar is a cat.'

c. Katten är *(**ett**) **däggdjur**.
cat.DEF is a mammal
'The cat is a mammal.'

The class of nouns that permit determinerless nominals is difficult to define. It contains nouns for nationality, profession, political or religious affiliation, hobbies, etc. I will refer to them as 'role nouns'. There are a number of nouns which do not obviously fit into the category of role nouns, and which would not usually occur without a determiner, but which can be used in a predicative position without a determiner under certain circumstances. In these cases, a role reading is forced. It is only when such a role reading is totally improbable that the sentences will be infelicitous. Examples are provided in (6.62), with possible interpretations.

(6.62) a. Anders var **katt**.
Anders was cat
'Anders played the part of a cat in a play.'

b. Karin var **dammsugare**.
Karin was vacuum cleaner
'Karin attended the fancy-dress party dressed up as a vacuum cleaner.'

c. *De var **grupp**.
they were group
Cannot be interpreted as 'They functioned as a group.' or 'They played the role of a group.'

6.4.4.2. *Previous analyses*

Holmberg (1992) discusses examples of role nouns in relation to the indefinite noun phrases that could occur in the same predicative position. In any predicative noun phrase the specifier position contains a subject in underlying structure. This subject then moves into the clausal subject position. Holmberg assumes that the role nouns license this subject position directly. This gives the structure in (6.63), from where the specifier *Torun* moves into the specifier position of the containing IP, resulting is a sentence like *Torun är journalist* see (6.60a).

(6.63)

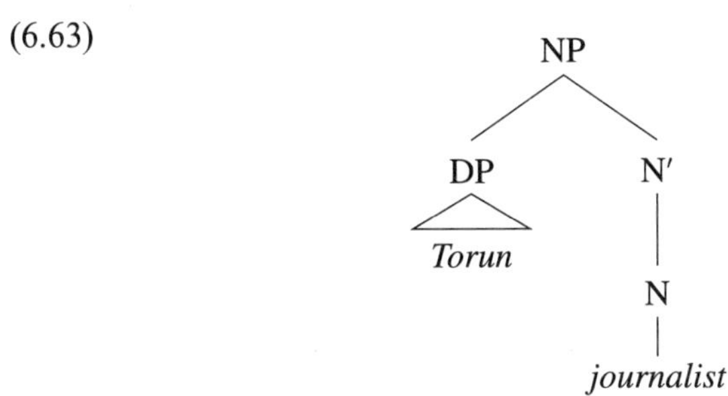

The nouns which can occur in predicative position but which are not role nouns are then assumed not to license a subject. Instead, an indefinite determiner must be introduced which licenses a specifier position for the subject. This gives the result in (6.64). The element in the specifier position of (6.64) can then move up to the specifier position of IP to yield a sentence like (6.61a).

(6.64)

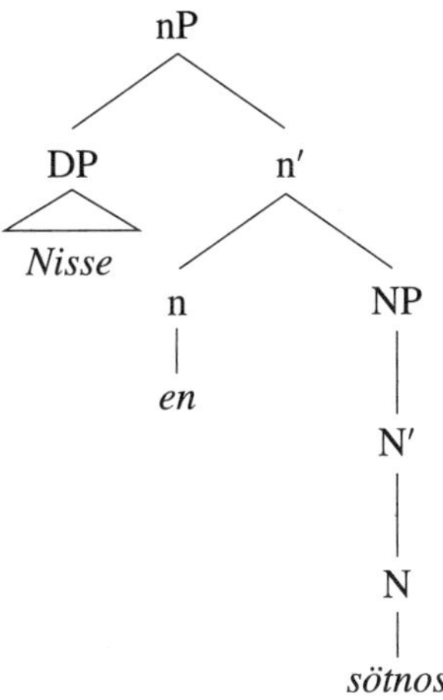

In Holmberg's account, the distinction between these two types of predicative noun phrases is categorial: one is an NP, a lexical projection; and one is nP, a functional projection. The nouns' ability or inability to license a specifier position causes this distinction. The non-argument noun phrases containing the indefinite determiner differ from identical argument noun phrases in that they contain a variable in the specifier position which is bound outside the noun phrase. An argument noun phrase must be closed; its specifier may not be bound outside the noun phrase. The difference between predicative noun phrases and noun phrases in argument position is then semantic in nature. It is defined in terms of open and closed expressions.

As mentioned in section 6.4.1.2, Delsing's (1993) initial assumption is that all non-argument noun phrases lack a determiner. It is to be expected, therefore, that he considers the role nouns, which do not require a determiner, to be examples of the basic predicative noun phrase. Delsing defines the nouns which do not require a determiner as 'classifying nouns' as opposed to 'descriptive nouns'. The latter do require an indefinite determiner in the same position. He claims that this element which obligatorily occurs with the descriptive nouns is actually different from the indefinite determiner which occurs in argument noun phrases. Delsing provides evidence in favour of the distinction between *en* in argument noun phrases and *en* in non-argument positions. Firstly, there is a prenominal element *ena* which can be viewed as a plural version of *en*. However, Delsing (1993: 33–5) claims that this element is only grammatical when the noun phrase occurs in a predicative position, or at least it sounds much better in non-argument positions. An example is given in (6.65) (Delsing's (24b)). The claim is then that only the predicatively used *en* has his form, and hence it can be said to be different from *en* used in argument noun phrases.

(6.65) Cia och Gunlög är **ena djävlar** på grammatik.
Cia and Gunlög are a.PL devils on grammar
'Cia and Gunlög are bloody good at grammar.'

Secondly, Delsing (1993: 35) gives examples where, according to his judgements, you need the indefinite determiner with non-count nouns in predicative position. In an argument position, it would not be possible to use an indefinite determiner with non-count nouns, he argues. A couple of his examples are provided in (6.66), with his grammaticality judgements.

(6.66) a. Det var ??(en) sur ved du skaffat.
it was a sour wood you procure
'You seem to have got hold of some green firewood.'

b. Det var ??(ett) starkt kaffe du lagar.
it was a strong coffee you cook
'You certainly make strong coffee.'

I actually prefer the versions of these sentences without the determiner, but this does not detract from Delsing's argument, since *en* is certainly possible in these examples.

Finally, Delsing (1993: 36) claims that the predicative *en* differs from that used in argument noun phrases in that it 'is always accompanied by an implicit argument'. This implicit argument can sometimes be spelled out. In argument noun phrases *en* is not associated with an implicit argument. Compare the sentences in (6.67).[10]

(6.67) a. Han var **mig** en lustig figur.
he was me a funny character
'I thought he was a funny character.'

b. *Jag träffade **mig** ena konstiga typer igår.
I met me a.PL strange character yesterday

I am not convinced that the generalization Delsing makes here is correct. I cannot see that all predicative noun phrases containing the indefinite determiner are accompanied by an implicit argument. This seems to me to be related to whether or not the noun in the predicative noun phrase is evaluative or not. Compare the sentences in (6.61). I cannot see that there is an implicit argument in (6.61b) and (6.61c). As the judgements in (6.68) show, the implicit argument can certainly not be made explicit in these two cases.

(6.68) a. Nisse är **mig** en sötnos.
Nisse is me a sweetie pie
'I really think Nisse is a sweetie pie.'

b. *Oscar är **mig** en katt.
Oscar is me a cat

c. *Katten är **mig** ett däggdjur.
cat.DEF is me a mammal

On the basis of the data discussed here, Delsing concludes that *en* in predicative noun phrases is not a surface determiner. However, at deep structure, it is a determiner, generated in the D position.[11] He makes a distinction between BASE-GENERATED DETERMINERS and ARTICLES. Base-generated determiners are what Delsing calls 'meaningful determiners', namely, all determiners except the articles.[12] Articles, on the other hand, are D elements which are inserted at surface structure in argument noun phrases to satisfy the criterion that all argument noun phrases must have a filled D position. They can be referred to as 'expletive determiners'. In this sense, *en* as it occurs in predicative noun phrases is not an ARTICLE. Delsing refers to it as the NON-ARGUMENTAL INDEFINITE DETERMINER. He then modifies the claim I have quoted as (6.28) to that given here as (6.69) (Delsing 1993: 65).

(6.69) **Argument rule**:
All arguments must have a filled determiner position at S-structure

This means then that predicative noun phrases containing the indefinite *en* do indeed have a filled D position and hence are DPs. There is now nothing to require a predicative noun phrase not to have a determiner. However, the element which fills this position is unusual in that, even though it is in Delsing's terms not a meaningful determiner, it is base-generated there. In argument noun phrases, the same element would have been inserted at surface structure.

The only nouns that require this non-argumental indefinite determiner are what Delsing terms 'descriptive' nouns. 'Classifying' nouns normally occur without any determiner in predicative position. I presume that this information would be part of the nouns' semantic specification in the lexicon. However, it would be a feature which influences the syntactic structure of noun phrases in which they occur. Some form of rule would state that if a descriptive noun is to occur in a non-argument position, it will need a base-generated *en* in its sister D position.

I assume that the distinction between determinerless predicatives and predicatives with the non-argument indefinite determiner is made in categorial terms in Delsing's analysis. When the noun is classifying and hence does not require a determiner at any level there is no D projection, so that the whole phrase is of category NP. The descriptive nouns, on the other hand, which require a determiner must form DPs. The distinction between these predicative DPs and the identical argument DPs lies in the fact that in one case the determiner – the predicatively used *en* – is base-generated there (predicative noun phrases) and in the other case the article is inserted there in surface structure (argument noun phrases).

6.4.4.3. *Conclusions and proposed analysis*

The two accounts discussed in section 6.4.4.2 have in common the basic assumption that there is a definable class of nouns which permit determinerless noun phrases in predicative positions. The proposals differ as to how and where this distinction should be specified, but in both cases the nouns which can occur in determinerless noun phrases are specified as different in some way. Below I will discuss how this type of solution could be formulated within the framework that I am using here. I will, however, argue in favour of an alternative type of account.

For all role nouns, it holds that they would also have to be specified as 'ordinary' nouns, since they can all occur in argument positions as well, both definite and indefinite ones. This is illustrated in (6.70), to be compared with (6.60).

(6.70) a. **En dålig journalist** kan göra mycken skada.
a bad journalist can do much damage
'A bad journalist can do much damage.'

b. **Denna gamla lärare** borde ha gått i pension.
this old teacher ought have gone in pension
'This old teacher should have retired.'

c. **Ett begåvat fotbollsproffs** kan tjäna nästan hur mycket som helst.
a talented professional football player can earn almost how much as most
'A talented professional football player can earn almost any amount.'

In terms of the formalism I have used so far, this means the role nouns would have to be specified as N[DEF *u*], since they can have the same syntactic distribution as any other N[DEF *u*]. Secondly, these nouns could be specified as, say, N[ROLE +]. Any noun with the feature value [ROLE +] could then be assumed to lack a value for the feature DEF, since it has no potential for referentiality, and therefore the [DEF +] vs. [DEF –] distinction can be said not to be applicable. The distinction could then be made between a noun with the feature value [DEF *u*], which, when combined with the appropriate element, can receive the value '+' or '–' for the feature DEF through unification, and elements which lack the potential to be specified for DEF. In a sense, then, a role noun would lack the feature DEF in the same way that, say, a verb phrase does.[13] The feature matrices for a role noun like *journalist* would be as in (6.71a). Every such noun would also have one specification which permits it to occur in ordinary noun phrases, and which requires it to have a determiner in these cases. This is provided in (6.71b). Note that this is also the specification for a noun which does not normally permit a role reading, such as *katt*.

(6.71) a. *journalist*
$$\left[\begin{array}{ll}\text{CAT} & \left[\begin{array}{ll}\text{HEAD} & noun \left[\begin{array}{ll}\text{ROLE} & + \\ \text{PRD} & +\end{array}\right] \\ \text{SUBJ} & \langle\ \rangle \\ \text{SPR} & \langle\ \rangle \\ \text{COMPS} & \langle\ \rangle\end{array}\right]\end{array}\right] \quad \text{(see (6.60))}$$

b. *journalist*
$$\left[\begin{array}{ll}\text{CAT} & \left[\begin{array}{ll}\text{HEAD} & noun\ [\text{DEF } u] \\ \text{SUBJ} & \langle\ \rangle \\ \text{SPR} & \langle det \rangle \\ \text{COMPS} & \langle\ \rangle\end{array}\right]\end{array}\right] \quad \text{(see (6.70))}$$

Verbs like *be* would then select for an NP[PRD +], which can consist either of an N[ROLE +] (as in (6.60)) or of an indefinite determiner and a N[DEF *u*] (as in (6.61)). Definite nouns would be specified as [PRD –] since these cannot occur in predicative positions (though see Holmberg's discussion of noun phrases containing prenominal genitives which may occur in predicative positions; 1992: 67–71). A noun phrase projected from a specification such as that in (6.71b) would be unspecified for PRD but in non-argument positions it would inherit the value [PRD –] from the verb through unification.

In this account, the difference between the two types of noun phrases is then made not in terms of category or bar level, but in terms of a feature. When premodification is present, the N[ROLE +] cannot be chosen, since strong adjectives, as well as weak ones, require their sister N′ to select a determiner (see section 6.3.1). The difference between predicative indefinite noun phrases and indefinite noun phrases in argument position would not be made in terms of a difference in determiners, but in terms of another feature PRD.

A solution can thus be formulated in terms of my HPSG analysis which resembles those proposed by Holmberg (1992) and Delsing (1993) in that the lexicon contains some form of specification of one class of nouns as different inasmuch as they can occur as determinerless nominals in predicative positions. There are, however, reasons not to adopt such an analysis. As we saw in (6.62), there are certain nouns which do not obviously fit into the category of role nouns, but which can be used in a predicative position without a determiner. In these cases, a role reading is forced. It is only when such a role reading is totally improbable that the sentences will be infelicitous. The restrictions which specify which non-definite nouns can occur without a determiner in these constructions is related to whether or not a particular semantic interpretation is plausible. Under the solution proposed above, this would have the undesirable consequence that even a noun like *dammsugare* 'vacuum cleaner' would have to occur as two entries in the lexicon, once as [DEF *u*] and once as [ROLE +].

Instead, I propose that there is an interpretation rule which is activated when certain verbs which may take a predicative NP complement are followed by a determinerless noun phrase, that is, a nominal element specified as [DEF *u*]. The effect of this semantic rule would be a role reading. If a role reading is not plausible, the interpretation of the sentence fails. My proposal for role nouns is then very similar to that which I proposed, following Cooper (1984), for non-agreeing subjects.

6.5. Conclusions

Crucial to my analysis of definite noun phrases in chapter 5 is the fact that DEF is a semantic feature in the sense that it performs the function of a determiner semantically. A consequence of this conclusion is that we would not expect a definite determiner to occur with an indefinite noun, or the other way around. This led me to conclude that a noun like *mus*, which lacks the morphological marker for definiteness, is in fact not strictly speaking indefinite. It can combine with certain definite determiners and must therefore be unspecified for definiteness rather than indefinite.

In this chapter, I have shown that the fact that a noun like *mus* is not specified as [DEF –], but as [DEF *u*], makes the right predictions for the distribution of bare singular non-definite nouns. Bare singular non-definite nouns cannot function as argument noun phrases. In order to be referential, a nominal in argument position must be specified as either [DEF +] or [DEF –]. The value for this feature can be inherited from a noun or a determiner, but it must be present on the nominal projection in order for it to be a legal argument noun phrase. However, if we assume that Swedish non-definite nouns are [DEF *u*] rather than [DEF –], then the feature value [DEF –] could not be inherited from a noun. From this follows that an indefinite argument noun phrase needs a determiner. This is indeed the correct prediction as the examples in (6.72) show.

(6.72) a. *(**En**) **journalist** har skrivit boken.
a journalist has written book.DEF
'The book is written by a journalist.'

b. Anders kittlade *(**en**) **kompis**.
Anders tickled a friend
'Anders tickled a friend.'

In section 6.2.3 I provided an HPSG account which makes the correct predictions about non-definite nouns in argument positions.

In a non-argument position, a nominal need not be specified as [DEF +] or [DEF –], since it does not refer, but ascribes a property to another noun phrase. This means that we expect determinerless non-definite nominals to be allowed in predicative positions. There does indeed turn out to be a class of nouns in Swedish which naturally occur without a determiner in predicative positions. An example is provided in (6.73).

(6.73) Oscar är **rörmokare**.
Oscar is plumber
'Oscar is a plumber.'

This has led a number of people to assume that these nouns are specified in the lexicon as being different from other non-definite nouns. I concluded, however, that this is not an appropriate solution since any non-definite noun can occur in this position as long as a special semantic interpretation is available. This interpretation can be called a ROLE READING. Examples such as those in (6.74) make implausible a lexical distinction between nouns which can occur in determinerless nominals and those which cannot.

(6.74) a. Anders var **häst**.
Anders was horse
'Anders played the role of a horse (in a play).'

b. Karin är **tandborste**.
Karin is tooth brush
'Karin is dressed up as a toothbrush (at a fancy-dress party).'

Another conclusion which has been drawn by some linguists on the basis of the fact that determinerless nominals may occur in predicative positions is that predicative noun phrases are of a different category from those that occur in argument positions. A problem with this assumption is the fact that non-definite noun phrases may have identical shapes in predicative and argument positions. This is difficult to account for in an analysis where the two types of noun phrases are assumed to have different structure. Examples are provided in (6.75).

(6.75) a. Oscar är **en katt**. Predicative
Oscar is a cat
'Oscar is a cat.'
b. **En katt** åt upp kycklingen. Argument
a cat ate up chicken.DEF
'A cat ate the chicken.'

For these reasons, I proposed in section 6.4.4.3 that predicative noun phrases are of the same category as argument noun phrases. The difference is captured by a feature, PRD, which the noun phrase receives through unification from the verb which selects it. Predicative positions can be assumed not to permit definite noun phrases, in other words, [DEF +] $\supset$ ¬[PRD +]. When a bare singular non-definite noun occurs in a predicative position, normal interpretation rules fail. However, if a role reading based on that noun is available, then this special interpretation rule applies and the sentence is interpreted.

The adjectives which occur in indefinite noun phrases, that is, strong adjectives, resemble the weak adjectives of definite noun phrases in that they require the presence of a determiner. This can only be illustrated with the kind of nouns that do not require a determiner for independent reasons. Examples like (6.73) can thus be used and (6.76) shows that, when the noun is preceded by an adjective, the determiner is required.

(6.76) Oscar är *(**en**) **skicklig rörmokare**.
Oscar is a skilful plumber
'Oscar is a skilful plumber.'

In section 6.3.3 I provided feature specifications for strong adjectives which make the correct predictions in this respect.

There are a number of different types of non-definite nouns which appear to violate the generalization that non-definite nouns must be accompanied by a determiner in argument positions. I discussed plural and non-count nouns briefly in section 6.4.1. However, the only conclusion I drew was that the semantic issues involved are too complex to be dealt with appropriately in this book.

Another type of seeming counterexample to the generalisation was discussed in section 6.4.2. It is illustrated here by (6.77).

(6.77) **Buss** är **billigt**, men **tåg** är **dyrt**.
buss.COM.SG is cheap.NT.SG but train.NT.SG is expensive.NT.SG
'It is cheap to go by bus, but it is expensive to go by train.'

Here non-definite singular nouns occur in subject position without a determiner. In such sentences, an adjective in predicative position always appears in the neuter singular form, even though predicative adjectives normally agree with their subjects in Swedish. Associated with the subjects of such clauses is a propositional reading in which the subject functions as the object. In these examples, I assume that the noun is specified as [DEF *u*] and hence lacks a positive or negative value for the feature DEF which is crucial for a nominal's ability to refer. Just as in the case of the role nouns, this means that normal interpretation rules fail. Instead, if there is a propositional reading available, the sentence will be accepted and the non-agreement permitted.

The matter is not as straightforward as this, because the subject position of non-agreeing sentences may be filled by a subject which contains a determiner, as long as the noun phrase is indefinite. The sentence in (6.78) is an example of this.

(6.78) **En** **burk** **öl** om dagen är bara **nyttigt**.
a.COM.SG can.COM.SG beer per day is only wholesome.NT.SG
'A can of beer a day is only good for you.'

From such examples, I concluded that there is a special instance of the indefinite article which lacks a value for the feature DEF. This means that the subject noun phrase in (6.78) is like that in (6.77) in that the subject lacks a value for DEF. As long as there is a plausible propositional reading, the sentence can still be interpreted.

A final type of determinerless non-definite nominal, exemplified in (6.79), was dealt with in section 6.4.3.

(6.79) Anders gillar **banan**.
Anders likes banana.SG
'Anders likes bananas.'

In these cases, there is no special semantic interpretation, so that a solution along the lines proposed for examples like (6.73), (6.74) and (6.77) is not plausible. As (6.80) shows, the possible combinations are very limited, and I therefore assume that these are idiomatic combinations which are listed in the lexicon.

(6.80) *Anders tog / lämnade banan.
Anders took left behind banana.SG

7
CONCLUSION

The aim of this book was to provide a theoretical analysis of Swedish noun phrases. A theoretical analysis implies the use of a theoretical framework providing suitable tools to make it possible, for instance, to define categories, to state generalizations in exact terms, and also to make it easier to verify the account against further data. The advantages of using an established framework are, to my mind, quite obvious. An established framework will have been tried and tested on a wide variety of data, which means that an analysis of new data can easily be compared with analyses of similar constructions from other languages. This is especially important when dealing with as small a sample as I do here: a subset of the noun phrases of one language.

There are a number of reasonably well-defined syntactic theories to choose from, but in this case, a detailed study of the data made some of the theories appear less plausible candidates to someone who does not have an *a priori* reason to work within any particular framework. This detailed study takes up chapters 2, 3 and 4 of this book and those chapters are intended to be as free from theory-specific assumptions as possible.

Two main issues were crucial in the choice of theoretical framework. These were the status of the nominal definite ending, DEF, and the head status of noun phrases. The major consideration related to DEF was whether this element is sufficiently similar to non-bound elements in order to justify a representation of it as an element which differs from a syntactic element simply in that it is bound and therefore requires a phonological host. I concluded that the answer to this was negative. DEF has a number of characteristics that cannot be captured if it is assigned syntactic status, albeit as a bound element. Instead, I concluded that the behaviour and distribution of DEF show that it is governed by a different set of rules from independent syntactic determiners. This, to my mind, can only be accounted for in a framework where DEF can easily be represented as the instantiation of a feature.[1] Hence a theory with a well-developed account of feature percolation appeared to be the obvious choice. In spite of the use of features in the most recent versions of Minimalism (Chomsky 1995: chapter 4), this in my view makes theories like Categorial Grammar, Generalized Phrase Structure Grammar, Head-driven Phrase Structure Grammar or Lexical-Functional Grammar more likely candidates than recent versions of transformational grammar. In recent transformational accounts, elements which have traditionally been considered morphological elements are assumed to have full syntactic status; they are only distinguished from other syntactic elements by being bound. A consequence of this is that the distinction between morphological rules and syntactic rules has been reduced to near non-existence. Another result of this approach is that transformational accounts tend to suffer from underdeveloped theories of feature percolation, so that when elements like DEF are indeed assumed to be base-generated on a host (see aspects of Delsing's 1993 analysis) the details of how this is done, or of how the feature which it instantiates is spread, are unclear. I therefore decided on the basis of the discussion in chapter 3 not to adopt a transformational approach.

The conclusion that can be drawn from my discussion in chapter 4 of the head status of Swedish noun phrases was disappointing. With respect to the Swedish data, there was evidence in both directions. It became clear on the basis of the data discussed that there are a number of crucial properties which a noun phrase receives from the noun. This is obvious also from the fact that a number of the people who have argued for a DP account have also argued for a two-headed analysis. With respect to the traditional headedness criteria, my conclusion was that the only criterion which points convincingly in the direction of D as the head relates to governing relationships, or subcategorization, within the noun phrase. Definite determiners in Swedish appear to govern certain features on their nominal sisters, or, in an alternative account, determiners subcategorize for their nominal sisters. In most theoretical approaches, this means that D must be the head and the nominal the complement sister. However, another option is to reconsider the assumption that selectional behaviour is a clear sign of head status. In fact, there is one theoretical framework, namely Head-driven Phrase Structure Grammar (HPSG), which does not follow standard assumptions about selection. Within this theory, there are well-defined mechanisms which allow modifiers and also specifiers to select their sisters. In the case of specifiers, the selection is bi-directional, so that a head sister can also select its specifier. The specifier selects its sister through a head feature SPEC and the nouns select their specifiers through a valence feature SPR. The relevant feature for modifiers is MOD. This then means that the selectional behaviour displayed within Swedish noun phrases can be accounted for in HPSG without assuming that D is the head. This book then provides such an analysis, and attempts to show that not only is such an analysis possible, it also has certain advantages over the standard DP analyses.

A crucial assumption in this analysis is that the DEF feature represented on nouns is semantic, or functional, in the sense that it can function as a semantic determiner in the same way that English *the* does. It is this property of the definite ending which allows definite nouns in Swedish to function as full noun phrases. Since nouns lacking the definite ending cannot function as full noun phrases the way that definite nouns can, I conclude that they are not actually indefinite, but non-definite. If the feature [DEF +] functions as a semantic determiner, I would want to assume that a feature [DEF –] would also function as a semantic determiner. This means that I have described the non-definite nouns as [DEF *u*]. This view of non-definite nouns turns out to make accurate predictions about the distribution of indefinite determiners (see chapter 6), and also about the nouns themselves (they can occur with both definite and indefinite determiners).

The advantages of the NP analysis are most obvious with respect to noun phrases containing adjectives (section 5.4). In Swedish, adjectives carry different morphological marking in definite and indefinite noun phrases. I argue, however, that this is not the result of the presence of the nominal definiteness feature. For one thing, the adjectival feature does not have the semantic function which the nominal definiteness feature has. However, the issue of how to refer to the adjectival definiteness feature (traditionally referred to as WEAK/STRONG) does not arise in the NP analysis proposed here. In this analysis, the distribution of the adjectival forms is correctly predicted without having to make specific reference to an adjectival feature. Instead the distribution of the adjectival form is captured in terms of what kind of determiner the adjective requires its nominal to combine with. This solution requires reference only to the definiteness feature which can be manifested on determiners and nouns and which is required independently. This solution is made possible by the selection mechanisms found in HPSG which allow determiners and nominals to select each other bi-directionally and modifiers to select their sisters uni-directionally.

The analysis in this book is based on a narrow range of data, namely noun phrases containing determiners and other prenominal elements only. Two important and complex noun phrase types have been left out; namely, those containing relative clauses and those containing prenominal genitives. However, I believe that the issues that I have considered and accounted for are of fundamental importance, so that this analysis should form a solid basis from which to proceed. I hope to have shown that a non-transformational account of Swedish noun phrases is quite plausible. Furthermore, such an analysis can be formulated assuming that N is the head of the noun phrase and turns out to have some advantages over existing DP analyses of Swedish and related languages. Given that there are certainly some aspects of headedness that undoubtedly belong to the noun – hence the many 'dual headed' DP analyses (such as Abney 1987, Radford 1993 and Netter 1994) – unless one has other reasons to assume the existence of a functional head – such as uniformity across categories – an NP analysis seems preferable.

NOTES

1 Introduction

1 It would, of course, be misguided to claim that I begin my study without any theoretical assumptions. I do, for instance, assume that some form of X-bar based phrase structure grammar is appropriate (as used in different ways in Lexical-Functional Grammar, Head-driven Phrase Structure Grammar (HPSG) and most versions of transformational grammar). This is by no means a necessary assumption in a theoretical framework, as the existence of Categorial Grammar and different versions of dependency grammar (Hudson 1984, Hudson 1990, Nikula 1986) show.

2 In this book, I will number examples as (N.n), which is the nth example in chapter N. In order to avoid confusion with section numbering, all references to (sub)sections will contain the word 'section', and all numbers of examples will appear within parentheses.

3 Throughout this book, I will use 'transformational' to refer to work within the Chomskyan generative tradition. Depending on the date of the article referred to, this means Standard Theory, Extended Standard Theory, Government and Binding, Principles and Parameters or Minimalist assumptions (Chomsky 1965, 1982a, 1982b, 1986a, 1986b, 1992, 1995). I have found it impossible to refer to the different stages in each case, since it is impossible to say when a new name for the theory becomes the accepted term. The use of the term 'transformational' does, of course, not mean that I want to get involved in a discussion about whether there really are any transformations as such in a Minimalist account of syntactic structures.

4 The idea that D is the head of the noun phrase is not unique to transformational theory though. Hudson (1984, 1987) also promotes this idea, working within the dependency framework of Word Grammar. DP proposals have also been made for Norwegian and German noun phrases within HPSG by Svenonius (1992a, 1992c) and Netter (1994), respectively.

5 There are many dialects of Swedish which do permit *denna musen*, and in others, possibly including standard Swedish, the other proximal demonstrative *den här* would be preferred to *denna* in the spoken language.

6 Throughout this book, I will use the singular common gender form of determiners to refer generically to all forms of that particular element. Hence *den* here is used to refer to *den* 'the/that.COM.SG', *det* 'the/that.NT.SG' and *de* 'the/that.PL'.

2 Determiners and Modifiers

1 For a critical discussion of the lack of distinction between 'form' and 'function' in Loman's approach, see Lødrup (1989: 63–65).

2 Loman (1956: 228) is aware of some of these difficulties.

3 In section 2.2.2, I will take complementary distribution with core determiner to be one possible criterion for determiner status, and I will return to *mången* at that point.

4 For the time being, I will follow traditional terminology and refer to nouns like *gris* 'pig' (as opposed to *grisen* 'pig.DEF') as indefinite. Later I will, however, claim that they are more accurately described as non-definite.

5 In (2.15c) and (2.15d), there are scope ambiguities:

c. OSCAR WANT [ALMOST [KILL HER]]
OSCAR ALMOST [WANT KILL HER]
d. OSCAR SEEM [ALMOST [ANGRY WITH HER]]
OSCAR ALMOST [SEEM ANGRY WITH HER].

6 Another difference is that *en/ett* are the only cardinal numbers to have a morphological distinction between neuter and non-neuter. However, this seems insignificant since Swedish does not make a gender distinction in the plural.

7 Prescriptivists might claim that *ena* should only be used in opposition to *den andra* 'the other', i.e. to mean 'one out of two'. I do not think this reflects common usage, though. To me the sequence of sentences below is perfectly acceptable.

Han köpte bara den ena boken av Tolkien.
he bought only the one-out-of-X book.DEF by Tolkien
De andra två tänkte han köpa senare.
the other two thought he buy later
'He only bought one of the books by Tolkien. He thought he'd buy the other two later.'

8 However, for a much wider interpretation of the notion of determiner, see Keenan and Faltz (1985: 227–49).

9 See note 5 in chapter 1.

10 The example in (2.31a) sounds less natural than (2.30a), but there is a crucial difference in acceptability between (2.31a) and (2.31b) which cannot be explained if *här* and *där* are analysed as adjectives.

11 This argument about the status of determiners goes back to the debate between Postal (1969), who said that pronouns were really intransitive determiners, and Sommerstein (1972), who turned the argument round and said that the two types of element were similar, but that they should therefore both be analysed like typical pronouns, namely as basically nominal in nature.

12 It has been suggested that the examples in (2.35) are best treated as apposition of two noun phrases, *denna/detta* (which can be used pronominally) and *min övertygelse/vår kommittés slutgiltiga beslut*. For arguments against such an analysis, see Börjars (1990).

The construction containing a determiner and a PrenGen sounds formal. Examples like ??*dessa mina sockor* 'these my socks' or *varje mitt leksakståg* 'every my toy train' therefore sound distinctly odd.

13 Compare note 11 in this chapter.

14 For an analysis proposed within a Lexical-Functional Grammar (LFG) framework, in which the Norwegian possessive or genitive element is assumed to head the phrase, but where it is not assumed to be a determiner, see Lødrup (1989: 51–6). He refers to Langendoen and Langsam (1984) for a similar analysis for English.

15 I am grateful to Masja Koptjevskaja-Tamm for pointing these examples out to me.

16 Holmberg (1992: 68) also points out that if the noun phrase contains an adjective as in (i):

(i) Per är Johans nya lärare.
Per is Johan's new teacher

then the predicational reading is not available. This is based on the grammaticality judgement in (ii):

(ii) ??Per är Johans nya lärare och Lisa är också Johans nya lärare.
Per is Johan's new teacher and Lisa is also Johan's new teacher

17 They can also be nominalized and occur with full or partial noun morphology, but this is not of interest to the present discussion.

18 The only elements which were defined as determiners in section 2.2.2 which can carry the genitive *-s* of an understood nominal in this way are *varenda* and *varannan*. These words derive from combinations of the determiner *var* and the elements *enda* and *annan*, respectively. The latter two elements are members of the determiner field in Loman's terms, namely PK5. The behaviour of attributes in position classes 4 to 6 of Loman's determiner field will be discussed in section 2.4.

19 The possibilities of co-ordinating determiners are very limited. A conjunctive co-ordination seems to be possible only for demonstratives, as in (i). The other determiners allow disjunctive co-ordination as in (ii), but not conjunction as in (iii).

(i) den här och den där musen
this and that mouse
(ii) varje eller ingen mus
every or no mouse
(iii) *en och någon mus
a/one and some mouse

Since most determiners in Swedish can also function as pronouns, this test is difficult to apply. The result may be a case of co-ordinated NPs rather than co-ordinated determiners. For the NP *denna och någon bil* 'this and some car' there are in principle two possible analyses: $[[\textit{denna}]_{\text{NP}}\ \textit{och}\ [\textit{någon bil}]_{\text{NP}}]_{\text{NP}}$ and $[[[\textit{denna}]_{\text{DET}}\ \textit{och}\ [\textit{någon}]_{\text{DET}}]_{\text{DET}}\ \textit{bil}]_{\text{NP}}$. The latter of these two readings would appear to be impossible.

3 Definite Feature or Definite Article

1 In the Chomskyan tradition, the distinction between affix and clitic is not of the same importance since elements which are undoubtedly affixes in the traditional terminology, e.g. the English past tense ending *-ed*, are still found under their own node in syntactic trees.

2 There is also another, largely independent, tradition in which a different set of criteria for clitic status is used, identifying a different set of elements. This approach can be traced back to Kayne (1975). A number of recent applications of this approach can be found in the papers in the following three volumes: van Riemsdijk (1991), Hellan (1993) and Rizzi (1993).

3 Both Hellan and Svenonius refer to data from Norwegian, but the two languages are sufficiently similar to make their accounts directly relevant to Swedish.

4 Klavans (1985) does state, however, that some clitics, e.g. Spanish verbal clitics, seem to have a lexical domain. In the Spanish example it is V. However, further research leads her to claim that the lexical, rather than phrasal, domain of certain clitics 'reflects the fact that these clitics lexically joined to their hosts' (Klavans 1983: 107; the wording of the articles indicates that Klavans 1985 had already been submitted to *Language* when Klavans 1983 was written.) Klavans thus distinguishes between LEXICAL CLITICS and POSTLEXICAL CLITICS, where the lexical clitics resemble affixes in that they come out of the lexicon as one unit with their hosts, and are not joined to it in the syntax. The main aim of my investigation is to establish the syntactic structure of Swedish noun phrases. This means that I am, in simplified terms, interested in finding out whether DEF is part of the syntax of Swedish, or whether it is added to the noun in the morphology, i.e., under Klavans's assumptions, in the lexicon. From this it follows that the distinction between lexical clitics and affixes will be less central to my discussion than it is to Klavans's. Furthermore, this distinction is more subtle and difficult to make than that between (postlexical) clitics on the one hand and affixes (and lexical clitics) on the other. Klavans (1983) discusses the notion of lexical clitics with special reference to particle clitics in Ngiyambaa, where there is phonological evidence supporting the distinction between lexical and postlexical clitics. This type of evidence is, as far as I can see, not available in Swedish. In what follows, I shall therefore concentrate on the distinction between Klavans's postlexical clitics and affixes. It should also be pointed out here that some of the problems are related to terminology more than anything else. For a different approach to the distinction between types of bound elements which avoids a number of these problems, see Börjars and Vincent (1993).

5 Zwicky and Pullum (1983) make a further distinction between two types of clitics. A SIMPLE CLITIC is one that has exactly the same distribution as a corresponding full form. A clitic which either does not have a corresponding form or which has different distribution from a corresponding form is termed a SPECIAL CLITIC. Since DEF must be a special clitic according to this definition, I will only be concerned here with the criteria Zwicky and Pullum (1983) put forward for clitics in general. The distinction in Zwicky (1977) is slightly different and more subtle and also uses the notion BOUND WORD.

6 An example of how this basic assumption can cause difficulties can be found in Nevis and Joseph (1993).

7 Börjars and Vincent (1993) in fact argue that the result of applying the Zwicky and Pullum type criteria is best captured in terms of two parameters referring to the way in which the element is positioned. On the basis of the possible values for these two parameters, natural classes can be distinguished. Some of these natural classes correspond to core cases of affixes and clitics, whereas the elements of other classes share certain features with traditional clitics and others with archetypal affixes.

8 This is certainly true for Standard Swedish (*Rikssvenska*), but in a number of northern Swedish dialects adjectives may carry the definite ending (Delsing 1988: 66, 1993: 91).

9 Carstairs (1981) uses a terminology that is neutral as to whether an item is an affix or a clitic. He uses APPENDAGE as a collective form to cover both these categories of bound forms. The term ANCHOR then refers to the stem or host word of the appendage.

10 Carstairs' Characteristic 6 says that bound forms 'are often members of a relatively small closed system, one of whose members must always appear at the relevant place in the structure' (1981: 4). On the basis of this characteristic, Carstairs makes a second, more tentative, claim, the Openness Claim (1981: 18). The claim is that bound forms with Characteristic 6 never have Characteristic 2b, but must have 2a instead. According to Carstairs' initial definition of a Strictly Closed System (1981: 18), the Swedish DEF would not be a member of a closed class, since the other member of that class, i.e. 'INDEF' (though for a different view of the lack of definiteness, see section 5.3.3.1), is never realized as anything but zero. Since the form of Carstairs's Openness Claim and the characteristic of DEF can be expressed in the following way:

(i) IF Characteristic 6 THEN NOT Characteristic 2a

from the fact that we know:

(ii) NOT Characteristic 6

we cannot conclude anything from the implication in (i) (since this says nothing about what follows, if anything, from NOT Characteristic 6).

Carstairs later in the same article (1981: 34–43) discusses the possibility of a redefinition of the notion of closed class to include bound forms which had been ruled out by the Strictly Closed System definition. He is aware of the problem of finding a new definition which yields the correct results without being *ad hoc* and therefore does not specify in detail the new Loosely Closed System. Thus it is not clear whether the Swedish DEF would still belong to the (Loosely) Closed System. This means that Carstairs's second claim is not directly relevant here.

11 The difference in shape of DEF **within** (3.13a) and (3.13b), respectively, can be defined in terms of phonology: *råtta* and *öga* end in a short unstressed vowel and therefore get the form of DEF that lacks the initial short unstressed vowel. The variation **between** (3.13a), (3.13b) and (3.14), on the other hand, cannot be explained in terms of phonology.

12 Though see note 4 in this chapter about Klavans's (1983) distinction between lexical and postlexical clitics.

13 Referring to *den* as the prenominal definite article is not uncontroversial. The element is homophonous to a demonstrative determiner. Indeed, Santelmann (1992) claims that the two are in fact not distinct. I will return to this issue in section 5.3.

14 This irregularity cannot be related to whether the name has a definite article in the original language or not; *der Rhein*, *la Seine* and *the Thames*. It does seem to be the case that the names of rivers which can take DEF cannot be used without it unless it is preceded by *floden*: **Thames flyter genom London*. However, the situation is further complicated by the fact that there are names of rivers that can occur with DEF but which still cannot occur without it, even in a combination with *floden*, as in:

Nilen / *Floden Nil flyter genom Kairo.
Nile.DEF river.DEF Nile flows through Cairo

15 An alternative explanation for the facts in (3.32) could be that *station* and *grammofon* in these cases do carry the definite ending, but that the /e/ has been deleted to give:

station-n grammofon-n
station-DEF record.player-DEF

If this is the case, one might expect the phonological rules of Swedish to realize this as:

[staʃʊːnː] [gramːʊfɔːnː]

There are, however, problems with this analysis (cf. Börjars 1988: §2.2.4).

16 In some analyses where definite and indefinite determiners are found in different positions (e.g. Delsing 1988), DEF occurs in the same position as definite determiners. However, this need not be the case (cf. Santelmann 1992).

Holmberg (1987) treats DEF like a syntactic determiner, and like other syntactic determiners, DEF is found in the specifier position of the noun phrase. In this analysis, DEF differs from the other determiners in that it is generated to the right of the head noun.

17 Constructions where syntactic determiners co-occur with DEF are often referred to as 'double articulation', 'double definiteness', 'double determination' or, in the Scandinavian literature 'overdetermination' (the term is *overbestemd* (Norwegian) or *överbestämd* (Swedish); see for instance Lundeby 1965, Hultman 1966 and Hansen 1966). For a discussion of this notion with respect to Swedish and other Scandinavian languages and the relevant Balkan languages, see Börjars (1994).

18 In (3.40), *bänkar* in the second co-ordinated noun phrase cannot be interpreted as a definite noun phrase, as one would expect if the definite affix functioned as the determiner for the co-ordinated nouns.

19 *Hink och spade* is every child's standard equipment for a day in the sand box or on the beach. The main stress falls on the second conjunct only, and not equally on both parts as in normal co-ordination.

20 Many dialects of Swedish have lost number agreement in predicative position so that the singular common gender form (the morphologically unmarked form) is used instead:

Oscar och Kisse är trött.
Oscar and Kisse are tired.COM.SG

21 There are exceptions: Zwicky (1987) treats 's as an inflexional affix, and Carstairs (1987) concludes that the possessive of nouns with a plural ending in *-s* are inflexional genitives but other instances of the possessive are clitics.

22 I am grateful to Mirjana Kočoska for her native speaker judgements on Macedonian and to Martin French for his help with ideas about and data on all the Balkan languages.

It is not uncommon to treat Bulgarian and Macedonian as one language, but as we shall see, there are interesting differences between the two with respect to the phenomenon being examined here which makes the distinction justified.

23 In Macedonian, there are independent prenominal demonstratives, like *onoj* 'that'. These demonstratives also have cliticized unstressed forms, which are either translated as 'this' or 'that', or 'this over here' or 'that over there' (Lunt 1952: 40–3).

24 The genitive forms are in parentheses, because this category has been lost almost totally in spoken Faroese, having been replaced by prepositional constructions. (For a discussion of this and attempts by purists to reintroduce the genitive, see Barnes 1994. [This is referred to in the book in which it occurs as 'Barnes with Weyhe', but for simplicity's sake I will refer to it here as Barnes (1994)]). In Icelandic, the comparable pattern is not marked in this way.

25 With respect to the Macedonian data in (3.68a), there are different reactions from native speakers, but the crucial thing for my discussion here is that they all appear to involve irregularities.

26 Though compare Elson (1976), who states that even though DEF in Bulgarian and Macedonian behave like clitics in a number of ways, with respect to junctural properties, their behaviour is not consistent with traditional assumptions about clitics.

27 Though see note 5 in chapter 1.

28 According to Kress (1982: 174), the use of the prenominal definite article is literary. In the spoken language, the definite end article, or a demonstrative pronoun (*sá*, *sú* or *það*) is more common.

29 'Double definition' refers to co-occurrence of DEF and a syntactic determiner.

30 I will refer to this element as *i* here, after its shape in M.NOM.SG.

31 The two forms are *e* and *të*, where *të* is identical to the indefinite paradigm. If we simplify matters slightly, we can say that the *e* form occurs when the particle follows the head noun,

but is separated from it (by e.g. a possessive pronoun). For a more detailed account of the two forms, and a neat generalization stating their distribution, see Morgan (1984).

32 Throughout this chapter, I have ignored the use of definite determiners with superlative forms. This use of the determiner complicates the issue substantially, especially in Romanian. The reason that I have decided not to deal with superlatives is that I think the status of the definite determiners preceding superlatives needs thorough examination. Definite determiners in this position may not be full definite determiners. For instance, they do not appear to trigger definiteness effects. In both Swedish and English such 'definite' noun phrases can occur in contexts otherwise not permitted for definite noun phrases. This is shown in (i) and (ii).

(i) Det fanns de mest exklusiva viner i hans källare.
there existed the most exclusive wines in his cellar
(ii) There were the most exclusive wines in his cellar.

For a discussion of definiteness, reference and superlatives, see Hawkins (1978).

33 The solution to this problem adopted by Delsing (1993) is to argue that the elements which I take to be syntactic determiners are, in fact, not determiners. I do not, however, agree with his arguments.

34 The only exception to this might be order, which indicate that the DEFs of the Insular Scandinavian languages show certain clitic-like properties.

35 I am grateful to Bob Borsley for having pointed this out to me, and to Winifred Davies for her native speaker judgements on Welsh noun phrases.

The definite article in Welsh is *y* (before consonants) or *yr* (before vowels) for masculine, feminine and plural nouns. When the definite article follows a vowel, i.e. if the last sound of the preceding word is a vowel, it is realized as *'r* for all genders and numbers. Since the appropriate form of 'and' in this case is *a*, the definite article is realized as *'r*. The change in the initial sound of feminine nouns following the definite article is due to soft mutation: *merch* 'daughter', but *y ferch* 'the daughter'.

36 Note, however, that Delsing (1993: 129–30) assumes that in some constructions DEF is base-generated on the noun.

4 The Head of the Noun Phrase

1 The detailed use of X-bar theory varies greatly between these theories, for instance with respect to the so-called functional categories. HPSG use these very sparingly, if at all. Instead such elements as would head functional nodes in transformational analyses are represented as features or are assigned to a category which does not participate in X-bar schemas in the same way, e.g. markers (like complementizers, Pollard and Sag 1994: 44–6). In LFG (Bresnan 1995), and as far as I can tell in recent versions of Minimalism (Chomsky 1995: chapter 4), they are assumed to be restricted to C, I and D. In Government and Binding and in many versions of Minimalism the use of functional categories is unrestricted.

There are also other differences in the use of X-bar theory. In HPSG, for instance, there is no explicit way of referring to bar level and in LFG, all elements in an X-bar rule (including heads) are assumed to be optional unless required by some independent principle.

2 Even though this is assumed to be the general structure of phrases, some exceptions may be allowed within the theory. In analyses where phrases are headed by function elements, which have traditionally been analysed as specifiers (i.e. an element which combines with X′ to form an X″), there are arguments for assuming that the remaining lexical projection is of bar level one (see Fukui and Speas 1986).

A clearer case of a phrase type that violates standard X-bar assumptions is, in my opinion, that of co-ordinated structures. For detailed arguments to this effect, see Borsley (1995).

3 This is not assumed to be the case in modern transformational theory, where a number of options for the placement of adjuncts are used, e.g. adjunction to the maximal projection,

the specifier position; and in some analyses, an adjective is assumed to head its own projection within which the noun is the complement.

4 HPSG differs from the other major theories with respect to the notion subcategorized element, cf. note 10 in this chapter.

5 This is not strictly speaking true of approaches in which a lexical head has co-head status with respect to the functional head of which it is a complement, see e.g. Grimshaw (1991) and Bresnan (1995). Multi-headed analyses of noun phrases have been proposed in some detail in Abney (1987) and Radford (1993). I will discuss the notion of headedness with respect to such analyses in section 4.2.3.

6 In this book, I will follow the practice of using lower case for the names of phrases in their traditional use and capitalized or abbreviated versions for theoretical units. Hence the major issue of this chapter is whether a noun phrase should be considered a Noun Phrase or a Determiner Phrase.

7 Compare also the notion 'extended projection' (Grimshaw 1991) and a similar notion in LFG (Bresnan 1995).

8 Though in some ways the notion of external subcategorization is closely related to the notion of distributional equivalence, discussed by Zwicky (1985a) and Hudson (1987). In both cases, the issue is which constituent of the phrase can be said to be the external representative of the phrase (see also Zwicky 1993: 5).

9 I disregard figurative usage here, as in *The tape recorder has just eaten my favourite tape*, though it could be claimed that in such examples *my favourite tape* has been 'reanalysed' as a [+EDIBLE] noun.

10 One exception to this is HPSG (Pollard and Sag 1987, 1994). In earlier standard versions of this theory, the head constituent at every bar level, be it lexical or phrasal, carries a SUBCAT feature, the value of which is a list of the elements required by that constituent (Pollard and Sag 1987: 67–72). An intransitive verb like *sneeze* requires one noun phrase subject, and the value of its SUBCAT feature is therefore a list with one element. The phrase *Oscar sneezed* is saturated, and the value of its SUBCAT feature is an empty list. The SUBCAT value for a noun phrase is likewise an empty set. In Pollard and Sag (1994: 344ff.) a proposal by Borsley (1987, 1988) to introduce distinct SUBJ and COMPS features is adopted. In this version, a third feature SPEC through which specifiers are selected is also introduced.

11 In a number of theoretical approaches, subcategorization is not the only way in which elements can select each other. In HPSG (Pollard and Sag 1987, 1994), selectional restrictions can be defined not only between heads and complements, but also between modifiers and their sisters and between specifiers and their sisters. I will return to these notions in HPSG in chapters 5 and 6, since my analysis of Swedish noun phrases will rely crucially on their existence.

In transformational theory, the Specifier-Head relationship is also increasingly used not only for feature sharing, but also to define selectional restrictions.

12 In Cann's terms, articles 'L-select' their nominal complements. Cann's notion of L-selection covers subcategorization, Θ-marking and form government. I will return to L-selection in section 4.2.5.

13 However, when Cann (1993) applies the subcategorizand definition to verb phrases, the fact that verbs can be either transitive or intransitive is taken as evidence that the V is the head with respect to subcategorization. 'For example in V+NP constructions, noun phrases partition the set of verbs into partially disjoint (and non-null) subsets of transitive and intransitive verbs' (Cann 1993: 49). (In a note, Cann points out that NP is used in the traditional sense of a noun phrase. In his terms it would be a DetP.) It is not clear to me, why in this quote, 'noun phrases' cannot be substituted by 'nouns' (or 'nominal elements') and 'verb' by 'demonstrative' to use the same argument as evidence for the head status of demonstratives.

14 This view is not present in modern transformational grammar, where what is traditionally viewed as morphological marking, e.g. the 3rd person present tense *-s* in English, is assigned syntactic status and differs from other syntactic elements, e.g. a modal verb, only in being morphologically bound. In the most recent forms of Minimalism (Chomsky 1995: chapter 4), even though features play a much more important role, they do not have the same properties and are not governed by the same constraints as in feature-based approaches like GPSG, HPSG and LFG.

15 All the feature co-occurrence restrictions discussed here work in terms of 'legal subtrees'. Therefore, it is not entirely appropriate to use words like 'percolate' or 'spread'. Rather, the principles licence subtrees in which the nodes consist of a legal combination of sets of feature specifications. However, to keep the terminology simple, I will use terms that imply that the features move around in trees.

16 In a more recent article, Zwicky (1993) makes this separation of different aspects of headedness more formal (see the discussion in section 4.5).

17 The cases he refers to have in other approaches been discussed in terms of a distinction between affixes and clitics.

18 In analyses such as those proposed by Abney (1987) and Radford (1993), there is a sense in which even this feature can be inherited from a non-head. Radford (1989, 1993: 98) criticizes Abney's use of an inheritance principle for these cases. However, in his own analysis, he assumes that at any level a noun phrase can have two heads. A noun phrase like *these students* has an immediate head, the D *these*, and an ultimate head, the N *students*. The category of the whole phrase is DNP, Determinate Noun Phrase. In this solution, then, there is a sense in which the category as a whole has inherited a categorial feature [+N] from a non-head sister. The dual-headedness notion is not further formalized by Radford. For instance, there is no definition of what element may function as an ultimate head, and there are no criteria to distinguish between an immediate head and an ultimate head. The resulting dual headedness is strongly reminiscent of that created by Abney's (1987) notions s-projection and c-projection.

19 Verbs do not agree with their subjects in Swedish:

(i) En gris / Den grisen / Ett djur / Det djuret / De grisarna / djuren äter.
a pig / that pig / an animal / that animal / those pigs / animals eat

A predicative adjective, on the other hand does agree with the subject for number and gender in Standard Swedish (but see note 20 in chapter 3), and therefore the gender and number features are indirectly relevant for the verb phrase:

(ii) En gris är hungrig / *hungrigt / *hungriga.
a pig(COM.SG) is hungry.COM.SG NT.SG PL
(iii) Ett djur är *hungrig / hungrigt / *hungriga.
an animal(NT.SG) is
(iv) Alla grisarna/djuren är *hungrig / *hungrigt / hungriga.
all pigs/animals are

For a discussion of how this should be dealt with in the syntax, see Cooper (1984: 42–6).

20 The example in (4.9c) is overtly marked for singular on the noun only if one assumes that the absence of a plural marker indicates singular. Of course, one might want to say that there is some kind of zero marking also in the plural in (4.9b). However, similar examples in English have been used as evidence that the determiner should be considered the morphosyntactic locus, e.g. *this sheep* vs. *these sheep*.

21 However, since the other value of this feature, [SG], is never marked overtly in Swedish it seems inappropriate to assume the presence of a ∅ marker for [PL].

22 For a more detailed discussion of the nature of the definiteness features of the adjective, see section 5.4.

23 In section 2.2.2, I found that the determiner criteria which apply to elements like *vi* 'we' and *ni* 'you.PL' indicate that they do behave like other determiners. Still, the criteria do not say anything about whether the elements selected by the criteria are of category D or NP_{PRON}.

24 Facts relating to *wh*-determiners have also been used by Cowper (1987) to argue in favour of a DP analysis of English. Delsing (1988: 58–9) refers to data similar to those presented here to support the DP analysis of Swedish noun phrases which he proposes within a transformational framework.

25 The proposal put forward by Di Sciullo and Williams (1987) differs slightly from the others in that it is not actually formulated as non-head inheritance. Instead it makes the non-head into a head with respect to the feature in question. This is similar to syntactic analyses in which one element is assumed to be the head with respect to certain features, as in Netter's (1994) account of German noun phrases.

26 The demand that the head must be unspecified for the feature might seem to provide

evidence against an NP analysis of noun phrases such as *denna mus* 'this mouse' where the noun could be assumed to be specified as [DEF]. In this case, the necessary inheritance of the [+DEF] feature from the non-head determiner to the NP node would be excluded by the non-head percolation principles, since the head sister would not be unspecified for the feature. However, in section 5.3.3 I will argue that a noun like *mus* in a noun phrase like *denna mus* is not [DEF], but rather unspecified for definiteness. Hence, this cannot be taken as an argument in favour of a DP analysis. It should be noted that if *mus* was [DEF], this would give problems also for a DP analysis.

27 This is under the traditional view that a head–modifier relationship holds between N and A. As mentioned in section 4.1, analyses exist where this is assumed to be a head–complement relationship. In this case, the A is assumed to be the head.

28 The issue of ellipsis in these constructions will de discussed in section 4.2.7, where the closely related notion 'obligatory constituent' is dealt with.

29 MODIFIER is the term Hudson (1984) uses to refer to any non-head word in each pair of head and dependent, or in his terminology, any 'non-head member of a companion relation'.

30 Though see the discussion in section 4.4 of Payne's (1993a) objections to Corbett's (1993) conclusions.

31 Abney (1987: 77) acknowledges this and provides references to literature where similar ideas have been expressed. However, he also states that he was unaware of this literature when he developed his ideas.

32 Since Word Grammar is a framework based on dependency relations rather than constituents, this does not lead to a DP analysis as such. However, the dependency relations that hold within the noun phrase could be translated into a tree structure, which in terms of X-bar syntax would be a DP.

33 The terminology, but not the analysis, is borrowed from Montague (1973).

34 Note that this type of feature distribution could not be accounted for by non-head inheritance as discussed in section 4.2.3, since it is not the case that N is unspecified for the relevant feature.

35 For instance, Szabolcsi (1987) argues that the Hungarian noun phrase is a projection of a functional category CN of which the definite article is the head. The complement of CN is another functional projection, IN″, which is headed by nominal agreement morphology. Horrocks and Stavrou (1987) assume that the parallels which exist between clauses and noun phrases are subject to parametric variation. Under their analysis, nominal D corresponds to clausal C in Greek, but to clausal I in English. Both these proposals will be discussed in this subsection.

36 Szabolcsi translates these sentences as 'For x = Peter, I saw x's hat' and 'For which x, I saw x's hat' respectively.

37 For the Hungarian data, Abney refers to the article later to appear as Szabolcsi (1987).
One of Abney's arguments is based on the claim that possessor agreement in many languages is parallel to subject–verb agreement. For the languages referred to by Abney this is correct, but in a number of languages the formal similarities are between possessor agreement and object, rather than subject, agreement. Seiler (1983) provides an overview of the two types of parallels based on a sample of North American languages. He provides a semantic explanation for the difference between possessive-objective and possessive-subject affinities.

38 This is a simplified version of the analysis provided by Abney (1987: 23). There is also a refined version (Abney 1987: 223), where *-ing* is assumed to attach to a VP to convert it into an NP. This means that the complement of the determiner in this version of the analysis is of the category NP rather than VP.

39 There is still disagreement about other functional categories within the noun phrase though. Q(uantifier), Num(ber), K(for Case), and Card(inality) have been suggested as other possible functional heads within the noun phrase as well as different types of nominal Agr(eement) nodes (cf. e.g. Bhatt 1990, Corbett 1993, Delsing 1991a, Ritter 1991). Also the discussion of whether or not adjectives are heads that select NPs is still in progress (a good overview of these arguments in general and how they relate to the Scandinavian languages in particular can be found in Delsing 1992.)

40 Though Netter (1994) provides a type of DP analysis within HPSG (see section 4.2.1). His analysis will be discussed in sections 5.2.3.3, 5.3.3.3 and 5.4.3.3. Svenonius's (1992a, 1992c)

analysis of Norwegian noun phrases in terms of the Edge Feature Principle is an example of a DP analysis of noun phrases formulated roughly in terms of HPSG.

41 I will return to a discussion of Borsley's (1988) arguments for a distinction between specifiers and subjects in section 5.5.2.

42 Since I do not think that the structural position of *bara* is a straightforward matter, I have only assigned a category label to the phrase with which *bara* combines, but not to the resulting string. I am concerned here exclusively with the linear position of *bara*.

43 I refer here to head-to-head movement analyses like:

$[_{DP}\ [_{D}\ \textit{mus}_{i}\textit{-en}\ ]\ [_{NP}\ [_{N'}\ [_{N}\ t_i\ ]]]]$
mouse-DEF

In my analysis, there is no room for such movement, since I concluded in chapter 3 that *-en* does not have any independent syntactic status.

44 In Ernst's terminology, 'specifier' refers to a subset of the set of functional categories. According to him, there are three types of functional categories: those that head their own projections, those that are realized as features on some other category, and those that are specifiers. The term 'SPEC' he uses to refer to the position in a tree which is a sister of X′ and a daughter of X″.

45 The criteria in 3b and 5 refer to the same data; the difference is whether one assumes that the features in question are present as a result of subcategorization or government. The data referred to is:

denna mus
this(DEF) mouse.INDEF

46 If criteria 7 and 8 are narrowed to exclude ellipsis according to Zwicky (1985a), then N is the head according to both criteria.

47 One might want to claim that there is some form of *wh*-movement out of noun phrases in Swedish in examples like (i), which should be compared to (ii) where the whole noun phrase has moved:

(i) vad_i har ni [$\mathbf{t}_i$ för bil]
what have you for car

(ii) $[\text{vad för bil}]_i$ har ni $\mathbf{t}_i$
what for car have you

I have discussed this type of construction in Börjars (1992), where I conclude that it is only for subcategorization purposes that one might want to consider *vad* a D heading a DP. This type of construction does not, therefore, contribute any new arguments in favour of a DP analysis for Swedish noun phrases. The subcategorization criterion is already listed in table 4.1 as evidence in favour of D as the head.

5 Features in Definite Noun Phrases

1 In Pollard and Sag (1987), SYNSEM was split into two, SYNTAX and SEMANTICS.

2 The exact ID schema used in Pollard and Sag (1994) for determiners is the schema used for *markers* generally, i.e. elements like complementiser. It is ID schema 4 (Pollard and Sag 1994: 402), but its exact structure is not really of relevance here.

3 The status of *den där* and *den här* as lexical units was argued for in section 2.2.3.

4 This restriction also holds for adjectives in indefinite noun phrases, a point to which I will return in section 6.3.

In (5.6) I gloss the adjectival marking as DEF, but in section 5.4 I will discuss the nature of this adjectival feature and conclude that it is distinct from the definiteness feature marked on nominal elements.

5 As Lars-Olof Delsing has pointed out to me, in restricted use, A+N.DEF combinations can be used without an article; the resulting NP then has very specific reference.

6 Delsing (1988) assumes a more complex structure than that in (5.10). In that analysis, there is an Intervening ArtP between D and N, and DEF is generated in Art. A definite noun phrase must be a full DP in his analysis. This means that *mus* moves from N to Art, where it

attaches to *-en, mus-en* then moves further into D, so that the result forms a full definite DP. In more recent work, Delsing (1989, 1992) posits a structure in which the D takes an NP complement in noun phrases without any attributive modifiers, so that (5.10) is the correct representation for such noun phrases.

7 In Delsing (1988), this position is Art (cf. note 6 in this chapter).

8 It is not clear to me how this type of selection is defined. Nor is it obvious what Santelmann means by 'the definite noun phrase', whether it is the DP or the NP. In the introduction to her article, she states that 'she will use the generic term "noun phrase" to refer to the phrase as a whole, when the distinction between DP and NP is not important' (Santelmann 1992: 100). Normally, selectional restrictions are assumed to hold between a lexical element and its sister or the head of its sister. This would mean that the definiteness features under D^0 would be responsible for the selection of DEF in Num^0.

9 This rule is taken from the summary of rules at the end of the article. In this summary, a separate rule deals with indefinite nouns, which may under certain circumstances function as noun phrases (see chapter 6). In an earlier section dealing with noun phrases consisting of just one noun, Cooper (1984: 121) proposes a slightly different formulation for these rules:

R1.1 $\underset{\alpha}{N^2} \rightarrow \underset{\alpha}{N'}$

If β= {DEF, −PL, γNEUTER}, then α = {DEF, −PL, +NEUTER}
If β= {DEF, +PL, γNEUTER}, then α = {DEF, −PL, +NEUTER} or $\alpha=\beta$

Otherwise $\alpha=\beta$

R1.2 $\underset{\alpha}{N^1} \rightarrow \underset{\alpha}{N}$

In R1.1 the special conditions make sure that indefinite singular nouns must, and indefinite plural nouns may, yield noun phrases which are specified as [+NEUTER], regardless of the gender of the noun itself. This is to ensure that the correct agreement patterns are predicted for bare indefinite nouns (cf. discussion in section 6.4.2).

With reference to noun phrases consisting of a definite noun, however, the combination of R1.1 and R1.2 yields a different structure from the rule in (5.12). R1.1 and R1.2 result in a structure in which a noun phrase like *musen* has internal structure, whereas (5.12) produces a tree in which there is no intermediate level between N^2 and N.

10 The interpretation is formulated in terms of $[\![N^1]\!]$, rather than $[\![N]\!]$, because the interpretation also applies to a syntactic rule involving a prenominal determiner and an adjective.

11 This is my direct translation of the German *kongruente Projektionen.*

12 This is my translation from the German original.

13 The relationship between the two trees in (5.17) is assumed not to be transformational in nature. Rather, the 'collapsed' tree is generated instead of the full tree under the appropriate circumstances (Svenonius 1992c: 155, n. 9).

14 In the lexicon, *musen* is only specified as [INDEF], but through unification with an element which requires an N which is $[^{+\text{DEF}}_{-\text{INDEF}}]$ the noun receives the necessary specification for [DEF].

15 As mentioned in section 5.2.2.1, this is also partly true for Delsing (1993).

16 There are also arguments in favour of defining selection in terms of syntactic categories. Some verbs, for instance select a clausal complement with a particular complementizer, rather than a semantically similar complement with a different complementizer.

17 Certain nouns select further elements through their COMPS and SUBJ features. A predicative noun will require a subject and a noun like, for instance, *execution* may have one element (PP[*of*]) on its COMPS list.

18 This is one of the ways suggested briefly by Pollard and Sag (1987) for dealing with plural common nouns and mass nouns in English.

19 Note that I assume that nouns subcategorize for *det*, rather than *DetP*. Pollard and Sag (1994: section 1.7) do opt for a phrasal category, but since I assume that one characteristic of determiners is that they cannot be modified I refer to it as a lexical category. This makes determiners more similar to complementizers, or 'markers' as these are called by Pollard and Sag.

In all HPSG representations, I will abbreviate the attribute-value matrices (AVMs) to represent only features of interest to the discussion at that point. For more details on how the valence and HEAD features fit into the total description of a sign, I refer to Pollard and Sag (1987, 1994).

20 This fact may be related to the fact that *devour* is more specific than *eat*, but this relationship is too vague to base a syntactic rule on. We cannot make a general rule like 'the less specific term will allow an ontologically necessary role to be unexpressed, whereas a more specific term will not.' Such a statement may not even be true in the sense that we may find specific elements which permit optional elements on the SUBCAT list, whereas corresponding less specific elements do not. But even if it is correct as a tendency, it is not strong enough to form the basis of a grammatical rule.

21 In the transformational literature, the importance of the presence of morphological marking for zero argument noun phrases has often been over-emphasized. Gilligan (1987) studied the pro-drop property in a fairly representative sample of 100 languages. Of these, 90 languages were pro-drop in the sense that they allowed null thematic subjects. In only 65 of these languages could pro-drop be related to agreement morphology. For a discussion of the problems associated with a standard transformational analysis of pro-drop in a language which does not make use of agreement morphology, such as Vietnamese, see Rosén (1996).

22 Netter (1994: 313–15) does consider functional categories like determiners to be heads, since they subcategorize for their sisters. In this way, he avoids the additional selection mechanisms used by Pollard and Sag (1994).

23 Netter does not refer to separate SUBJ and COMP lists.

24 I use 'almost all' here since, in spite of many recent claims to the contrary, I believe that co-ordinated structures lack a head in the sense it is used here (*pace* many recent claims: for evidence see e.g. Borsley 1995). Also, in recent LFG (Bresnan 1995), since all elements are assumed to be optional unless required by an independent principle, headless phrases may occur.

25 An exception is LFG, where subcategorization is expressed in terms of functional rather than syntactic categories.

26 For a discussion of this notion with respect to the languages of Europe in general, see the articles in Plank (1995). In that volume, the articles by van der Auwera and Börjars (the latter expanded as Börjars 1994) make special reference to the Scandinavian languages.

27 At an earlier point in his thesis, Delsing defines the Argument Rule, which states that all arguments must have a filled determiner position at S-structure (1993: 65). Determiners in non-argumental noun phrases, he claims, 'are generated in a determiner position at D-structure, but . . . such noun phrases normally do not require a determiner at S-structure.' Most relevant at this point is his claim about argument noun phrases: 'Contrary to non-arguments, all arguments seem to have a determiner at S-structure. I will thus assume that all meaningful determiners, like demonstratives, numerals and pronouns are base generated in a determiner position at D-structure.' I am not sure I can follow the internal argument here, but more importantly it does not seem consistent with his later analysis of demonstratives (or indeed numerals). For further discussion of his account of non-argument noun phrases, see sections 6.2.2 and 6.4.2.2.

28 Delsing (1993) does not actually provide any arguments for the assumption that demonstratives are not definite. This may follow from the fact that they are, in his analysis, basically adjectival in nature, and from the assumption that adjectives are not definite. Adjectives in definite noun phrases will be marked for some feature, say 'weak', and if demonstratives are adjectives, one might expect them to be marked for 'weak' as well. For a discussion of Delsing's account of weak adjectives, see section 5.4.2.1.

29 Delsing (1993: 185200) distinguishes between two types of pronominal quantifiers: partitive and pseudopartitive. I find it difficult to apply semantic criteria for such a distinction to *denna,* but a syntactic criterion, according to Delsing, is that in partitive constructions the nominal occurs in its definite form. This means that *denna* must be a partitive quantifier in *denna mannen* 'this man.DEF'.

Note that in this structure, Delsing does appear to assume that DEF is generated under the D node, and not as the definite form of a noun. It is not clear to me when DEF is base-generated in N, and when it is not (see my discussion of Delsing's analysis in section 5.2.2.1).

30 This is a specific fact about Swedish. There are languages in which more subtle distinctions can be expressed by means of morphological determiners. One such language is Macedonian; see Lunt (1952: 41).

31 Since I assume that a determiner cannot be modified and cannot subcategorize for any element other than that of which it is the specifier, determiners lack valence features like SUBJ, COMPS and SPR. In sections 4.2.2 and 4.2.6 I have already suggested that determiners could be considered pronouns, i.e. NPs, rather than Dets. I will return to this issue briefly in section 5.5.2, but the exact categorial status of determiners is not of crucial importance to the issues discussed here.

32 The nouns are not specified for person since they can combine with elements like *vi* 'we' and *ni* 'you.PL' as in *vi möss* 'we mice' and *ni möss* 'you mice'. In section 2.2.2 I argued that these elements are first- and second-person determiners.

33 Another context where a determiner is required for independent reasons is when the noun is preceded by an adjective. I refer to section 5.4.3 for a detailed discussion of such constructions.

34 In this structure I have assumed that APs attach at N′ level. If one assumes that adjectives actually head the complement of D, taking an NP complement, then this problem becomes even worse since it will occur both in the AP and the NP. If adjectives are assumed to be adjoined to NP, then the expansion from N′ to NP will always be empty.

In a theory involving movement, a possessor could be generated in the Spec–NP position. It would then be assumed to move up to Spec–DP, parallel to the way in which subjects are assumed to be generated in Spec–VP and move up to Spec–IP. However, in this chapter, I am assuming an analysis without syntactic movement.

35 This is not true for Insular Scandinavian, as the following two examples show (from Barnes 1994 and Kress 1982 respectively):

(i) gamli bátur-in — Faroese
old boat-DEF
'the old boat'

(ii) mikli maður-inn — Icelandic
great man-DEF
'the great man'

36 There are some apparent exceptions to this generalization in Swedish, which I will discuss in section 5.5.1.

37 Kester (1992) also proposes that the weak adjectival endings are related to the assignment of Case.

38 This should be compared to HPSG approaches to be discussed in sections 5.4.3.2 and 5.4.3.3, where, in a sense, the opposite generalization is made and nouns (and in some cases also determiners) are assumed to be marked for [DECL WK/STR] just like adjectives (Netter 1994, Pollard and Sag 1994).

39 The *-a* ending in ambiguous between [WK, SG] and [WK/STR, PL], but the zero article with plural nouns is associated with an indefinite interpretation.

40 *Några* 'some' is an indefinite determiner. The position in which *några kalla* occurs only allows indefinite noun phrases in Swedish.

41 Delsing (1989) does not provide any details about the circumstances under which this lowering is permitted.

42 It is not absolutely clear to me how the adjective receives its weak morphology in Delsing's most recent analyses (1992, 1993). It cannot be through definiteness agreement defined in terms of Spec–Head agreement with the NP. Firstly, Delsing (1993: 84) claims that one of the advantages of his analysis is that agreement can be done in identical ways for attributive and predicative APs. Since predicative adjectives may not carry weak morphology, they do not agree in terms of definiteness. Hence I assume that definiteness is not one of the agreement features. Secondly, the fact that a weak adjective may occur with a non-definite noun (as in *denna hungriga mus* 'this hungry.WK mouse') is a further sign that it cannot be accounted for by Spec–Head agreement with the NP.

The preceding determiner does govern the adjective (though a Deg projection may intervene), so that it could potentially assign Case as in Delsing's previous analyses.

However Delsing (1992: 38, 1993: 106–7) explicitly states that the only projection which is assigned Case is the DP. AP and NP receive it through percolation.

Hence I assume that weak morphology is the result of some feature assigned under government by the determiner. If this is the case, it would be interesting to have details about how this feature is distributed when attributive adjectives occur recursively or when a DegP intervenes between the determiner and the AP (see (5.26) in section 5.3.2.1). Even though this might be thought of as just a technical matter, the issue of whether it can be done without the features [WK/STR] also spreading to the noun is important. In section 5.4.3.2, I discuss the issue of [WK/STR] marking on nouns.

43 There are two exceptions to this, namely, the rule which expands a vocative N^2 and the rule which introduces the type of indefinite noun phrase which may disagree with a predicative adjective. These will be discussed in section 6.4.2.

44 Two facts of Swedish makes this distinction less obvious to the eye than that illustrated by (5.66) and (5.67). Firstly, the plural agreement marker on the adjective is identical in shape to the marker for [WK] (which is identical for singular and plural). Secondly, plural adjectives like plural nouns may occur without a determiner and are then interpreted generically. This means that structures like (5.64a) may be grammatical, but with a limited number of adjectives and in an indefinite, plural interpretation: (i) is grammatical, with a parallel interpretation to that of the noun phrase in (ii).

(i) Blinda bör få mer hjälp av samhället.
blind.PL ought receive more help by society

(ii) Blinda människor bör få mer hjälp av samhället.
blind.STR.PL human.being.PL ought receive more help by society

45 Note that the use of the feature names WEAK and STRONG here has nothing to do with the notion of weak and strong features as used in Minimalism (Chomsky 1995).

46 For a list of the different kinds of prenominal modifiers which do not inflect, see Thorell (1973).

47 A number of difficult issues are associated with noun phrases like the subject of (5.76a), for example: what is the relation between bare plurals in generic and non-generic use? Do either, or both, involve zero determiners? Obviously, the status of the strong adjectives which occur in these noun phrases will depend on what analysis one assigns to the noun phrase as a whole. In section 6.3.1 I will discuss a number of analyses which have been proposed for noun phrases like these. However, without entering on a detailed discussion of these possible analyses at this stage, I still maintain that a strong adjective ending in *-a* represents a different form from a weak adjective ending in *-a*.

48 As pointed out in section 2.3 these elliptical adjectives can take the possessive *'s* which would otherwise appear on the noun. In section 3.4 I argued that this is due to certain facts about the distribution of *'s* and should not be viewed as an indication that the adjective has been nominalized.

49 Note that adjectives may productively form compounds with nouns in certain dialects spoken in Northern Sweden (see Delsing 1993: 122–3).

50 I will use Netter's abbreviations *we* and *st* when discussing his account, even though I have used WK and STR to refer to the same feature values.

51 Of course, for *den* to combine with *hungriga musen, musen* would have to have the value [FCOMPL −], but that is not a problem, since *musen* is unspecified for FCOMPL in the lexicon and can hence receive either value through unification.

52 As pointed out in section 4.2.3, features do not 'move' in frameworks such as HPSG and GPSG. The principles that govern feature distribution put constraints on local trees rather than move features. However, I will use terms like percolate which imply movement for the sake of convenience.

53 As already pointed out, in Delsing's (1992, 1993) analysis, it is the A which is the head, and the NP is found in the specifier position of the AP.

54 There is an alternative approach, adopted by Delsing (1989), namely to assume that the adjectival marking is an instantiation of Case.

55 It should be pointed out that this problem is not specific to a DP analysis. It is actually even more obvious in an NP analysis if we follow the restrictions on feature distribution which we have assumed in this section. In an NP analysis, under these assumptions, a

specifier would have to assign a feature to a modifier of the element of which it is a specifier.

56 This argument is not specific to the assumption that adjectives are marked for Case. It could also be phrased in terms of definiteness marking.

57 Similar data for Norwegian is provided by Svenonius (1992c: 151).

58 A number of these so-called predeterminers may also follow a determiner. When they do, there is often a difference in meaning, which may be explicable in terms of scope. If *halva* is preceded by a definite article, as in *den halva gamla ostbiten,* the meaning of the noun phrase differs from that of (5.102a). The sentence in (5.102a) implies that half the piece of cheese is gone, but the other half is still there. In *Den halva ostbiten var borta,* the implication is that there never was more than half a piece of cheese present in the first place. In the case of another pre-modifier, *hela* 'whole' there is a more substantial change in meaning; when used after a determiner, be it definite or indefinite, it means 'unbroken, without cracks'.

59 One of Borsley's arguments for making a distinction between subjects and specifiers is indeed the fact that subjects are obligatory whereas specifiers are not. He does, however, assume that determiners are specifiers in this respect (1988: 15).

60 As already stated in section 5.2.3.4, I believe that the relation between morphological marking and the possibility of leaving an element unexpressed should not be made too direct.

61 There is one determiner, *denna* 'this', which can under certain circumstances co-occur with a possessive as in:

(i) denna min övertygelse
this my conviction

(ii) detta vår ordförandes slutgiltiga beslut
this our chair person's final decision

However, this is a marked construction, available only with this one determiner. Furthermore, in HPSG, the noun is assumed to combine with the specifier first, so that linearly the subject will be further from the head noun than the specifier. This is necessary in order to make sure that the correct predictions are made about the position of the subjects and specifiers of predicative phrases. However, in examples such as (i) and (ii), if they are assumed to be standard noun phrases with both a specifier and a subject, then they violate the general rule that subjects precede specifiers. For an alternative analysis of such noun phrases, see Börjars (1990).

62 This led, for instance, Holmberg (1986) to posit two different indefinite articles for English, one which occurs in predicative positions, and one which occurs in other contexts.

63 I have not discussed the use of the feature value [−DEF] yet, since I claim that this is not a feature which occurs in definite noun phrases. In fact, I assume that this feature is not part of any noun's lexical specification. Constructions involving [−DEF] elements (determiners) will be the focus of chapter 6.

6 Features in Indefinite Noun Phrases

1 In (6.1b) a singular interpretation of *murmeldjur* is intended. If *murmeldjur* is assumed to be plural, then the sentence is grammatical without a determiner, and receives a generic interpretation.

2 In this article, Delsing assumes that noun phrases have three heads, to give the structure $[_{DP}\,[_{ArtP}\,[_{NP}]]]$. All determiners which are assumed to be present in deep structure are generated in the Art slot. If they are marked as [+DEF] they may move to D and hence the resulting noun phrase is a DP. Indefinite determiners, on the other hand, cannot move. This means that there is nothing to fill the D position in indefinite noun phrases, hence there is no D projection. An indefinite noun phrase is therefore an ArtP.

3 In Delsing's account, *en* is not always the standard indefinite article. There are some noun phrases in Swedish where he claims that *en* fills a different function. I will return to this issue in section 6.4.4.

4 It should be pointed out here that this conclusion is not so obvious when it comes to noun

phrases headed by plural or non-count nouns. Such noun phrases will be discussed briefly in section 6.4.1.

5 There is also a stressed version of *några*, which corresponds in meaning to the stressed *some* [sʌm] in Standard English.

6 In (6.32), I gloss *är* as 'is' in (a) and (b) and as 'are' in (c), since these would be the correct forms in English. There is however, no distinction made in the Swedish examples.

7 This holds true also for the cases where the subject is a bare plural noun. Since I have not provided an analysis for bare plurals, I will not discuss them in detail here either. However, regardless of what type of analysis is adopted for bare plurals, the general idea behind the discussion here will apply to them as well.

8 A possible objection to this claim might be that since I have allowed *en* to have a lexical entry where it is specified as [DEF *u*], there is nothing in principle to stop me from assuming a similar second entry for definite determiners which combine with N′ [DEF *u*], e.g. *denna*. If *denna* also had an entry like (6.49), *denna mus* 'this mouse' would be [DEF *u*] and would be expected to be grammatical in non-agreeing constructions. However, since *en* may occur also in other constructions where it alternates with a determinerless indefinite noun phrase, I believe that there are good reasons to assume dual status for *en* which cannot be extended to other determiners. Other linguists have made a similar claim about the status of the indefinite article, e.g. Hellan (1986), Holmberg (1986) and Delsing (1993) (though in section 6.4.4.2, I am critical about the arguments used by Delsing).

9 In (6.53a), *brev* is to be interpreted as a singular noun. The plural form of *brev* is identical, and if the plural interpretation is imposed on *brev* in (6.53a), the sentence is grammatical.

10 To me, (6.67b), without *mig* is perfectly grammatical, which would go against Delsing's argument that the plural form of *en* is restricted to predicative positions.

11 I use the more 'old-fashioned' term 'deep structure' here, even though Delsing (1993) does use 'D-structure'. This is in order to avoid confusion with D as an abbreviation for determiner, as in 'D position'. The notions of deep and surface structure are assumed not to be relevant in a more recent version of Chomsky's theory, the Minimalist program (Chomsky 1992, 1995).

12 Though, as discussed in section 5.3.2.1, demonstratives are adjectives rather than determiners in Delsing's (1993) analysis.

13 There is another possible solution in which role nouns could be assumed always to be [DEF *u*], in the sense that the value u(nspecified) for DEF indicates an inability to refer. In this case, the [DEF *u*] nouns which may not normally occur as determinerless predicatives would have to be specified as [ROLE −]. The nouns which can function either as arguments or as determinerless predicatives could then simply be unspecified for the feature ROLE, so that they are available both to elements requiring an N[ROLE −] and to elements requiring an N[ROLE +]. In this solution, for all determiners which select a [DEF *u*] nominal, this nominal would also have to be specified as [ROLE −]. Furthermore, a verb like *vara* would have to be specified as selecting either a NP[DEF ±] or NP[ROLE +].

7 Conclusion

1 The easiest way to talk about this is in terms of the definite ending representing the feature DEF. I do not, however, wish to imply an incremental approach to morphology; quite to the contrary, I see many advantages to a realizational approach.

REFERENCES

Abney, S. R. 1987. The English noun phrase in its sentential aspect. Ph. D. dissertation, MIT.

Ahrenberg, L. 1992. The formalization of Field Grammar. In J. Louis-Jensen and J. H. W. Poulsen (eds), *The Nordic languages and Modern Linguistics*. Tórshavn: Føroya Fróðskaparfelag. 119–30.

Allén, S. 1958. Indelningen av nusvenskans pronomen. *Arkiv för nordisk filologi* **73**: 51–70.

Anderson, S. R. 1982. Where's morphology? *Linguistic Inquiry* **13**: 571–612.

Anderson, S. R. 1993. Wackernagel's revenge: clitics, morphology and the syntax of the second position. *Language* **69**: 68–98.

Anderson, S. R. 1996. How to put your clitics in their place or why the best account of second position clitics may be something like the optimal one. *The Linguistic Review* **13**: 165–91.

Anward, J. and Linell, P. 1976. Om lexikaliserade fraser i svenskan. *Nysvenska studier* **55–6**: 77–119.

Anward, J. and Swedenmark, J. 1997. ¡Kasus nej, bestämdhet ja! Om möjliga modeller av nominalböjningens utveckling i svenskan. In P. Åström (ed.), *Studier i svensk språkhistoria* 4 (MINS 44), Stockholm University, Department of linguistics. 21–34.

Auwera, J. van der 1990. Coming to terms. Habilitation thesis, University of Antwerp.

Auwera, J. van der 1994. On double definiteness in Dutch, Lebanese, Arabic, Swedish and Danish. In F. Plank (ed.), *EUROTYP Working Papers VII: Double articulation*. University of Konstanz. 113–20.

Bach, E. 1983. Generalized Categorial Grammars and the English auxiliary. In F. Heny and B. Richards (eds), *Linguistic Categories: Auxiliaries and related Puzzles*. Vol. 2. Dordrecht: Reidel. 101–20.

Baker, M. C. 1988. *Incorporation. A Theory of Grammatical Function Changing*. Chicago: The University of Chicago Press.

Baker, M. C. and Hale, K. L. 1990. Relativized minimality and pronoun incorporation. *Linguistic Inquiry* **21**: 289–97.

Baltin, M. R. 1989. Heads and projection. In M. R. Baltin and A. S. Kroch (eds), *Alternative Conceptions of Phrase Structure*. Chicago: The University of Chicago Press. 1–16.

Baltin, M. R. and Kroch, A. R. (eds) 1989. *Alternative conceptions of phrase structure*. Chicago: The University of Chicago Press.

Barnes, M. P. with E. Weyhe 1994. Faroese. In E. König and J. van der Auwera (eds), *The Germanic Languages*. London: Routledge. 190–218.

Bauer, L. 1988. *Introducing Linguistic Morphology*. Edinburgh: Edinburgh University Press.

Beckman, N. 1952. *Svensk språklära för den högre elementarundervisningen*. Stockholm.

Bhatt, C. 1990. Kasuszuweisung in der DP. *Klagenfurter Beiträge zur Sprachwissenschaft* **15–16**: 1–23.

Bloomfield, L. 1933. *Language*. London: Allen and Unwin.

Börjars, K. E. 1988. Stress, segment duration and syllable structure. Doctoraalscriptie (M. A. dissertation), University of Leiden.

Börjars, K. E. 1990. Types of complements in Swedish Determiner Phrases. In J. van Lit, R. Mulder and R. Sybesma (eds), *LCJL 2 Proceedings*. Department of General Linguistics, University of Leiden. 1–12.

Börjars, K. E. 1991. Complementation in the Scandinavian languages. In N. B. Vincent and K. E. Börjars (eds), *EUROTYP Working Papers III.2*. University of Manchester. 65–90.

Börjars, K. E. 1992. D selecting a PP complement. In A. Holmberg (ed.), *Papers from the Workshop on the Scandinavian Noun Phrase*. [DGL-UUM-Report 32] Department of General Linguistics, University of Umeå. 1–19.

Börjars, K. E. 1994. Swedish double determination in a European typological perspective. *Nordic Journal of Linguistics. Special issue on typology* **17**: 219–52.

Börjars, K. E. 1997. One (more) reason why we need morphology. In W. U. Dressler, M.

Prinzhorn and J. R. Rennison (eds), *Advances in Morphology*. Berlin: Mouton de Gruyter. 111–29.

Börjars, K. E. and Vincent, N. B. 1993. Towards a parametrization of the clitic-affix distinction. Paper presented at the Autumn Meeting of the Linguistics Association of Great Britain, Bangor, September 1993.

Börjars, K. E., Vincent, N. B. and Chapman, C. 1997 Paradigms, periphrasis and pronominal inflection: a feature-based account. In G. Booij and J. van Marle (eds), *Yearbook of morphology 1996*. Dordrecht: Kluwer. 155–80.

Borsley, R. D. 1987. Subjects and complements in HPSG. CSLI Technical Report No 107–87. Stanford, Ca: CSLI Publications.

Borsley, R. D. 1988. Subjects, complements, and specifiers in HPSG. Unpublished ms. University of Wales, Bangor.

Borsley, R. D. 1993. Heads in Head-driven Phrase Structure Grammar. In G. G. Corbett, N. M. Fraser and S. McGlashan (eds), *Heads in Grammatical Theory*. Cambridge: CUP. 186–203.

Borsley, R. D. 1995. In defence of coordinate structures. *Linguistic Analysis* **24**: 218–46.

Bouma, G. 1988. Modifiers and specifiers in Categorial Grammar. *Linguistics* **26**: 21–46.

Bresnan, J. 1970. On complementizers: toward a syntactic theory of complement types. *Foundations of Language* **6**: 297–321.

Bresnan, J. 1995. Lexical-Functional Grammar. Ms. Stanford University. (Barcelona ESSLLI version).

Cann, R. 1989. Splitting heads. *Occasional Papers*. The Linguistics Department, University of Edinburgh.

Cann, R. 1993. Patterns of headedness. In G. G. Corbett, N. M. Fraser and S. McGlashan (eds), *Heads in Grammatical Theory*. Cambridge: CUP. 44–72.

Carlson, G. N. 1977. Reference to kinds in English. Ph. D. dissertation, University of Massachusetts at Amherst.

Carstairs, A. 1981. *Notes on Affixes, Clitics, and Paradigms*. Bloomington: Indiana University Linguistics Club.

Carstairs, A. 1987. Diachronic evidence and the affix-clitic distinction. In A. G. Ramat, O. Carruba and G. Bernini (eds), *Papers from the 7th International Conference on Historical Linguistics*. Amsterdam: John Benjamins. 151–62.

Carstens, V. 1990. The morphology and syntax of Determiner Phrases in Swahili. Ph. D. dissertation, UCLA.

Chomsky, N. 1965. *Aspects of the Theory of Syntax*. Cambridge, Ma: MIT Press.

Chomsky, N. 1982a (rev. ed.). *Lectures on Government and Binding*. [Series in Generative Grammar.] Dordrecht: Foris.

Chomsky, N. 1982b. *Some Concepts and Consequences of the Theory of Government and Binding*. [Linguistic Inquiry Monographs 6] Cambridge, Ma: MIT Press.

Chomsky, N. 1986a. *Knowledge of Language – Its Nature, Origin, and Use*. [Convergence.] New York: Praeger.

Chomsky, N. 1986b. *Barriers*. [Linguistic Inquiry monographs.] Cambridge, Ma: MIT Press.

Chomsky, N. 1992. A minimalist program for linguistic theory. *MIT Occasional Papers in Linguistics* **1**. Cambridge, Ma: MIT.

Chomsky, N. 1995. *The Minimalist Program*. Cambridge, Ma: MIT Press.

Cooper, R. 1982. Wholewheat* syntax (*unenriched with inaudibilia). In P. Jacobson and G. Pullum (eds), *The Nature of Syntactic Representation*. Dordrecht: Reidel. 59–77.

Cooper, R. 1984. Svenska nominalfraser och kontext-fri grammatik. *Nordic Journal of Linguistics* **7**: 115–44.

Cooper, R. 1986. Swedish and the Head-Feature Convention. In L. Hellan and K. K. Christensen (eds), *Topics in Scandinavian Syntax*. Dordrecht: Reidel. 31–52.

Corbett, G. G. 1979. The agreement hierarchy. *Journal of Linguistics* **15**: 203–24.

Corbett, G. G. 1991. *Gender*. Cambridge: CUP.

Corbett, G. G. 1993. The head of Russian numeral expressions. In G. G. Corbett, N. M. Fraser and S. McGlashan (eds), *Heads in Grammatical Theory*. Cambridge: CUP. 11–35.

Corver, N. 1990. The syntax of left branch extractions. Ph. D. thesis, Katholieke Universiteit Brabant, The Netherlands.

Cowper, E. A. 1987. Pied piping, feature percolation and the structure of the noun phrase. *Canadian Journal of Linguistics/Revue canadienne de Linguistique* **32**: 321–38.

Déchaine, R.-M. 1996. Compositional morphology. Paper presented at The 7th International Morphology Meeting, Vienna, February 16–18.
Delsing, L.-O. 1988. The Scandinavian noun phrase. *Working Papers in Scandinavian Syntax* **42**. 57–79.
Delsing, L.-O. 1989. A DP analysis of the Scandinavian noun phrase. Paper presented at The NP Colloquium, Manchester University, 18–19 September.
Delsing, L.-O. 1991. Quantification in the Swedish noun phrase. *Working Papers in Scandinavian Syntax* **47**: 89–117.
Delsing, L.-O. 1992. On attributive adjectives in Scandinavian and other languages. In A. Holmberg (ed.), *Papers from the Workshop on the Scandinavian Noun Phrase*. [DGL-UUM-Report 32.] Department of General Linguistics, University of Umeå. 20–44.
Delsing, L.-O. 1993. The internal structure of noun phrases in the Scandinavian languages. Ph. D. thesis, Lund University.
Di Sciullo, A.-M. and Williams, E. 1987. *On the Definition of Word*. Cambridge, Ma: MIT Press.
Diderichsen, P. 1946. *Elementær dansk grammatik*. Copenhagen: Gyldendal.
Dik, S. C. 1980. Seventeen sentences: basic principles and application of Functional Grammar. In E. M. Moravcsik and J. R. Wirth (eds), *Syntax and Semantics 13. Current Approaches to Syntax*. New York: Academic Press. 45–75.
Dik, S. C. 1989. *The Theory of Functional Grammar. Part I: The Structure of the Clause*. Dordrecht: Foris.
Dobrovie-Sorin, C. 1987. A propos de la structure du groupe nominal en roumain. *Rivista di Grammatica Generativa* **12**: 123–52.
Dowty, D. R. 1988. Type raising. In R. T. Oehrle, E. Bach and D. Wheeler (eds), *Categorial Grammars and Natural Language Structures*. Dordrecht: Reidel. 153–97.
Dowty, D. R., Wall, R. E. and Peters, S. (eds) 1981. *Introduction to Montague Semantics*. Dordrecht: Reidel.
Dryer, M. S. 1989. Article-noun order. In C. Wiltshire, R. Graczyk and B. Music (eds), *Papers from the 25th Annual Regional Meeting of the Chicago Linguistic Society. Part One: The General Session*. [CLS 25.] Chicago: Chicago Linguistic Society. 83–97.
Elson, M. J. 1976. The definite article in Bulgarian and Macedonian. *Slavic and East European Journal* **20**: 273–9.
Ernst, T. 1984. *Towards an Integrated Theory of Adverb Position in English*. Bloomington: Indiana University Linguistics Club.
Ernst, T. 1991. A phrase structure theory for tertiaries. In S. D. Rothstein (ed.), *Syntax and Semantics 25. Perspectives on Phrase Structure. Heads and Licensing*. San Diego: Academic Press. 189–208.
Faarlund, J. T. 1977. Embedded clause reduction and Scandinavian gender agreement. *Journal of Linguistics* **13**: 239–57.
Fenchel, K. 1989. Nominal Hydras. A GPSG approach to agreement in the German NP. In C. Wiltshire, R. Graczyk and B. Music (eds), *Papers from the 25th Annual Regional Meeting of the Chicago Linguistic Society. Part One: The General Session*. [CLS 25.] Chicago: Chicago Linguistic Society. 133–44.
Fiva, T. 1987. *Possessor Chains in Norwegian*. Oslo: Novus.
Fjelstad, A. and Hervold, K. 1989. *Norsk for svensker*. Lund: Studentlitteratur.
Fukui, N. and Speas, M. 1986. Specifiers and projections. In N. Fukui, T. R. Rapoport and E. Sagey (eds), *MIT Working Papers in Linguistics. Papers in Theoretical Linguistics 8*. 128–72.
Gazdar, G., Klein, E., Pullum, G. and Sag, I. 1985. *Generalized Phrase Structure Grammar*. Oxford: Blackwell.
Gilligan, G. M. 1987. A cross-linguistic approach to the pro-drop parameter. Ph.D. dissertation, University of Southern California.
Giusti, G. 1992. *Heads and Modifiers among Determiners: Evidence from Romanian and German*. University of Venice Working Papers in Linguistics.
Grimshaw, J. 1991. Extended projections. Ms. Brandeis.
Grosu, A. 1988. On the distribution of genitive phrases in Rumanian. *Linguistics* **26**: 931–49.
Haider, H. 1988a. Matching projections. In A. Cardinaletti, G. Cinque and G. Giusti (eds), *Constituent structure*. [Papers from the 1987 GLOW conference.] Dordrecht: Foris. 101–22.
Haider, H. 1988b. Die Struktur der deutschen Nominalphrase. *Zeitschrift für Sprachwissenschaft* **7**: 32–59.

Halpern, A. 1992a. Topics in the placement and morphology of clitics. Ph. D. dissertation, Stanford University.

Halpern, A. 1992b. The Balkan definite article and pseudo-second position. In L. A. Buszard-Welcher, L. Wee and W. Weigel (eds), *Proceedings of the Eighteenth Annual Meeting of the Berkeley Linguistics Society*. [BLS 18.] Berkeley: Berkeley Linguistics Society.

Halpern, A. L. and Zwicky, A. M. (eds) 1996. *Approaching Second. Second Position Clitics and Related Phenomena*. Stanford, Ca: CSLI Publications.

Hansen, A. 1966. Overbestemdhed. *Arkiv för nordisk filologi* **81**: 201–13.

Harris, Z. S. 1951. *Methods in Structural Linguistics*. Chicago: The University of Chicago Press.

Haugen, E. 1976. *The Scandinavian Languages – An Introduction to their History*. London: Faber and Faber.

Haugen, E. 1982. *Scandinavian Language Structures – A Comparative Historical Survey*. Minneapolis: University of Minnesota Press.

Hawkins, J. A. 1978. *Definiteness and Indefiniteness: A Study in Reference and Grammaticality Prediction*. London: Croom Helm.

Hellan, L. 1986. The headedness of NPs in Norwegian. In P. Muysken and H. van Riemsdijk (eds), *Features and Projections*. Dordrecht: Foris. 89–122.

Hellan, L. (ed.) 1993. *Eurotyp Working Papers VIII.4: Clitics in Germanic and Slavic*. Katholieke Universiteit Brabant, The Netherlands.

Hellan, L. 1993. On clitics. Paper presented at The XIVth Scandinavian Conference on Linguistics, University of Gothenburg, 16–21 August.

Hockett, C. A. 1958. *A Course in Modern Linguistics*. New York: Macmillan.

Holmberg, A. 1986. Word order and syntactic features in the Scandinavian languages and English. Ph. D. thesis, Stockholm University.

Holmberg, A. 1987. The structure of NP in Swedish. *Working Papers in Scandinavian Syntax* **33**: 1–23.

Holmberg, A. 1992. On the structure of predicate NP. In A. Holmberg (ed.), *Papers from the Workshop on the Scandinavian Noun Phrase*. [DGL-UUM-Report 32.] Department of General Linguistics, University of Umeå. 58–71.

Horrocks, G. and Stavrou, M. 1987. Bounding theory and Greek syntax: evidence for *wh*-movement in NP. *Journal of Linguistics* **23**: 79–108.

Hudson, R. A. 1993. Do we have heads in our minds? In G. G. Corbett, N. M. Fraser and S. McGlashan (eds), *Heads in Grammatical Theory*. Cambridge: CUP. 266–92.

Hudson, R. A. 1984. *Word Grammar*. Oxford: Blackwell.

Hudson, R. A. 1987. Zwicky on heads. *Journal of Linguistics* **23**: 109–32.

Hudson, R. A. 1990. *English Word Grammar*. Oxford: Blackwell.

Hulthén, L. 1948. *Studier i jämförande nunordisk syntax II*. [Göteborgs Högskolas Årsskrift LIII [1947: 4]. Gothenburg: University of Gothenburg/Elanders Boktryckeri Aktiebolag.

Hultman, T. 1966. Obestämt, bestämt och överbestämt. *Arkiv för nordisk filologi* **81**: 214–28.

Jackendoff, R. 1977. *X-bar Syntax: S Study of Phrase Structure*. Cambridge, Mass: MIT Press.

Kaisse, E. M. 1983. The English auxiliaries as sentential clitics. In J. F. Richardson, M. Marks and A. Chukerman (eds), *CLS Parasession on the Interplay of Phonology, Morphology and Syntax*. Chicago: Chicago Linguistics Society. 96–102.

Kathol, A. 1991. Verbal and adjectival passives in German. In Jonathan Bobaljik and Anthony Bures, *Papers from the Third Student Conference in Linguistics. MIT Working Papers in Linguistics* Vol. 14. 115–30.

Kathol, A. 1994. Agreement in HPSG revisited. Unpublished ms. Ohio State University.

Kayne, R. 1975. *French Syntax*. Cambridge, Ma: MIT Press.

Keenan, E. L. 1974. The functional principle: generalizing the notion of 'subject of'. In M. W. La Gay, R. A. Fox and A. Bruck (eds), *Papers from the Tenth Regional Meeting of the Chicago Linguistics Society*. [CLS 10.] Chicago: Chicago Linguistic Society. 298–309.

Keenan, E. L. and Faltz, L. 1978. Logical Types for Natural Language. UCLA Occasional Papers in Linguistics **3**. Department of Linguistics, University of California at Los Angeles.

Keenan, E. L. and Faltz, L. M. 1984. *Logical Types for Natural Language*. Dordrecht: Reidel.

Keenan, E. L. and Faltz, L. M. 1985. *Boolean Semantics for Natural Language*. Dordrecht: Reidel.

Kester, E.-P. 1992. Adjectival inflection and dummy affixation in Germanic and Romance languages. In A. Holmberg (ed.), *Papers from the Workshop on the Scandinavian Noun*

Phrase. [DGL-UUM-Report 32.] Department of General Linguistics, University of Umeå. 72–87.

Klavans, J. L. 1979. On clitics as words. In P. R. Clyne, W. F. Hanks and C. L. Hofbauer (eds), *The Elements: A Parasession on Linguistic Units and Levels*. Chicago: Chicago Linguistics Society. 68–80.

Klavans, J. L. 1983. The morphology of cliticization. In J. F. Richardson, M. Marks and A. Chukerman (eds), *CLS Parasession on the Interplay of Phonology, Morphology and Syntax*. Chicago: Chicago Linguistics Society. 103–19.

Klavans, J. L. 1985. The independence of syntax and phonology in cliticization. *Language* **61**: 95–120.

Kolliakou, D. 1994. The syntax of Modern Greek noun phrases. Paper presented at The Autumn Meeting of the Linguistics Association of Great Britain, University of Salford, 5–7 April 1994.

Kornai, A. and Pullum, G. K. 1990. The X-bar theory of phrase structure. *Language* **66**: 24–51.

Kress, B. 1982. *Isländische Grammatik*. München: Max Hueber Verlag.

Langendoen, D. T. and Langsam, Y. 1984. The representation of constituent structures for finite-state parsing. *Proceedings of COLING 84*. Stanford, Ca.

Lehmann, C. 1982. Universal and typological aspects of agreement. In H. Seiler and F.-J. Stachowiak (eds), *Apprehension: das sprachliche Erfassen von Gegenständer. Vol II: Die Techniken und ihr Zusammenhang in Einzelsprachen*. Tübingen: Günter Narr. 201–67.

Lieber, R. 1980. The organization of the lexicon. Ph. D. dissertation, MIT. Distributed by the Indiana University Linguistics Club, Bloomington.

Ljung, M. and Ohlander, S. 1971. *Allmän grammatik*. Lund: Liber Läromedel.

Lockwood, W. B. 1977. *An Introduction to Modern Faroese*. Tórshavn: Føroya Skúlabókagrunnur.

Lødrup, H. 1989. *Norske hypotagmer: en LFG-beskrivelse av ikke-verbale hypotagmer*. [Oslostudier i språkvitenskap.] Oslo: Novus.

Loman, B. 1956. Om relationen mellan ordföljd och betydelse hos framförställda attributiva bestämningar till substantiviska huvudord. *Arkiv för nordisk filologi* **71**: 218–44.

Loman, B. 1964. Adjektivkombinationer. In C.-C. Elert (ed.), *Förhandlingar vid sammankomst för att dryfta frågor rörande svenskans beskrivining 1*. [Svenskans beskrivning 1.] Stockholm: Stockholm University. 72–81.

Longobardi, G. 1994. Reference and proper names: a theory of N-movement in syntax and logical form. *Linguistic Inquiry* **25**: 609–65.

Lundeby, E. 1965. *Overbestemt substantiv i norsk og de andre nordiske språk*. Oslo: Universitetsforlaget.

Lunt, H. G. 1952. *A Grammar of the Macedonian Literary Language*. Skopje.

Lyons, C. 1985. A possessive parameter. *Sheffield Working Papers in Language and Linguistics* **2**: 98–104.

Lyons, C. 1986. The syntax of English genitive constructions. *Journal of Linguistics* **22**: 123–43.

Lyons, C. 1989. Phrase structure, possessives and definiteness. *York Papers in Linguistics* **14**: York University, UK 221–9.

Lyons, C. 1992. Some thoughts on the DP hypothesis. Ms, University of Salford.

Lyons, C. in press. *Definiteness*. Cambridge: CUP.

Lyons, J. 1977. *Semantics 1–2*. Cambridge: CUP.

Lyttkens, I. A. and Wulff, F. A. 1885. *Svenska språkets ljudlära och beteckningslära, jämte en avhandling om aksent*. Lund: Gleerups.

McCloskey, J. 1982. The syntax of inflection in Modern Irish. *Proceedings of the 13th Conference of the North Eastern Conference of Linguistics*. [NELS 13] University of Massachusetts, Amherst.

Maier, P. and Steffens, P. 1989. Zur Syntax pränominaler Elemente in einer kategorialen Unifikationsgrammatik des Deutschen. *IWBS Report* no.70. Stuttgart: IBM Germany Scientific Center.

Malmgren, S.-G. 1990. *Adjektiviska funktioner i svenskan*. [Nordistica Gothoburgensia 14.] Gothenburg: Acta Universitatis Gothoburgensis.

Marantz, A. 1984. *On the nature of Grammatical Relations*. Cambridge, Ma: MIT Press.

Miller, P. H. 1992a. *Clitics and Constituents in Phrase Structure Grammar*. New York: Garland.

Miller, P. H. 1992b. Morphological marking misses the head. Paper presented at the West Coast Conference on Formal Linguistics, Stanford.

Montague, R. 1973. The proper treatment of quantification in ordinary English. In J. Hintikka, E. Moravcsik and P. Suppes (eds), *Approaches to natural language*. [Proceedings of the 1970 Stanford workshop on grammar and semantics.] Dordrecht: Reidel. 221–42.

Morgan, J. 1984. Some problems of agreement in English and Albanian. In C. Brugman and M. Macaulay (eds), *Proceedings of the Tenth Annual Meeting of the Berkeley Linguistics Society*. [BLS 10.] Berkeley: Berkeley Linguistics Society. 233–47.

Netter, K. 1994. Towards a theory of functional heads: German nominal phrases. In J. Nerbonne, K. Netter and C. Pollard (eds), *German in Head-driven Phrase Structure Grammar*, Stanford, Ca: CSLI Publications. 297–340.

Nevis, J. A. and Joseph, B. D. 1993. Wackernagel affixes: evidence from Balto-Slavic. *The Yearbook of Morphology 1992*. 93–111.

Nichols, J. 1986. Head-marking and dependent-marking grammar. *Language* **62**: 56–119.

Nikula, H. 1986. *Dependensgrammatik*. [Ord och Stil. Språkvårdssamfundets skrifter 16.] Malmö: Liber Förlag.

Nilsson, K. G. 1968. Noun and article in Swedish. *Studia Linguistica* **22**: 51–63.

Östergren, O. 1919. *Nusvensk ordbok*. Stockholm: Wahlström och Widstrand.

Partee, B. and Rooth, M. 1983. Generalized conjunction and type ambiguity. In R. Baeuerle, C. Schwarze and A. von Stechow (eds), *Meaning, Use and Interpretation of Language*. Berlin: de Gruyter. 361–83.

Payne, J. R. 1993a. The headedness of noun phrases: slaying the nominal hydra. In G. G. Corbett, N. M. Fraser and S. McGlashan (eds), *Heads in Grammatical Theory*. Cambridge: CUP. 114–39.

Payne, J. R. 1993b. Categorial headhunting. Ms., University of Manchester. Prepared for the Antwerp meeting of EUROTYP Theme Group VII.

Payne, J. R. 1993c. Nouns and noun phrases. In R. E. Asher and J. M. Y. Simpson (eds), *The Encyclopaedia of Language and Linguistics*. Oxford: Pergamon Press. 2848–55.

Payne, J. R. and Börjars, K. E. 1994. Swedish noun phrases meet Categorial Grammar. In A. Holmberg and C. Hedlund (eds), *Proceedings from the Workshop on Scandinavian Syntax*. University of Gothenburg. 111–25.

Perridon, H. 1989. Reference, definiteness and the noun phrase in Swedish. Ph. D. thesis, University of Amsterdam.

Plank, F. 1992. Possessives and the distinction between determiners and modifiers (with special reference to German). *Journal of Linguistics* **28**: 453–68.

Plank, F. 1995. Double articulation. In F. Plank (ed.), *EUROTYP Working Papers VII: Double Articulation*. University of Konstanz. 1–60.

Plank, F. (ed.) 1995. *EUROTYP Working Papers VII: Double Articulation*. University of Konstanz.

Platzack, C. 1982. Transitive adjectives in Swedish: a phenomenon with implications for the theory of abstract Case. *Linguistic Review* **2**: 39–56.

Pollard, C. and Sag, I. A. 1987. *Information-based Syntax and Semantics. Vol. 1: Fundamentals*. Stanford, Ca: CSLI.

Pollard, C. and Sag, I. A. 1994. *Head-driven Phrase Structure Grammar*. Stanford: CSLI and Chicago: University of Chicago Press.

Postal, P. M. 1969. On so-called 'pronouns" in English. In D. A. Reibel and S. A. Schane (eds), *Modern Studies in English. Readings in Transformational Grammar*. Englewood Cliff, NJ: Prentice-Hall. 201–24.

Pullum, G. K. 1985. Assuming some version of X-bar theory. In W. H. Eilfort, P. D. Kroeber and K. L. Peterson (eds), *Papers from the General Session at the Twenty-first Regional Meeting of the Chicago Linguistic Society*. [CLS 21.] Chicago: Chicago Linguistic Society. 323–353.

Radford, A. 1989. The syntax of attributive adjectives in English: abnegating Abney. Paper presented at The Noun Phrase Colloquium, University of Manchester, September 1989.

Radford, A. 1993. Head-hunting: on the trail of the nominal Janus. In G. G. Corbett, N. M. Fraser and S. McGlashan (eds), *Heads in Grammatical Theory*. Cambridge: CUP. 73–113.

Renzi, L. 1989. The Rumanian article as a Balkanism. In U. Klenk, K.-H. Körner and W. Thümmel (eds), *Variatio Linguarum. Beiträge zu Sprachvergleich und Sprachentwicklung*. [Festschrift zum 60. Geburtstag van Gustav Ineichen.] 217–25.

Riemsdijk, H. van (ed.) 1991. *EUROTYP Working Papers VIII.2: Clitics and their hosts.* Katholieke Universiteit Brabant, The Netherlands.

Ritter, E. 1991. Two functional categories in noun phrases: evidence from Modern Hebrew. In S. D. Rothstein (ed.), *Syntax and Semantics 25. Perspectives on Phrase Structure. Heads and Licensing.* San Diego: Academic Press. 37–62.

Rizzi, L. 1990. *Relativized Minimality.* Cambridge, Ma: MIT Press.

Rizzi, L. (ed.) 1993. *EUROTYP Working Papers VIII.3: Clitics in Romance and Germanic.* Katholieke Universiteit Brabant, The Netherlands.

Roberts, L. 1992. Pseudo-adjuncts, applicatives and type raising. Paper presented at The Spring Meeting of the Linguistics Association of Great Britain, Brighton Polytechnic, April.

Robinson, J. J. 1970. Dependency structures and transformational rules. *Language* **46**: 259–85.

Rosén, V. 1996. Analyzing what's not there: the treatment of empty pronouns in GB theory. In L. Heltoft and H. Haberland (eds), *Proceedings of the Thirteenth Scandinavian Conference of Linguistics*, Department of Languages and Culture, Roskilde University. 135–46.

Sadock, J. M. 1991. *Autolexical Syntax. A Theory of Parallel Grammatical Representations.* [Studies in Contemporary Linguistics.] Chicago: The University of Chicago Press.

Sag, I. A. and Fodor, J. D. 1995. Extraction without traces. Ms. Stanford University.

Santelmann, L. 1992. *Den*-support: an analysis of double determiners in Swedish. In A. Holmberg (ed.), *Papers from the Workshop on the Scandinavian Noun Phrase.* [DGL-UUM-Report 32.] Department of General Linguistics, University of Umeå. 100–18.

SAOL. 1981. (10th ed.) *Svenska Akademins ordlista över svenska språket.* Stockholm: P. A. Norstedt & Söners Förlag.

Scatton, E. A. 1980. On the shape of the Bulgarian definite article. In C. Chvany and R. Brecht (eds), *Morphosyntax in Slavic.* Columbus, Oh: Slavica. 204–11.

Seiler, H. 1983. Possessivity, subject and object. *Studies in Language* **7**: 89–117.

Shieber, S. 1986. *An Introduction to Unification-based Approaches to Grammar.* Stanford, Ca: CSLI.

Siewierska, A. 1991. *Functional Grammar.* London and New York: Routledge.

Sigurðsson, H. A. 1992. Aspects of the DP analysis of the Icelandic NP. In A. Holmberg (ed.), *Papers from the Workshop on the Scandinavian Noun Phrase.* [DGL-UUM-Report 32.] Department of General Linguistics, University of Umeå. 119–44.

Sommerstein, A. H. 1972. On the so-called definite article in English. *Linguistic Inquiry* **3**: 197–209.

Spencer, A. J. 1991. *Morphological Theory. An Introduction to Word Structure in Generative Grammar.* Oxford: Blackwell.

Steedman, M. 1985. Dependency and coordination in the grammar of Dutch and English. *Language* **61**: 523–68.

Stowell, T. 1989. Subjects, specifiers, and X-bar theory. In M. R. Baltin and A. R. Kroch (eds), *Alternative conceptions of Phrase Structure.* Chicago: The University of Chicago Press. 232–62.

Stowell, T. 1991. Determiners in NP and DP. In K. Leffel and D. Bouchard (eds), *Views on Phrase Structure.* Dordrecht: Kluwer Academic Publishers. 37–56.

Strandskogen, Å.-B. and Strandskogen, R. 1980. *Norsk grammatikk for utlendinger.* Oslo: Gyldendal Norsk Forlag A/S.

Svenonius, P. 1992a. The structure of the Norwegian noun phrase. Paper presented at The Seventh Workshop on Comparative Germanic Syntax, Stuttgart.

Svenonius, P. 1992b. The extended projection of N: identifying the head of the noun phrase. *Working Papers in Scandinavian Syntax* **49**: 95–121.

Svenonius, P. 1992c. The distribution of definite marking. In A. Holmberg (ed.), *Papers from the Workshop on the Scandinavian Noun Phrase.* [DGL-UUM-Report 32.] Department of General Linguistics, University of Umeå. 135–64.

Szabolcsi, A. 1981. The possessive construction in Hungarian: a configurational category in a non-configurational language. *Acta Linguistica Academiae Scientiarum Hungaricae* **31**: 261–89.

Szabolcsi, A. 1984. The possessor that ran away from home. *The Linguistic Review* **3**: 89–102.

Szabolcsi, A. 1987. Functional categories in the noun phrase. In I. Kenesei (ed.), *Approaches to Hungarian. Volume two: Theories and Analyses.* Szeged: Jate. 167–89.

Taraldsen, K. T. 1990. D-projections and N-projections in Norwegian. In J. Mascaró and

M. Nespor (eds), *Grammar in Progress, GLOW Essays for Henk van Riemsdijk*. Dordrecht: Foris. 419–31.
Taraldsen, K. T. 1991. Two arguments for functional heads. *Lingua* **84**: 85–108.
Teleman, U. 1969. *Definita och indefinita attribut i nusvenskan*. Lund: Studentlitteratur.
Thorell, O. 1973. *Svensk grammatik*. Stockholm: Esselte Studium.
Uriagereka, J. 1988. On Government. Ph. D. dissertation, University of Connecticut, Storrs.
Valois, D. 1990. The internal syntax of DP and adjective placement in French and English. *Proceedings of the 21st Conference of the North Eastern Conference of Linguistics*. [NELS 21.] University of Massachusetts, Amherst, Mass.
Vennemann, T. and Harlow, R. 1977. Categorial Grammar and consistent basic *VX* serialization. *Theoretical Linguistics* **4**: 227–254.
Vincent, N. B. and Börjars, K. E. 1997. Double case and the 'wimpiness' of morphology. Paper presented at the LFG 97 conference, San Diego, June 1997.
Wackernagel, J. 1892. Über ein Gesetz der indogermanischen Wortstellung. *Indogermanische Forschungen* **1**: 333–436.
Wells, R. S. 1947. Immediate constituents. *Language* **23**: 81–177.
Wessén, E. 1970. *Schwedische Sprachgeschichte. Band III: Grundriß einer historischen Syntax*. Berlin: de Gruyter.
Wood, M. M. 1993. *Categorial Grammar*. London: Routledge.
Zeevat, H. 1988. Combining Categorial Grammar and unification. In U. Reyle and C. Rohrer (eds), *Natural Language Parsing and Linguistic Theories*. Dordrecht: Reidel. 202–29.
Zwicky, A. M. 1977. *On Clitics*. Bloomington: Indiana University Linguistics Club.
Zwicky, A. M. 1985a. Heads. *Journal of Linguistics* **21**: 1–29.
Zwicky, A. M. 1985b. Clitics and particles. *Language* **61**: 283–305.
Zwicky, A. M. 1987. Suppressing the Zs. *Journal of Linguistics* **23**: 133–48.
Zwicky, A. M. 1988. Direct reference to heads. *Folia Linguistica* **22**: 397–404.
Zwicky, A. M. 1993. Heads, bases and functors. In G. G. Corbett, N. M. Fraser and S. McGlashan (eds), *Heads in grammatical theory*. Cambridge: CUP. 292–315.
Zwicky, A. M. and Pullum, G. K. 1983. Cliticization vs. inflection: English *n't*. *Language* **59**: 502–13.

INDEXES

GENERAL INDEX

INDEX OF LANGUAGES

AUTHOR INDEX

INDEX
THEORIES, RULES, PRINCIPLES DENOTED BY AN ABBREVIATION